The Way We Lived

Volume II
1865–Present

The Way We Lived

Essays and Documents
in American Social History
Third Edition

Frederick M. Binder
City University of New York, College of Staten Island

David M. Reimers
New York University

D. C. HEATH AND COMPANY
Lexington, Massachusetts   Toronto

Address editorial correspondence to

D. C. Heath and Company
125 Spring Street
Lexington, MA 02173

Acquisitions Editor: James Miller
Development Editor: Lauren Johnson
Production Editor: Heather Garrison
Designer: Kenneth Hollman
Photo Researcher: Bruce Carson
Production Coordinator: Richard Tonachel
Permissions Editor: Margaret Roll

International Standard Book Number: 0–669–39715–6

Library of Congress Catalog Number: 94-72796

10 9 8 7 6 5

Preface

History courses have traditionally emphasized the momentous events of our past. Wars and laws, technological advances and economic crises, ideas and ideologies, and the roles of famous heroes and infamous villains have been central to these studies. Yet what made events momentous is the impact they had on society at large, on people from all walks of life. Modern scholars' growing attention to social history is in part a recognition that knowledge of the experiences, values, and attitudes of these people is crucial to gaining an understanding of our past.

America's history as reflected in the everyday lives of its people provides the focus of these volumes. In preparing a work of selected readings, we have had to make choices as to which episodes from our past to highlight. Each of those included, we believe, was significant in the shaping of our society. Each of the essays is followed by original documents that serve several purposes. They provide examples of the kinds of source materials used by social historians in their research; they help to illuminate and expand upon the subject dealt with in the essays; and they bring the reader into direct contact with the people of the past—people who helped shape, and people who were affected by, the "momentous events."

Our introduction to each essay and its accompanying documents is designed to set the historical scene and to call attention to particular points in the selections, raising questions for students to ponder as they read. A list of suggested readings follows after each of the major divisions of the text. We trust that these volumes will prove to be what written history at its best can be—interesting and enlightening.

We are pleased to note that favorable comments by faculty and students as well as the large number of course adoptions attest to the success of our first two editions. Quite naturally, we thus have no desire in our third edition to alter the basic focus, style, and organization of *The Way We Lived*. Those essays that we and our readers consider to have been the earlier editions' very best remain intact. We believe that the new selections will identify and clarify significant issues in America's social history even more effectively than those they replaced.

F. M. B.
D. M. R.

Contents

Part I *The Emergence of an Urban, Industrial Society, 1865–1920*   **1**

1   Reconstruction and Free Plantation Labor   5

ESSAY   7
Peter Kolchin, "Free Plantation Labor"

DOCUMENTS   19
A Letter "To My Old Master," c. 1865 • The Black Code of St. Landry's Parish, 1865 • Dedicated Teachers, Determined Students, 1869

2   The Last Frontier   25

ESSAY   27
Jack Chen, "Linking a Continent and a Nation"

DOCUMENTS   40
Flush Times in Nevada, c. 1862 • Heading East Out of Kansas, 1895 • A Montana Cowtown, 1899

3   Indian Schools: "Americanizing" the Native American   46

ESSAY   48
Robert A. Trennert, "Educating Indian Girls at Nonreservation Boarding Schools, 1878–1920"

DOCUMENTS   61
Rules for Indian Schools, 1890 • A Government Official Describes Indian Race and Culture, 1905 • Cause for Hope: The Establishment of Tribal Colleges, 1994

4   Woman's Sphere: Woman's Work   68

ESSAY   70
Margery W. Davies, "Office Work After the Civil War"

DOCUMENTS   82
"Is Not Woman Destined to Conduct the Rising Generation?" 1844 • Only Heroic Women Were Doctors Then (1865), 1916 • Women's Separate Sphere, 1872

5   Life and Labor in Industrial America   89
    ESSAY   90
    Bonnie Mitelman, "Rose Schneiderman and the Triangle Fire"

    DOCUMENTS   99
    Tenement Cigarmakers, c. 1890 • "Our Daily Life Is Not
    a Pleasant One," 1902 • An Italian Bootblack's Story, 1902

6   The Triumph of Racism   106
    ESSAY   108
    Keith Weldon Medley, "The Birth of 'Separate but Equal'"

    DOCUMENTS   117
    The Atlanta Exposition Address, 1895 • A Call for Equality,
    1905 • "I Want to Come North," 1917

7   War and Society, 1917–1918   121
    ESSAY   123
    David M. Kennedy, "The Doughboys' War: 'An Extraordinary
    Interlude'"

    DOCUMENTS   136
    Diary of an Unknown Aviator, 1918 • German-American
    Loyalty, 1917 • Letters from Mennonite Draftees, 1918

    Part I   Suggestions for Further Reading   142

Part II *Modern American Society,*
            1920–Present   **145**

8   Intolerance: A Bitter Legacy of Social Change   149
    ESSAY   151
    David Chalmers, "The Hooded Knights Revive Rule by
    Terror in the Twenties"

    DOCUMENTS   160
    The Klan's Fight for "Americanism," 1926 • Congress
    Debates Immigration Restriction, 1921 • National-Origins
    Formula Reaffirmed, 1951

9   Morals and Manners in the 1920s   166
    ESSAY   167
    John D'Emilio and Estelle Friedman, "The Sexual Revolution"

DOCUMENTS   177
Happiness in Marriage, 1926 • Moving Pictures Evoke
Concern, 1922 • Prohibition Nonobserved, 1931

10   The Depression Years   183
ESSAY   185
Steven Mintz and Susan Kellogg, "America's Families Face
the Great Depression"
DOCUMENTS   196
The Great Depression in Philadelphia, 1933 • The Okies
in California, 1939 • The Bronx Slave Market, 1935

11   World War II: The Home Front   203
ESSAY   205
William O'Neill, "The People Are Willing"
DOCUMENTS   215
Joining the Navy (1939), c. 1991 • "Well, we never met
Rosie" (1941–1945), c. 1991 • Juvenile Delinquency During
the War, 1944

12   The Internment of Japanese-Americans:
Executive Order 9066   217
ESSAY   219
Commission on Wartime Relocation and Internment
of Civilians, "Personal Justice Denied"
DOCUMENTS   236
In Support of Evacuation, 1942 • Exclusion and
Internment Upheld, 1944 • President Ronald Reagan's
Apology, 1988

13   Moving to Suburbia: Dreams and Discontents   242
ESSAY   244
Kenneth Jackson, "The Baby Boom and the Age of
the Subdivision"
DOCUMENTS   257
Little Boxes, 1962 • The Problem That Has No Name,
1963 • Segregation in the Suburbs, 1994

Contents

14   The Black Struggle for Equality   263

ESSAY   265
Jane Stevenson, "Rosa Parks Wouldn't Budge"

DOCUMENTS   278
School Segregation Ruled Unconstitutional, 1954 •
Opposition to the Civil Rights Bill, 1964 • Growing Up Black
in the South: A Remembrance, 1977

15   The Revival of Feminism   284

ESSAY   286
William H. Chafe, "The Revival of Feminism"

DOCUMENTS   299
In Support of ERA, 1970 • A Woman's Right to Abortion,
1973 • President George Bush Opposes Abortion, 1989

16   America's Latest Immigrants   306

ESSAY   308
Stanley Karnow, "Orange County's Little Saigon: Bridging
Two Worlds"

DOCUMENTS   317
An Undocumented Mexican Immigrant: Miguel Torres,
1977 • Senator Simpson on Immigration, 1981

Part II Suggestions for Further Reading   321

Part I

The Emergence of an Urban, Industrial Society 1865–1920

AFTER THE CIVIL WAR, AMERICANS TURNED THEIR ATTENTION to building a new social order for the defeated Confederacy. Former slaves hoped for a society in which they would be treated as equals and would enjoy the fruits of their labor. Following the stormy Reconstruction years, however, white Southern Democrats again took control of their state governments, imposing severe limitations on the rights of blacks. Later, around the turn of the century, Southern whites, with Northern compliance, relegated blacks to second-class citizenship, segregated them in public life, and removed them from political affairs. For most blacks the postwar labor system closely resembled the pre–Civil War conditions; by law, they were free, but the harshness of their lives had barely eased since slavery days.

Elsewhere, westward expansion accelerated. The Indians of the Great Plains found their land coveted, just as the Cherokees and other eastern Indians had years before, and ultimately had no more success in stopping the advance of white miners, cattlemen, and farmers. Even as the last of the Indian wars came to an end, Native Americans found themselves confined to reservations and subjected to pressures to pattern their lives after those of white Americans.

In the nation's cities and towns, industrialization continued apace after 1865. This period saw social and economic changes so substantial that by World War I a majority of Americans lived in urban areas and earned their living in factories and businesses. For those engaged in manual labor, working conditions often proved extremely hazardous. A growing number of the new urban wage earners were women, but they were confined to certain "female" occupations, such as stenography, typing, teaching, retail selling, and nursing.

As in the years before the Civil War, people immigrated from Europe and Asia in search of new opportunities in the United States. Many immigrants continued to arrived from England, Ireland, and Germany, but after 1896 the majority of newcomers came from eastern and southern Europe. For the most part, they settled in the burgeoning industrial cities of the Northeast and Middle West, but immigrants populated all regions of America, where they strove to adapt to new and sometimes strange and hostile environments.

Europeans were not the only people on the move in these years. Southern blacks, facing poverty and racial discrimination at home, began to emigrate north around 1880. When World War I curtailed

3

European immigration and created a labor shortage in the nation's industries, the black move north accelerated. Although these migrants usually found a better life in their new surroundings, they nonetheless discovered that Northern cities had their own forms of racial discrimination.

The readings that follow explore the major changes noted above. The essays and documents focus on the new Southern labor system, the settlement of the last frontier, the westward movement's impact on Indian life and culture, the consequences of industrial growth for both men and women workers, and the migration of peoples from abroad and of blacks from the South to the North. Part I concludes with a look at how America's participation in World War I altered the lives of soldiers and civilians.

Chapter 1

Reconstruction and Free Plantation Labor

The Civil War eliminated slavery but left undecided the question of what agrarian labor system would replace it in the devastated South. Peter Kolchin's essay "Free Plantation Labor" describes how Alabama freedmen (former slaves) and their erstwhile masters established relationships to maintain the productivity of the land. As you read, consider the aspirations, fears, and misunderstandings that governed the behavior of blacks, Southern whites, and Southern-based representatives of the federal government working for the Freedmen's Bureau. Although salaried agricultural labor and tenant farming made an appearance on Alabama plantations, it was sharecropping that came to dominate agriculture in that state and much of the rest of the South. Sharecropping ultimately proved an unproductive system of land management, crushing black farmers and their families under a yoke of debt and poverty for generations to come. Yet, as Kolchin's essay points out, both blacks and whites initially found the system attractive. Why?

The first document is a letter from a freed slave to his former master. The letter speaks eloquently of the conditions and humiliations that he had endured in the past and also of the better life that he has built for himself. How would you describe the general tone of the letter?

Although even the most tenacious plantation owners recognized that slavery was finished and that the South needed a new system of labor, few white Southerners could accept the freedmen as social and political equals. In 1865–1866, Southern politicians established Black Codes to ensure white supremacy. The second document is the Black Code of St. Landry's Parish, Louisiana. To what extent does this document support the claim of some Northern Radical Republicans that the Black Codes amounted to nothing less than the continuation of slavery? The code explains part of the motivation for the passage of the Reconstruction amendments and laws by the Republican-controlled federal government. It also provides clues to the fate in store for Southern blacks after 1877, when the last federal troops left the South and Reconstruction ended.

The third document consists of letters from two Northern schoolteachers, who were among the hundreds who traveled south after the war under the auspices of the Freedmen's Bureau and several private philanthropic agencies. What do these documents and the Kolchin essay indicate about the goals of the newly freed blacks? What actions did the freedmen take to achieve their objectives?

Beginning in the 1890s, the freedmen lost the rights and opportunities they had won during the ten years following the Civil War, as Southern whites began systematically to disfranchise blacks and to institutionalize segregationist and discriminatory practices. Whites prohibited blacks from voting, segregated them in public life, denied them justice in the courts, and placed their children in underfunded "colored schools." Although blacks never accepted these conditions as permanent, over half a century would pass before their march toward full equality resumed with the promise of significant success.

E S S A Y

Free Plantation Labor

Peter Kolchin

I

Despite the migration of Negroes to Alabama's towns and cities, the most important question to blacks in 1865 concerned the role of the rural freedmen. The end of the Civil War found general confusion as to their status. "You have been told by the Yankees and others that you are free," one planter declared to his Negroes in April 1865. "This may be so! I do not doubt that you will be freed in a few years. But the terms and time of your ultimate freedom is not yet fully and definitely settled. Neither you nor I know what is to be the final result." Even if free, the Negroes' position in society remained to be determined. Presumably they would continue to till the land, for agriculture, especially cotton, was the mainstay of the state's economy and would continue as such for years. But it was not clear under what new system the land would be cultivated.

In the spring of 1865, before the arrival of Freedmen's Bureau officials, Union officers played the greatest role in establishing the new order. Throughout the state, they informed whites that the Negroes really were free and gathered blacks together to tell them of their new rights. "All persons formerly held as slaves will be treated in every respect as entitled to the rights of freedmen, and such as desire their services will be required to pay for them," announced Lieutenant Colonel C. T. Christensen in a typical statement from Mobile.

The army also served as the precursor of the Freedmen's Bureau in establishing the new agricultural labor system, according to which freedmen were to work under yearly contracts with their employers, supervised by federal officials. Varieties of this contract system had already been tested in certain Union-occupied portions of the South before the end of the war, and in April Thomas W. Conway, general superintendent of freedmen for the Department of the Gulf, arrived in Montgomery to inaugurate it in Alabama. But it was late summer before the Freedmen's Bureau was fully established throughout the state, and until then the task of supervising relations between planters and freedmen rested primarily with the army. Officers advised blacks to remain on their plantations "whenever the persons by whom they are employed recognize their rights and agree to compensate them for their services." Similar circulars, although not always so friendly in tone, were issued from other parts of the state. Brevet Major General R. S. Granger ordered that all contracts between freedmen and planters must be in writing. He added bluntly that "[t]hose found unemployed will be arrested and set to work." But officers were usually vague in recommending what the compensation of the freedmen, or their working relations with planters, should be. Conditions varied widely from one location to another during the first few months after the war as individual army officers, Freedmen's Bureau officials, and planters exercised their own discretion.

Observers generally noted a demoralization of labor during the spring and summer of 1865, which they frequently associated with the early migration of freedmen. Upon his arrival in Montgomery, Conway noted a "perfect reign of idleness on the part of the negroes." Other Bureau officials joined planters in declaring that blacks either would not work or would at best make feeble symbolic gestures toward work. Southern whites, and some Northern ones as well, complained that Negroes refused to work and were "impudent and defyant." In one piedmont county, the commander of the local militia warned that "[t]he negroes are becoming very impudent and unless something is done very soon I fear the consequences." White Alabamians frequently confused black "impudence" with outright revolt, but organized violence did occasionally occur.

Events on the Henry Watson plantation, a large estate in the blackbelt county of Greene, illustrate the behavior of freedmen during the first few months after the war. "About the first of June," wrote John Parrish to his brother-in-law Henry Watson, who was vacationing in Germany, "your negroes rebelled against the authority" of the overseer George Hagin. They refused to work and demanded his removal. As Parrish was ill at the time, he induced a friend of Watson's, J. A. Wemyss, to go to the plantation and attempt to put things in order. "He made a sort of compromise bargain with the negroes," Parrish reported, "agreeing that if they would remain he would give them part of the crop, they should be clothed and fed as usual, and that Mr. Hagan [sic] should have no authority over them. . . . All hands are having a good easy time, not doing half work." Six days later Parrish reported that "they have again rebelled." When Wemyss informed them firmly that they must submit to the overseer's authority, at first they "amiably consented," but soon they once again objected— "their complaints were universal, very ugly"—and seventeen of them left for nearby Uniontown, where a federal garrison was stationed. Meanwhile, a Freedmen's Bureau agent had arrived in Greensboro. Parrish brought him to the plantation, where he "modified the contract in the negroes['] fav[or] & made them sign it with their marks." The modified contract granted the laborers one-eighth of the crop.

When Watson finally returned from Germany to take charge of matters himself, he was totally disgusted with what he found. The Negroes "claim of their masters full and complete compliance on their part," he complained, "but forget that they agreed to do anything on theirs and are all idle, doing nothing, insisting that they shall be fed and are eating off their masters." Finding such a state of affairs more than he could tolerate, he decided to rent the plantation to overseer Hagin and "have nothing to do with the hiring of hands or the care of the plantation." Hagin, in turn, later broke up the plantation and sublet individual lots to Negro families.

II

Southern whites, long accustomed to thinking of their slaves as faithful and docile servants, were quick to blame outsiders for any trouble. As early as April 1862, a north Alabama planter had noted that the Union soldiers "to a great extent demoralized the negroes. . . . The negroes were delighted with them and since they left enough can be seen to convince one that the Federal army[,] the negroes and white Southern people cannot inhabit the same country." After the war, planters continued to complain about the harmful influence of the army. The presence of black troops was especially unpalatable to former slave owners. "[N]egroes will *not work* surrounded [by] black troops encouraging them to insubordination," complained one outraged resident of a blackbelt community.

Although Alabama whites were deeply humiliated by the presence of Yankees and black troops in their midst, there was little foundation to the complaints about outside agitation. Indeed, federal officials often cooperated directly with planters and local authorities in attempting to keep blacks in line. Army officers urged Negroes to stay on their plantations. Freedmen's Bureau agents frequently assisted in keeping order, too. "My predecessors here worked with a view to please the white citizens, at the expense of, and injustice to, the Freedmen," complained a shocked Bureau assistant superintendent shortly after his arrival in Tuskegee. "They have invariably given permission to inflict punishment for insolence or idleness, and have detailed soldiers to tie up and otherwise punish the laborers who have, in the opinion of the employers, been *refractory.*" [Freedmen's Bureau] Commissioner [O. O.] Howard later explained that the Bureau "came to the assistance of the Planters" and succeeded in making the blacks "reliable laborers under the free system." He added that "[t]he good conduct of the millions of freedmen is due to a large extent to our officers of the Army and the Bureau."

A more substantial cause of the demoralization of labor was the mistrust existing between freedman and planter. Where this mistrust was minimal—that is, where planters and freedmen had relatively close ties and where planters readily acknowledged the changed condition of their relations—Negroes continued to work well. More often than not it was the small planter, who worked in the field beside his employees and knew them personally, who managed to remain on good terms with them. But few planters were willing to accept all the implications of the overthrow of slavery. "Thus far," pronounced the state's leading newspaper [*Daily Selma Times*] in October, "we are sorry to say that experience teaches that the negro in a free condition will not work on the old plantations." Another newspaper agreed that freedom had made the blacks "dissatisfied, listless, improvident, and unprofitable drones." Throughout the state, whites refused to believe that Negroes would work without the compulsion of slavery.

Some planters continued to hope that emancipation could either be rescinded or delayed, and "consequently told the negroes they were not free." Others recognized the de jure passing of slavery and concentrated on making the condition of the freedmen as near as possible to that of slaves. Upon his arrival in Montgomery, Conway noted that "the Planters appeared disinclined to offer employment, except with guarantees that would practically reduce the Freedmen again to a state of bondage."

Early contracts between planters and freedmen reflected the disbelief of whites in the possibility of free black labor and their desire to maintain slavery in fact, if not in name. Some planters reached "verbal agreements" with freedmen to continue as they had, without recompense. It was also relatively easy, before the Freedmen's Bureau was firmly established, for planters to lure former slaves into signing contracts that essentially perpetuated their condition. "Today I contracted with Jane and Dick to serve the remainder of the year, such being the federal law," Sarah Espy of the mountain county of Cherokee wrote in her diary in July. "I give them their victuals and clothing, the proceeds of their patches[,] and they are to proceed as heretofore." Similar contracts were made in other regions, and numerous Freedmen's Bureau officials reported upon arrival at their posts that Negroes were working without pay. The practice was summarized in a report to [Assistant Commissioner Wager] Swayne: "We find that the agreements they [the freedmen] have been working under (some of them since last April) are merely a paper drawn up by their late owners," wrote Captain J. W. Cogswell, "in which the negro promises to work for an indefinite time for nothing but his board and clothes, and the white man agrees to do nothing."

When some compensation was provided, as was the case more often than not, it almost always involved a share of the crop. There seems to have been little or no experimentation with wage labor during the first few months after the war. The initial reason for the immediate widespread adoption of sharecropping was simple: the defeated South did not have sufficient currency to pay laborers in cash. Cropping provided a convenient mode of paying freedmen without any money transactions.

Partly for the same reason and partly from tradition, most early contracts specified that food and medical care would be provided by the planter. In addition to being a continuation of the old plantation paternalism, this provision also conformed to the wishes of the Freedmen's Bureau. Shortly after his arrival in Montgomery, Swayne drew up a list of proposed labor regulations. One was that "[p]art of the compensation is required to be in food and medical attendance, lest the improvident leave their families to suffer or the weak are obliged to purchase at unjust rates what they must immediately have." The concern of the Freedmen's Bureau for the welfare of the freedmen, superimposed upon the legacy of slave paternalism and combined with the shortage of currency, insured that early contracts would give Negroes, in addition to their share of the crop, "quarters, fuel, necessary clothes, [and] medical attendance in case of sickness."

Although the size of the shares freedmen received in 1865 varied considerably, it was almost always very small. W. C. Penick agreed to pay his laborers one-quarter of the crop, but such liberality was rare during the summer of 1865. More typical was the contract between Henry Watson and his more than fifty adult blacks, which promised them one-eighth of the crop. In other cases shares varied from one-quarter to one-tenth of the crop.

In addition to appropriating the greater portion of the freedmen's labor, planters were concerned with maintaining control over their lives. "I look upon slavery as gone, gone, gone, beyond the possibility of help," lamented one planter. He added reassuringly, however, that "we have the power to pass stringent police laws to govern the negroes—This is a blessing—For they must be controlled in some way or white people cannot live amongst them." Such an outlook did not necessarily represent a conscious effort to thwart the meaning of freedom, for whites had been conditioned by years of slavery to look upon subservience as the only condition compatible with Negro, or any plantation, labor. Nevertheless, the effect was the same. Early contracts often included provisions regulating the behavior of laborers. A typical one provided that "all orders from the manager are to be promptly and implicitly obeyed under any and all circumstances" and added "[i]t is also agreed that none of the said negroes will under any circumstances leave the plantation without a written permission from the manager." If any of them quit work before the expiration of the contract, he was to forfeit all his wages. Some contracts gave planters authority to whip refractory Negroes.

It is only as a response to such attempts to perpetuate slave conditions that the seeming demoralization of black labor can be understood. Although whites pointed at idle or turbulent Negroes and repeated that they did not comprehend the meaning of freedom, the lack of comprehension was on the part of Alabama's whites. Blacks lost little time in demonstrating their grasp of the essentials of freedom and the tactical flexibility their new condition provided. Just as many felt compelled to leave their old plantations immediately after the war to prevent old relations from being perpetuated, so did they find it necessary to establish at the outset that they would not labor under conditions that made them free in name but slave in fact.

III

In December 1865 events reached something of a crisis as planters continued to strive for a return to the methods of prewar days and blacks continued to resist. Planter-laborer relationships were tense during the summer and fall, but with contracts entered into after the war due to expire on 31 December, the approach of the new year heralded an especially difficult time. Negroes now had the experience of over half a year as freedmen in dealing with planters. They also had the backing of the Freedmen's Bureau, which, if generally ambivalent about the precise position of the freedman in Southern society, refused to sanction his essential reenslavement. The culmination of the demoralization of labor and the mass migrations of 1865 was the refusal of many blacks to contract for the following year.

One reason Negroes were slow to contract was that many of them expected the plantations of their ex-masters to be divided among them at the start of the year. While this idea proved to be a total misconception, it was neither so ludicrous nor so far-fetched a notion as white Alabamians portrayed it. Southern whites themselves had contributed greatly to the expectation by warning during the war that defeat would result in the confiscation of their lands. Commissioner Howard had originally intended to turn over confiscated and abandoned lands to the freedmen, and it was only when President Johnson directly countermanded this policy in the autumn of 1865 that the Bureau reversed itself and began restoring the lands in its possession to the original owners. As the end of the year approached, Freedmen's Bureau officials carefully explained to Negroes that they were not to be given land and advised them to contract for moderate wages.

White Alabamians responded to the black desire for land by exaggerating the extent to which the freedmen expected confiscation, playing up every minor incident, and predicting ominously that New Year's would bring a black uprising. They complained of Negroes arming themselves, and in at least one area whites organized armed patrols to defend themselves against an imagined impending Negro insurrection. Other observers, however, denied any threat of an uprising, and according to [reformer] Carl Schurz rumors were "spread about impending negro insurrections evidently for no other purpose than to serve as a pretext for annoying police regulations concerning the colored people."

The refusal of the freedmen to contract in December in no way presaged a rebellion, but merely expressed their reluctance to repeat their unhappy experience of the past half-year. Without careful Freedmen's Bureau supervision, the contract system threatened to become little more than an opportunity for whites to take advantage of illiterate and ignorant blacks. As Swayne wrote, with what turned out to be something of an underestimation of the abilities of the newly freed slaves, "[c]ontracts imply bargaining and litigation, and at neither of these is the freedman a match for his Employer." For this reason, the assistant commissioner [Swayne] reported, planters "so vigorously demanded contracts there was danger they would not undertake to plant at all without them."

That the fears of insurrection consisted chiefly of groundless rumors became evident when New Year's day passed without the slightest hint of trouble. To the astonishment and relief of whites, freedmen rushed to contract during the first few days of 1866 and then settled down to work. "The praiseworthy conduct of the negroes has surprised many," declared the Selma *Morning Times* in an editorial that typified the general white response. The demoralizing effects of emancipation about which whites had complained so bitterly vanished in a matter of days. "One thing is obvious," recorded a surprised planter; "the negroes, who are hired are farming and working much better than any one predicted they would work." Other white Alabamians agreed. From Tuskegee, the local Freedmen's Bureau agent boasted that "the Freedmen have commenced work with such a zeal as to merit the praise and approbation of the Planters. Planters say to me [']my negroes have never done so well as they are doing now.[']"

But if planters rejoiced that their laborers were hard at work, the freedmen had won a signal victory that was noticed by the more perceptive whites. "I think the negro hire was very high," complained future Democratic Governor George S. Houston; "[I] never had any idea of paying that much for negroes." He was right. Gone were the days when a typical contract gave the laborers one-eighth of the crop, or merely bed and board. By refusing to contract until the last moment, the freedmen had thrown their prospective employers into a panic and forced a significant alteration in the terms of the ultimate settlement. Although neither so well concerted nor organized, the process had essentially the same effect as a massive general strike.

Aside from the presence of the Freedmen's Bureau, which made blatant cheating by planters more difficult, the prevailing shortage of labor proved an inestimable boon to the freedmen. In 1866, as throughout most of the early postwar period, the pressure was on the planter to find laborers rather than on the Negro to find employment. Freedmen could feel relatively free in refusing to contract on what they regarded as unsatisfactory terms or in leaving employers with whom they were unhappy. Labor stealing, or enticing freedmen to change employers for higher wages, was a persistent complaint among planters. Occasionally, blacks were even able to strike for higher wages, as in the mountain county of Cherokee, "where they bound themselves together, under a penalty of fifty lashes, to be laid on the naked back, not to contract to work for any white man during the present harvest, for less than two dollars per day."

As had been the case in 1865, the terms of working arrangements varied widely among plantations. Both the lower and upper limits of the pay scale, however, were substantially higher than they had been. Half, or perhaps slightly more than half, of the contracts provided for a division of the crop. In such cases, the laborer almost always received a larger share than he had in 1865. Although there are examples of freedmen receiving as little as one-sixth of the crop, the prevailing portion—when, as was usual in 1866, the laborer provided nothing but his own labor—was one-quarter. For the first time, many planters contracted to pay their employees money wages rather than a portion of the crop. A typical small planter recorded that he paid his eight field hands an average of ten dollars per month for men and fifty dollars a year for women, in addition to food. In other cases where Negroes worked for wages, the rate of compensation usually ranged from seven to fifteen dollars per month for men, and somewhat less for women.

IV

The economic disadvantage of sharecropping to the Negro became evident in 1866 as the bright prospects of winter and spring faded in the summer. By August the cotton crop, which once seemed so promising, had been reduced by unseasonal rains to half its usual size, and autumn saw the second straight crop failure. As the extent of the disaster became clear, whites across the state began to decide that free blacks were not working well after all. The *Clarke County Journal*, for example, noted that although freedmen had labored satisfactorily during the winter and spring, now they seemed stubborn and lazy. "What is the matter with the freedmen?" it queried.

The contract system provided innumerable opportunities for friction between planters and freedmen—especially sharecroppers—in time of crisis. True, there were occasional touching instances when planters looked after former slaves. One white wrote to Swayne that an ex-slave of his who had left him after the war "because he would not 'feel free' if he did not" was "about to be imposed upon by an unprincipled man, who is about to employ him for the next year for far less than he is worth. . . . Please write to me," begged the distressed planter in a letter asking the assistant commissioner for advice. "I am willing to put myself to some trouble to protect my former faithful slave." Most planters, however, were primarily interested in receiving the maximum possible labor from the freedmen at minimal cost, even if it involved cheating, violence, and brutality.

The most common complaint of the freedmen was that either after the main labor on the crop was done or when it came time to divide the crop, planters would drive them off the plantations, frequently charging them with some technical violation of contract. Unlike wage earners, who were relatively secure, sharecroppers could be discharged and deprived of any compensation whatsoever. Temporary laborers could then be hired either by the day or week to finish up any remaining work. From Greene County, in the blackbelt, a Freedmen's Bureau agent reported "I find many, many men who employed them [freedmen] are arresting them . . . in a large majority of cases without cause" and sending them to sit in jail until the crop was sold. Although in some instances Bureau officials, or even the courts, mediated between planters and freedmen and were able to secure for the latter some payment, many injustices went unnoticed or unredressed.

The cyclical pattern established in 1865–1866 was repeated with some variations the following year. In December 1866, blacks once again were reluctant to contract. Although many of them now had the additional experience of being cheated out of their share of the crop, the absence of any illusions over the possibility of land confiscation enabled most blacks and planters to come to agreements more quickly and with less bitter feeling on both sides than they had the previous year. By spring, whites were rejoicing over Alabama's good fortune and praising her Negroes for their hard work and reliability. "The freedmen, according to universal testimony, are working better than they did last year," reported the *Daily Selma Messenger* with satisfaction.

There was an almost universal return to sharecropping in 1867, although a very few planters and freedmen continued, despite the shortage of currency, to experiment with wages. Some Freedmen's Bureau officials, who felt that Negroes fared better economically on wages, and some white Alabamians, who supported the system under which blacks were most carefully supervised, continued to advocate wage labor. With very few exceptions, however, planters and freedmen ignored their pleas. Arrangements granting the laborers one-quarter of the crop were most widespread, although in a few instances freedmen contracted to provide their own food and receive half the crop.

Sharecropping triumphed because both planters and freedmen favored the system. To the average planter it continued to be a more feasible labor system than wages, if for no other reason than the shortage of currency. In addition, many whites felt that shares gave blacks an interest in the crop, thus providing them with an incentive to work. Most blacks apparently preferred cropping, despite the economic disadvantages, because it allowed them greater control of their own lives. Because of his interest in the crop, the sharecropper required less supervision. In contrast to the wage laborer, who was a hired hand clearly in a subordinate position to his employer, the cropper was the partner of the landowner in a joint business venture that provided the freedman with opportunities for greater individual discretion, dignity, and self-respect. For this reason, Negroes considered the cropper a notch above the wage laborer in the social scale. "I am not working for wages," declared one freedman to his employer, as he explained why he had a right to leave the plantation at will to attend political meetings, "but am part owner of the crop and as I have all the rights that you or any other man has I shall not suffer them abridged."

V

As in 1866, the cotton crop of 1867 was a poor one. By fall, planters had once again begun to complain about the inefficiencies of freedmen as laborers. "The cause of the cotton crop being so inferior is the inefficiency of labor and the bad season [is] more on account of labor than anything else," lamented George Hagin, the ex-overseer who had rented Henry Watson's plantation. "There has been a few of the old negroes that lived on the place before that have worked very well but the younger ones are worth nothing." A correspondent of the Union Springs *Times* proclaimed free labor a failure.

Once again, planters drove freedmen from their homes without pay. "Negroes are now being dismissed from the plantations[,] there being nothing more for them to do," explained one blackbelt resident. He added calmly that "[t]hey will all be turned loose without homes[,] money or provisions[;] at least no meat." From the northwest corner of the state, 114 Negroes appealed for assistance to Major General John Pope, who in April had assumed command of the Third Military District,* comprising Alabama, Georgia, and Florida. They explained that "unless some person in whom we can place the utmost confidence be appointed to superintend the settling up of our affairs, we do not feel that justice will be done us." In 1867, for the first time, many blacks were also fired for voting Republican or attending political meetings.

Occasionally, through unusual persistence or intelligence, blacks were able to enlist the aid of the Freedmen's Bureau and resist arbitrary discharge. Bernard Houston, a sharecropper on an Athens plantation, told his landlord, "I shall not suffer myself to be turned off[,] and under legal advice and the advice of assistant Commissioner of [the] Freedmans Bureau I shall stay there until the crop is matured[,] gathered and divided according to contract." The planter protested lamely that he objected to the Negro's being "disobedient" and denied that politics had anything to do with the situation, but a month later he complained to Swayne that the freedman was "yet on the place acting in utter and entire disobedience of orders & the necessary discipline of the plantation."

---

*Provisions of the First Reconstruction Act of 1867 divided the former Confederacy—Tennessee excepted—into five military districts, each under a commander responsible for protecting life and property.

In numerous other cases, freedmen were less fortunate. Freedmen's Bureau agents tried to come to the assistance of persecuted blacks, but there were simply too few agents for the job. Furthermore, since the procedure for handling grievances was not clear, Bureau representatives were not sure how best to dispose of them. Some turned cases over to the civil courts. In general, however, this method proved unsatisfactory. "[B]esides the slow process of the Law, there stands in the way the difficulty of obtaining counsel," explained one Bureau agent. "The Freedmen as a general thing have no mean[s] to pay a fee: consequently they submit to the swindle simply because they cannot purchase justice." The sub-assistant commissioner at Huntsville sent discharged freedmen back to their plantations and told them to stay there. In other locations, officials tried to mediate between laborers and planters. "I notify the parties concerned to appear at this office together, and try either to effect an understanding, or a settlement," explained one Bureau official. He reported that he had "so far been fortunate, to prevent any injustice to be done." But for every such settlement, many other grievances undoubtedly went unheard.

The cumulative effects of three years of substandard crops became increasingly evident during the late autumn and early winter of 1867–1868, a period of considerable tension because of the meeting of the Radical Constitutional Convention in December and the election to ratify the new constitution in February. The problem was no longer that freedmen were reluctant to contract, but rather that planters were unwilling or unable to plant. Their universal reaction to poor crops and low profits was to plan to cut back on planting operations. Unemployment among Negroes threatened to reach serious proportions for the first time since the war. . . .

VI

Hidden behind the daily monotony of agricultural labor, significant changes occurred in the lives of black plantation workers during their first few years of freedom. These changes were evident both in their relations with their employers and in their relations with each other. All of them can, with little inaccuracy and only slight ambiguity, be called moves toward independence. These moves, as much class as racial in nature, represented not only the desire of blacks to be free of white control, but also of ex-slave plantation laborers to be free of planter control.

"Freedom has worked great changes in the negro, bringing out all his inherent savage qualities," proclaimed the Mobile *Daily Register* in 1869. Certainly a growing physical restlessness and self-consciousness among black plantation workers—reinforced by the political emancipation brought about under congressional Reconstruction—were very evident. They were no longer willing to be imposed upon by their former owners. From the end of the war laborers, such as those on the Henry Watson plantation, had revolted against working under their old overseers. But the increasing

17

number of white complaints of Negro "impudence," "insolence," and "insubordination," and the increasing readiness of black laborers to resort to violence and organization when faced with an unpalatable situation, testified to their growing self-assertiveness and confidence. In December 1867, for example, planters in Russell County, who were forced to cut back on planting operations because of poor crops the previous year, complained that their laborers were "seizing and holding property upon some of the places. They are generally armed." A year later, a revolt in the same area had to be put down by military force.

This desire of agricultural laborers for independence, which led them to choose sharecropping over wages even though they usually fared better economically under a wage system, was one of the greatest causes of other changes in modes of life and labor on the plantation. Before the war, field hands on large plantations had usually lived in rows of cabins grouped together. They had worked together in a slave gang, under the authority of an overseer and perhaps a driver. Their lives had been, by and large, collective. After the war, black plantation laborers quickly indicated their preference for a more individual form of life. They objected to working under the control of an overseer. They also objected to the regimented nature of the work gang and the Negro quarters. These had been accepted "in the days of slavery, when laborers were driven by overseers by day, and penned like sheep at night, and not allowed to have any will of their own," reported one Freedmen's Bureau agent. "But now, being *free* to think and act for themselves, they feel their individual responsibility for their conduct, and the importance of maintaining a good character." He noted that fights frequently broke out among Negroes forced to live among others against their will.

Many planters found it necessary or useful to break up the former slave quarters and allow laborers to have individual huts, scattered across the plantations. The process was far from complete by the end of the 1860s, but the trend was unmistakable. As early as the spring of 1867, an article in the Montgomery *Daily Advertiser* described certain changes that had occurred in the appearance of one plantation community. "You do not see as large gangs together as of old times, but more frequently squads of five or ten in a place, working industriously without a driver," wrote the correspondent. "Several large land owners have broken up their old 'quarters' and have rebuilt the houses at selected points, scattered over the plantation. . . ."

Although most black sharecroppers continued to provide only their labor and receive food and clothing in addition to their usual quarter of the crop, the late 1860s saw the introduction of a new cropping arrangement that would, in a matter of years, be widely adopted. Early in 1868, a Freedmen's Bureau official noted that there "does not seem to be as much uniformity in the tenor of contracts as last year." He wrote that although "some give the freedmen one-fourth of the crop and provide rations as

18

was customary last year . . . others give one third of [the] crop, and require the laborers to furnish their own rations; and some give one half, the laborers bearing an equal share of the expense." The result was to remove the cropper still further from the wage laborer, and accentuate his role as a partner of the planter in a joint business venture.

Such changes in working and living conditions were sometimes fostered by planters themselves. Some, like Henry Watson, found it impossible to adjust to a new situation in which they did not have total control over their labor force. Under such circumstances, it was tempting for them to adopt whatever system would permit the least contact between employer and laborer, even if it resulted in more of the very independence that so troubled them. A correspondent from the blackbelt county of Hale reported to the Mobile *Daily Register* in 1869 that "everything appears experimental. . . . Many planters have turned their stock, teams, and every facility for farming, over to the negroes, and only require an amount of toll for the care of their land, refusing to superintend, direct, or even, in some cases, to suggest as to their management."

By the late 1860s, then, old patterns of agricultural relationships had been irreparably shattered, and the outlines of new ones had emerged. The logical culmination of emancipation for the plantation workers—the acquisition of their own land—remained for most an illusory dream. But within the confines of the plantation system great changes had occurred in the lives of the black laborers. They themselves had helped bring about most of these changes by demonstrating that they were not willing to continue in a position of complete subservience to their former owners. As one white planter lamented succinctly of the freedmen, "[T]hey wish to be free from restraint." That wish was a potent one in the years immediately following the Civil War.

DOCUMENTS

A Letter
"To My Old Master," c. 1865

TO MY OLD MASTER, COLONEL P. H. ANDERSON,
BIG SPRING, TENNESSEE

Sir: I got your letter, and was glad to find that you had not forgotten Jourdon, and that you wanted me to come back and live with you again, promising to do better for me than anybody else can. I have often felt uneasy about you. I thought the Yankees would have hung you long before this, for harboring Rebs they found at your house. I suppose they never

SOURCE: L. Maria Child, *The Freedmen's Book* (1865).

heard about your going to Colonel Martin's to kill the Union soldier that was left by his company in their stable. Although you shot at me twice before I left you, I did not want to hear of your being hurt, and am glad you are still living. It would do me good to go back to the dear old home again, and see Miss Mary and Miss Martha and Allen, Esther, Green, and Lee. Give my love to them all, and tell them I hope we will meet in the better world, if not in this. I would have gone back to see you all when I was working in the Nashville Hospital, but one of the neighbors told me that Henry intended to shoot me if he ever got a chance.

I want to know particularly what the good chance is you propose to give me. I am doing tolerably well here. I get twenty-five dollars a month, with victuals and clothing; have a comfortable home for Mandy—the folks call her Mrs. Anderson—and the children—Milly, Jane, and Grundy—go to school and are learning well. The teacher says Grundy has a head for a preacher. They go to Sunday school, and Mandy and me attend church regularly. We are kindly treated. Sometimes we overhear others saying, "Them colored people were slaves" down in Tennessee. The children feel hurt when they hear such remarks; but I tell them it was no disgrace in Tennessee to belong to Colonel Anderson. Many darkeys would have been proud, as I used to be, to call you master. Now if you will write and say what wages you will give me, I will be better able to decide whether it would be to my advantage to move back again.

As to my freedom, which you say I can have, there is nothing to be gained on that score, as I got my free papers in 1864 from the Provost-Marshal-General of the Department of Nashville. Mandy says she would be afraid to go back without some proof that you were disposed to treat us justly and kindly; and we have concluded to test your sincerity by asking you to send us our wages for the time we served you. This will make us forget and forgive old scores, and rely on your justice and friendship in the future. I served you faithfully for thirty-two years, and Mandy twenty years. At twenty-five dollars a month for me, and two dollars a week for Mandy, our earnings would amount to eleven thousand six hundred and eighty dollars. Add to this the interest for the time our wages have been kept back, and deduct what you paid for our clothing, and three doctor's visits to me, and pulling a tooth for Mandy, and the balance will show what we are in justice entitled to. Please send the money by Adam's Express, in care of V. Winters, Esq., Dayton, Ohio. If you fail to pay us for faithful labors in the past, we can have little faith in your promises in the future. We trust the good Maker has opened your eyes to the wrongs which you and your fathers have done to me and my fathers, in making us toil for you for generations without recompense. Here I draw my wages every Saturday night; but in Tennessee there was never any pay-day for the Negroes any more than for the horses and cows. Surely there will be a day of reckoning for those who defraud the laborer of his hire.

In answering this letter, please state if there would be any safety for my Milly and Jane, who are now grown up, and both good-looking girls. You know how it was with poor Matilda and Catherine. I would rather stay here and starve—and die, if it come to that—than have my girls brought to shame by the violence and wickedness of their young masters. You will also please state if there has been any schools opened for the colored children in your neighborhood. The great desire of my life now is to give my children an education, and have them form virtuous habits.

Say howdy to George Carter, and thank him for taking the pistol from you when you were shooting at me.

FROM YOUR OLD SERVANT,
JOURDON ANDERSON

The Black Code of St. Landry's Parish, 1865

Whereas it was formerly made the duty of the police jury to make suitable regulations for the police of slaves within the limits of the parish; and whereas slaves have become emancipated by the action of the ruling powers; and whereas it is necessary for public order, as well as for the comfort and correct deportment of said freedmen, that suitable regulations should be established for their government in their changed condition, the following ordinances are adopted, with the approval of the United States military authorities commanding in said parish, viz:

SECTION 1.   *Be it ordained by the police jury of the parish of St. Landry,* That no negro shall be allowed to pass within the limits of said parish without a special permit in writing from his employer. Whoever shall violate this provision shall pay a fine of two dollars and fifty cents, or in default thereof shall be forced to work four days on the public road, or suffer corporeal punishment as provided hereinafter.

SECTION 2.   *Be it further ordained,* That every negro who shall be found absent from the residence of his employer after 10 o'clock at night, without a written permit from his employer, shall pay a fine of five dollars, or in default thereof, shall be compelled to work five days on the public road, or suffer corporeal punishment as hereinafter provided.

SECTION 3.   *Be it further ordained,* That no negro shall be permitted to rent or keep a house within said parish. Any negro violating this provision shall be immediately ejected and compelled to find an employer; and any

SOURCE: U.S. Congress, *Senate Executive Document No. 2* (Washington, D.C., 1865), 93–94.

person who shall rent, or give the use of any house to any negro, in violation of this section, shall pay a fine of five dollars for each offence.

SECTION 4.   *Be it further ordained,* That every negro is required to be in the regular service of some white person, or former owner, who shall be held responsible for the conduct of said negro. But said employer or former owner may permit said negro to hire his own time by special permission in writing, which permission shall not extend over seven days at any one time. Any negro violating the provisions of this section shall be fined five dollars for each offence, or in default of the payment thereof shall be forced to work five days on the public road, or suffer corporeal punishment as hereinafter provided.

SECTION 5.   *Be it further ordained,* That no public meetings or congregations of negroes shall be allowed within said parish after sunset; but such public meetings and congregations may be held between the hours of sunrise and sunset, by the special permission in writing of the captain of patrol, within whose beat such meetings shall take place. This prohibition, however, is not intended to prevent negroes from attending the usual church services, conducted by white ministers and priests. Every negro violating the provisions of this section shall pay a fine of five dollars, or in default thereof shall be compelled to work five days on the public road, or suffer corporeal punishment as hereinafter provided.

SECTION 6.   *Be it further ordained,* That no negro shall be permitted to preach, exhort, or otherwise declaim to congregations of colored people, without a special permission in writing from the president of the police jury. Any negro violating the provisions of this section shall pay a fine of ten dollars, or in default thereof shall be forced to work ten days on the public road, or suffer corporeal punishment as hereinafter provided.

SECTION 7.   *Be it further ordained,* That no negro who is not in the military service shall be allowed to carry fire-arms, or any kind of weapons, within the parish, without the special written permission of his employers, approved and indorsed by the nearest or most convenient chief of patrol. Any one violating the provisions of this section shall forfeit his weapons and pay a fine of five dollars, or in default of the payment of said fine, shall be forced to work five days on the public road, or suffer corporeal punishment as hereinafter provided.

SECTION 8.   *Be it further ordained,* That no negro shall sell, barter, or exchange any articles of merchandise or traffic within said parish without the special written permission of his employer, specifying the articles of sale, barter or traffic. Any one thus offending shall pay a fine of one dollar for each offence, and suffer the forfeiture of said articles, or in default of the payment of said fine shall work one day on the public road, or suffer corporeal punishment as hereinafter provided.

SECTION 9.   *Be it further ordained,* That any negro found drunk within the said parish shall pay a fine of five dollars, or in default thereof shall work five days on the public road, or suffer corporeal punishment as hereinafter provided.

SECTION 10.   *Be it further ordained,* That all the foregoing provisions shall apply to negroes of both sexes.

SECTION 11.   *Be it further ordained,* That it shall be the duty of every citizen to act as a police officer for the detection of offences and the apprehension of offenders, who shall be immediately handed over to the proper captain or chief of patrol.

SECTION 12.   *Be it further ordained,* That the aforesaid penalties shall be summarily enforced, and that it shall be the duty of the captains and chiefs of patrol to see that the aforesaid ordinances are promptly executed.

SECTION 13.   *Be it further ordained,* That all sums collected from the aforesaid fines shall be immediately handed over to the parish treasurer.

SECTION 14.   *Be it further ordained,* That the corporeal punishment provided for in the foregoing sections shall consist in confining the body of the offender within a barrel placed over his or her shoulders, in the manner practiced in the army, such confinement not to continue longer than twelve hours, and for such time within the aforesaid limit as shall be fixed by the captain or chief of patrol who inflicts the penalty.

SECTION 15.   *Be it further ordained,* That these ordinances shall not interfere with any municipal or military regulations inconsistent with them within the limits of said parish.

SECTION 16.   *Be it further ordained,* That these ordinances shall take effect five days after their publication in the *Opelousas Courier.*

Dedicated Teachers,
Determined Students, 1869

RALEIGH, N.C., FEB. 22, 1869

It is surprising to me to see the amount of suffering which many of the people endure for the sake of sending their children to school. Men get very low wages here—from $2.50 to $8 per month usually, while a first rate hand may get $10, and a peck or two of meal per week for rations— and a great many men cannot get work at all. The women take in sewing and washing, go out by day to scour, etc. There is one woman who supports three children and keeps them at school; she says, "I don't care how hard I has to work, if I can only sen[d] Sallie and the boys to school looking respectable." Many of the girls have but one decent dress; it gets washed

SOURCE: Edward L. Pierce, "The Freedmen at Port Royal," *Atlantic Monthly* 12 (September 1869): 306–307.

and ironed on Saturday, and then is worn until the next Saturday, provided they do not tear it or fall in the mud; when such an accident happens there is an absent mark on the register. . . . One may go into their cabins on cold, windy days, and see daylight between every two boards, or feel the rain dropping through the roof; but a word of complaint is rarely heard. They are anxious to have the children "get on" in their books, and do not seem to feel impatient if they lack comforts themselves. A pile of books is seen in almost every cabin, though there be no furniture except a poor bed, a table and two or three broken chairs.

MISS M. A. PARKER

CHARLOTTESVILLE, VA., OCT. 17, 1866

Mrs. Gibbins (a colored native teacher) is very much liked by the colored people here. Her nature is so noble, that she is not so liable to stimulate petty jealousy among her people as many might under similar circumstances. . . . I think she is doing well in her new sphere of duty, especially in the matter of government. She has a kind of magnetism about her which is a good qualification for a teacher. She is really a fine reader of easy readings, and I should choose her to prepare scholars for me in that line, from among nine-tenths of those engaged in this work, so far as I have known her. She intends to pursue her studies in the evening with my help.

ANNA GARDNER

Chapter 2

The Last Frontier

From eastern North Dakota south to the Texas panhandle and west to the Rocky Mountains lay the Great Plains, a region at one time considered so bleak and uninhabitable that travelers referred to it as the "Great American Desert." In time, however, it would prove a source of immense wealth in minerals, grains, and livestock. This last American frontier—the land of the miner, the farmer, and the cowboy—by the late 1800s underwent a dramatic transformation paralleling change in the large cities and smoking factories of the urban, industrial East.

American literature and folklore have immortalized those who settled and tamed the Great Plains—the miners and their wide-open towns; the sod-house farmers; and, above all, the cowboys. But we all too often overlook the racial and ethnic diversity of those who built the West. Moreover, we forget what a critical role technology played in developing this region. The railroad, for example, was among the most important factors propelling the westward movement. In the essay "Linking a Continent and a Nation," Jack Chen highlights the role of Chinese immigrants in building the transcontinental railroad. How does Chen's de-

scription compare to popular depictions in western novels, in the movies, and on television?

The story of mining, like that of cattle raising and farming, was one of initial boom and prosperity for some, followed by bust for many. Like the other ventures, mining added to the nations's wealth—$1,242,872,032 in gold and $901,160,660 in silver were unearthed between 1860 and 1890. At the same time, it enriched the nation's folklore. In 1862, before he took the pen name Mark Twain, Samuel Clemens worked as a reporter for the Virginia City (Nevada) Enterprise. *In the first document, taken from his book* Roughing It, *Clemens describes Virginia City, America's premier mining town and home of the world's richest vein of silver, the Comstock Lode.*

Farmers also benefited from technology—steel plows to cut rough sod, windmills to pump water from deep in the ground, and barbed wire to fence off land on the treeless plains. In order to obtain these and other new, American-built agricultural tools such as threshers, harvesters, and binders, the settlers had to borrow money. Farmers could tolerate loneliness, brutally harsh weather, insects, and even debt, given the certainty of a rich harvest. However, beginning in 1887, when a series of arid summers devastated the region, hundreds of debt-ridden farmers abandoned their land, and many headed back East. The second document, an article by contemporary journalist William Allen White, describes such a scene. What can you conclude from the first two documents about the role of risk in agriculture and mining during the last half of the nineteenth century?

The last document, by Theodore Roosevelt, tells about a typical "cow town," Miles City, Montana. A romantic view of cowboys, it also reveals much about the ethnic diversity of the new Westerners. How does Roosevelt's picture add to the essay by Jack Chen?

ESSAY

Linking a Continent
and a Nation

Jack Chen

Without the "Chinamen's" knowledge and respect for explosive powders, ability to work on the side of near vertical cliffs at dizzying heights and survive hardships which white men could not endure, the Central Pacific would never have been completed when it was but much later.

R. W. HOWARD, *The Great Iron Trail*

The Chinese filled swamps, cut into mountains, dug tunnels, built bridges. As one historian notes, "The work was so obviously needed and all groups and areas vied with each other to build a railroad in their area, so that they would have welcomed the devil himself had he built a road. The lack of white laborers was too evident to cause even the most ardent anti-Chinese to resent their employment on such work."

ROBERT E. WYNNE, *Reaction to the Chinese in the Pacific Northwest and British Columbia*

The expansion of the railroad system in the United States was astonishingly swift. England had pioneered the building of railways and for a time was the acknowledged leader in the field, but from the moment the first locomotive was imported into the United States in 1829 the farsighted saw railways as the obvious solution for transport across the vast spaces of the American continent. By 1850, 9,000 miles of rails had been laid in the eastern states and up to the Mississippi. The California Gold Rush and the opening of the American West made talk about a transcontinental line more urgent. As too often happens, war spurred the realization of this project.

The West was won. California was a rich and influential state, but a wide unsettled belt of desert, plain, and mountains, separated it and Oregon from the rest of the states. As the economic separation of North and South showed, this situation was fraught with danger. It could lead to a political rift. In 1860, it was cheaper and quicker to reach San Francisco from Canton in China—a sixty-day voyage by sea—than from the Missouri River, six months away by wagon train. The urgent need was to link

California firmly with the industrialized eastern states and their 30,000 miles of railways. A railway would cut the journey to a week. The threat of civil war loomed larger between North and South over the slavery issue. Abraham Lincoln's Republican administration saw a northern transcontinental railway as a means to outflank the South by drawing the western states closer to the North. In 1862, Congress voted funds to build the 2,500-mile-long railway. It required enormous resourcefulness and determination to get this giant project off the drawing boards. Not much imagination was required to see its necessity, but the actual building presented daunting difficulties. It was calculated that its cost would mount to $100 million, double the federal budget of 1861.

It was Theodore Judah, described by his contemporaries as "Pacific Railroad Crazy," who began to give substance to the dream. An eastern engineer who had come west to build the short Sacramento Valley Railroad, he undertook a preliminary survey and reported that he had found a feasible route crossing the Sierra by way of Dutch Flat. But the mainly small investors who supported his efforts could not carry through the whole immense undertaking. With rumors of civil war between North and South, San Francisco capitalists, mostly Southerners, boycotted the scheme as a northern plot, and pressed for a southern route. Then the Big Four, Sacramento merchants, took up the challenge: Leland Stanford as president, C. P. Huntington as vice-president, Mark Hopkins as treasurer, and Charles Crocker, in charge of construction, formed the Central Pacific Railway Company. Judah was elbowed out.

The Big Four came as gold seekers in 1849 or soon after but found that there was more money to be made in storekeeping than in scrabbling in the rocks in the mountains. As Republicans, they held the state for the Union against the secessionists. Leland Stanford, the first president of the Central Pacific, was also the first Republican governor of California.

The beginnings were not auspicious. The Union Pacific was building from Omaha in the East over the plains to the Rockies, but supplies had to come in by water or wagon because the railways had not yet reached Omaha. The Civil War now raged and manpower, materials and funds were hard to get. The Indians were still contesting invasion of their lands. By 1864, however, with the Civil War ending, these problems were solved. The UP hired Civil War veterans, Irish immigrants fleeing famine and even Indian women, and the line began to move westward.

The Central Pacific, building eastward from Sacramento, had broken ground on January 8, 1863, but in 1864, beset by money and labor problems, it had built only thirty-one miles of track. It had an even more intractable manpower problem than the UP. California was sparsely populated, and the gold mines, homesteading, and other lucrative employments offered stiff competition for labor. Brought to the railhead, three out of every five men quit immediately and took off for the better prospects of the new

Nevada silver strikes. Even Charles Crocker, boss of construction and raging like a mad bull in the railway camps, could not control them. In the winter of 1864, the company had only 600 men working on the line when it had advertised for 5,000. Up to then, only white labor had been recruited and California white labor was still motivated by the Gold Rush syndrome. They wanted quick wealth, not hard, regimented railway work. After two years only fifty miles of track had been laid.

James Strobridge, superintendent of construction, testified to the 1876 Joint Congressional Committee on Chinese Immigration: "[These] were unsteady men, unreliable. Some would not go to work at all. . . . Some would stay until pay day, get a little money, get drunk and clear out." Something drastic had to be done.

In 1858, fifty Chinese had helped to build the California Central Railroad from Sacramento to Marysville. In 1860, Chinese were working on the San Jose Railway and giving a good account of themselves, so it is surprising that there was so much hesitation about employing them on the Central Pacific's western end of the first transcontinental railway. Faced with a growing crisis of no work done and mounting costs, Crocker suggested hiring Chinese. Strobridge strongly objected: "I will not boss Chinese. I don't think they could build a railroad." Leland Stanford was also reluctant. He had advocated exclusion of the Chinese from California and was embarrassed to reverse himself. Crocker, Huntington, Hopkins, and Stanford, the "Big Four" of the Central Pacific, were all merchants in hardware, dried goods, and groceries in the little town of Sacramento. Originally, they knew nothing about railroad building, but they were astute and hard-headed businessmen. Crocker was insistent. Wasted time was wasted money. The CP's need for labor was critical. The men they already had were threatening a strike. Finally fifty Chinese were hired for a trial.

Building the Transcontinental Railroad

In February 1865, they marched up in self-formed gangs of twelve to twenty men with their own supplies and cooks for each mess. They ate a meal of rice and dried cuttlefish, washed and slept, and early next morning were ready for work filling dump carts. Their discipline and grading—preparing the ground for track laying—delighted Strobridge. Soon fifty more were hired, and finally some 15,000 had been put on the payroll. Crocker was enthusiastic: "They prove nearly equal to white men in the amount of labor they perform, and are much more reliable. No danger of strikes among them. We are training them to all kinds of labor: blasting, driving horses, handling rock as well as pick and shovel." Countering Strobridge's argument that the Chinese were "not masons," Crocker pointed out that the race that built the Great Wall could certainly build a railroad culvert. Up on the Donner Pass today the fine stonework embankments built by the Chinese are serving well after a hundred years.

Charles Nordhoff, an acute observer, reports Strobridge telling him, "[The Chinese] learn all parts of the work easily." Nordhoff says he saw them "employed on every kind of work. . . . They do not drink, fight or strike; they do gamble, if it is not prevented; and it is always said of them that they are very cleanly in their habits. It is the custom, among them, after they have had their suppers every evening, to bathe with the help of small tubs. I doubt if the white laborers do as much." As well he might. Well-run boardinghouses in California in those days proudly advertised that they provided guests with a weekly bath.

Their wages at the start were $28 a month (twenty-six working days), and they furnished all their own food, cooking utensils, and tents. The headman of each gang, or sometimes an American employed as clerk by them, received all the wages and handed them out to the members of the work gang according to what had been earned. "Competent and wonderfully effective because tireless and unremitting in their industry," they worked from sun-up to sundown.

All observers remarked on the frugality of the Chinese. This was not surprising in view of the fact that, with a strong sense of filial duty, they came to America in order to save money and return as soon as possible to their homes and families in China. So they usually dressed poorly, and their dwellings were of the simplest [construction]. However, they ate well: rice and vermicelli (noodles) garnished with meats and vegetables; fish, dried oysters, cuttlefish, bacon and pork, and chicken on holidays, abalone meat, five kinds of dried vegetables, bamboo shoots, seaweed, salted cabbage, and mushroom, four kinds of dried fruit, and peanut oil and tea. This diet shows a considerable degree of sophistication and balance compared to the beef, beans, potatoes, bread, and butter of the white laborers. Other supplies were purchased from the shop maintained by a Chinese merchant contractor in one of the railway cars that followed them as they carried the railway line forward. Here they could buy pipes, tobacco, bowls, chopsticks, lamps, Chinese-style shoes of cotton with soft cotton soles, and ready-made clothing imported from China.

On Sundays, they rested, did their washing, and gambled. They were prone to argue noisily, but did not become besotted with whiskey and make themselves unfit for work on Monday. Their sobriety was much appreciated by their employers.

Curtis, the engineer in charge, described them as "the best roadbuilders in the world." The once skeptical Strobridge, a smart, pushing Irishman, also now pronounced them "the best in the world." Leland Stanford described them in a report on October 10, 1865, to [President] Andrew Johnson:

> As a class, they are quiet, peaceable, patient, industrious, and economical. More prudent and economical [than white laborers] they are contented with less wages. We find them organized for

30

mutual aid and assistance. Without them, it would be impossible to complete the western portion of this great national enterprise within the time required by the Act of Congress.

Crocker testified before the congressional committee that "if we found that we were in a hurry for a job of work, it was better to put on Chinese at once." All these men had originally resisted the employment of Chinese on the railway.

Four-fifths of the grading labor from Sacramento to Ogden was done by Chinese. In a couple of years more, of 13,500 workers on the payroll 12,000 were Chinese. They were nicknamed "Crocker's Pets."

Appreciating Chinese Skills

The Chinese crews won their reputation the hard way. They outperformed Cornish men brought in at extra wages to cut rock. Crocker testified,

> They would cut more rock in a week than the Cornish miners, and it was hard work, bone labor. [They] were skilled in using the hammer and drill, and they proved themselves equal to the very best Cornish miners in that work. They were very trusty, they were intelligent, and they lived up to their contracts.

Stanford held the Chinese workers in such high esteem that he provided in his will for the permanent employment of a large number on his estates. In the 1930s, some of their descendants were still living and working lands now owned by Stanford University.

The Chinese saved the day for Crocker and his colleagues. The terms of agreement with the government were that the railway companies would be paid from $16,000 to $48,000 for each mile of track laid. But there were only so many miles between the two terminal points of the projected line. The Union Pacific Company, working with 10,000 mainly Irish immigrants and Civil War veterans, had the advantage of building the line through Nebraska over the plains and made steady progress. The Central Pacific, after the first easy twenty-three miles between Newcastle and Colfax, had to conquer the granite mountains and gorges of the Sierra Nevada and Rockies before it could emerge onto the Nevada-Utah plains and make real speed and money. The line had to rise 7,000 feet in 100 miles over daunting terrain. Crocker and the Chinese proved up to the challenge. After reaching Cisco, there was no easy going. The line had to be literally carved out of the Sierra granite, through tunnels and on rock ledges cut on the sides of precipices.

Using techniques from China, they attacked one of the most difficult parts of the work: carrying the line over Cape Horn [promontory], with its sheer granite buttresses and steep shale embankments, 2,000 feet above the American River canyon. There was no foothold on its flanks. The indomitable Chinese, using age-old ways, were lowered from above in rope-held baskets, and there, suspended between earth and sky, they began to chip away with hammer and crowbar to form the narrow ledge that was later laboriously deepened to a shelf wide enough for the railway roadbed, 1,400 feet above the river.

Behind the advancing crews of Chinese builders came the money and supplies to keep the work going. This was an awesome exercise in logistics. The Big Four, unscrupulous, dishonest, and ruthless on a grand scale, were the geniuses of this effort. The marvel of engineering skill being created by Strobridge and his Chinese and Irish workers up in the Sierra was fed by a stream of iron rails, spikes, tools, blasting powder, locomotives, cars, and machinery. These materials arrived after an expensive and hazardous eight-month, 15,000-mile voyage from East Coast ports around Cape Horn to San Francisco, thence by river boat to Sacramento, and so to the railhead by road.

The weather, as well as the terrain, was harsh. The winter of 1865–1866 was one of the severest on record. Snow fell early, and storm after storm blanketed the Sierra Nevada. The ground froze solid. Sixty-foot drifts of snow had to be shoveled away before the graders could even reach the roadbed. Nearly half the work force of 9,000 men were set to clearing snow.

In these conditions, construction crews tackled the most formidable obstacle in their path: building the ten Summit Tunnels on the twenty-mile stretch between Cisco, ninety-two miles from Sacramento and Lake Ridge just west of Cold Stream Valley on the eastern slope of the summit. Work went on at all the tunnels simultaneously. Three shifts of eight hours each worked day and night.

The builders lived an eerie existence. In *The Big Four*, Oscar Lewis writes,

> Tunnels were dug beneath forty-foot drifts and for months, 3,000 workmen lived curious mole-like lives, passing from work to living quarters in dim passages far beneath the snow's surface. . . . [There] was constant danger, for as snows accumulated on the upper ridges, avalanches grew frequent, their approach heralded only by a brief thunderous roar. A second later, a work crew, a bunkhouse, an entire camp would go hurtling at a dizzy speed down miles of frozen canyon. Not until months later were the bodies recovered; sometimes groups were found with shovels or picks still clutched in their frozen hands.

On Christmas Day, 1866, the papers reported that "a gang of Chinamen employed by the railroad were covered up by a snow slide and four or five [note the imprecision] died before they could be exhumed." A whole camp of Chinese railway workers was enveloped during one night and had to be rescued by shovelers the next day.

No one has recorded the names of those who gave their lives in this stupendous undertaking. It is known that the bones of 1,200 men were shipped back to China to be buried in the land of their forefathers, but that was by no means the total score. The engineer John Gills recalled that "at Tunnel No. 10, some 15–20 Chinese [again, note the imprecision] were killed by a slide that winter. The year before, in the winter of 1864–65, two wagon road repairers had been buried and killed by a slide at the same location."

A. P. Partridge, who worked on the line, describes how 3,000 Chinese builders were driven out of the mountains by the early snow. "Most . . . came to Truckee and filled up all the old buildings and sheds. An old barn collapsed and killed four Chinese. A good many were frozen to death." One is astonished at the fortitude, discipline and dedication of the Chinese railroad workers.

Many years later, looking at the Union Pacific section of the line, an old railwayman remarked, "There's an Irishman buried under every tie of that road." Brawling, drink, cholera, and malaria took a heavy toll. The construction crew towns on the Union Pacific part of the track, with their saloons, gambling dens, and bordellos, were nicknamed "hells on wheels." Jack Casement, in charge of construction there, had been a general in the Civil War and prided himself on the discipline of his fighting forces. His work crews worked with military precision, but off the job they let themselves go. One day, after gambling in the streets on payday (instigated by professional gamblers) had gotten too much out of hand, a visitor, finding the street suddenly very quiet, asked him where the gamblers had gone. Casement pointed to a nearby cemetery and replied, "They all died with their boots on." It was still the Wild West.

It is characteristic that only one single case of violent brawling was reported among the Chinese from the time they started work until they completed the job.

The Central Pacific's Chinese became expert at all kinds of work: grading, drilling, masonry, and demolition. Using black powder, they could average 1.18 feet daily through granite so hard that an incautiously placed charge could blow out backward. The Summit Tunnel work force was entirely composed of Chinese, with mainly Irish foremen. Thirty to forty worked on each face, with twelve to fifteen on the heading and the rest on the bottom removing material.

The Donner tunnels, totaling 1,695 feet, had to be bored through solid rock, and 9,000 Chinese worked on them. To speed the work, a new and untried explosive, nitroglycerin, was used. The tunnels were completed in November 1867, after thirteen months. But winter began before the way could be opened and the tracks laid. That winter was worse than the preceding one, but to save time it was necessary to send crews ahead to continue building the line even while the tunnels were being cut. Therefore,

3,000 men were sent with 400 carts and horses to Palisade Canyon, 300 miles in advance of the railhead. "Hay, grain and all supplies for men and horses had to be hauled by teams over the deserts for that great distance," writes Strobridge. "Water for men and animals was hauled at times 40 miles." Trees were felled and the logs laid side by side to form a "corduroy" roadway. On log sleds greased with lard, hundreds of Chinese manhandled three locomotives and forty wagons over the mountains. Strobridge later testified that it "cost nearly three times what it would have cost to have done it in the summertime when it should have been done. But we shortened the time seven years from what Congress expected when the act was passed."

Between 10,000 and 11,000 men were kept working on the line from 1866 to 1869. The Sisson and Wallace Company (in which Crocker's brother was a leading member) and the Dutch merchant Cornelius Koopmanschap of San Francisco procured these men for the line. Through the summer of 1866, Crocker's Pets—6,000 strong—swarmed over the upper canyons of the Sierra, methodically slicing cuttings and pouring rock and debris to make landfills and strengthen the foundations of trestle bridges. Unlike the Caucasian laborers, who drank unboiled stream water, the Chinese slaked their thirst with weak tea and boiled water kept in old whiskey kegs filled by their mess cooks. They kept themselves clean and healthy by daily sponge baths in tubs of hot water prepared by their cooks, and the work went steadily forward.

Crocker has been described as a "hulking, relentless driver of men." But his Chinese crews responded to his leadership and drive and were caught up in the spirit of the epic work on which they were engaged. They cheered and waved their cartwheel hats as the first through train swept down the eastern slopes of the Sierra to the meeting of the lines. They worked with devotion and self-sacrifice to lay that twenty-odd miles of track for the Central Pacific Company in 1866 over the most difficult terrain. The cost of those miles was enormous—$280,000 a mile—but it brought the builders in sight of the easier terrain beyond the Sierra and the Rockies. Here costs of construction by veteran crews were only half the estimated amount of federal pay.

By summer 1868, an army of 14,000 railway builders was passing over the mountains into the great interior plain. Nine-tenths of that work force was Chinese. More than a quarter of all Chinese in the country were building the railway.

When every available Chinese in California had been recruited for the work, the Central Pacific arranged with Chinese labor contractors in San Francisco to get men direct from China and send them up to the railhead. It was evidently some of these newcomers who fell for the Piute Indian's tall tales of snakes in the desert "big enough to swallow a man easily." Thereupon "four or five hundred Chinese took their belongings and struck out to return directly to Sacramento," reports the *Alta California.* "Crocker and Company had spent quite a little money to secure them and they sent men on horseback after them. Most of them came back again kind of quieted down, and after nothing happened and they never saw any of the snakes, they forgot about them." At least one Chinese quit the job for a similar reason. His daughter, married to a professor of Chinese art, told me that her father had worked on the railway but quit because "he was scared of the bears." He later went into domestic service.

By September 1868, the track was completed for 307 miles from Sacramento, and the crews were laying rails across the plain east of the Sierra. Parallel with the track layers went the telegraph installers, stringing their wires on the poles and keeping the planners back at headquarters precisely apprised of where the end of the track was.

The Great Railway Competition

On the plains, the Chinese worked in tandem with all the Indians Crocker could entice to work on the iron rails. They began to hear of the exploits of the Union Pacific's "Irish terriers" building from the east. One day, the Irish laid six miles of track, they were told. The Chinese of the Central Pacific topped this with seven. "No Chinaman is going to beat us," growled the Irish, and the next day, they laid seven and a half miles of track. They swore that they would outperform the competition no matter what it did.

Crocker taunted the Union Pacific that his men could lay ten miles of track a day. Durant, president of the rival line, laid a $10,000 wager that it could not be done. Crocker took no chances. He waited until the day before the last sixteen miles of track had to be laid and brought up all needed supplies for instant use. Then he unleashed his crews. On April 28, 1869, while Union Pacific checkers and newspaper reporters looked on, a combined gang of Chinese and eight picked Irish rail handlers laid ten miles and 1,800 feet more of track in twelve hours. This record was never surpassed until the advent of mechanized track laying. Each Irishman that day walked a total distance of ten miles, and their combined muscle handled sixty tons of rail.

So keen was the competition that when the two lines approached each other, instead of changing direction to link up, their builders careered on and on for 100 miles, building lines that would never meet. Finally, the government prescribed that the linkage point should be Promontory [Point], Utah.

Competition was keen, but there seems to be no truth in the story that the Chinese and Irish in this phase of work were trying to blow each other up with explosives. It is a fact, however, that when the two lines were very near each other, the Union Pacific blasters did not give the Central Pacific men timely warning when setting off a charge, and several Chinese were hurt. Then a Central Pacific charge went off unannounced and several

Irishmen found themselves buried in dirt. This forced the foremen to take up the matter and an amicable settlement was arranged. There was no further trouble.

On May 10, 1869, the two lines were officially joined at Promontory [Point], north of Ogden in Utah. A great crowd gathered. A band played. An Irish crew and a Chinese crew were chosen to lay the last two rails side by side. The last tie was made of polished California laurel with a silver plate in its center proclaiming it "The last tie laid on the completion of the Pacific Railroad, May 10, 1869." But when the time came it was nowhere to be found. As consternation mounted, four Chinese approached with it on their shoulders and they laid it beneath the rails. A photographer stepped up and someone shouted to him "Shoot!" The Chinese only knew one meaning for that word. They fled. But order was restored and the famous ceremony began; Stanford drove a golden spike into the last tie with a silver hammer. The news flashed by telegraph to a waiting nation. But no Chinese appears in that famous picture of the toast celebrating the joining of the rails.

Crocker was one of the few who paid tribute to the Chinese that day: "I wish to call to your minds that the early completion of this railroad we have built has been in large measure due to the poor, despised class of laborers called the Chinese, to the fidelity and industry they have shown." No one even mentioned the name of Judah.

The building of the first transcontinental railway stands as a monument to the union of Yankee and Chinese-Irish drive and know-how. This was a formidable combination. They all complemented each other. Together they did in seven years what was expected to take at least fourteen.

In his book on the building of the railway, John Galloway, the noted transportation engineer, described this as "without doubt the greatest engineering feat of the nineteenth century," and that has never been disputed. David D. Colton, then vice-president of the Southern Pacific, was similarly generous in his praise of the Chinese contribution. He was asked, while giving evidence before the 1876 congressional committee, "Could you have constructed that road without Chinese labor?" He replied, "I do not think it could have been constructed so quickly, and with anything like the same amount of certainty as to what we were going to accomplish in the same length of time."

And, in answer to the question, "Do you think the Chinese have been a benefit to the State?" West Evans, a railway contractor, testified, "I do not see how we could do the work we have done, here, without them; at least I have done work that would not have been done if it had not been for the Chinamen, work that could not have been done without them."

It was heroic work. The Central Pacific crews had carried their railway 1,800 miles through the Sierra and Rocky mountains, over sagebrush desert and plain. The Union Pacific built only 689 miles, over much easier terrain.

It had 500 miles in which to carry its part of the line to a height of 5,000 feet, with another fifty more miles in which to reach the high passes of the Black Hills. With newly recruited crews, the Central Pacific had to gain an altitude of 7,000 feet from the plain in just over 100 miles and make a climb of 2,000 feet in just 20 miles.

All this monumental work was done before the age of mechanization. It was pick and shovel, hammer and crowbar work, with baskets for earth carried slung from shoulder poles and put on one-horse carts.

For their heroic work, the Chinese workmen began with a wage of $26 a month, providing their own food and shelter. This was gradually raised to $30 to $35 a month. Caucasians were paid the same amount of money, but their food and shelter were provided. Because it cost $0.75 to $1.00 a day to feed a white unskilled worker, each Chinese saved the Central Pacific, at a minimum, two-thirds the price of a white laborer (1865 rates). Chinese worked as masons, dynamiters, and blacksmiths and at other skilled jobs that paid white workers from $3 to $5 a day. So, at a minimum, the company saved about $5 million by hiring Chinese workers.

Did this really "deprive white workers of jobs" as anti-Chinese agitators claimed. Certainly not. In the first place, experience had proved that white workers simply did not want the jobs the Chinese took on the railroad. In fact, the Chinese created jobs for white workers as straw bosses, foremen, railhandlers, teamsters, and supervisors.

The wages paid to the Chinese were, in fact, comparable to those paid unskilled or semiskilled labor in the East (where labor was relatively plentiful), and the Chinese were at first satisfied. Charles Nordhoff estimated that the frugal Chinese could save about $13 a month out of those wages. The *Alta California* estimated their savings at $20 a month and later, perhaps, as wages increased, they could lay aside even more. With a bit of luck, a year and a half to two years of work would enable them to return to China with $400 to buy a bit of land and be well-to-do farmers.

But the Chinese began to learn the American way of life. On one occasion in June 1867, 2,000 tunnelers went on strike, asking for $40 a month, an eight-hour day in the tunnels, and an end to beating by foremen. "Eight hours a day good for white man, all same good for Chinese," said their spokesman in the pidgin English common in the construction camps. But solidarity with the other workers was lacking, and after a week the strike was called off when the Chinese heard that Crocker was recruiting strikebreakers from the eastern states.

When the task was done, most of the Chinese railwaymen were paid off. Some returned to China with their hard-earned savings, and the epic story of building the Iron Horse's pathway across the continent must have regaled many a family gathering there. Some returned with souvenirs of the great work, chips of one of the last ties, which had been dug up and split up among them. Some settled in the little towns that had grown up along the line of the railway. Others took the railway to seek adventure further east and south. Most made their way back to California and took what jobs they could find in that state's growing industries, trades, and other occupations. Many used their traditional and newly acquired skills on the other transcontinental lines and railways that were being swiftly built in the West and Midwest. This was the start of the diaspora of the Chinese immigrants in America.

The Union and Central Pacific tycoons had done well out of the building of the line. Congressional investigation committees later calculated that, of $73 million poured into the Union Pacific coffers, no more than $50 million could be justified as true costs. The Big Four and their associates in the Central Pacific had done even better. They had made at least $63 million and owned most of the CP stock worth around $100 million and 9 million acres of land grants to boot.

Ironically, the great railway soon had disastrous results for the Chinese themselves. It now cost only $40 for an immigrant to cross the continent by rail and a flood of immigrants took advantage of the ease and cheapness of travel on the line the Chinese had helped to build. The labor shortage (and resulting high wages) in California turned into a glut. When the tangled affairs of the Northern Pacific line led to the stock market crash of Black Friday, September 19, 1873, and to financial panic, California experienced its first real economic depression. There was devastating unemployment, and the Chinese were made the scapegoats.

Building Other Lines

The expansion of the railroads was even faster in the following decade. In 1850, the United States had 9,000 miles of track. In 1860, it had 30,000. In 1890, it had over 70,000 miles. Three years later, it had five transcontinental lines.

The first transcontinental railway was soon followed by four more links: (1) the Southern Pacific–Texas and Pacific, completed in 1883 from San Francisco to Texas by way of Yuma, Tucson, and El Paso; (2) the Atcheson, Topeka, and Santa Fe, completed in 1885 from Kansas City to Los Angeles via Santa Fe and Albuquerque; (3) the Northern Pacific completed in 1883 from Duluth, Minnesota, to Portland, Oregon; and (4) the Great Northern (1893). The skill of the Chinese as railroad builders was much sought after, and Chinese worked on all these lines. Some 15,000 worked on the Northern Pacific, laying tracks in Washington, Idaho, and Montana; 250 on the Houston and Texas line; 600 on the Alabama and Chattanooga line; 70 on the New Orleans line. Nearly 500 Chinese were recruited for the Union Pacific even after the lines were joined. Many worked in the Wyoming coal mines and during the summer months doubled as track laborers. They carried the Southern Pacific lines over the burning Mojave Desert. They helped link San Francisco with Portland in 1887.

The Canadian Pacific seized the chance to enlist veteran Chinese railwaymen from the Southern Pacific and Northern Pacific railroads and also brought Chinese workers direct from China. In 1880, some 1,500 were working on that line, increasing to 6,500 two years later. Casualties were heavy on this line. Hundreds lost their lives while working on it.

Chinese railwaymen helped on the Central and Southern Pacific's main line down the San Joaquin Valley in 1870 and 1871. They worked on the hookup to Los Angeles and the loop with seventeen tunnels over the Tehachapi Pass completed in 1876. On this line, 1,000 Chinese worked on the 6,975-foot San Fernando Tunnel, the longest in the West. This rail link between San Francisco and Los Angeles, tapping the rich Central Valley, played a major role in the development of California's agriculture, later its biggest industry. They worked on the line north from Sacramento along the Shasta route to Portland, which was reached in 1887. In 1869, the Virginia and Truckee line employed 450 Chinese, veterans of the Central Pacific, to grade its track. When the Virginia and Truckee's Carson and Colorado branch line was planned from Mound House to Benton, its tough manager Yerington arranged with the unions for the grading to be done by white labor to Dayton and by Chinese from Dayton on south. "If the entire line had to be graded by white labor, I would not think of driving a pick into the ground, but would abandon the undertaking entirely," he said.

Chinese laborers worked on the trans-Panamanian railway, which linked the Pacific and the Atlantic before the Panama Canal was completed. This railway played a major role in speeding up the economic development of the United States, but it was not built without sacrifice: hundreds of the Chinese builders died of fever and other causes during its construction.

This by no means completes the list of contributions of the Chinese railway workers. The transcontinental lines on which they worked "more than any other factor helped make the United States a united nation," writes the *Encyclopedia Britannica* ["Railways"]. They played a major role in building the communications network of iron roads that was the transport base of American industrial might in the twentieth century.

Speaking eloquently in favor of the Chinese immigrants, Oswald Garrison Villard said,

> I want to remind you of the things that Chinese labor did in opening up the Western portion of this country. . . . [They] stormed the forest fastnesses, endured cold and heat and the risk of death at hands of hostile Indians to aid in the opening up of our northwestern empire. I have a dispatch from the chief engineer of the Northwestern Pacific telling how Chinese laborers went out into eight feet of snow with the temperature far below zero to carry on the work when no American dared face the conditions.

And these men were from China's sun-drenched south, where it never snows.

In certain circles, there has been a conspiracy of silence about the Chinese railroadmen and what they did. When U.S. Secretary of Transportation John Volpe spoke at the "Golden Spike" centenary, not a single Chinese American was invited, and he made no mention in his speech of the Chinese railroad builders.

DOCUMENTS

Flush Times* in Nevada, c. 1862

Six months after my entry into journalism that grand "flush times" of Silverland began, and they continued with unabated splendor for three years. All difficulty about filling up the "local department" ceased, and the only trouble now was how to make the lengthened columns hold the world of incidents and happening that came to our literary net every day. Virginia had grown to be the "livest" town, for its age and population, that America had ever produced. The sidewalks swarmed with people— to such an extent, indeed, that it was generally no easy matter to stem the human tide. The streets themselves were just as crowded with quartz-wagons, freight-teams, and other vehicles. The procession was endless. So great was the pack, that buggies frequently had to wait half an hour for an opportunity to cross the principal street. Joy sat on every countenance, and there was a glad, almost fierce, intensity in every eye, that told of the money-getting schemes that held sway in every heart. Money was as plenty as dust; every individual considered himself wealthy, and a melancholy countenance was nowhere to be seen. There were military companies, fire companies, brass bands, banks, hotels, theaters, "hurdy-gurdy houses,"** wide-open gambling-palaces, political pow-wows, civic processions, street-fights, murders, inquests, riots, a whiskeymill every fifteen steps, a Board of Aldermen, a Mayor, a City Surveyor, a City Engineer, a Chief of the Fire Department, with First, Second, and Third Assistants, a Chief of Police, City Marshal, and a large police force, two Boards of Mining Brokers, a dozen breweries, and a half dozen jails and

SOURCE: Samuel L. Clemens, *Roughing It 2* (New York: Harper and Brothers, 1890): 11–13, 16–19.

*The term *flush times* refers to the silver and gold boom in Nevada in the 1860s.

**Hurdy-gurdy houses* is a slang term for dance halls.

station-houses in full operation, and some talk of building a church. The "flush times" were in magnificent flower! Large fireproof brick buildings were going up in the principal streets, and the wooden suburbs were spreading out in all directions. Town lots soared up to prices that were amazing.

The great "Comstock lode" stretched its opulent length straight through the town from north to south, and every mine on it was in diligent process of development. One of these mines alone employed six hundred and seventy-five men, and in the matter of elections the adage was, "as the 'Gould & Curry' [mine] goes, so goes the city." Laboring-men's wages were four and six dollars a day, and they worked in three "shifts" or gangs, and the blasting and picking and shoveling went on without ceasing, night and day.

The "city" of Virginia roosted royally midway up the steep side of Mount Davidson, seven thousand two hundred feet above the level of the sea, and in the clear Nevada atmosphere was visible from a distance of fifty miles! It claimed a population of fifteen thousand to eighteen thousand, and all day long half of this little army swarmed the streets like bees and the other half swarmed the drifts and tunnels of the "Comstock," hundreds of feet down in the earth directly under those same streets. . . .

My salary was increased to forty dollars a week. But I seldom drew it. I had plenty of other resources, and what were two broad twenty-dollar gold pieces to a man who had his pockets full of such and a cumbersome abundance of bright half-dollars besides? (Paper money has never come into use on the Pacific coast.) Reporting was lucrative, and every man in the town was lavish with his money and his "feet."* The city and all the great mountainside were riddled with mining-shafts. There were more mines than miners. True, not ten of these mines were yielding rock worth hauling to a mill, but everybody said, "Wait till the shaft gets down where the ledge comes in solid, and then you will see!" So nobody was discouraged. These were nearly all "wildcat" mines, and wholly worthless, but nobody believed it then. The "Ophir," the "Gould & Curry," the "Mexican," and other great mines on the Comstock lode in Virginia and Gold Hill were turning out huge piles of rich rock every day, and every man believed that his little wildcat claim was as good as any on the "main lead" and would infallibly be worth a thousand dollars a foot when he "got down where it came in solid." Poor fellow! he was blessedly blind to the fact that he would never see that day. So the thousand wildcat shafts burrowed deeper and deeper into the earth day by day, and all men were beside themselves with hope and happiness. How they labored, prophesied, exulted! Surely nothing like it was ever seen before since the world began.

*Shares of stock in wildcat mines were measured in feet.

Every one of these wildcat mines—not mines, but holes in the ground over imaginary mines—was incorporated and had handsome engraved "stock" and the stock was salable, too. It was bought and sold with a feverish avidity on the boards every day. You could go up on the mountainside, scratch around and find a ledge (there was no lack of them), put up a "notice" with a grandiloquent name on it, start a shaft, get your stock printed, and with nothing whatever to prove that your mine was worth a straw, you could put your stock on the market and sell out for hundreds and even thousands of dollars. To make money, and make it fast, was as easy as it was to eat your dinner. Every man owned "feet" in fifty different wildcat mines and considered his fortune made. Think of a city with not one solitary poor man in it! One would suppose that when month after month went by and still not a wildcat mine (by wildcat I mean, in general terms, *any* claim not located on the mother vein, *i.e.*, the "Comstock") yielded a ton of rock worth crushing, the people would begin to wonder if they were not putting too much faith in their prospective riches; but there was not a thought of such a thing. They burrowed away, bought and sold, and were happy.

New claims were taken daily, and it was the friendly custom to run straight to the newspaper offices, give the reporter forty or fifty "feet" and get him to go and examine the mine and publish a notice of it. They did not care a fig what you said about the property so [long as] you said something. Consequently we generally said a word or two to the effect that the "indications" were good, or that the ledge was "six feet wide," or that the rock "resembled the Comstock" (and so it did—but as a general thing the resemblance was not startling enough to knock you down!). . .

There was *nothing* in the shape of a mining claim that was not salable. We received presents of "feet" every day. If we needed a hundred dollars or so, we sold some; if not we hoarded it away, satisfied that it would ultimately be worth a thousand dollars a foot. I had a trunk about half full of "stock." When a claim made a stir in the market and went up to a high figure, I searched through my pile to see if I had any of its stock—and generally found it.

Heading East
Out of Kansas, 1895

There came through Emporia yesterday two old-fashioned "mover wagons," headed east. The stock in the caravan would invoice four horses, very poor and very tired; one mule, more disheartened than the horses; and one sad-eyed dog, that had probably been compelled to rustle his own precarious living for many a long and weary day.

A few farm implements of the simpler sort were in the wagon, but nothing that had wheels was moving except the two wagons. All the rest of the impedimenta had been left upon the battlefield, and these poor stragglers, defeated but not conquered, were fleeing to another field, to try the fight again.

These movers were from western Kansas—from Gray County, a county which holds a charter from the state to officiate as the very worst, most desolate, God-forsaken, man-deserted spot on the sad old earth. They had come from that wilderness only after a ten years' hard, vicious fight, a fight which had left its scars on their faces, had beat their bodies, had taken the elasticity from their steps, and left them crippled to enter the battle anew.

For ten years they had been fighting the elements. They had seen it stop raining for months at a time. They had heard the fury of the winter wind as it came whining across the short burned grass, and their children huddling in the corner. They have strained their eyes watching through the long summer days for the rain that never came. They have seen that big cloud roll up from the southwest about one o'clock in the afternoon, hover over the land, and stumble away with a few thumps of thunder as the sun went down. They have tossed through hot nights wild with worry, and have arisen only to find their worst nightmares grazing in reality on the brown stubble in front of their sun-warped doors.

They had such high hopes when they went out there; they are so desolate now—no, not now, for now they are in the land of corn and honey. They have come out of the wilderness, back to the land of promise. They are now in God's own country down on the Neosho, with their wife's folks, and the taste of apple butter and good cornbread and fresh meat and pie—pie-plant [rhubarb] pie like mother used to make—gladdened their shrunken palates last night. And real cream, curdling on their coffee saucers last night for supper, was a sight so rich and strange that it lingered in their dreams, wherein they walked beside the still water, and lay down in green pastures.

SOURCE: From William Allen White, Emporia (Kansas) *Gazette*, June 15, 1895.

A Montana Cowtown, 1899

A true "cow town" is worth seeing,—such a one as Miles City, for instance, especially at the time of the annual meeting of the great Montana Stock-raisers' Association. Then the whole place is full to overflowing, the importance of the meeting and the fun of the attendant frolics, especially the horse-races, drawing from the surrounding ranch country many hundreds of men of every degree, from the rich stock-owner worth his millions to the ordinary cowboy who works for forty dollars a month. It would be impossible to imagine a more typically American assemblage, for although there are always a certain number of foreigners, usually English, Irish, or German, yet they have become completely Americanized; and on the whole it would be difficult to gather a finer body of men, in spite of their numerous shortcomings. The ranch-owners differ more from each other than do the cowboys; and the former certainly compare very favorably with similar classes of capitalists in the East. Anything more foolish than the demagogic outcry against "cattle kings" it would be difficult to imagine. Indeed, there are very few businesses so absolutely legitimate as stock-raising and so beneficial to the nation at large; and a successful stock-grower must not only be shrewd, thrifty, patient, and enterprising, but he must also possess qualities of personal bravery, hardihood, and self-reliance to a degree not demanded in the least by any mercantile occupation in a community long settled. Stockmen are in the West the pioneers of civilization, and their daring and adventurousness make the after settlement of the region possible. The whole country owes them a great debt. . . .

The bulk of the cowboys themselves are South-westerners; but there are also many from the Eastern and the Northern States, who, if they begin young, do quite as well as the Southerners. The best hands are fairly bred to the work and follow it from their youth up. Nothing can be more foolish than for an Easterner to think he can become a cowboy in a few months' time. Many a young fellow comes out hot with enthusiasm for life on the plains, only to learn that his clumsiness is greater than he could have believed possible; that the cowboy business is like any other and has to be learned by serving a painful apprenticeship; and that this apprenticeship implies the endurance of rough fare, hard living, dirt, exposure of every kind, no little toil, and month after month of the dullest monotony. For cowboy work there is need of special traits and special training, and young Easterners should be sure of themselves before trying it: the struggle for existence is very keen in the far West, and it is no place for men who lack the ruder, coarser virtues and physical qualities, no matter how intellectual

SOURCE: Theodore Roosevelt, *Ranch Life and the Hunting-Trail* (New York: Century Co., 1899), 7, 10–11. Reprinted University Mircofilms, Ann Arbor, Michigan, 1966.

or how refined and delicate their sensibilities. Such are more likely to fail there than in older communities. Probably during the past few years more than half of the young Easterners who have come West with a little money to learn the cattle business have failed signally and lost what they had in the beginning. The West, especially the far West, needs men who have been bred on the farm or in the workshop far more than it does clerks or college graduates.

Some of the cowboys are Mexicans, who generally do the actual work well enough, but are not trustworthy; moreover, they are always regarded with extreme disfavor by the Texans in an outfit, among whom the intolerant caste spirit is very strong. Southern-born whites will never work under them, and look down upon all colored or half-caste races. One spring I had with my wagon a Pueblo Indian, an excellent rider and roper, but a drunken, worthless, lazy devil; and in the summer of 1886 there were with us a Sioux half-breed, a quiet, hard-working, faithful fellow, and a mulatto, who was one of the best cow-hands in the whole round-up.

Chapter 3

Indian Schools: "Americanizing" the Native American

The white settlers' movement onto the Great Plains devastated Native American tribes who had roamed the area for centuries. As on previous frontiers farther east, the Indians resisted the encroachment with some initial success, their most notable victory the defeat of General George Custer at the Little Bighorn River in 1876. However, the whites' superior manpower and technology, fueled by their desire to fulfill a "manifest destiny" to develop the entire continent, overcame the Native Americans, and in the end the whites removed virtually all of them to reservations.

During the 1870s and 1880s, even while the last Indian wars raged, the federal government passed legislation and instituted policies designed to solve the "Indian problem" by "Americanizing" them—assimilating them into American society. The federal government encouraged them, sometimes forcefully, to ex-

change their lands, held by the tribe as a whole, for individual holdings which they were expected to farm. Equally important, the government sought to educate their children away from their traditional cultures and provide them with the skills, knowledge, and attitudes deemed necessary for the new way of life that the dominant white culture dictated.

By 1881 the federal government operated 106 Indian day and boarding schools to accomplish these objectives. Although most of the schools were on or adjacent to reservation land, white educators placed their greatest faith in non-reservation boarding schools far removed from parental and tribal influences. Robert A. Trennert's essay. "Educating Indian Girls at Nonreservation Boarding Schools, 1878–1920" provides a detailed view of this policy in action. What do you think the advocates of Indian education meant by "assimilation"? To what does the author attribute the failure of the government's Indian-school policies during this period?

The first document consists of excerpts from the "Rules for Indian Schools" set forth by the Bureau of Indian Affairs (1890). What attitudes toward their mission and toward Native American youth would these instructions likely engender in the minds of the teachers who read them? In what ways does each of the rules cited contribute to the broad objectives of the government's Indian-education policies? What can you conclude about the immediate and long-term objectives of Indian education?

Although the government expressed its land and educational policies in positive terms, these principles in fact reflected the prevailing belief that the Native American culture was inferior. At the turn of the century, many social scientists had adapted Darwin's biological theories of evolution to explain social development, drawing conclusions totally rejected by their counterparts today. Specifically, they developed a theoretical hierarchy of superior and inferior races that placed northern Europeans at the top and Indians, blacks, and southern and eastern Europeans, among others, at the bottom. The second document, a 1905 report of the Board of Indian Commissioners, typifies the attitudes underlying governmental policies until the 1930s. This report sheds light on the basis for Indian policy and reveals much of the rationale for the immigration-restriction and racial-segregation laws of the era.

Many factors explain why, by the 1920s, Native Americans found themselves mired in poverty at the bottom of the economic ladder: the failure of the federal government's Indian-education policies, the poor land conditions under which they were expected to become independent farmers, and the racism and discrimination meted out by the dominant white culture. During the 1930s, however, conditions began to improve. The Indian Reorganization Act of 1934 called for the establishment of tribal governments and the election of tribal leaders, a decision that exemplified a more enlightened view of Native American culture and reflected the New Deal government's concern for the poor and disadvantaged.

After World War II, Native Americans, like other minority groups, orga-nized to proclaim their cultural identity and to demand full civil rights, economic opportunities, and the preservation of their culture. As a result, new Indian tribal colleges sprang up. As the final document reveals, despite limited financial re-sources, these institutions have managed to offer Native Americans real hope for a better future. In what significant ways do the new colleges differ from the old Indian boarding schools? What about them elicits such enthusiasm among Na-tive Americans?

ESSAY

Educating Indian Girls at Nonreservation Boarding Schools, 1878–1920

Robert A. Trennert

During the latter part of the nineteenth century the Bureau of Indian Affairs made an intensive effort to assimilate the Indian into American society. One important aspect of the government's acculturation program was Indian education. By means of reservation day schools, reservation boarding schools, and off-reservation industrial schools, the federal government attempted to obliterate the cultural heritage of Indian youths and replace it with the values of Anglo-American society. One of the more notable aspects of this program was the removal of young Indian women from their tribal homes to government schools in an effort to transform them into a government version of the ideal American woman. This program of assimilationist education, despite some accomplishments, generally failed to attain its goals. This study is a review of the education of Indian women at the institutions that best typified the government program—the off-reservation industrial training schools. An under-standing of this educational system provides some insight into the impact of the acculturation effort on the native population. Simultaneously, it illustrates some of the prevalent national images regarding both Indians and women.

The concept of educating native women first gained momentum among eighteenth-century New England missionaries who recommended that Indian girls might benefit from formal training in housekeeping. This idea matured to the point that, by the 1840s, the federal government had

SOURCE: Robert A. Trennert, "Educating Indian Girls at Nonreservation Boarding Schools, 1878–1920," *Western Historical Quarterly*, 13 (July 1982): 169–90. Copyright by the Western History Association. Reprinted by permission.

committed itself to educating Indian girls in the hope that women trained as good housewives would help their mates assimilate. A basic premise of this educational effort rested on the necessary elimination of Indian culture. Although recent scholarship has suggested that the division of labor between the sexes within Indian societies was rather equitable, mid-nineteenth-century Americans accepted a vision of Native American women as slaves toiling endlessly for their selfish, slovenly husbands and fathers in an atmosphere of immorality, degradation, and lust. Any cursory glance at contemporary literature provides striking evidence of this belief. Joel D. Steele, for example, in his 1876 history of the American nation described Indian society in the following terms: "The Indian was a barbarian. . . . Labor he considered degrading, and fit only for women. His squaw, therefore, built his wigwam, cut his wood, and carried his burdens when he journeyed. While he hunted or fished, she cleared the land . . . and dressed skins."

Government officials and humanitarian reformers shared Steele's opinion. Secretary of the Interior Carl Schurz, a noted reformer, stated in 1881 that "the Indian woman has so far been only a beast of burden. The girl, when arrived at maturity, was disposèd of like an article of trade. The Indian wife was treated by her husband alternately with animal fondness, and with the cruel brutality of the slave driver." Neither Steele nor Schurz was unique in his day; both expressed the general opinion of American society. From this perspective, if women were to be incorporated into American society, their sexual role and social standing stood in need of change.

The movement to educate Indian girls reflected new trends in women's education. Radical changes in the economic and social life of late nineteenth-century America set up a movement away from the traditional academy education of young women. Economic opportunity created by the industrial revolution combined with the decline of the family as a significant economic unit produced a demand for vocational preparation for women. The new school discipline of "domestic science," a modern homemaking technique, developed as a means to bring stability and scientific management to the American family and provide skills to the increasing number of women entering the work force. In the years following the Civil War, increased emphasis was placed on domestic and vocational education as schools incorporated the new discipline into their curriculum. Similar emphasis appeared in government planning for the education of Indian women as a means of their forced acculturation. However, educators skirted the question of whether native women should be trained for industry or homemaking.

During the 1870s, with the tribes being confined to reservations, the government intensified its efforts to provide education for Indian youth of both sexes. The establishment of the industrial training schools at the end of the decade accelerated the commitment to educate Indian women. These schools got their start in 1878 when Captain Richard Henry Pratt, in charge of a group of Indian prisoners at Fort Marion, Florida, persuaded the government to educate eighteen of the younger male inmates at Hampton Normal Institute, an all-black school in Virginia, run by General Samuel C. Armstrong. Within six months Pratt and Armstrong were pleased enough with the results of their experiment to request more students. Both men strongly believed that girls should be added to the program, and Armstrong even went so far as to stipulate that Hampton would take more Indian students only on condition that half be women. At first Indian Commissioner Ezra A. Hayt rejected the proposal, primarily because he questioned the morality of allowing Indian women to mix with black men, but Armstrong's argument that "without educated women there is no civilization" finally prevailed. Thus, when Pratt journeyed west in the fall of 1878 to recruit more students, he fully expected half to be women.

Pratt was permitted to enlist fifty Indian students on his trip up the Missouri River. Mrs. Pratt went along to aid with the enlistment of girls. Although they found very little problem in recruiting a group of boys, they had numerous difficulties locating girls. At Fort Berthold, for instance, the Indians objected to having their young women taken away from home. Pratt interpreted this objection in terms of his own ethnocentric beliefs, maintaining that Indian tribes made their "squaws" do all the work. "They are too valuable in the capacity of drudge during the years they should be at school to be spared to go," he reported. Ultimately it required the help of local missionaries to secure four female students. Even then there were unexpected problems. As Pratt noted, "One of the girls [age ten] was especially bright and there was a general desire to save her from the degradation of her Indian surroundings. The mother [age twenty-six] said that education and civilization would make her child look upon her as a savage, and that unless she could go with her child and learn too, the child could not come." Pratt included both mother and daughter. Not all the missionaries and government agents, however, shared Pratt's enthusiasm. At Cheyenne River and other agencies a number of officials echoed the sentiments of Commissioner Hayt regarding the morality of admitting girls to a black school, and they succeeded in blocking recruitment. As a result, only nine girls were sent to Hampton.

Although the educational experiences of the first Indian girls to attend Hampton have not been well documented, a few things are evident. The girls were kept under strict supervision and were separated from the boys except during times of classroom instruction. In addition, the girls were kept apart from black pupils. Most of the academic work was focused on learning the English language, and the girls also received instruction in household skills. The small number of girls, of course, made it difficult to implement a general educational plan. Moreover, considerable opposition remained to educating Indian women at Hampton. Many prominent reformers expected confrontations, or even worse, love affairs, between black and red. Others expressed concern that Indian students in an all-black setting would not receive sufficient incentive and demanded they have the benefit of direct contact with white citizens.

Captain Pratt himself wanted to separate the Indians and blacks, and despite the fact that no racial trouble surfaced at Hampton, he pressured the government to create a school solely for Indians. Indian contact with blacks did not fit in with his plans for native education, and he reminded Secretary Schurz that Indians could become useful citizens only "through living among our people." The government consented, and in the summer of 1879 Pratt was authorized to open a school at Carlisle Barracks, Pennsylvania, "provided both boys and girls are educated in said school." Thus, while Hampton continued to develop its own Indian program, it was soon accompanied by Carlisle and other all-Indian schools.

Under the guidance of General Armstrong at Hampton and Captain Pratt at Carlisle, a program for Indian women developed over a period of several years. Although these men differed on the question of racial mixing, they agreed on what Indian girls should be learning. By 1880, with fifty-seven Indian girls at Carlisle and about twenty at Hampton, the outlines of the program began to emerge. As rapidly as possible the girls were placed in a system that put maximum emphasis on domestic chores. Academic learning clearly played a subordinate role. The girls spent no more than half a day in the classroom and devoted the rest of their time to domestic work. At Carlisle the first arrivals were instructed in "the manufacture and mending of garments, the use of the sewing machine, laundry work, cooking, and the routine of household duties pertaining to their sex."

Discipline went hand in hand with work experience. Both Pratt and Armstrong possessed military backgrounds and insisted that girls be taught strict obedience. General Armstrong believed that obedience was completely foreign to the native mind and that discipline was a corollary to civilization. Girls, he thought, were more unmanageable than boys because of their "inherited spirit of independence." To instill the necessary discipline, the entire school routine was organized in martial fashion, and every facet of student life followed a strict timetable. Students who violated the rules were punished, sometimes by corporal means, but more commonly by ridicule. Although this discipline was perhaps no more severe than that in many non-Indian schools of the day, it contrasted dramatically with tribal educational patterns that often mixed learning with play. Thus, when Armstrong offered assurances that children accepted "the penalty gratefully as part of his [her] education in the good road," it might be viewed with a bit of skepticism.

Another integral part of the program centered on the idea of placing girls among white families to learn by association. The "outing" system, as it was soon called, began almost as quickly as the schools received students. Through this system Pratt expected to take Indian girls directly from their traditional homes and in three years make them acceptable for placement in public schools and private homes. By 1881 both Carlisle and Hampton were placing girls in white homes, most of which were located in rural Pennsylvania or New England. Here the girls were expected to become independent, secure a working knowledge of the English language, and acquire useful domestic skills. Students were usually sent to a family on an individual basis, although in a few cases several young women were placed in the same home. Emily Bowen, an outing program sponsor in Woodstock, Connecticut, reveals something of white motives for participation in the service. Miss Bowen, a former teacher, heard of Pratt's school in 1880 and became convinced that God had called upon her to "lift up the lowly." Hesitating to endure the dangers of the frontier, she volunteered instead to take eight Indian girls into her home to "educate them to return and be a blessing to their people." Bowen proposed to teach the girls "practical things, such as housework, sewing, and all that is necessary to make home comfortable and pleasant." In this manner, she hoped, the girls under her charge would take the "true missionary spirit" with them on their return to their people.

Having set the women's education program in motion, Pratt and his colleagues took time to reflect on just what result they anticipated from the training. In his 1881 report to Commissioner Hiram Price, Pratt charted out his expectations. Essentially he viewed the education of native girls as a supportive factor in the more important work of training boys. To enter American society, the Indian male needed a mate who would encourage his success and prevent any backsliding. "Of what avail is it," Pratt asked, "that the man be hard-working and industrious, providing by his labor food and clothing for his household, if the wife, unskilled in cookery, unused to the needle, with no habits of order or neatness, makes what might be a cheerful, happy home only a wretched abode of filth and squalor?" Pratt charged Indian women with clinging to "heathen rites and superstitions" and passing them on to their children. They were, in effect, unfit as mothers and wives. Thus, a woman's education was supremely important, not so much for her own benefit as for that of her husband. Pratt did acknowledge that girls were required to learn more than boys. An Indian male needed only to learn a single trade; the woman, on the other hand, "must learn to sew and to cook, to wash and iron, she must learn lessons of neatness, order, and economy, for without a practical knowledge of all these she cannot make a home."

The size of the girls' program increased dramatically during the 1880s. The government was so taken with the apparent success of Carlisle and Hampton that it began to open similar schools in the West. As the industrial schools expanded, however, the women's program became institutionalized, causing a substantial deviation from the original concept. One reason for this change involved economic factors. The Indian schools, which for decades received $167 a year per student, suffered a chronic lack of funds; thus, to remain self-sufficient, they found themselves relying upon student labor whenever possible. Because they already believed in the educational value of manual labor, it was not a large step for school officials to begin relying upon student labor to keep the schools operating. By the mid-1880s, with hundreds of women attending the industrial schools, student labor had assumed a significant role in school operations. Thus, girls, originally expected to receive a useful education, found themselves becoming more important as an economic factor in the survival of the schools.

The girls' work program that developed at Hampton is typical of the increasing reliance on Indian labor. By 1883 the women's training section was divided into such departments as sewing, housekeeping, and laundry, each in the charge of a white matron or a black graduate. The forty-one girls assigned to the sewing department made the school's bedding, wardrobe, and curtains. At Winona Lodge, the dormitory for Indian girls that also supported the housework division, the matron described the work routine as follows: "All of the Indian girls, from eight to twenty-four years old, make their own clothes, wash and iron them, care for their rooms, and a great many of them take care of the teachers' rooms. Besides this they have extra work, such as sweeping, dusting, and scrubbing the corridors, stairs, hall, sewing-room, chapel, and cleaning other parts of the building." In addition, a large group of Indian girls worked in the school laundry doing the institution's wash.

Conditions were even more rigorous at western schools where a lack of labor put additional demands on female students. At Genoa, Nebraska, the superintendent reported that the few girls enrolled in that school were kept busy doing housework. With the exception of the laundry, which was detailed to the boys, girls were responsible for the sewing and repair of garments, including their own clothes, the small boys' wear, underwear for the large boys, and table linen. The kitchen, dining room, and dormitories were also maintained by women students. Similar circumstances prevailed at Albuquerque, where Superintendent P. F. Burke complained of having to use boys for domestic chores. He was much relieved when enough girls enrolled to allow "the making of the beds, sweeping, and cleaning both the boys' and girls' sleeping apartments." Because of inadequate facilities there were no girls enrolled when the Phoenix school opened in 1891; but as soon as a permanent building was constructed, Superintendent Wellington Rich requested twenty girls "to take the places now filled by boys in the several domestic departments of the school." Such uses of student labor were justified as a method of preparing girls for the duties of home life.

Some employees of the Indian Service recognized that assembly line chores alone were not guaranteed to accomplish the goals of the program. Josephine Mayo, the girls' matron at Genoa, reported in 1886 that the work program was too "wholesale" to produce effective housewives. "Making a dozen beds and cleaning a dormitory does not teach them to make a room attractive and homelike," she remarked. Nor did cooking large quantities of a single item "supply a family with a pleasant and healthy variety of food, nicely cooked." The matron believed that Indian girls needed to be taught in circumstances similar to those they were expected to occupy. She therefore suggested that small cottages be utilized in which girls could be instructed in the care of younger students and perform all the duties of a housewife. Although Mayo expressed a perceptive concern for the inherent problems of the system, her remarks had little impact on federal school officials. In the meantime, schools were expected to run effectively, and women continued to perform much of the required labor.

Not all the girls' programs, of course, were as routine or chore oriented as the ones cited above. Several of the larger institutions made sincere efforts to train young Indian women as efficient householders. Girls were taught to care for children, to set tables, prepare meals, and make domestic repairs. After 1896 Haskell Institute in Kansas provided women with basic commercial skills in stenography, typing, and bookkeeping. Nursing, too, received attention at some schools. A number of teachers, though conventional in their views of Indian women's role, succeeded in relaxing the rigid school atmosphere. Teachers at Hampton, for instance, regularly invited small groups of girls to their rooms for informal discussions. Here girls, freed from the restraints of the classroom, could express their feelings and receive some personal encouragement. Many institutions permitted their girls to have a dress "with at least some imitation of prevailing style" and urged them to take pride in their appearance.

The industrial schools reached their peak between 1890 and 1910. During this period as many as twenty-five nonreservation schools were in operation. The number of Indian women enrolled may have reached three thousand per annum during this period and females composed between 40 and 50 percent of the student body of most schools. The large number of young women can be attributed to several factors: girls were easier to recruit, they presented fewer disciplinary problems and could be more readily placed in the "outing" system, and after 1892 they could be sent to school without parental consent.

Women's education also became more efficient and standardized during the 1890s. This was due in large part to the activities of Thomas J. Morgan, who served as Indian commissioner from 1889 to 1893. Morgan advocated the education of Indian women as an important part of the acculturation process, believing that properly run schools could remove girls from the "degradation" of camp life and place them on a level with "their more favored white sisters." The commissioner hoped to accomplish this feat by completely systematizing the government's educational program. "So far as possible," he urged, "there should be a uniform course of study, similar methods of instruction, the same textbooks, and a carefully organized and well understood system of industrial training." His suggestions received considerable support, and by 1890, when he issued his "Rules for Indian Schools," the standardization of the Indian schools had begun. Morgan, like Pratt before him, fully expected his concept of education to rapidly produce American citizens. The results were not what the commissioner expected. While standardization proved more efficient, it also exacerbated some of the problems of the women's educational program.

Under the direction of Morgan and his successors, the Indian schools of the era became monuments to regimentation from which there was no escape. This development is obvious in the increasing emphasis on military organization. By the mid-nineties most girls were fully incorporated into the soldierly routine. As one superintendent noted, all students were organized into companies on the first day of school. Like the boys, the girls wore uniforms and were led by student officers who followed army drill regulations. Every aspect of student life was regulated. Anna Moore, a Pima girl attending the Phoenix Indian School, remembered life in the girls' battalion as one of marching "to a military tune" and having to drill at five in the morning. Most school officials were united in their praise of military organization. Regimentation served to develop a work ethic; it broke the students' sense of "Indian time" and ordered their life. The merits of military organization, drill, and routine in connection with discipline were explained by one official who stated that "it teaches patriotism, obedience, courage, courtesy, promptness, and constancy."

Domestic science continued to dominate the women's program. Academic preparation for women never received much emphasis by industrial school administrators despite Morgan's promise that "literary" training would occupy half the students' time. . . . One reason for the lack of emphasis on academics was that by 1900 many school administrators had come to feel that Indians were incapable of learning more. One school superintendent did not consider his "literary" graduates capable of accomplishing much in white society, while another educator described the natives as a "child race."

The extent to which every feature of the girls' program was directed toward the making of proper middle-class housewives can be seen in the numerous directives handed down by the government. By the early twentieth century every detail of school life was regulated. In 1904 Superintendent of Indian Schools Estelle Reel issued a three-page circular on the proper method of making a bed. Much of this training bore little relationship to the reservation environment to which students would return. A few programs were entirely divorced from reality. The cooking course at Sherman Institute in California, for instance, taught girls to prepare formal meals including the serving of raw oysters, shrimp cocktails, and croquettes. In another instance, Hampton teachers devoted some of their energies to discussing attractive flower arrangements and the proper selection of decorative pictures.

Another popular program was the "industrial" cottage. These originated in 1883 at Hampton when the school enrolled several married Indian couples to serve as examples for the students. The couples were quartered in small frame houses while learning to maintain attractive and happy homes. Although the married students did not long remain at Hampton, school officials began to use the cottages as model homes where squads of Indian girls might practice living in white-style homes. By 1900 similar cottages were in use at western schools. The industrial cottage at Phoenix, for example, operated a "well-regulated household" run by nine girls under a matron's supervision. The "family" (with no males present) cleaned and decorated the cottage, did the regular routine of cooking, washing, and sewing, and tended to the poultry and livestock in an effort "to train them to the practical and social enjoyment of the higher life of a real home."

The outing system also continued to be an integral part of the girls' program. As time went on, however, and the system was adopted at western locations, the original purposes of the outings faded. Initially designed as a vehicle for acculturation, the program at many locations became a means of providing servants to white householders. At Phoenix, for example, female pupils formed a pool of cheap labor available to perform domestic services for local families. From the opening of the school in 1891, demands for student labor always exceeded the pool's capacity. One superintendent estimated that he could easily put two hundred girls to work. Moreover, not all employers were interested in the welfare of the student. As the Phoenix superintendent stated in 1894, "The hiring of Indian youth is not looked upon by the people of this valley from a philanthropic standpoint. It is simply a matter of business." In theory, school authorities could return pupils to school at any time it appeared they were not receiving educational benefits; but as one newspaper reported, "What a howl would go up from residents of this valley if the superintendent would exercise this authority."

Even social and religious activities served an educational purpose. When Mrs. Merial Dorchester, wife of the superintendent of Indian schools, made a tour of western school facilities in the early 1890s, she recommended that school girls organize chapters of the King's Daughters, a Christian service organization. Several institutions implemented the program. At these locations girls were organized by age into "circles" to spend spare time producing handcrafted goods for charity. School officials supported such activity because the necessity of raising their own funds to pay dues instilled in the girls a spirit of Christian industry. The manufacture of goods for charity also enhanced their sense of service to others. Said one school superintendent, the organization is "effective in furnishing a spur to individual effort and makes the school routine more bearable by breaking the monotony of it." Although maintaining a nonsectarian stance, the schools encouraged all types of religious activity as an effective method of teaching Christian values and removing the girls from the home influence.

An important factor in understanding the women's program at the industrial schools is the reaction of the girls themselves. This presents some problems, however, since most school girls left no record of their experiences. Moreover, many of the observations that have survived were published in closely controlled school magazines that omitted any unfavorable remarks. Only a few reliable reminiscences have been produced, and even these are not very informative. Despite such limitations, however, several points are evident. The reaction of Indian girls to their education varied greatly. Some came willingly and with the approval of their parents. Once enrolled in school, many of these individuals took a keen interest in their education, accepted discipline as good for them, and worked hard to learn the ways of white society. An undetermined number may have come to school to escape intolerable conditions at home. Some evidence suggests that schools offered safe havens from overbearing parents who threatened to harm their children. For other girls the decision to attend a nonreservation school was made at considerable emotional expense, requiring a break with conservative parents, relatives, and tribesmen. In a few cases young women even lost their opportunity to marry men of their own tribe as they became dedicated to an outside lifestyle.

Many girls disliked school and longed to return home. The reasons are not hard to find. The hard work, discipline, and punishment were often oppressive. One Hopi girl recalled having to get down on her knees each Saturday and scrub the floor of the huge dining hall. "A patch of floor was scrubbed, then rinsed and wiped, and another section was attacked. The work was slow and hard on the knees," she remembered. Pima schoolgirl [Anna] Moore experienced similar conditions working in the dining hall at Phoenix: "My little helpers and I hadn't even reached our teen-aged years yet, and this work seemed so hard! If we were not finished when the 8:00 a.m. whistle sounded, the dining room matron would go around strapping us while we were still on our hands and knees. . . . We just dreaded the sore bottoms." In a number of instances, teachers and matrons added to the trauma by their dictatorial and unsympathetic attitudes. A few girls ran away from school. Those who were caught received humiliating punishment. Runaway girls might be put to work in the school yard cutting grass with scissors or doing some other meaningless drudgery. In a few cases recalcitrant young ladies had their hair cut off. Such experiences left many girls bitter and anxious to return to the old way of life.

The experiences of Indian girls when they returned home after years of schooling illustrate some of the problems in evaluating the success of the government program. For many years school officials reported great success for returned students. Accounts in articles and official documents maintained that numbers of girls had returned home, married, and established good homes. The Indian Bureau itself made occasional surveys purporting to show that returned students were doing well, keeping neat homes, and speaking English. These accounts contained a certain amount of truth. Some graduates adapted their education to the reservation environment and succeeded quite well. Many of these success stories were well publicized. There is considerable evidence to suggest, however, that the reports were overly optimistic and that most returning girls encountered problems.

A disturbingly large number of girls returned to traditional life upon returning home. The reasons are rather obvious. As early as 1882, the principal of Hampton's Indian Division reported that "there is absolutely no position of dignity to which an Indian girl after three years' training can look forward to with any reasonable confidence." Although conditions improved somewhat as time went on, work opportunities remained minimal. Girls were usually trained in only one specialty. As the superintendent of the Albuquerque school reported, girls usually returned home with no relevant skills. Some spent their entire school stay working in a laundry or sewing room, and though they became expert in one field, they had nothing to help them on the reservation. As the Meriam Report* later noted, some Indian girls spent so much time in school laundries that the institutions were in violation of state child labor laws. In another instance, one teacher noted how girls were taught to cook on gas ranges, while back on the reservation they had only campfires.

Moreover, the girls' educational achievements were not always appreciated at home. Elizabeth White tells the story of returning to her Hopi home an accomplished cook only to find that her family shunned the cakes and pies she made in place of traditional food, called her "as foolish as a white woman," and treated her as an outcast. As she later lamented, her school-taught domestic skills were inappropriate for the Hopis. Girls who refused to wear traditional dress at home were treated in like manner. Under these circumstances, many chose to cast off their learning, to marry, and return to traditional living. Those young women who dedicated them-

*The 1928 Meriam Report was an intense study of the conditions of American Indians and the operations of the Bureau of Indian Affairs, conducted by the Institute for Government Research under the auspices of the Department of the Interior.

selves to living in the white man's style often found that reservations were intolerable, and unable to live in the manner to which they had become accustomed, they preferred to return to the cities. Once there the former students tended to become maids, although an undetermined number ended up as prostitutes and dance hall girls.

Employment opportunities for educated Indian women also pointed up some of the difficulties with the industrial schools. In fairness, it must be admitted that trained women probably had more opportunities than their male counterparts. Most of those who chose to work could do so; however, all positions were at the most menial level. If a girl elected to live within the white community, her employment choices were severely limited. About the only job available was that of domestic service, a carry-over from the outing system. In this regard, the Indian schools did operate as employment agencies, finding jobs for their former students with local families. Despite the fact that some Indian women may have later come to feel that their work, despite its demeaning nature, provided some benefits for use in later life, many of their jobs proved unbearably hard. After being verbally abused, one former student wrote that "I never had any Lady say things like that to me." Another reported on her job, "I had been working so hard ever since I came here cleaning house and lots of ironing. I just got through ironing now I'm very tired my feet get so tired standing all morning." Unfortunately, few respectable jobs beyond domestic labor were available. Occasionally girls were trained as nurses or secretaries only to discover that they could find no work in Anglo society.

The largest employer of Indian girls proved to be the Indian Bureau. Many former students were able to secure positions at Indian agencies and schools; in fact, had it not been for the employment of former students by the paternalistic Indian service, few would have found any use for their training. The nature of the government positions available to Indian girls is revealing. Almost all jobs were menial in nature; only a few Indian girls were able to become teachers, and none worked as administrators. They were, rather, hired as laundresses, cooks, seamstresses, nurses' helpers, and assistant matrons. Often these employees received little more than room, board, and government rations, and even those who managed to be hired as teachers and nurses received less pay than their white counterparts. . . . Indian girls could find work, but only in the artificial environment of Indian agencies and schools located at remote western points and protected by a paternalistic government. Here they continued to perform tasks of domestic nature without promise of advancement. Nor were they assimilated into the dominant society as had been the original intent of their education.

School administrators were reluctant to admit the failings of the system. As early as the 1880s some criticism began to surface, but for the most part it was lost in the enthusiasm for training in a nonreservation environment.

After 1900, however, critics became more vocal and persistent, arguing that the Indian community did not approve of this type of education, that most students gained little, and that employment opportunities were limited at best. More important, this type of education contributed little to the acculturation effort. As one opponent wrote, "To educate the Indian out of his [or her] home surroundings is to fill him with false ideas and to endow him with habits which are destructive to his peace of mind and usefulness to his community when the educational work is completed." Commissioner Leupp (1905–1909) was even more vocal. He generally accepted the increasingly prevalent theory that Indians were childlike in nature and incapable of assimilating into white society on an equal basis. Leupp suggested that the system failed to produce self-reliant Indians and, instead of giving Indian children a useful education, protected them in an artificial environment. Other school officials echoed the same sentiments. In this particular respect it was suggested that boarding school students were provided with all the comforts of civilization at no cost and thus failed to develop the proper attitude toward work. Upon returning to the reservations, therefore, they did not exert themselves and lapsed into traditionalism.

Despite increasing criticism, the women's educational program at the nonreservation schools operated without much change until after 1920. Girls were still taught skills of doubtful value, were hired out as maids through the outing system, did most of the domestic labor at the schools, and returned to the reservation either to assume traditional life or accept some menial government job. By the late twenties, however, the movement to reform Indian education began to have some impact. Relying upon such studies as the 1928 Meriam Report, reformers began to demand a complete change in the Indian educational system. Among their suggestions were that industrial boarding schools be phased out and the emphasis on work training be reduced. Critics like [future Commissioner of Indian Affairs] John Collier argued that the policy of removing girls from their homes to educate them for a life among whites had failed. Instead, girls were discouraged from returning to the reservation and had received little to prepare them for a home life. Collier's arguments eventually won out, especially after he became Indian commissioner in 1933. Thus ended this particular attempt to convert Native American women into middle-class American housewives. . . .

DOCUMENTS

Rules for Indian Schools, 1890

General Rules

39. The Sabbath must be properly observed. There shall be a Sabbath school or some other suitable service every Sunday, which pupils shall be required to attend. The superintendent may require employés to attend and participate in all the above exercises; but any employé declining as a matter of conscience shall be excused from attending and participating in any or all religious exercises. . . .

41. All instruction must be in the English language. Pupils must be compelled to converse with each other in English, and should be properly rebuked or punished for persistent violation of this rule. Every effort should be made to encourage them to abandon their tribal language. To facilitate this work it is essential that all school employés be able to speak English fluently, and that they speak English exclusively to the pupils, and also to each other in the presence of pupils.

42. Instruction in music must be given at all schools. Singing should be a part of the exercises of each school session, and wherever practicable instruction in instrumental music should be given.

43. Except in cases of emergency, pupils shall not be removed from school either by their parents or others, nor shall they be transferred from a Government to a private school without special authority from the Indian Office.

44. The school buildings should be furnished throughout with plain, inexpensive, but substantial furniture. Dormitories or lavatories should be so supplied with necessary toilet articles, such as soap, towels, mirrors, combs, hair, shoe, nail, and tooth brushes, and wisp brooms, as to enable the pupils to form exact habits of personal neatness.

45. Good and healthful provisions must be supplied in abundance; and they must well cooked and properly placed on the table. A regular bill of fare for each day of the week should be prepared and followed. Meals must be served regularly and neatly. Pains should be taken not only to have the food healthful and the table attractive, but to have the bill of fare varied. The school farm and dairy should furnish an ample supply of vegetables, fruits, milk, butter, cottage cheese, curds, eggs, and poultry. Coffee and tea should be furnished sparingly; milk is preferable to either, and children can be taught to use it. Pupils must be required to attend meals promptly after proper attention to toilet, and at least one employé must be in the dining room during each meal to supervise the table manners of

SOURCE: U.S. Bureau of Indian Affairs, "Rules for Indian Schools," *Annual Report of the Commissioner of Indian Affairs, 1890* (Washington, D.C., 1890), cxlvi, cl–clii.

the pupils and to see that all leave the table at the same time and in good order. . . .

47. So far as practicable, a uniform style of clothing for the school should be adopted. Two plain, substantial suits, with extra pair of trousers for each boy, and three neat, well-made dresses for each girl, if kept mended, ought to suffice for week-day wear for one year. For Sunday wear each pupil should be furnished a better suit. The pupils should also be supplied with underwear adapted to the climate, with night clothes, and with handkerchiefs, and, if the climate requires it, with overcoats and cloaks and with overshoes.

48. The buildings, outhouses, fences, and walks should at all times be kept in thorough repair. Where practicable, the grounds should be ornamented with trees, grass, and flowers.

49. There should be a flag staff at every school, and the American flag should be hoisted, in suitable weather, in the morning and lowered at sunset daily.

50. Special hours should be allotted for recreation. Provision should be made for outdoor sports, and the pupils should be encouraged in daily healthful exercise under the eye of a school employé; simple games should also be devised for indoor amusement. They should be taught the sports and games enjoyed by white youth, such as baseball, hopscotch, croquet, marbles, bean bags, dominoes, checkers, logomachy, and other word and letter games, and the use of dissected maps, etc. The girls should be instructed in simple fancy work, knitting, netting, crocheting, different kinds of embroidery, etc.

51. Separate play grounds, as well as sitting rooms, must be assigned the boys and the girls. In play and in work, as far as possible, and in all places except the school room and at meals, they must be kept entirely apart. It should be so arranged, however, that at stated times, under suitable supervision, they may enjoy each other's society; and such occasions should be used to teach them to show each other due respect and consideration, to behave without restraint, but without familiarity, and to acquire habits of politeness, refinement, and self-possession. . . .

53. Corporal punishment must be resorted to only in cases of grave violations of rules, and in no instances shall any person inflict it except under the direction of the superintendent, to whom all serious questions of discipline must be referred.* Employés may correct pupils for slight misdemeanors only.

---

*In some of the more advanced schools it will be practicable and advisable to have material offenses arbitrated by a school court composed of the advanced students, with school employés added to such court in very aggravated cases. After due investigation, the amount of guilt should be determined and the quantity of punishment fixed by the court, but the approval of the superintendent shall be necessary before the punishment is inflicted, and the superintendent may modify or remit but may not increase the sentence.

54. Any pupil twelve years of age or over, guilty of persistently using profane or obscene language; of lewd conduct; stubborn insubordination; lying; fighting; wanton destruction of property; theft; or similar misbehavior, may be punished by the superintendent either by inflicting corporal punishment or imprisonment in the guardhouse; but in no case shall any unusual or cruel or degrading punishment be permitted. . . .

Industrial Work

56. A regular and efficient system of industrial training must be a part of the work of each school. At least half of the time of each boy and girl should be devoted thereto—the work to be of such character that they may be able to apply the knowledge and experience gained, in the locality where they may be expected to reside after leaving school. In pushing forward the school-room training of these boys and girls, teachers, and especially superintendents, must not lose sight of the great necessity for fitting their charges for the every-day life of their after years.

57. A farm and garden, if practicable an orchard also, must be connected with each school, and especial attention must be given to instruction in farming, gardening, dairying, and fruit growing.

58. Every school should have horses, cattle, swine, and poultry, and when practicable, sheep and bees, which the pupils should be taught to care for properly. The boys should look after the stock and milk the cows, and the girls should see to the poultry and the milk.

59. The farm, garden, stock, dairy, kitchen, and shops should be so managed as to make the school as nearly self-sustaining as practicable, not only because Government resources should be as wisely and carefully utilized as private resources would be, but also because thrift and economy are among the most valuable lessons which can be taught Indians. Waste in any department must not be tolerated.

60. The blacksmith, wheelwright, carpenter, shoemaker, and harness maker trades, being of the most general application, should be taught to a few pupils at every school. Where such mechanics are not provided for[,] the school pupils should, so far as practicable, receive instruction from the agency mechanics.

61. The girls must be systematically trained in every branch of housekeeping and in dairy work; be taught to cut, make, and mend garments for both men and women; and also be taught to nurse and care for the sick. They must be regularly detailed to assist the cook in preparing the food and the laundress in washing and ironing.

62. Special effort must be made to instruct Indian youth in the use and care of tools and implements. They must learn to keep them in order, protect them properly, and use them carefully.

A Government Official Describes Indian
Race and Culture, 1905

We believe that the strength of our American life is due in no small part to the fact that various and different race elements have entered into the making of the American the citizen of the United States in the twentieth century. No one racial stock is exclusively in control in our land. The typical modern American is a fine "composite," with race elements drawn from many sources. We do not believe that the Government of the United States in dealing with its Indian wards would act righteously or wisely if it were to attempt to crush out from those who are of Indian descent all the racial traits which differentiate the North American Indian from the other race stocks of the world. Certain conceptions of physical courage, a certain heroic stoicism in enduring physical pain, an inherited tendency to respect one's self, even if that tendency shows itself at times in unwarrantable conceit, are race traits which have value, if the people who have them become civilized and subject themselves to the laws of social morality and to the obligation of industrial efficiency, which are essential if any race stock or any group of families is to hold its own in the modern civilized world.

But the facts seem to us to be that good results are to be hoped for not by keeping the North American Indians peculiar in dress or in customs. We think that the wisest friends of the Indian recognize with great delight and value highly the art impulse in certain Indian tribes, which has shown itself in Indian music, in Indian art forms—such as the birchbark canoe, in Indian basketry, and more rarely in Indian pottery. But we firmly believe that the way to preserve the best of what is distinctively characteristic in the North American Indians is to civilize and educate them, that they may be fit for the life of the twentieth century under our American system of self-government. Because we value the elements for good which may come into our American life through the stock of North American Indians, we wish to see children of Indian descent educated in the industrial and practical arts and trained to habits of personal cleanliness, social purity, and industrious family life. We do not believe that it is right to keep the Indians out of civilization in order that certain picturesque aspects of savagery and barbarism may continue to be within reach of the traveler and the curious, or even of the scientific observer. In the objectionable "Indian dances" which are breaking out afresh at many points we see not a desirable maintenance of racial traits, but a distinct reversion toward barbarism and superstition. We believe that while the effort should never be made to "make

SOURCE: U.S. Department of Interior, "Board of Indian Commissioners' Reports," in *Annual Reports* (June 30, 1905), H. Doc. 20: 59th Cong., 1st sess., 17–18.

a white man out of an Indian," in the sense of seeking to do violence to respect to parents or a proper or intelligent regard for what is fine in the traits and the history of one's ancestors, it is still most desirable that all the Indians on our territory should come as speedily as possible to the white man's habits of home-making, industry, cleanliness, social purity, and family integrity.

Precisely as all intelligent American patriots have seen danger to our national life in the attempt, wherever it has been made, to perpetuate in the United States large groups of foreign-born immigrants who try to keep their children from learning English and seek to perpetuate upon our territory (at the cost of true Americanism for their children) what was characteristic in the life of their own people on other continents and in past generations, precisely as in such cases we feel that the hope of our American system lies in the public schools and such educational institutions as shall maintain standards of public living that inevitably bring the children of foreign-born immigrants into the great body of English-speaking, home-loving, industrious, and pure-minded Americans—precisely so does it seem to us that all the efforts of the Government, and far more of distinctive missionary effort on the part of the Christian people of this country than has ever yet been used with this end in view, should be steadily employed in the effort to make out of the Indian children of this country intelligent, English-speaking, industrious, law-abiding Americans. We believe that the breaking up of tribal funds as rapidly as practicable will help toward this end. Even if many of the Indians do for a time misuse money while they are learning how to use it properly, even if some of them squander it utterly, we believe that there is hope for the Indians in the future only as by education, faith in work, and obedience to Christian principles of morality and clean living, their children shall come to have the social standards and the social habits of our better American life throughout the land.

Our task is to hasten the slow work of race evolution. Inevitably, but often grimly and harshly by the outworking of natural forces, the national life of the stronger and more highly civilized race stock dominates in time the life of the less civilized, when races like the Anglo-Saxon and the Indian are brought into close contact. In our work for the Indians we want to discern clearly those influences and habits of life which are of the greatest advantage in leading races upward into Christian civilization; and these influences and habits we wish to make as strongly influential as possible, and as speedily as possible influential upon the life of all these American tribes. It is not unreasonable to hope that through governmental agencies and through the altruistic missionary spirit of one of the foremost Christian races and governments of the world much can be done to hasten that process of civilization which natural law, left to itself, works out too slowly and at too great a loss to the less-favored race. We want to make the conditions for our less-favored brethren of the red race so favorable that the social forces which have developed themselves slowly and at great expense of time and life in our American race and our American system of government shall be made to help in the uplifting of the Indians and to shorten that interval of time which of necessity must elapse between savagery and Christian civilization.

Cause for Hope: The Establishment of Tribal Colleges, 1994

ROSEBUD RESERVATION, S.D.—There are no ivy walls or fraternity houses on the campus of Sinte Gleska University. It is a small, horseshoe-shaped jumble of aging mobile homes, a log building and squat Government housing. In the parking lot sit weathered pickups and rusting old cars.

But the college is the jewel of the Rosebud reservation, a dry, shadowless stretch in western South Dakota where the clouds are stingy with rainfall and relentless winds rattle the flimsy walls of tar-paper shacks and house trailers.

Some 750 students are enrolled in this college, where Irene Garrett, who grew up in a shack without running water or electricity in the reservation town of Mission, teaches the writings of Linda Hogan, an Osage; Lisa Cook-Lynn, a Lower Brule Sioux; and Simon Ortiz, a Hopi.

"This is one of the most wonderful revolutions in Indian Country, the right to educate on our own terms," said Dr. David Gipp of the American Indian Higher Education Committee.

The first tribal college opened on the Navajo reservation in Arizona in 1968. Today there are 26 such colleges, with more than 16,000 Indian students. While the institutions started as community colleges granting associate degrees, three of them, including Sinte Gleska (SIN-teh GLES-ka), offer four-year bachelor's programs and have recently expanded to offer master's degrees.

Perhaps the colleges' greatest success has been a transformation in the way Indians view school. For generations, Indians have been suspicious of formal education, a legacy that dates to the Government boarding schools, where native languages were forbidden and teachers denigrated tribal culture.

"We're about restoring culture," said Cheryl Crazybull, the vice president of Sinte Gleska, where the Lakota language is a required subject.

As a child, Ms. Garrett never saw an Indian teacher. "I remember one teacher demanding that I look her in the eye," she said. "She didn't know that we consider that a sign of disrespect."

SOURCE: Dirk Johnson, "In Bleak Area in South Dakota, Indians Put Hopes in Classroom," *New York Times,* July 3, 1994. Copyright © 1994 by The New York Times Company. Reprinted by permission.

After high school, Ms. Garrett won a scholarship to attend college in Albany, where she encountered only one other Indian, an Oneida from upstate New York, and quit in 1971 after two years.

She came home, took a job with a Federal agency and gave up on college. But the next year, Sinte Gleska opened. Ms. Garrett, a single mother, enrolled.

Today she tells her students, many of whom are single parents, "If you don't have day care, bring your kids to class."

And when the students are busy reading in class, or writing essays, the teacher plays with the children.

Chapter 4

Woman's Sphere: Woman's Work

During the final decades of the nineteenth century, America's urban growth and expanding industrial economy opened innumerable jobs in the private and public sectors. For many white men with ambition, intelligence, and education, the choice of careers was broad and the chance of success promising. For immigrants, for blacks, for poor youth off the farm, and for women, however, opportunities expanded in a much more limited way. The barriers of ethnicity, race, sex, and inadequte schooling were formidable.

Margery W. Davies's essay "Office Work After the Civil War" recounts the feminization of clerical work during these decades. She illustrates the relationship between the increasing numbers of women in the office work force and significant developments in American society: the rise of urban industrialism, the decline of the family farm, the impact of technology on the home and workplace, and the "drastic changes in the scale and shape of business enterprise." At the same time, she illuminates how, despite expanding employment opportunities, the popular perception of a separate woman's sphere continued to restrict women to particular occupations. What does Davies identify as the most significant factors in transforming clerical work from a male-dominated to a female-dominated occupation? What made this kind of work attractive to women?

The popular belief in the notion of "women's work" required some justification for admitting females to certain jobs. Teaching, as Davies notes, preceded office work as the first "literacy-required" occupation deemed suitable to a woman's nature. In the first document, Horace Mann, Secretary of the Massachusetts Board of Education and famous crusader for public schooling, applauds the entry of women as teachers in the primary grades, a position for which he believed they were particularly fit. Though this Annual Report was written in 1844, it expressed attitudes toward women that would remain common throughout the rest of the century. Note the reference to woman's special qualities with which "the Author of nature preadapted her." By the Civil War, the schoolmistress had almost completely replaced the schoolmaster in the nation's public elementary schools, a development that highlights the persuasiveness of Mann's argument. Of course, differences in salaries might also have exerted influence as communities hired teachers: in 1861, the average salary for male teachers in rural districts was $6.30 per week; for women, it was $4.05. In urban districts, men earned $18.00 per week; women, only $6.91.

Women attempting to enter prestigious, traditionally male occupations often met with considerable resistance and drew on huge stores of courage in their perseverance. The second document is a 1916 newspaper account of the recollections of Dr. Anna Manning Comfort, who graduated in the first class of the New York Medical College and Hospital for Women in 1865. How did the perception of a separate place for women within the medical profession shift between 1865 and 1916?

Although popular beliefs about women's natural capacities supported their entry into teaching, clerical jobs, nursing, factory work, librarianship, social work, and even medicine, they were also used to exclude women from positions of leadership in those fields, to deny them the right to vote, and to bar their entry into other professions. In 1872 the United States Supreme Court upheld a decision of the Illinois courts denying Myra Bradwell a license to practice law on the grounds of her sex. The third document presents Supreme Court Justice Bradley's majority opinion in support of the Court's decision. Notice that his argument rested heavily on traditional perceptions of women's natures.

The Court's decision in Bradwell v. Illinois *set back women's rights, yet the era saw victories as well. That same year (1872), the Illinois legislature removed all restrictions to women's entry into the professions. Similar actions were taken in other states. In 1869 Arabella Mansfield of Iowa had become the first woman licensed to practice law. By 1891 the nation boasted two hundred licensed women lawyers. (Of course, the figure represented less than 1 percent of all the nation's attorneys.) The struggle has continued well into our own century. How would you describe popular beliefs today concerning separate spheres for men and women in the home, in politics, and in the world of work?*

ESSAY

Office Work After the Civil War

Margery W. Davies

The last third of the nineteenth century witnessed drastic changes in the scale and shape of business enterprise. The small and highly competitive firms that had dominated production in the antebellum United States gave way to giant corporations integrated vertically and horizontally in the merger movement that swept through industry during the 1890s. In the steel, oil, tobacco, food, and meat-packing sectors, to name just a few, such corporations enjoyed virtual monopolies.

As is now well known, profound changes in production techniques accompanied the rise of the trusts. But innovation was not restricted to the shop floor. It also reached upwards into the office, for the increase in the volume of business, coupled with the development of regional, national, and international markets, led to a proliferation of correspondence and inspired the need for more accurate record keeping. As the amount and geographic range of a firm's activities grew, it became more difficult for that firm to conduct the bulk of its transactions in person. While face-to-face business contacts by no means disappeared, a businessman might choose to pay a bill, order merchandise, or confirm an appointment in writing rather than in person, particularly when the transaction took place between cities. Even after the invention of the telephone, many businesses preferred to keep a written record of transactions rather than having to rely on memory.

As a firm's operations expanded and became more complex, accurate records of its transactions became more important. A small entrepreneurial butcher did not need very complex records. He might keep a list of which customers owed him money and how much, and of how many pounds of beef and how many pounds of pork he could expect each week from various meat-slaughterers, but he would not need much more. A large meat-packing firm, however, required more complex records: how many head

SOURCE: Margery W. Davies, *Women's Place Is at the Typewriter: Office Work and Office Workers, 1870–1930.* Copyright © 1982 by Temple University. Reprinted by permission of Temple University Press.

of cattle were fattening in pens in Omaha or Kansas City, and how many were being driven across the plains from points farther west; how much the workers in the slaughterhouses were being paid; how many refrigerated cars were on their way to the eastern cities, and how many on their way back. These records had to be accurate and up-to-date, for the managers needed detailed information at their fingertips in order to make plans for the future. Furthermore, . . . firms required elaborate records to guard against fraud both by their own employees and by the companies with which they did business.

Among the outstanding features of the reorganization of the office was the division of businesses into departments. This became necessary as firms grew so large and complex that it was no longer possible for one capitalist, or even a small group, to make all the decisions. The ultimate control of a firm's capital and direction still rested with the owner or owners, but the more mundane operations were decentralized into various functionally defined departments. The Pennsylvania Railroad management, for example, one of the first to introduce this method of organization, instituted separate offices for accounting and for the supervision of roadbeds and moving stock. It also worked out a more elaborate structure of relations between the major departments and their ancillary units.

These organizational innovations were accompanied by the subdivision of clerical labor. Before the Civil War there had been four basic clerical jobs in the office: copyist, bookkeeper, messenger or office boy, and clerk. This relatively simple range of occupations was expanded and elaborated following the war, with the division of labor most pronounced in the largest offices. File clerks, shipping clerks, billing clerks and other "semiskilled" workers began to appear. The exact pattern that the division of labor followed in a particular office depended, of course, on the nature of the business at hand. An insurance company might have many billing or file clerks, but no shipping clerks whatsoever; a mail-order house would use an army of shipping and file clerks, but no billing clerks since orders were paid in advance.

Not surprisingly, the most popular change resulted from the introduction of the typewriter. Once it was adopted, stenographers and typists quite rapidly replaced copyists. A stenographer's job consisted of taking dictation, usually from a firm's manager or owner, although occasionally also from a higher-level clerical worker, and then transcribing the notes into a letter, report, or whatever. For a while, it was considered rude or disrespectful for a firm to type its correspondence, and some dictation was at first transcribed in a fine longhand. Before long, however, typewriting became the accepted mode of business correspondence, and handwritten letters yielded to typewritten ones. The stenographer was in effect a direct replacement for a copyist, since in general stenography encompassed transcription as well as dictation. The integration of these

71

tasks came about not only because many different systems of shorthand were in use, but also because stenographers tended to add individual quirks or shortcuts to the system being used. Hence the stenographer might be the only one who could read his or her notes. At first glance it would seem that the shift from copyist to stenographer involved no further division of labor. But the fact that typists were being hired as well as stenographers suggests even greater specialization. Take the example of a manufacturer with outstanding debts from thirty customers. He might decide to send each of them a dunning letter couched in the strongest language instead of an invoice with "Third and Final Notice" stamped on it in red ink. He might dictate this letter to a stenographer, who would transcribe it in longhand and pass it on, along with the names and addresses of the overdue debtors, to two or three typists, who would produce as many copies of the letter as necessary. The result was that what had once been done by one kind of clerk, a copyist, was now done by two, a stenographer and a typist. In this example, the typists execute the bulk of the task at hand, and the manufacturer congratulates himself on the efficiency of his system and on the money saved by using a stenographer only where necessary and by using typists whenever possible.

This increasing division of labor constituted a basic change in the organization of office work. In antebellum offices clerical workers were responsible for a wide range of tasks and in some cases their work bore the aspects of a craft. But the division and redivision of clerical tasks meant that an individual clerical worker performed only a small number of tasks in a larger range of operations. This reorganization of work was uneven. It first appeared immediately before the Civil War (the Erie Railroad) and was clearly taking hold by the 1870s. Thus the post–Civil War expansion and consolidation of capitalism drastically rearranged the office by partitioning firms into departments and dividing up clerical work into specialized tasks. Another factor which did much to alter the appearance of clerical work, and which had some influence on the changing nature of that work, was technological innovation, with the typewriter being far and away the most important of the new office machines. . . .

One of the ways women entered clerical work was by mastering the typewriter and then finding a job as a typist. When Mark Twain bought his first typewriter in early 1875, the salesman had a "type girl" on hand to demonstrate the machine to prospective customers. And in late 1875 this ad for the Remington typewriter appeared in the *Nation:*

CHRISTMAS PRESENT
for a boy or girl
And the benevolent can, by the gift of a "Type-Writer" to a poor, deserving young woman, put her at once in the way of earning a good living as a copyist or corresponding clerk.

No invention has opened for women so broad and easy an avenue to profitable and suitable employment as the "Type-Writer," and it merits the careful consideration of all thoughtful and charitable persons interested in the subject of work for woman.

Mere girls are now earning from $10 to $20 per week with the "Type-Writer," and we can at once secure good situations for one hundred expert writers on it in court-rooms in this city.

The public is cordially invited to call and inspect the working of the machine, and obtain all information at our showrooms.

But in 1875 and for a few years thereafter, the typewriter was still thought of as a frill by most businessmen. It was not until the 1880s that typewriters were manufactured and sold in large numbers.

In the 1880s, also, the employment of women in offices began to climb sharply. . . . This coincidence has led some analysts to conclude that the invention of the typewriter was basically responsible for the employment of women in offices in the United States. For example, a pamphlet put out by the Women's Bureau of the United States Department of Labor asserts that "not only . . . has the typewriter revolutionized modern business methods but it has *created* an occupation calling for more women than have been employed as a result of any other invention." Bruce Bliven, the author of a history of the typewriter, recounts the story of how the New York YWCA started training young women typists in 1881. Far from succumbing to mental and physical breakdowns under the strain of their new occupation, as some observers had warned, these women quickly found jobs. The YWCA was soon deluged with many more requests for typists than it could fill. Bliven concludes that "the revolution came rather quietly, on high-buttoned shoes, accompanied not by gunfire or bombs bursting in air, but by a considerable amount of rather obnoxious snickering."

Just as it would be a mistake to say that the typewriter was responsible for the growth of offices after the Civil War, so would it be erroneous to credit it with the employment of women in those offices. . . . [F]emale employment was increasing rapidly throughout the clerical occupations, and not just among stenographers and typists.

Although the typewriter was not responsible for the employment of women as clerical workers, its existence probably facilitated or eased the entrance of women into offices. It was such a new machine that it had not been "sex-typed" as masculine. Thus women who worked as typists did not face the argument that a typewriter was a machine fit only for men. In fact, it was not too long afterwards that women were claimed to be more manually dexterous and tolerant of routine than men and therefore more suited, by virtue of their very natures, to operate typewriters.

Changes in the structure of capitalism in the United States brought women into offices. The expansion and consolidation of capitalist firms after the Civil War caused a rapid increase in the amount of correspondence and record keeping required by those firms. This in turn resulted in the growth of offices and an immediate increase in the need for clerical workers. That, in short, explains the demand. Where was the supply to come from?

The basic skill required of clerical workers was literacy. The supply therefore had to come from those segments of the population that had some education, and at this time[,] women, as well as men, had advanced schooling. In fact, . . . the number of women high school graduates exceeded that of men during the last decades of the nineteenth century.

And women's labor was cheaper than men's. Patriarchal social relations devalued the labor of women compared to that of men from similar backgrounds. The reasons for this are legion. First of all, there was the widespread belief that women were simply, and by the very nature of things, inferior to men. In addition, women were often thought to be working for "pin money" with which to make frivolous purchases. Since they were not thought to be supporting themselves or their families, there was nothing the matter with paying them low wages. Then there was the argument that women were not serious members of the labor force: they would be returning to an exclusively domestic life either as soon as they married or, at the very latest, as soon as they bore children. Such transient workers did not deserve the higher wage with which an employer might try to attract and keep a more steadfast male worker. Finally, women's depressed wages did drive them back into the home, where they again became available to fill a subordinate position within the domestic division of labor. Whether or not this worked to the ultimate benefit of men, it certainly provided them with short-term benefits.

On the face of it, the cheapness of labor ought to explain why employers preferred women over men. But women's labor in the United States has always come cheaper than men's, so that it is not immediately obvious why employers did not always show preference for females. There must be a further reason why employers started to favor women for certain clerical positions.

The supply of literate male labor was simply not large enough to fill the great demand for office workers. The expansion of capitalist firms created not only a much larger need for clerical workers, but also an increased demand for managerial personnel. As is clear from the discussion of the proliferation of hierarchical structures within late nineteenth-century firms, the managerial corps necessitated by this new system of finely delegated authority expanded mightily. An educated man, faced with the choice among positions within the office hierarchy, was unlikely to choose to be a typist instead of a manager, who was higher-paid and invested with a fair degree of authority and power. The expansion of capitalist firms, coupled with the growth of cities at the end of the nineteenth century, also led to a rise in the number of jobs ancillary to business operations. Lawyers are an excellent example: in 1870 there were 40,736 lawyers in the United States, all but five of whom were men. By 1900 there were almost three times as many lawyers, 114,640, over 99 percent of whom were men. There had been one lawyer for every 307 people employed in all occupations in the United States in 1870; by 1900 there was one lawyer for every 254 such persons. Thus a man who had enough education and literacy skills (the ability to spell reasonably well, to write [in] a legible hand, to do basic arithmetic accurately) to obtain a job as a clerical worker was also probably educated enough to at least aspire to, and in many cases to attain, a managerial or professional position. As a consequence, the supply of men available for clerical work was considerably diminished.

Furthermore, fewer boys than girls were graduating from high school in the United States. . . . If high school and college graduations are considered together, more men than women were receiving secondary school diplomas or better during the years 1870 and 1880. But in 1890 and 1900, the number of women receiving high school diplomas or better had outstripped the number of men. Despite the fact that consistently far more men than women graduated from college, the number of women finishing high school grew to so outweigh the number of men that the surplus of male over female college graduates was cancelled out. In addition, the men who were reaching those high educational levels were likely to be supplying the demand for managers and professionals. Thus the demand for managers and professionals and the fact that more women than men were reaching relatively high levels of formal education combine to explain why it was that the ever-increasing demand for clerical workers was met by women.

Other factors, though secondary, also influenced feminization. First of all, the employment of women as clerks in the United States Treasury Department during the Civil War established a precedent that may have eased the entrance of women into offices ten and fifteen years later. The employment of female clerks in the Treasury Department showed that it was possible for women to work in offices. Women had gotten a toe in the office door. As a result, when structural changes in capitalism produced a dramatic rise in the demand for clerical workers, it was slightly easier for women to push the door wide open.

A second factor that facilitated—as opposed to caused—the employment of women was the invention and production of the typewriter. Women were employed in increasing numbers throughout the entire gamut of clerical occupations, and not just as typists. The process that underlay the employment of women in offices was similar to that which underlay the successful manufacture of a typewriter in the first place—the expansion and consolidation of capitalist firms. But the fact that the typewriter was sex-neutral, without historical ties to workers of either sex, meant that female typists did not have to meet the argument that they were operating a man's machine.

Finally, the reorganization of the division of labor within the office may have abetted its feminization. It is possible that if offices had simply expanded without being reorganized, women would have had a more difficult time entering clerical work. The reorganization of many offices often resulted in a redivision of clerical labor and in the creation of new jobs, from stenographers and typists to file clerks, billing clerks, and the like. Since many of these jobs, or at least their labels, had not existed before the growth of the office, they were not defined as men's jobs. Women who took such positions did not face the argument that they were taking over men's work.

Nonetheless, the roots of the feminization of clerical work lay in political-economic conditions that were independent of the job itself. Changes in the structure of capitalism caused a rapid increase in the demand for clerical workers, a demand that was met in part by an available supply of literate women. Furthermore, it seems that many employers were only too glad to employ female labor in place of more costly male labor. The feminization of clerical work was not intrinsic to the job itself, despite ideological justifications that arose after the fact. By its very nature, clerical work was neither men's work nor women's work.

Clerical jobs were available to women, but, for feminization to occur, women had to be available to take the jobs. A variety of factors produced a supply of women to fill the demand. The economic decline of small, family-owned farms and businesses frequently forced daughters into the labor force. Clerical work was generally seen as more desirable than industrial work, and this spurred women of working-class origins to seek clerical jobs. Productive work in the home was on the decline, making the labor of both working-class and non-working-class women available for jobs outside the domestic sphere. And clerical work was one of the few options for literate women seeking jobs that required literate workers. . . .

Although the decline of the small, independent farmer as a class had hardly begun in earnest, by the end of the nineteenth century the large cities of the East were already beginning to feel the effects. The new homesteads of the West absorbed only some of the eastern farmers forced off their land. Others who found they could no longer make ends meet were already moving into the cities in the waning years of the nineteenth century, although it was not until the twentieth that displaced small farmers really began to swell the urban labor force. The ranks of clerical workers included people of small-farm origins from the outset.

The situation of small-business proprietors differed significantly from that of farmers. From 1870 to 1930 they not only held their own numerically and as a proportion of the labor force but, in fact, grew. Although the class as a whole maintained itself through the years, . . . individual members of the classic petite bourgeoisie did not always manage to make ends meet, much less prosper. Thousands of fledgling businesses were started by hopeful entrepreneurs; almost as many failed.

These small entrepreneurs lived in constant dread of failure and imposed long hours on themselves and their families in order to fend off financial disaster. "But the average life of these old middle-class, especially urban, units in the twentieth century is short; the coincidence of family unit and work-situation among the old middle class is a pre-industrial fact. So even as the centralization of property contracts their 'independence,' it liberates the children of the old middle class's smaller entrepreneurs."

Some of those children were "liberated" to become clerical workers. The endemic financial insecurity of many small businessmen often meant not only that their children were reluctant to follow them in an unstable occupation, but also, in many cases, that the children were forced to support themselves. Thus the classic petite bourgeoisie contributed to the pool of people available for work in offices. . . .

For many daughters of working-class families, however, membership in the labor force was nothing new. The vast majority of working-class families were unable to afford the luxury of keeping out of the labor force an unmarried daughter whose labor was not essential to the maintenance of the home. Single working-class women were expected to enter the labor force as a matter of course. In fact, a writer in 1929 considered it a sign of the improved condition of the working class that its children were staying in school longer and longer, rather than entering the labor force out of economic necessity:

> The rising standard of living of manual workers has made it possible for more of them to provide their children with the high school education necessary to clerical positions, and the popular belief in education as the open sesame to opportunity has been an incentive to increased high school attendance. This increase in the high school population—the rate of which, within the last thirty years, has been about twenty times the rate of the increase in the population—has thrown upon the vocational market thousands of girls with a high school education, a large proportion of whom aspire to clerical positions.

The main reason working-class girls "aspired" to clerical work was that it paid better than most jobs open to women. In 1883, at the very beginning of the influx of large numbers of women into clerical work, female office workers in Boston were relatively well off compared to women in other working-class occupations. Copyists in personal service earned an average weekly wage of $6.78, bookkeepers earned $6.55, cashiers earned $7.43, and clerks (it is not clear from the available information whether "clerks" refers to clerks in offices or stores, or both) earned $5.28. Although a highly skilled craft-worker in manufacturing, such as a button-hole-maker for men's shirts, could earn as much as $10.00, most women working in manufacturing did not make over $5.00, and some made considerably less. These wages do not take into account the shorter hours women in offices enjoyed, a factor that would make their average hourly wage even better when compared to that of other working-class women. In 1910 a study of the incomes and expenditures of 450 Boston working women found that clerical work was second only to professional occupations in annual net income.

In addition to better wages, clerical work brought higher status than many other "female" occupations, such as factory work, domestic service, and clerking in stores. The argument has been made that this higher status was a result of a cleaner work environment, shorter hours, such benefits as vacation and sick leave, and the notion that clerical work could lead to promotions of some importance in the business world. Whether or not such analyses are correct, the fact that clerical work enjoyed higher status does not seem to be in question. . . . [A]t least some working-class women saw clerical work not only as more prestigious, but even as a means of rising out of the working class itself. . . .

In *The Long Day: The Story of a New York Working Girl*, Dorothy Richardson also saw clerical work as a means of escaping the drudgery of working-class jobs. Her heroine started out in jobs that were typical of most turn-of-the-century working women: making artificial flowers or paper boxes and working first as a sales clerk and then as a demonstrator of a new brand of tea or coffee in a department store. Determined to better her position, she took a night-school course in stenography and studied English grammar and composition on her own. After having attained a typing speed of one hundred words a minute, she sought her first clerical job. It "paid me only six dollars a week, but it was an excellent training-school, and in it I learned self confidence, perfect accuracy, and rapidity. Although this position paid me two dollars less than what I had been earning brewing tea and coffee and handing it over the counter, and notwithstanding the fact that I knew of places where I could go and earn ten dollars a week, I chose to remain where I was." Armed with clerical experience, she then moved on to a fifteen-dollar-a-week stenographic position at a publishing house. It was at this point in her life that Richardson's heroine started writing and selling articles. Richardson's account shows not only that she considered clerical work to be a cut above other kinds of working-class jobs, but also that she believed that one could use office work as a means of moving from a purely working-class job to a higher position with some autonomy.

The number of women available to work in offices was also augmented by the decline of productive work in the home. For farm families, there was ample work both in the field and in the home to keep the various family members busy. In addition to all of the chores that accompanied farming itself, there was a lot of work that served to keep the family self-sufficient and relatively independent of the market. Even after rural Americans no longer performed such tasks as weaving cloth or making candles, which had been part of the normal household's work in the seventeenth and eighteenth centuries, much still remained. Vegetables and fruits were preserved, butter and cheese were made, some furniture was constructed from scratch, and almost everyone's clothes were handmade. In addition, the absence of running water, central heating, and electricity meant that water had to be carried from a well or pump, wood chopped to supply cooking and heating needs, and kerosene lamps filled and kept in good running order. There was plenty of work to keep parents and children occupied most of the time.

But with the move from country to city that was well under way by the end of the nineteenth century, productive work done in the home began to decrease. The same growth of industrialism that drew a labor force to the cities resulted in the mass production of consumer goods. Items that had been produced in the home were now available in stores. Canned goods, bakery bread, and readymade clothing gained gradual acceptance in more and more urban homes, despite the fact that a kitchen garden plot was a common feature of many urban dwellings into the twentieth century. Even more important changes, perhaps, were running water and indoor plumbing, central heating, and electrical wiring, all of which became standard features of more and more urban homes, beginning with those of the well-to-do.

The decrease of productive work in the home had its most dramatic effect on women. "Woman's place is in the home" made economic sense when there was plenty of work to be done. But as domestic work diminished, women who remained there began to lose their productive function in society. In fact, as [historian] Gerda Lerner has pointed out, one of the long-term developments of the nineteenth century was the elevation of this nonproductive function of women to a symbol of high status and wealth. The "lady" was living testament to her husband's or father's ability to earn money and to a relatively high place in the class structure.

A woman's ability to enjoy nonproductive leisure was determined, of course, by her family's economic position. Booth Tarkington's Alice Adams and her parents were anxious that she should enjoy just as much leisure and luxury as the town's bourgeois daughters.* A good example of the

---

*Booth Tarkington's novel *Alice Adams* was published in 1921.

way Alice liked to spend her time is this account of her activities on the morning of a high-class dance given by one of the girls in town.

> "Where are you going?" [asked her mother.]
> "Oh, I've got lots to do. I thought I'd run out to Mildred's to see what she's going to wear tonight, and then I want to go down and buy a yard of chiffon and some narrow ribbon to make new bows for my slippers—you'll have to give me some money."

Alice would have preferred to spend her time on such frivolous errands, but her family's financial straits sent her into the labor market, her hopes of rising into the bourgeoisie dashed. The relatively small amount of productive work done in the Adams home permitted the grown daughter to spend most of her time in leisure activities, at least for a while. And when Alice entered the labor force, she was able to do so because her labor was not needed in the home.

During the period from 1870 to 1930, the number of occupations open to women was relatively limited. In general, women found employment in factory work of various kinds, in the smaller manufacturing concerns that employed sweated labor, behind the counter in retail stores, in domestic service, in nursing, in clerical work, in teaching, and to a very small degree in some of the higher-level professions. Manufacturing and other factory work, as well as domestic service, did not require literacy. And in positions where neither bills nor orders were written out, neither did retail selling. A literate woman who used her education in her work was restricted to a narrow range of occupational choices. Among these options, the better-paid were clerical work, teaching, and the various professions.

The teaching and professional positions that were open to women absorbed a small proportion of the female labor force. . . . In fact, teaching was the only occupation requiring literacy that in any way rivaled clerical work as an employer of women after the Civil War. . . . [T]eaching employed more women than did the clerical occupations until 1900, after which the number of female clerical workers rose so dramatically that teaching fell far behind. [Scholar] Elizabeth Baker argues that women may have preferred clerical work to teaching because of the severe restrictions placed on the personal and social life of teachers. Women teachers were not allowed to smoke, to drink, or, in some instances, to "keep company" with men. Those who married were often asked to leave their jobs. And sometimes "the new view of science and religion which they were bringing to the classroom from their college and university experience was opposed. Conditions such as these prompted many young girls to take up stenography instead of teaching when they graduated from high school; and it is not surprising that more than 100,000—a sixth of the teachers—were reported to have left the profession every year."

There is also some evidence that teachers were paid less than clerical workers. In 1912 the superintendent of schools in Council Bluffs, Iowa, argued that the student who completed the high school's business course was in a better economic position than the one who chose the classical course: "If a graduate of the classical course in the . . . high school had decided to teach in the public schools of the same city, under the most favorable circumstances possible[,] she could not have commenced teaching until one year after graduation. Her salary for the third year after graduation could not have been more than fifty dollars per month for nine months, or $450 per year. The average pupil (female) who graduated from the business department of the high school would have received for the same year an annual salary of slightly over $660. A male graduate of the same year would have received an annual salary of slightly over $840. You may judge for yourself of the economic efficiency from the standpoint of salary."

That women's low level of employment in the professions was due in part to outright discrimination is made clear by a study of women in government service published in 1920. It indicates that the federal government primarily hired women as clerical workers and goes on to demonstrate that the civil service examinations themselves (a prerequisite to government employment) discriminated against women and shunted them into clerical positions. . . .

Some of the very institutions where literacy skills were taught and polished led directly to clerical work. Both private commercial schools and the commercial track of public high schools trained girls and young women for clerical work. Commercial schools, where skills such as arithmetic, penmanship, and bookkeeping were taught, had been established in the United States by the 1840s and 1850s. Their doors were open to both men and women. Men were urged to obtain an education that would give them a solid start in their climb to success in the business world. Women were encouraged to apply their brains to pursuits other than gracing the domestic circle, or, in the case of working-class women, to aspire to jobs that would liberate them from the drudgery of the factory or sweatshop. In the latter half of the nineteenth century, such institutions were very successful. By 1890 there were over 80,000 students enrolled in commercial schools (by comparison enrollment in grades nine to twelve of public and private high schools totaled 298,000). Women made up only 4 percent of the 6,460 students enrolled in commercial schools in 1871, but they accounted for 32 percent of the 96,135 enrolled in 1894–95.

By the twentieth century, private business schools were being supplanted by other institutions. University business schools were offering training to aspiring capitalists and managers, while public high schools were initiating commercial education departments to teach clerical skills. By 1915 enrollment in the commercial courses of public high schools outstripped that in private commercial schools. In these high school courses girls predominated. In 1902–3 they already made up 54 percent of the total; in 1930 this had increased to 67 percent. It has been argued that public commercial education furthered the feminization of clerical work. Not only did the commercial courses provide clerical training for girls, but school guidance materials often funneled girls into commercial courses and advised them to plan for clerical jobs. . . .

For some women, participation in the labor force afforded psychological benefits such as increased independence and self-reliance. This, however, should not distract attention from the central fact of working-class life: most women worked because they had to.

DOCUMENTS

"Is Not Woman Destined to Conduct the Rising Generation?" 1844

One of the most extraordinary changes which have taken place in our schools, during the last seven years, consists in the great proportionate increase in the number of female teachers employed.

In 1837, the number of male teachers in all our public schools, including
summer and winter terms, was, ...2370
Of females. 3591
In the school year 1843–4, it was,—males, ...2529
Females. 4581
Increase in the number of male teachers 159
Increase in the number of female teachers 990
During the same time, the number of schools, in the State, has
increased only. 418

This change in public sentiment, in regard to the employment of female teachers, I believe to be in accordance with the dictates of the soundest philosophy. Is not woman destined to conduct the rising generation, of both sexes, at least through all the primary stages of education? Has not the Author of nature preadapted her, by constitution, and faculty, and temperament, for this noble work? What station of beneficent labor can she aspire to, more honorable, or more congenial to every pure and gen-

SOURCE: Horace Mann, *"Eighth Annual Report of the Secretary of the Board of Education (1844),"* in *Life and Words of Horace Mann*, vol. 3, ed. Mary Mann (Boston, 1891), 426–29.

erous impulse? In the great system of society, what other part can she act, so intimately connected with the refinement and purification of the race? How otherwise can she so well vindicate her right to an exalted station in the scale of being; and cause that shameful sentence of degradation by which she has so long been dishonored, to be repealed? Four-fifths of all the women who have ever lived, have been the slaves of man—the menials in his household, the drudges in his field, the instruments of his pleasure, or, at best, the gilded toys of his leisure days in court or palace. She has been outlawed from honorable service, and almost incapacitated, by her servile condition, for the highest aspirations after usefulness and renown. But a noble revenge awaits her. By a manifestation of the superiority of moral power, she can triumph over that physical power which has hitherto subjected her to bondage. She can bless those by whom she has been wronged. By refining the tastes and sentiments of man, she can change the objects of his ambition; and, with changed objects of ambition, the fields of honorable exertion can be divided between the sexes. By inspiring nobler desires for nobler objects, she can break down the ascendency of those selfish motives that have sought their gratification in her submission and inferiority. All this she can do, more rapidly, and more effectually than it can ever be done in any other way, unless through miracles, by training the young to juster notions of honor and duty, and to a higher appreciation of the true dignity and destiny of the race.

The more extensive employment of females for educating the young, will be the addition of a new and mighty power to the forces of civilization. It is a power, also, which, heretofore, to a very great extent, has been unappropriated; which has been allowed, in the administration of the affairs of men, to run to waste. Hence it will be an addition to one of the grandest spheres of human usefulness, without any subtraction from other departments—a gain without a loss. For all females—the great majority—who are destined, in the course of Providence, to sustain maternal relations, no occupation or apprenticeship can be so serviceable; but, in this connection, it is not unworthy of notice, that, according to the census of Massachusetts, there are almost eight thousand more females than males belonging to the State.

But if a female is to assume the performance of a teacher's duties, she must be endowed with high qualifications. If devoid of mental superiority, then she inevitably falls back into that barbarian relation, where physical strength measures itself against physical strength. In that contest, she can never hope to succeed; or, if she succeeds, it will be only as an Amazon, and not as a personification of moral power. Opportunities, therefore, should be everywhere opened for the fit qualification of female teachers; and all females possessing in an eminent degree, the appropriate natural endowments, should be encouraged to qualify themselves for this sacred work. Those who have worthily improved such opportunities, should be rewarded with social distinction and generous emoluments. Society cannot do less than this, on its own account, for those who are improving its condition; though for the actors themselves, in this beneficent work, the highest rewards must forever remain where God and nature have irrevocably placed them—in the consciousness of well-doing.

Could public opinion, on this one subject, be rectified, and brought into harmony with the great law of Christian duty and love, there are thousands of females amongst us, who now spend lives of frivolity, of unbroken wearisomeness and worthlessness, who would rejoice to exchange their days of painful idleness for such ennobling occupations; and who, in addition to the immediate rewards of well-doing, would see, in the distant prospect, the consolations of a life well spent, instead of the pangs of remorse for a frivolous and wasted existence.

Only Heroic Women Were Doctors Then (1865), 1916

Changes in the position of women in the world in the last fifty years were emphasized by Dr. Anna Manning Comfort, graduate of the New York Medical College and Hospital for Women in its first class in 1865, at a luncheon in her honor, given by the Faculty and Trustees of the college at Delmonico's yesterday. Dr. Comfort was graduated at the age of 20, and she is only in the early seventies, alert and well preserved, though she has had a vigorous career, has been married, and is the mother of three children.

"Students of today have no idea of conditions as they were when I studied medicine," said Dr. Comfort. "It is difficult to realize the changes that have taken place. I attended the first meeting when this institution was proposed, and was graduated from the first class. We had to go to Bellevue Hospital for our practical work, and the indignities we were made to suffer are beyond belief. There were 500 young men students taking post-graduate courses, and we were jeered at and catcalled, and the 'old war horses,' the doctors, joined the younger men.

"We were considered aggressive. They said women did not have the same brains as men and were not trustworthy. All the work at the hospital was made as repulsively unpleasant for us as possible. There were originally six in the class, but all but two were unable to put up with the treatment to which we were subjected and dropped out. I trembled when-

SOURCE: "Only Heroic Women Were Doctors Then," *The New York Times*, 9 April 1916.

84

ever I went to the hospital and I said once that I could not bear it. Finally the women went to the authorities, who said that if we were not respectfully treated they would take the charter from the hospital!

"As a physician there was nothing that I could do that satisfied people. If I wore square-toed shoes and swung my arms they said I was mannish, and if I carried a parasol and wore a ribbon in my hair they said I was too feminine. If I smiled they said I had too much levity, and if I sighed they said I had no sand.

"They tore down my sign when I began to practice, the drug stores did not like to fill my prescriptions, and the older doctors would not consult with me. But that little band of women made it possible for the other women who have come later into the field to do their work. When my first patients came and saw me they said I was too young, and they asked in horrified tones if I had studied dissecting just like the men. They were shocked at that, but they were more shocked when my bills were sent in to find that I charged as much as a man.

"I believe in women entering professions," said Dr. Comfort, "but I also believe in motherhood. For the normal woman it is no more of a tax to have a profession as well as family life than it is for a man to carry on the multitudinous duties he has outside the family. I had three sons of my own and two adopted ones, and I am as proud of my motherhood as of my medical career. I gave as much of my personality to my children in an hour as some mothers do in ten. My children honored me and have been worth while in the world."

There were many expressions of esteem for Dr. Comfort and she was overcome when it was announced that money had been raised for an Anna Manning Comfort scholarship in the hospital.

Letters of regret were read from John Burroughs and Colonel Theodore Roosevelt among others.

"I believe in women in the medical profession, and in politics, and in all worthy pursuits," said John Burroughs.

"I am amazed to learn that this is the only institution in this State, and one of two in the United States, exclusively for the woman medical student," said Colonel Roosevelt. "There should be others and women of refinement would be drawn into the profession who will not study medicine in a co-educational college, and more women doctors are needed."

Dr. Walter G. Crump, who spoke of the need for medical colleges exclusively for women, said:

"We learn from the [1910] Flexner report that there is an overproduction of doctors, but nine out of ten of the women doctors practice. There are demands continually for women physicians which cannot be filled. They are needed in many places where women and girls are to be under a physician's care."

Dr. Mary A. Brinkman, who was one of the early graduates of the

85

college, spoke. She said she could corroborate many of the things told by Dr. Comfort. . . .

Women's Separate Sphere, 1872

The claim of the plaintiff, who is a married woman, to be admitted to practice as an attorney and counsellor-at-law, is based upon the supposed right of every person, man or woman, to engage in any lawful employment for a livelihood. The Supreme Court of Illinois denied the application on the ground that, by the common law, which is the basis of the laws of Illinois, only men were admitted to the bar, and the legislature had not made any change in this respect, but had simply provided that no person should be admitted to practice as attorney or counsellor without having previously obtained a license for that purpose from two justices of the Supreme Court, and that no person should receive a license without first obtaining a certificate from the court of some county of his good moral character. In other respects it was left to the discretion of the court to establish the rules by which admission to the profession should be determined. The court, however, regarded itself as bound by at least two limitations. One was that it should establish such terms of admission as would promote the proper administration of justice, and the other that it should not admit any persons, or class of persons, not intended by the legislature to be admitted, even though not expressly excluded by statute. In view of this latter limitation the court felt compelled to deny the application of females to be admitted as members of the bar. Being contrary to the rules of the common law and the usages of Westminster Hall* from time immemorial, it could not be supposed that the legislature had intended to adopt any different rule.

The claim that, under the fourteenth amendment of the Constitution, which declares that no State shall make or enforce any law which shall abridge the privileges and immunities of citizens of the United States, the statute law of Illinois, or the common law prevailing in that State, can no longer be set up as a barrier against the right of females to pursue any lawful employment for a livelihood (the practice of law included), assumes that it is one of the privileges and immunities of women as citizens to engage in any and every profession, occupation, or employment in civil life.

It certainly cannot be affirmed, as an historical fact, that this has ever been established as one of the fundamental privileges and immunities of

SOURCE: Justice Bradley's majority opinion in *Bradwell* v. *Illinois* (December 1872).
*Westminster Hall was the ancient seat of English law, established in the twelfth century.

the sex. On the contrary, the civil law, as well as nature herself, has always recognized a wide difference in the respective spheres and destinies of man and woman. Man is, or should be, woman's protector and defender. The natural and proper timidity and delicacy which belongs to the female sex evidently unfits it for many of the occupations of civil life. The constitution of the family organization, which is founded in the divine ordinance, as well as in the nature of things, indicates the domestic sphere as that which properly belongs to the domain and functions of womanhood. The harmony, not to say identity, of interests and views which belong, or should belong, to the family institution is repugnant to the idea of a woman adopting a distinct and independent career from that of her husband. So firmly fixed was this sentiment in the founders of the common law that it became a maxim of that system of jurisprudence that a woman had no legal existence separate from her husband, who was regarded as her head and representative in the social state; and, notwithstanding some recent modifications of this civil status, many of the special rules of law flowing from and dependent upon this cardinal principle still exist in full force in most States. One of these is, that a married woman is incapable, without her husband's consent, of making contracts which shall be binding on her or him. This very incapacity was one circumstance which the Supreme Court of Illinois deemed important in rendering a married woman incompetent fully to perform the duties and trusts that belong to the office of an attorney and counsellor.

It is true that many women are unmarried and not affected by any of the duties, complications, and incapacities arising out of the married state, but these are exceptions to the general rule. The paramount destiny and mission of woman are to fulfil the noble and benign offices of wife and mother. This is the law of the Creator. And the rules of civil society must be adapted to the general constitution of things, and cannot be based upon exceptional cases.

The humane movements of modern society, which have for their object the multiplication of avenues for woman's advancement, and of occupations adapted to her condition and sex, have my heartiest concurrence. But I am not prepared to say that it is one of her fundamental rights and privileges to be admitted into every office and position, including those which require highly special qualifications and demanding special responsibilities. In the nature of things it is not every citizen of every age, sex, and condition that is qualified for every calling and position. It is the prerogative of the legislator to prescribe regulations founded on nature, reason, and experience for the due admission of qualified persons to professions and callings demanding special skill and confidence. This fairly belongs to the police power of the State; and, in my opinion, in view of the peculiar characteristics, destiny, and mission of woman, it is within the province of the legislature to ordain what offices, positions, and callings shall be filled and discharged by men, and shall receive the benefit of those energies and responsibilities, and that decision and firmness which are presumed to predominate in the sterner sex.

For these reasons I think that the laws of Illinois now complained of are not obnoxious to the charge of abridging any of the privileges and immunities of citizens of the United States.

Chapter 5

Life and Labor in Industrial America

By the close of the nineteenth century, the benefits of industrialization had grown apparent. The United States had become a wealthy and powerful nation, a leader among the countries of the world. But it paid a price for this growth in terms of human suffering, a price that was only beginning to be realized. Working conditions were often abysmal; immigrant families engaged in cigar manufacturing, for example, both lived and labored in overcrowded, foul-smelling tenements. Factories and mines were designed with minimal concern for worker health and safety. Workers toiled long days at bare-subsistence wages, with virtually no compensation benefits or legal safeguards.

Bonnie Mitelman's article "Rose Schneiderman and the Triangle Fire" describes one of the most horrible examples of the consequences of such conditions. Although it focuses primarily on the tragedy of an industrial fire, the article also offers insights into working conditions in the garment industry, the attitudes of management toward their employees and workers toward their unions, and the circumstances that finally spurred public support and government action for workplace reform.

The first two documents illustrate that the hazards of the workplace were by no means restricted to the Greenwich Village garment district, but also included the tenement workshops of New York City and the coal mines of Pennsylvania. What attitude is reflected in the miner's statement, "We are American citizens and we don't go to hospitals and poorhouses"?

If working conditions were so bad here, why did so many immigrants come to America from Europe? We might find one answer in the third document, the story of Rocco Corresca, a poor Italian immigrant. What does his description of his first days in the United States indicate about the hardships experienced by the newcomers? In the end, what was the consequence of Rocco's success in America?

ESSAY

Rose Schneiderman and the Triangle Fire

Bonnie Mitelman

On Saturday afternoon, March 25, 1911, in New York City's Greenwich Village, a small fire broke out in the Triangle Waist Company, just as the 500 shirtwaist employees were quitting for the day. People rushed about, trying to get out, but they found exits blocked and windows to the fire escape rusted shut. They panicked.

As the fire spread and more and more were trapped, some began to jump, their hair and clothing afire, from the eighth and ninth floor windows. Nets that firemen held for them tore apart at the impact of the falling bodies. By the time it was over, 146 workers had died, most of them young Jewish women.

A United Press reporter, William Shepherd, witnessed the tragedy and reported, "I looked upon the heap of dead bodies and I remembered these girls were the shirtwaist makers. I remembered their great strike of last year in which these same girls had demanded more sanitary conditions and more safety precautions in the shops. These dead bodies were the answer."

The horror of that fire touched the entire Lower East Side ghetto community, and there was a profuse outpouring of sympathy. But it was Rose Schneiderman, an immigrant worker with a spirit of social justice and a powerful way with words, who is largely credited with translating the

SOURCE: Bonnie Mitelman, "Rose Schneiderman and the Triangle of Fire," *American History Illustrated* 16 (July 1981): 38–47. Reprinted through courtesy of Cowles Magazines, publisher of *American History Illustrated*.

ghetto's emotional reaction into meaningful, widespread action. Six weeks following the tragedy, and after years of solid groundwork, with one brilliant, well-timed speech, she was able to inspire the support of wealthy uptown New Yorkers and to swing public opinion to the side of the labor movement, enabling concerned civic, religious, and labor leaders to mobilize their efforts for desperately needed safety and industrial reforms.

The Triangle fire, and the deaths of so many helpless workers, seemed to trigger in Rose Schneiderman an intense realization that there was absolutely nothing or no one to help working women except a strong union movement. With fierce determination, and the dedication, influence, and funding of many other people as well, she battled to regulate hours, wages, and safety standards and to abolish the sweatshop system. In so doing, she brought dignity and human rights to all workers.

The dramatic "uprising of the 20,000" of 1909–10, in which thousands of immigrant girls and women in the shirtwaist industry had endured three long winter months of a general strike to protest deplorable working conditions, had produced some immediate gains for working women. There had been agreements for shorter working hours, increased wages, and even safety reforms, but there had not been formal recognition of their union. At Triangle, for example, the girls had gained a 52 hour week, a 12–15 percent wage increase, and promises to end the grueling subcontracting system. But they had not gained the only instrument on which they could depend for lasting change: a viable trade union. This was to have disastrous results, for in spite of the few gains that they seemed to have made, the workers won no rights or bargaining power at all. In fact, "The company dealt only with its contractors. It felt no responsibility for the girls."

There were groups as well as individuals who realized the workers' impotence, but their attempts to change the situation accomplished little despite long years of hard work. The Women's Trade Union League [WTUL] and the International Ladies' Garment Workers' Union, through the efforts of Mary Dreier, Helen Marot, Leonora O'Reilly, Pauline Newman, and Rose Schneiderman, had struggled unsuccessfully for improved conditions: the futility that the union organizers were feeling in late 1910 is reflected in the WTUL minutes of December 5 of that year.

A scant eight months after their historic waistmakers' strike, and three months before the deadly Triangle fire, a Mrs. Malkiel (no doubt Theresa Serber Malkiel, who wrote the legendary account of the strike, *The Diary of a Shirtwaist Striker: A Story of the Shirtwaist Makers' Strike in New York*) is reported to have come before the League to urge action after a devastating fire in Newark, New Jersey, killed twenty-five working women. Mrs. Malkiel attributed their loss to the greed and negligence of the owners and the proper authorities. The WTUL subsequently demanded an investigation of all factory buildings and it elected an investigation committee from the League to cooperate with similar committees from other organizations.

The files of the WTUL contain complaint after complaint about unsafe factory conditions; many were filled out by workers afraid to sign their names for fear of being fired had their employers seen the forms. They describe factories with locked doors, no fire escapes, and barred windows. The New York *Times* carried an article which reported that fourteen factories were found to have no fire escapes, twenty-three that had locked doors, and seventy-eight that had obstructed fire escapes. In all, according to the article, 99 percent of the factories investigated in New York were found to have serious fire hazards.

Yet no action was taken.

It was the Triangle fire that emphasized, spectacularly and tragically, the deplorable safety and sanitary conditions of the garment workers. The tragedy focused attention upon the ghastly factories in which most immigrants worked; there was no longer any question about what the strikers had meant when they talked about safety and sanitary reform, and about social and economic justice.

The grief and frustration of the shirtwaist strikers were expressed by one of them, Rose Safran, after the fire: "If the union had won we would have been safe. Two of our demands were for adequate fire escapes and for open doors from the factories to the street. But the bosses defeated us and we didn't get the open doors or the better fire escapes. So our friends are dead."

The families of the fire victims were heartbroken and hysterical, the ghetto's *Jewish Daily Forward* was understandably melodramatic, and the immigrant community was completely enraged. Their Jewish heritage had taught them an emphasis on individual human life and worth; their shared background in the *shtetl* [Jewish village in Eastern Europe] and common experiences in the ghetto had given them a sense of fellowship. They were, in a sense, a family—and some of the most helpless among them had died needlessly.

The senseless deaths of so many young Jewish women sparked within these Eastern Europeans a new determination and dedication. The fire had made reform absolutely essential. Workers' rights were no longer just socialist jargon: They were a matter of life and death.

The Triangle Waist Company was located on the three floors of the Asch Building, a 10-story, 135-foot-high structure at the corner of Greene Street and Washington Place in Greenwich Village. One of the largest shirtwaist manufacturers, Triangle employed up to 900 people at times, but on the day of the fire, only about 500 were working.

Leon Stein's brilliant and fascinating account of the fire, entitled simply *The Triangle Fire*, develops and documents the way in which the physical facilities, company procedures, and human behavior interacted to cause this great tragedy. Much of what occurred was ironic, some was cruel, some stupid, some pathetic. It is a dramatic portrayal of the eternal confrontation of the "haves" and the "have-nots," told in large part by those who survived.

Fire broke out at the Triangle Company at approximately 4:45 P.M. (because time clocks were reportedly set back to stretch the day, and because other records give differing times of the first fire alarm, it is uncertain exactly what time the fire started), just after pay envelopes had been distributed and employees were leaving their work posts. It was a small fire at first, and there was a calm, controlled effort to extinguish it. But the fire began to spread, jumping from one pile of debris to another, engulfing the combustible shirtwaist fabric. It became obvious that the fire could not be snuffed out, and workers tried to reach the elevators or stairway. Those who reached the one open stairway raced down eight flights of stairs to safety; those who managed to climb onto the available passenger elevators also got out. But not everyone could reach the available exits. Some tried to open the door to a stairway and found it locked. Others were trapped between long working tables or behind the hordes of people trying to get into the elevators or out through the one open door.

Under the work tables, rags were burning; the wooden floors, trim, and window frames were also afire. Frantically, workers fought their way to the elevators, to the fire escape, and to the windows—to any place that might lead to safety.

Fire whistles and bells sounded as the fire department raced to the building. But equipment proved inadequate, as the fire ladders reached only to the seventh floor. And by the time the firemen connected their hoses to douse the flames, the crowded eighth floor was completely ablaze.

For those who reached the windows, there seemed to be a chance for safety. The New York *World* describes people balancing on window sills, nine stories up, with flames scorching them from behind, until firemen arrived: "The nets were spread below with all promptness. Citizens were commandeered into service, as the firemen necessarily gave their attention to the one engine and hose of the force that first arrived. The catapult force that the bodies gathered in the long plunges made the nets utterly without avail. Screaming girls and men, as they fell, tore the nets from the grasp of the holders, and the bodies struck the sidewalks and lay just as they fell. Some of the bodies ripped big holes through the life nets."

One reporter who witnessed the fire remembered how,

A young man helped a girl to the window sill on the ninth floor. Then he held her out deliberately, away from the building, and let her drop. He held out a second girl the same way and let her drop. He held out a third girl who did not resist. They were all as unresisting as if he were helping them into a street car instead of into eternity. He saw that a terrible death awaited them in the flames and his was only a terrible chivalry. He brought around another girl to the window. I saw her put her arms around him and kiss him. Then he held her into space—and dropped her. Quick as a flash, he was on the window sill himself. His coat fluttered upwards—the air filled his trouser legs as he came down. I could see he wore tan shoes.

Those who had rushed to the fire escape found the window openings rusted shut. Several precious minutes were lost in releasing them. The fire escape itself ended at the second floor, in an airshaft between the Asch Building and the building next door. But too frantic to notice where it ended, workers climbed onto the fire escape, one after another until, in one terrifying moment, it collapsed from the weight, pitching the workers to their death.

Those who had made their way to the elevators found crowds pushing to get into the cars. When it became obvious that the elevators could no longer run, workers jumped down the elevator shaft, landing on the top of the cars, or grabbing for cables to ease their descent. Several died, but incredibly, some did manage to save themselves in this way. One man was found, hours after the fire, beneath an elevator car in the basement of the building, nearly drowned by the rapidly rising water from the firemen's hoses.

Several people, among them Triangle's two owners, raced to the roof, and from there were led to safety. Others never had that chance. "When Fire Chief Croker could make his way into the [top] three floors," states one account of the fire, "he found sights that utterly staggered him. . . . He saw as the smoke drifted away bodies burned to bare bones. There were skeletons bending over sewing machines."

The day after the fire, the New York *Times* announced that "the building was fireproof. It shows hardly any signs of the disaster that overtook it. The walls are as good as ever, as are the floors: nothing is worse for the fire except the furniture and 141 [*sic*] of the 600 men and girls that were employed in its upper three stories."

The building *was* fireproof. But there had never been a fire drill in the factory, even though the management had been warned about the possible hazard of fire on the top three floors. Owners Max Blanck and Isaac Harris had chosen to ignore these warnings in spite of the fact that many of their employees were immigrants who could barely speak English, which would surely mean panic in the event of a crisis.

The New York *Times* also noted that Leonora O'Reilly of the League had reported Max Blanck's visit to the WTUL during the shirtwaist strike, and his plea that the girls return to work. He claimed a business reputation to maintain and told the Union leaders he would make the necessary improvements right away. Because he was the largest manufacturer in the business, the League reported, they trusted him and let the girls return.

But the improvements were never made. And there was nothing that anybody could or would do about it. Factory doors continued to open in instead of out, in violation of fire regulations. The doors remained bolted during working hours, apparently to prevent workers from getting past the inspectors with stolen merchandise. Triangle had only two staircases where there should have been three, and those two were very narrow. Despite the fact that the building was deemed fireproof, it had wooden window frames, floors, and trim. There was no sprinkler system. It was not legally required.

These were the same kinds of conditions which existed in factories throughout the garment industry; they had been cited repeatedly in the complaints filed with the WTUL. They were not unusual nor restricted to Triangle; in fact, Triangle was not as bad as many other factories.

But it was at Triangle that the fire took place.

The *Jewish Daily Forward* mourned the dead with sorrowful stories, and its headlines talked of "funerals instead of weddings" for the dead young girls. The entire Jewish immigrant community was affected, for it seemed there was scarcely a person who was not in some way touched by the fire. Nearly everyone had either been employed at Triangle themselves, or had a friend or relative who had worked there at some time or another. Most worked in factories with similar conditions, and so everyone identified with the victims and their families.

Many of the dead, burned beyond recognition, remained unidentified for days, as searching family members returned again and again to wait in long lines to look for their loved ones. Many survivors were unable to identify their mothers, sisters, or wives; the confusion of handling so many victims and so many survivors who did not understand what was happening to them and to their dead led to even more anguish for the community. Some of the victims were identified by the names on the pay envelopes handed to them at quitting time and stuffed deeply into pockets or stockings just before the fire. But many bodies remained unclaimed for days, with bewildered and bereaved survivors wandering among them, trying to find some identifying mark.

Charges of first- and second-degree manslaughter were brought against the two men who owned Triangle, and Leon Stein's book artfully depicts the subtle psychological and sociological implications of the powerful against the oppressed, and of the Westernized, German-Jewish immigrants against those still living their old-world, Eastern European heritage. Ultimately, Triangle owners Blanck and Harris were acquitted of the charges against them, and in due time they collected their rather sizable insurance.

The shirtwaist, popularized by Gibson girls, had come to represent the new-found freedom of females in America. After the fire, it symbolized death. The reaction of the grief-stricken Lower East Side was articulated by socialist lawyer Morris Hillquit:

> The girls who went on strike last year were trying to readjust the conditions under which they were obliged to work. I wonder if there is not some connection between the fire and that strike. I wonder if the magistrates who sent to jail the girls who did picket duty in front of the Triangle shop realized last Sunday that some of the responsibility may be theirs. Had the strike been successful, these girls might have been alive today and the citizenry of New York would have less of a burden upon its conscience.

For the first time in the history of New York's garment industry there were indications that the public was beginning to accept responsibility for the exploitation of the immigrants. For the first time, the establishment seemed to understand that these were human beings asking for their rights, not merely troublemaking anarchists.

The day after the Triangle fire a protest meeting was held at the Women's Trade Union League, with representatives from twenty leading labor and civic organizations. They formed "a relief committee to cooperate with the Red Cross in its work among the families of the victims, and another committee . . . to broaden the investigation and research on fire hazards in New York factories which was already being carried on by the League."

The minutes of the League recount the deep indignation that members felt at the indifference of a public which had ignored their pleas for safety after the Newark fire. In an attempt to translate their anger into constructive action, the League drew up a list of forceful resolutions that included a plan to gather delegates from all of the city's unions to make a concerted effort to force safety changes in factories. In addition, the League called upon all workers to inspect factories and then report any violations to the proper city authorities and to the WTUL. They called upon the city to immediately appoint organized workers as unofficial inspectors. They resolved to submit the following fire regulations suggestions: compulsory fire drills, fireproof exits, unlocked doors, fire alarms, automatic sprinklers, and regular inspections. The League called upon the legislature to create the Bureau of Fire Protection and finally, the League underscored the absolute need for all workers to organize themselves at once into trade unions so that they would never again be powerless.

The League also voted to participate in the funeral procession for the unidentified dead of the Triangle fire.

The city held a funeral for the dead who were unclaimed. "More than 120,000 of us were in the funeral procession that miserable rainy April day," remembered Rose Schneiderman. "From ten in the morning until four in the afternoon we of the Women's Trade Union League marched in the procession with other trade-union men and women, all of us filled with anguish and regret that we had never been able to organize the Triangle workers."

Schneiderman, along with many others, was absolutely determined that this kind of tragedy would never happen again. With single-minded dedication, they devoted themselves to unionizing the workers. The searing example of the Triangle fire provided them with the impetus they needed to gain public support for their efforts.

They dramatized and emphasized and capitalized on the scandalous working conditions of the immigrants. From all segments of the community came cries for labor reform. Stephen S. Wise, the prestigious reform rabbi, called for the formation of a citizens' committee. Jacob H. Schiff, Bishop David H. Greer, Governor John A. Dix, Anne Morgan (of *the* Morgans) and other leading civic and religious leaders collaborated in a mass meeting at the Metropolitan Opera House on May 2 to protest factory conditions and to show support for the workers.

Several people spoke at that meeting on May 2, and many in the audience began to grow restless and antagonistic. Finally, 29-year-old Rose Schneiderman stepped up to the podium.

In a whisper barely audible, she began to address the crowd.

> I would be a traitor to these poor burned bodies, if I came here to talk good fellowship. We have tried you good people of the public and we have found you wanting. The old Inquisition had its rack and its thumbscrews and its instruments of torture with iron teeth. We know what these things are today: the iron teeth are our necessities, the thumbscrews the high-powered and swift machinery close to which we must work, and the rack is here in the fire-proof structures that will destroy us the minute they catch on fire.
>
> This is not the first time girls have burned alive in the city. Every week I must learn of the untimely death of one of my sister workers. Every year thousands of us are maimed. The life of men and women is so cheap and property is so sacred. There are so many of us for one job it matters little if 140-odd are burned to death.
>
> We have tried you, citizens; we are trying you now, and you have a couple of dollars for the sorrowing mothers and daughters and sisters by way of a charity gift. But every time the workers come out in the only way they know to protest against conditions which are unbearable, the strong hand of the law is allowed to press down heavily upon us.
>
> Public officials have only words of warning to us—warning that we must be intensely orderly and must be intensely peaceable,

and they have the workhouse just back of all their warnings. The strong hand of the law beats us back when we rise into the conditions that make life bearable.

I can't talk fellowship to you who are gathered here. Too much blood has been spilled. I know from my experience it is up to the working people to save themselves. The only way they can save themselves is by a strong working-class movement.

Her speech has become a classic. It is more than just an emotional picture of persecution; it reflects the pervasive sadness and profound understanding that comes from knowing, finally, the cruel realities of life, the perspective of history, and the nature of human beings.

The devastation of that fire and the futility of the seemingly successful strike that had preceded it seemed to impart an undeniable truth to Rose Schneiderman: They could not fail again. The events of 1911 seemed to have made her, and many others, more keenly aware than they had ever been that the workers' fight for reform was absolutely essential. If they did not do it, it would not be done.

In a sense, the fire touched off in Schneiderman an awareness of her own responsibility in the battle for industrial reform. This fiery socialist worker had been transformed into a highly effective labor leader.

The influential speech she gave did help swing public opinion to the side of the trade unions, and the fire itself had made the workers more aware of the crucial need to unionize. Widespread support for labor reform and unionization emerged. Pressure from individuals, such as Rose Schneiderman, as well as from groups like the Women's Trade Union League and the International Ladies' Garment Workers' Union, helped form the New York State Factory Investigating Commission, the New York Citizens' Committee on Safety, and other regulatory and investigatory bodies. The League and Local 25 (the Shirtwaist Makers' Union of the ILGWU) were especially instrumental in attaining a new Industrial Code for New York State, which became "the most outstanding instrument for safeguarding the lives, health, and welfare of the millions of wage earners in New York State and . . . in the nation at large."

It took years for these changes to occur, and labor reform did not rise majestically, Phoenix-like, from the ashes of the Triangle fire. But that fire, and Rose Schneiderman's whispered plea for a strong working-class movement, had indeed become the loud clear call for action.

DOCUMENTS

Tenement Cigarmakers, c. 1890

Take a row of houses in East Tenth Street. . . . They contained thirty-five families of cigarmakers, with probably not half a dozen persons in the whole lot of them, outside of the children, who could speak a word of English, though many had been in the country half a lifetime. This room with two windows giving on the street, and a rear attachment without windows, called a bedroom by courtesy, is rented at $12.25 a month. In the front room[,] man and wife work at the bench from six in the morning till nine at night. They make a team, stripping the tobacco leaves together; then he makes the filler, and she rolls the wrapper on and finishes the cigar. For a thousand they receive $3.75, and can turn out together three thousand cigars a week. The point has been reached where the rebellion comes in, and the workers in these tenements are just now on a strike, demanding $5.00 and $5.50 for their work. The manufacturer having refused, they are expecting hourly to be served with notice to quit their homes, and the going of a stranger among them excites their resentment, until his errand is explained. While we are in the house, the ultimatum of the "boss" is received. He will give $3.75 a thousand, not another cent. Our host is a man of seeming intelligence, yet he has been nine years in New York and knows neither English nor German. Three bright little children play about the floor.

His neighbor on the same floor has been here fifteen years, but shakes his head when asked if he can speak English. He answers in a few broken syllables when addressed in German. With $11.75 rent to pay for like accommodation, he has the advantage of his oldest boy's work besides his wife's at the bench. Three properly make a team, and these three can turn out four thousand cigars a week, at $3.75. This Bohemian has a large family; there are four children, too small to work, to be cared for. . . . [T]his Bohemian's butcher's bill for the week, with meat at twelve cents a pound . . . is from two dollars and a half to three dollars. . . . Here is a suite of three rooms, two dark, three flights up. The ceiling is partly down in one of the rooms. "It is three months since we asked the landlord to fix it," says the oldest son, a very intelligent lad who has learned English in the evening school. His father has not had that advantage, and has sat at his bench, deaf and dumb to the world about him except his own, for six years. He has improved his time and become an expert at his trade. Father, mother, and son together, a full team, make from fifteen to sixteen dollars a week. . . .

SOURCE: Jacob Riis, *How the Other Half Lives* (New York: Scribner's, 1903), 103–8.

Probably more than half of all the Bohemians in this city are cigar-makers, and it is the herding of these in great numbers in the so-called tenement factories, where the cheapest grade of work is done at the lowest wages, that constitutes at once their greatest hardship and the chief grudge of other workmen against them. . . .

Men, women and children work together seven days in the week in these cheerless tenements to make a living for the family, from the break of day till far into the night. Often the wife is the original cigarmaker from the old home, the husband having adopted her trade here as a matter of necessity, because, knowing no word of English, he could get no other work. As they state the cause of the bitter hostility of the trades unions, she was the primary bone of contention in the day of the early Bohemian immigration. The unions refused to admit the women, and, as the support of the family depended upon her to a large extent, such terms as were offered had to be accepted. The manufacturer has ever since industriously fanned the antagonism between the unions and his hands, for his own advantage. The victory rests with him, since the Court of Appeals decided that the law, passed a few years ago, to prohibit cigarmaking in tenements was unconstitutional, and thus put an end to the struggle. While it lasted, all sorts of frightful stories were told of the shocking conditions under which people lived and worked in these tenements, from a sanitary point of view especially, and a general impression survives to this day that they are particularly desperate. The Board of Health, after a careful canvass, did not find them so then. I am satisfied from personal inspection, at a much later day, guided in a number of instances by the union cigarmakers themselves to the tenements which they considered the worst, that the accounts were greatly exaggerated. Doubtless the people are poor, in many cases very poor; but they are not uncleanly, rather the reverse; they live much better than the clothing-makers in the Tenth Ward, . . .

"Our Daily Life Is Not a Pleasant One," 1902

I am thirty-five years old, married, the father of four children, and have lived in the coal region all my life. Twenty-three of these years have been spent working in and around the mines. My father was a miner. He died ten years ago from "miners' asthma [black lung disease]."

Three of my brothers are miners; none of us had any opportunities to acquire an education. We were sent to school (such a school as there was in those days) until we were about twelve years of age, and then we were

SOURCE: *Independent* 54 (June 12, 1902): 1407–10.

put into the screen room of a breaker to pick slate. From there we went inside the mines as driver boys. As we grew stronger we were taken on as laborers, where we served until able to call ourselves miners. We were given work in the breasts and gangways. There were five of us boys. One lies in the cemetery—fifty tons of top rock dropped on him. He was killed three weeks after he got his job as a miner—a month before he was to be married.

In the fifteen years I have worked as a miner I have earned the average rate of wages any of us coal heavers get. To-day I am little better off than when I started to do for myself. I have $100 on hand; I am not in debt; I hope to be able to weather the strike without going hungry.

I am only one of the hundreds you see on the street every day. The muscles on my arms are no harder, the callous on my palms no deeper than my neighbor's whose entire life has been spent in the coal region. By years I am only thirty-five. But look at the marks on my body; look at the lines of worriment on my forehead; see the gray hairs on my head and in my mustache; take my general appearance, and you'll think I'm ten years older.

You need not wonder why. Day in and day out, from Monday morning to Saturday evening, between the rising and the setting of the sun, I am in the underground workings of the coal mines. From the seams water trickles into the ditches along the gangways; if not water, it is the gas which hurls us to eternity and the props and timbers to a chaos.

Our daily life is not a pleasant one. When we put on our oil soaked suit in the morning we can't guess all the dangers which threaten our lives. We walk sometimes miles to the place—to the man way or traveling way, or to the mouth of the shaft on top of the slope. And then we enter the darkened chambers of the mines. On our right and on our left we see the logs that keep up the top and support the sides which may crush us into shapeless masses, as they have done to many of our comrades.

We get old quickly. Powder, smoke, after-damp, bad air—all combine to bring furrows to our faces and asthma to our lungs.

I did not strike because I wanted to; I struck because I had to. A miner— the same as any other workman—must earn fair living wages, or he can't live. And it is not how much you get that counts. It is how much what you get will buy. I have gone through it all, and I think my case is a good sample.

I was married in 1890, when I was 23 years old—quite a bit above the age when we miner boys get into double harness [married]. The woman I married is like myself. She was born beneath the shadow of a dirt bank; her chances for school weren't any better than mine; but she did have to learn how to keep house on a certain amount of money. After we paid the preacher for tying the knot we had just $185 in cash, good health and the good wishes of many friends to start us off.

Our cash was exhausted in buying furniture for housekeeping. In 1890 work was not so plentiful, and by the time our first baby came there was room for much doubt as to how we would pull out. Low wages, and not much over half time in those years, made us hustle. In 1890–91, from June to May, I earned $368.72. That represented eleven months' work, or an average of $33.52 per month. Our rent was $10 per month; store not less than $20. And then I had my oil suits and gum boots to pay for. The result was that after the first year and a half of our married life we were in debt. Not much, of course, and not as much as many of my neighbors, men of larger families, and some who made less money, or in whose case there had been sickness or accident or death. These are all things which a miner must provide for.

I have had fairly good work since I was married. I made the average of what we contract miners are paid; but, as I said before, I am not much better off than when I started.

In 1896 my wife was sick eleven weeks. The doctor came to my house almost every day. He charged me $20 for his services. There was medicine to buy. I paid the drug store $18 in that time. Her mother nursed her, and we kept a girl in the kitchen at $1.50 a week, which cost me $15 for ten weeks, besides the additional living expenses.

In 1897, just a year afterward, I had a severer trial. And mind, in those years, we were only working about half time. But in the fall of that year one of my brothers struck a gas feeder. There was a terrible explosion. He was hurled downward in the breast and covered with the rush of coal and rock. I was working only three breasts away from him and for a moment was unable to realize what had occurred. Myself and a hundred others were soon at work, however, and in a short while we found him, horribly burned over his whole body, his laborer dead alongside of him.

He was my brother. He was single and had been boarding. He had no home of his own. I didn't want him taken to the hospital, so I directed the driver of the ambulance to take him to my house. Besides being burned, his right arm and left leg were broken, and he was hurt internally. The doctors—there were two at the house when we got there—said he would die. But he didn't. He is living and a miner today. But he lay in bed just fourteen weeks, and was unable to work for seven weeks after he got out of bed. He had no money when he was hurt except the amount represented by his pay. All of the expenses for doctors, medicine, extra help and his living were borne by me, except $25, which another brother gave me. The last one had none to give. Poor work, low wages and a sickly woman for a wife had kept him scratching for his own family.

It is nonsense to say I was not compelled to keep him, that I could have sent him to a hospital or the almshouse. We are American citizens and we don't go to hospitals and poorhouses. . . .

An Italian Bootblack's Story, 1902

We came to Brooklyn to a wooden house in Adams Street that was full of Italians from Naples. [A man named] Bartolo had a room on the third floor and there were fifteen men in the room, all boarding with Bartolo. He did the cooking on a stove in the middle of the room and there were beds all around the sides, one bed above another. It was very hot in the room, but we were soon asleep, for we were very tired.

The next morning, early, Bartolo told us to go out and pick rags and get bottles. He gave us bags and hooks and showed us the ash barrels. On the streets where the fine houses are the people are very careless and put out good things, like mattresses and umbrellas, clothes, hats and boots. We brought all these to Bartolo and he made them new again and sold them on the sidewalk; but mostly we brought rags and bones. The rags we had to wash in the backyard and then we hung them to dry on lines under the ceiling in our room. The bones we kept under the beds till Bartolo could find a man to buy them.

Most of the men in our room worked at digging the sewer. Bartolo got them the work and they paid him about one quarter of their wages. Then he charged them for board and he bought the clothes for them, too. So they got little money after all.

Bartolo was always saying that the rent of the room was so high that he could not make anything, but he was really making plenty. He was what they call a padrone* and is now a very rich man. The men that were living with him had just come to the country and could not speak English. They had all been sent by the young man we met in Italy. Bartolo told us all that we must work for him and that if we did not the police would come and put us in prison.

He gave us very little money, and our clothes were some of those that were found on the street. Still we had enough to eat and we had meat quite often, which we never had in Italy. Bartolo got it from the butcher— the meat that he could not sell to other people—but it was quite good meat. Bartolo cooked it in the pan while we all sat on our beds in the evening. Then he cut it into small bits and passed the pan around, saying:

"See what I do for you and yet you are not glad. I am too kind a man, that is why I am so poor."

We were with Bartolo nearly a year, but some of our countrymen who had been in the place a long time said that Bartolo had no right to us and we could get work for a dollar and a half a day, which, when you make it *lire* (reckoned in the Italian currency) is very much. So we went away

SOURCE: *Independent* 54 (December 4, 1902): 2865–67.
Padrone is a labor boss who secured employment for immigrants.

one day to Newark and got work on the street. Bartolo came after us and made a great noise, but the boss said that if he did not go away soon the police would have him. Then he went, saying that there was no justice in this country.

We paid a man five dollars each for getting us the work and we were with that boss for six months. He was Irish, but a good man and he gave us our money every Saturday night. We lived much better than with Bartolo, and when the work was done we each had nearly $200 saved. Plenty of the men spoke English and they taught us, and we taught them to read and write. That was at night, for we had a lamp in our room, and there were only five other men who lived in that room with us.

We got up at half-past five o'clock every morning and made coffee on the stove and had a breakfast of bread and cheese, onions, garlic and red herrings. We went to work at seven o'clock and in the middle of the day we had soup and bread in a place where we got it for two cents a plate. In the evenings we had a good dinner with meat of some kind and potatoes. We got from the butcher the meat that other people would not buy because they said it was old, but they don't know what is good. We paid four or five cents a pound for it and it was the best, tho I have heard of people paying sixteen cents a pound.

When the Newark boss told us that there was no more work Francisco and I talked about what we would do and we went back to Brooklyn to a saloon near Hamilton Ferry, where we got a job cleaning it out and slept in a little room upstairs. There was a bootblack named Michael on the corner and when I had time I helped him and learned the business. Francisco cooked the lunch in the saloon and he, too, worked for the bootblack and we were soon able to make the best polish.

Then we thought we would go into business and we got a basement on Hamilton avenue, near the Ferry, and put four chairs in it. We paid $75 for the chairs and all the other things. We had tables and looking glasses there and curtains. We took the papers that have the pictures in and made the place high toned. Outside we had a big sign that said:

THE BEST SHINE FOR TEN CENTS

Men that did not want to pay ten cents could get a good shine for five cents, but it was not an oil shine. We had two boys helping us and paid each of them fifty cents a day. The rent of the place was $20 a month, so the expenses were very great, but we made money from the beginning. We slept in the basement, but got our meals in the saloon till we could put a stove in our place, and then Francisco cooked for us all. That would not do, tho, because some of our customers said that they did not like to smell garlic and onions and red herrings. I thought that was strange, but we had to do what the customers said. So we got the woman who lived upstairs to give us our meals and paid her $1.50 a week each. She gave the boys soup in the middle of the day—five cents for two plates. . . .

We had said that when we saved $1,000 each we would go back to Italy and buy a farm, but now that the time is coming we are so busy and making so much money that we think we will stay. We have opened another parlor near South Ferry, in New York. We have to pay $30 a month rent, but the business is very good. The boys in the place charge sixty cents a day because there is so much work.

Chapter 6

The Triumph of Racism

A TRIUMPH FOR WHITE SUPREMACY.

In the decades following the Civil War, while the northern and western states turned to industrialization with the aid of immigrant laborers, the South remained largely agricultural. Some white Southerners, like Henry Grady of the Atlanta Constitution, *urged the former Confederate states to follow the example of the rest of the nation and build cities, factories, and railroads. Indeed, the South did experience a modicum of industrial and urban growth before World War I. But the region still lagged behind the rapid pace of change elsewhere in the United States.*

In another way, too, the white South continued to look to the past. Once Congress admitted the ex-Confederate states back into the union and federal troops had withdrawn from the South, white Southerners were free to pursue a system of race relations more to their taste than that imposed by Radical Republicans during the Reconstruction era (1865–1876). This system stipulated that blacks be segregated in most areas of public life, be denied the right to vote, and generally be limited to working as landless farmers.

In his essay on the Supreme Court's Plessy v. Ferguson *decision (1896), Keith Weldon Medley points out that among the southern states, Postwar Louisiana offered the brightest hope for easing racial inequality. African Americans participated in politics and benefited from the integration of many public facilities for a number of years after the removal of federal troops. But soon the rising tide of white racism destroyed their dreams; as in other states around the turn of the century, Louisiana ultimately established a rigid system of white supremacy.*

It was one thing for white legislators to enact measures to disfranchise and segregate African Americans; it was another for these laws to receive the sanction of the United States Supreme Court. After all, the Fourteenth and Fifteenth amendments to the Constitution seem to preclude such legislation. Medley's essay centers on the case of Homer Plessy's challenge to Louisiana's separate coach law. How did the Supreme Court manage to conclude that segregation did not violate the Fourteenth Amendment, which supposedly guarantees equal protection of the law? What implications did the Plessy *decision hold for racial segregation in other areas of southern life?*

Even before the Court handed down the Plessy *decision, some blacks realized that disfranchisement and segregation were sweeping the South. The most well-known African American of his day, Booker T. Washington, was among them. In the first document, from his 1895 Atlanta Exposition address delivered before a large interracial crowd, Washington called for cooperation between the races in the economic sphere. Yet, at least for the immediate future, he accepted social separation for blacks. Why do you think that he advocated such an approach?*

In the second document, W. E. B. Du Bois, a founder of the National Association for the Advancement of Colored People (NAACP) and a black intellectual, argued for a different approach. What do you consider the most significant differences between his program and that espoused by Washington? In view of the conditions portrayed in the essay, do you think that any hope existed for the realization of Du Bois's program around the turn of the century?

While black leaders and intellectuals debated future programs and strategies, many Southern blacks took matters into their own hands and headed north. The third document is a letter from a black Mississippi mechanic to the Chicago Defender, *an influential black newspaper. The letter reflects the determination of African Americans to find a better life in the North, the reluctance of Southern whites to let them leave, and the key role that the* Defender *played in encouraging northward migration.*

E S S A Y

The Birth of "Separate but Equal"

Keith Weldon Medley

> "On Tuesday evening, a Negro named [Homer] Plessy was arrested by Private Detective Cain on the East Louisiana train and locked up for violating Section 2 of Act 111 of 1890, relative to separate coaches. . . . He waived examination yesterday before Recorder Monlin and was sent before the criminal court under $500 bond."

This modest announcement appeared in the New Orleans *Daily Picayune* on June 9, 1892. Little noticed at the time, it recorded a moment of tragic significance for the people of America. For it marked not only the end of an era that had begun with Reconstruction, but the start of a half-century in which the rights and hopes of black people in the South, briefly raised up by Reconstruction, were all but extinguished.

In time it would make famous the names of a New Orleans shoemaker and a judge from Massachusetts, as the joint label on the landmark Supreme Court decision *Plessy* v. *Ferguson*. The issue was apparently resolved by the Court in 1896. But the running racial and judicial struggle involved did not have its most dramatic climax until a half-century later, with the decision known as *Brown* v. *Board of Education*.

Confrontation over a place in a public conveyance suggests a parallel with Rosa Parks. But her refusal to give up her bus seat to a white passenger in Montgomery, Alabama, was partly triggered by happenstance. Plessy's action on that warm New Orleans afternoon a century ago was an act of civil disobedience carefully planed and orchestrated by a group of black Republicans, lawyers and journalists known in the French-speaking areas of New Orleans as the Comité des Citoyens.

The story of their case and of their calculated yet desperate judicial fight is rooted not merely in the history of what happened in the South after the Civil War, but in the texture of life in New Orleans itself. Even before the Civil War, New Orleans had been a rich, cosmopolitan trading port and a place where people of color had accomplished a great deal.

Originally French, then Spanish, then French again before being bought by Thomas Jefferson in 1803 (along with what would become half of the United States), it was a city with a remarkable mix of colors and cultures, as well as a penchant for violence and vice. On the eve of the war in 1860, the population was pushing 170,000, including 25,000 Irish and 20,000 German immigrants, and 15,000 African-American slaves about to be freed. But New

SOURCE: "The Sad Story of how 'Separate but Equal' was Born," by Keith Weldon Medley, from *Smithsonian* (February 1994) 104–117. Copyright © by Keith Weldon Medley. Reprinted by permission of the Author.

Orleans also had a greater concentration of free people of color than any other city in the Deep South, some 10,000 people who had gained their freedom well before the Civil War began.

Homer Plessy was born free in March 1862, only a month before Yankee gunboats overran the city's Mississippi River defenses, taking control of the port while the war lasted. Like Plessy's family, many black New Orleanians were French-speaking and Roman Catholic. Some had come from Haiti to escape the bloody revolution at the beginning of the 19th century, when Haitians won their independence from France. Some had fought in 1815 with Andrew Jackson against the British in the Battle of New Orleans. The majority were working class, but many were landowners, businessmen, skilled artisans.

Full Inheritances and Paternal Surnames

Though interracial marriage had been officially banned and streetcars segregated, the city had fewer social restrictions about intermingling between whites and blacks than other areas in the South. Many de facto marriages between the races lasted a lifetime; the children produced often received full inheritances and paternal surnames. Some were sent to Europe for their education. Some became rich and prominent citizens.

So hopes ran high on June 11, 1864, as thousands joyfully gathered in Congo Square, the site of weekend slave gatherings, to celebrate a great event: on May 9 of that year, Louisiana had approved an emancipation ordinance. Ratification of the 13th Amendment to the Constitution would come in 1865, followed by the 14th in 1868, which said that if you were born in the United States you were a citizen, and that no state could deprive you of your rights, liberty or property without due process of law. By 1870 the 15th Amendment made clear that no citizen could be deprived of the right to vote on the basis of race, color or previous condition of servitude.

In 1867 New Orleans removed the black stars previously used to designate the city's segregated streetcars. That was the year of the Reconstruction Act, passed by still-powerful Radical Republicans in Washington, which sent U.S. armies of occupation into the South and gave military commanders in five areas there the right to protect life and property with federal force. They set up a procedure to register voters and see that lately freed slaves were allowed to vote, held elections, established black schools, and created machinery whereby Southern states were to ratify the 14th Amendment. In New Orleans and all over the South, Army commanders had the power to appoint and dismiss local officials.

By 1869 when Homer Plessy was 7, New Orleans began experimenting with integrated public schools—the only Southern city to do so. Blacks served with whites on juries and public boards. New Orleans had an integrated police department with a color-blind municipal pay scale. Thanks to Reconstruction, too, Plessy grew to manhood while blacks, who made up most of the Republican Party in the South, voted enthusiastically in large numbers and served in high office. Between the years 1868 and 1896, racial intermarriage was made legal, and Louisiana elected 32 black state senators and 95 state representatives. It had the only black governor in U.S. history before the late 1980s. (In the same period the South as a whole voted 600 black state representatives into office and sent 16 black congressmen to Washington.)

Apparently Plessy left no papers. City records, however, tell a good deal about him and about the racially mixed, middle-class faubourg, or suburb, where he lived. He began making shoes in 1879, married Louise Bordenave in 1888 and attended Mass at St. Augustine's Catholic Church on St. Claude Street. The church had been established by whites and free people of color before the war; services were conducted in French and Latin. The newlyweds could afford to rent a house near the corner of Ursulines Street on North Claiborne Avenue in the Faubourg Tremé.

Outside the Plessys' bedroom window was Congregation Hall, home of Saturday night "grand dancing festivals" where, for 15 cents, New Orleanians swayed to the sounds of Professor Moret's String Band. By the 1890s, Tremé had become an integrated enclave of several races, numbering among its residents many musicians and artists, who tended to be radical and egalitarian. There were also a number of dramatic clubs and benevolent religious societies that would contribute heavily to the Comité des Citoyens, among them the Société des Francs Amis (Homer Plessy became its vice president), which provided medical and funeral expenses for dues-paying members.

Following the Civil War, the full-scale occupation of the South as a defeated nation, along with Reconstruction programs, cost the American taxpayers considerable money, not including the pay and maintenance of the 6,000-odd federal soldiers. Yet for years the Republican Party, dominated by former abolitionists, maintained the political power and the will necessary to try remaking the former Confederate States.

There was no swift and easy way, however, for four million ex-slaves, just freed and without education, to be integrated into a racist, bitterly defeated and economically collapsing South. Race hatred, intimidation and riots flared. The Ku Klux Klan spread pamphlets and terror, which eventually included the murder of influential Reconstruction figures both black and white. It also embarked on the systematic intimidation of newly enfranchised black voters. The power of the Republican Party in Southern states, overwhelmingly based on those same black voters, began to wane, and Southern Democrats started to take back the South. The power of Republicans in Washington, especially after the Recession of 1873, was vulnerable to Democrats who could claim that Reconstruction cost money and had no hope of success.

In the North there had been optimistic expectations for economic recovery in a free-labor South and for the immediate effects of black suffrage. "We need no vast expenditures. We need no standing army," Senator Richard

Yates, a Radical Republican, had once declared. "The ballot will finish the Negro question." By the early 1870s that was clearly not so, and just as clear was the fact that many states in the North and West, which as late as 1868 did not permit black suffrage or integration, would not long concern themselves with the rights of blacks in the South. After the ratification of the 15th Amendment, an Illinois newspaper expressed a prevalent Northern view: "The Negro is now a voter and a citizen. Let him hereafter take his chances in the battle of life."

The specific political event that brought an end to Reconstruction and the withdrawal of occupation troops from the South was the Presidential election of 1876. Republicans had dominated national politics since Lincoln. But in 1876 neither Republican Rutherford B. Hayes nor Democrat Samuel J. Tilden got enough undisputed electoral votes to win. A deal was made, known as the Hayes-Tilden Compromise. Hayes would become President by being ceded the electoral votes of a number of Southern states in return for recalling the armies of occupation (they departed in 1877) and yielding to Democrats the control of the last three Southern states—including Louisiana—still run by the Republican Party. For their part, Southern Democratic leaders in those states agreed to maintain civil rights policies.

Among them was Louisiana's Democratic gubernatorial candidate Francis T. Nicholls, an ex-Confederate general who lost an arm and a leg in the Civil War. Nicholls swore to uphold "equal rights and common interests" and to "obliterate the color line in politics." For a while he kept his word. But without the Reconstruction programs and the bayonets of the armies to support them, lately freed blacks were at a hopeless disadvantage. All over the South, the advances made in the 1870s began to be undone. The pace accelerated in 1883 when the Supreme Court, which was also changing its makeup, declared the civil rights enforcement act of 1875 unconstitutional. This meant that the federal government, lacking the means and will, pretty well got out of the business of making sure that the new civil rights laws were applied in the South.

The erosion of civil rights went more slowly in New Orleans than elsewhere. But the city began reestablishing segregated schools, and in 1890 Nicholls approved the Louisiana Legislature's passage of the Separate Car Act.

The act decreed "equal but separate accommodations for the white and colored races" on Louisiana railway cars. Under its terms any railway company that did not provide separate coaches for blacks and whites could be fined $500. Except for "nurses attending children of the other race," individual whites and blacks would be forbidden to ride together, or risk a $25 fine or 20 days in jail. It was the passage of this bill that finally launched Homer Plessy into history. The fight involved a black newspaper, *The Crusader,* the six remaining black state senators and ultimately the Comité des Citoyens, which coalesced around *The Crusader.*

At the State Capitol, Senator Henry Demas thundered at his fellow legislators: "Like the Jews, we have been driven from our houses and firesides, from our churches and schoolhouses . . . and from the elevated avenues of livelihood, and now, in order to reach the lowest depth of infamy . . . you are willing to forget that you are men and vote for the passage of this bill." But the Separate Car Act passed the Louisiana Senate by a vote of 23 to 6.

The Crusader was a formidable enemy. A weekly founded in 1889 by attorney Louis Martinet to combat the increasingly virulent racism of other New Orleans papers, it called itself "spicy, progressive, liberal, stalwart, fearless," and stood for "A Free Vote and Fair Count, Free Schools, Fair Wages, Justice and Equal Rights." It cost a nickel and carried classified ads for everything from pianos, sails, cotton scales and first communion wreaths to ointments that claimed to "relax"—straighten—the hair. *The Crusader's* star contributor was Rodolphe Desdunes. The son of a Cuban mother and a Haitian father, Desdunes worked as a customs agent by day and, with smoking pen, scribbled polemical columns by night. Hundreds of his articles, still preserved in the archives of Xavier University in New Orleans, offer a window into the desperate fight to keep civil rights from slipping away.

"Colored people have largely patronized the railroads heretofore," Desdunes wrote on July 19, 1890. "They can withdraw the patronage from these corporations and travel only by necessity." He proposed a boycott not unlike the one launched in Montgomery, Alabama, 70 years later.

The 1890s were not a good time to exercise civil disobedience in the American South, or to get on the wrong side of a mob, whether you were black or not. The year 1892 alone produced 226 mob murders, mostly of black men, the highest number in the recorded history of lynchings. In New Orleans, on March 14, 1891, a newspaper editor and a prominent attorney led a crowd of several thousand to Parish Prison. Angry over the acquittal of Italian immigrants accused of the killing of police chief David Hennessy, they broke in, hunted down a group of 11 Italians, shot them, then hanged some from streetlamps and shot them again. Mournfully reflecting on the mood in New Orleans, a black woman told a reporter: "Thank God it wasn't a nigger who killed the Chief."

To combat what became known as the "Jim Crow car law," *The Crusader* and the Comité des Citoyens acquired a small but influential membership. It involved C. C. Antoine, a former officer in the Union Army, who had served four years (1873–77) as Louisiana's lieutenant governor, and wealthy philanthropist Aristide Mary, who had financed lawsuits against other resegregated establishments.

The Comité also included sail manufacturer Arthur Estèves, who became its president. To fight the Jim Crow car law, it was prepared to solicit funds not only from benevolent, social and religious societies in town but from former abolitionists in such faraway cities as Washington, D.C., Chicago and San Francisco. About $3,000 was quickly raised to launch two test cases: one to challenge legal segregation of trains on interstate routes and one to challenge segregation on conveyances within the state. The aim: to "seek redemption" from the Supreme Court of the United States. "We find this the only means left us," a Comité statement concluded. "We must have recourse to it, or sink into a state of helpless inferiority."

It was a forlorn hope, but not as forlorn as it would become in the slow process of going through the legal system. For one thing, on the face of it, if you gave any thought to the intent of the men who wrote the 14th Amendment, the Separate Car Act seemed a clear violation of the constitutional rights of the black citizens of Louisiana. But public opinion in the North had changed rapidly, and so, in the years after 1877, had the makeup of the Supreme Court, which lost its reasonable mix of justices sympathetic to the subject of civil rights.

Some railroad companies initially had been against the bill. It was going to cost money to build and run extra cars—for the bill implied that if a half-empty "white" car was waiting, and even if only one black passenger showed up, he or she would have to have a whole separate-but-equal vehicle made available. In a city that had for so long seen so much racial mixing, railway conductors would now have to decide who was white and who was black—a touchy business, especially since some wives and husbands would not be allowed to ride together.

One of the reasons that Homer Plessy was picked for the job was that he had fair skin. Had it been left to chance, he probably could have ridden the train in the "whites only" section unnoticed. But by prearrangement between the Comité and the East Louisiana Railroad, everything was ready for him when he came.

On June 7, 1892, Plessy strolled to the Press Street depot, which included a restaurant and a combination waiting room and ticket office (both still open to him), bought a first-class ticket and, ignoring the new "Colored Only" sign, sat down in the coach reserved for whites. It was to depart at 4:15 P.M., cross a bridge spanning Lake Pontchartrain and pass through Abita Springs for a two-hour run to Covington.

Hardly had the train started moving when conductor J. J. Dowling approached Plessy. "Are you a colored man?" he asked. "Yes," answered Plessy. "Then you will have to retire to the colored car," said Dowling. Plessy stated that he had paid for his ticket and intended to ride to Covington. Dowling signaled the engineer to stop. A private detective, Captain Chris Cain, hired by the Comité, came aboard and warned Plessy: "If you are colored you should go into the car set apart for your race. The law is plain and must be obeyed."

When Plessy again refused, he was taken a half-mile down to Elysian Fields Avenue for booking at the Fifth Precinct Station. Members of the Comité met him, and a judge released him on temporary bail. The next day a story in a New Orleans daily described Plessy as a "snuff-colored descendant of Ham." After a hearing, Comité member Paul Bonseigneur plunked down a $500 bond (raised by putting his own house in hock) to guarantee Plessy's appearance for trial. Plessy was 30 years old. The future of constitutional rights for blacks in America would ride on his day in court.

Enter John Howard Ferguson, 54, the judge whose name would forever be linked to Plessy's in American history. The lawyer son of a shipowner on the island of Martha's Vineyard, Massachusetts, Ferguson had come South after hearing of opportunities there from returning Civil War soldiers. He was what Southerners called a carpetbagger—meaning anybody who came South after the fighting to administer the remade South or to look for profit in the South's adversity. He married the daughter of a prominent local attorney, a Louisiana Unionist noted for his condemnations of slavery, and began practicing law. Ferguson served in Governor Nicholls' 1876 Legislature. Eventually he campaigned for Murphy Foster, the man who replaced Nicholls as governor and engineered passage of the Separate Car Act. Ferguson was made a judge and assigned the Plessy case a month after Plessy's arrest.

But only a short time after becoming a judge, in another Comité-generated case, he ruled that the Separate Car Act was unconstitutional on trains that traveled through several states—because of the federal government's predominant interest in interstate commerce. The Comité celebrated the decision, and Louis Martinet chortled in print: "Jim Crow is dead as a doornail."

He was wrong. At Plessy's arraignment, Homer Adolph Plessy v. The State of Louisiana, one of Plessy's lawyers, James Walker, argued that neither the state nor any railroad conductor representing it had the right to deny Plessy's liberty on the basis of race, since Plessy was a citizen, and the 14th Amendment clearly said that "no state shall make or enforce any law which shall abridge the privileges or immunities of any citizen of the United States." Judge Ferguson did not agree. The state, he claimed, had a legal right to regulate railroad companies operating solely within the state. Plessy had not been deprived of his liberty. "He was simply deprived of the liberty of doing as he pleased, and of violating a penal statute with impunity."

A swift appeal was presented to the State Supreme Court, which instantly agreed with Ferguson's decision. The 14th Amendment guaranteed black individuals "equality" but did not guarantee "identity or community" with white society. The glum Comité now could look only northward to the Supreme Court of the United States in Washington. As time passed, Plessy's prospects grew worse.

In the decade leading up to 1896, when the case at last was argued before the Court, seven Justices had been replaced—mostly by men who shared the increasingly prevalent belief that Reconstruction had largely failed and that blacks must fend for themselves. The only holdovers from Reconstruction times were John Marshall Harlan of Kentucky, a Hayes appointee, and the aging Stephen J. Field, who had been appointed in 1863 by Lincoln.

Attorney Albion Tourgée, who eventually argued the case for the Comité, estimated that only one Justice would firmly lean to Plessy's side, three would be uncertain and five, frankly opposed. In a letter to Louis Martinet he added a foreboding postscript: "It is of the utmost importance that we should not have a decision *against* us as the court has *never* reversed itself on a constitutional question."

Tourgée was not the only one to notice the changing temper of the Supreme Court. In 1894 Louisiana again placed racial restrictions on marriage and prohibited citizens of opposite races from using the same railroad depot waiting rooms.

The Comité's chances dwindled as the climate of opinion changed, even among people of color. Voices in some quarters argued that resisting white supremacy always evoked harsher responses, and that the struggle for decent conditions was what mattered most, not integration. In 1895 Booker T. Washington, head of Tuskegee Institute, publicly called for accommodation with segregation. Washington argued that in the face of white hatred, integration simply stirred up opposition. The main thing was to concentrate on making segregated schools work, on learning trades and on getting ahead in life.

But the Comité had pledged to see the case to the end. By late fall 1895 everything was in place. Albion Tourgée, with lawyers S. F. Phillips and F. D. McKenny, had filed final papers for the October 1895 term in Homer A. Plessy v. J. H. Ferguson. Tourgée went before the Supreme Court in April 1896. State arguments were made my Louisiana's Attorney General M. J. Cunningham and lawyers Lionel Adams and Alexander Porter Morse.

On May 18 the Court issued a ruling. With only one dissent it granted states the right to forcibly segregate people of different races. Writing for the majority, Justice Henry Billings Brown, appointed by Benjamin Harrison, dismissed Plessy's 14th Amendment claims and, as precedent, pointed to the existence of separate schools in the District of Columbia and the longstanding bans on interracial marriage. The only test of such segregation, he said, would be whether or not the regulations were reasonable. The Court also stated that "legislation is powerless to eradicate racial instincts or to abolish distinctions based upon physical differences." As for determining who was black or white, that was left to the discretion of each state.

The lone dissenter was Justice John Marshall Harlan. "The destinies of two races in this country," Harlan wrote, "are indissolubly linked together, and the interests of both require that the common government of all shall not permit the seeds of race hate to be planted under the sanction of law. . . . The thin disguise of 'equal' accommodations for passengers in railroad coaches will not mislead anyone, nor atone for the wrong this day done."

The decision was remanded to the Supreme Court of Louisiana on September 28, 1896. The Comité issued a final statement: "In passing laws which discriminate between its citizens," it declared, "the State was wrong. . . . Notwithstanding this decision . . . we, as freemen, still believe that we were right, and our cause is sacred."

On January 11, 1897, Homer Plessy returned to court for sentencing. By then, times had changed dramatically. The Comité had disbanded; *The Crusader* had ceased publication. All over the South, white supremacists were firmly in control of the Legislatures. Judge Ferguson had stepped down in 1896, and Judge Joshua Baker was presiding. Plessy changed his plea to guilty, paid a $25 fine and walked out into the brave new world of a segregated Louisiana.

Those in the black community who thought racial separation would bring peace were in for a rude awakening. Emboldened by the Supreme Court's Plessy decision, in February 1898 Louisiana called a constitutional convention in New Orleans to lay down a blueprint for white supremacy. Endorsed by Governor Foster, the delegates made it illegal to run an integrated school, allocated state money as a "pension fund" for the relatives of Confederate soldiers, declared the Louisiana Democratic Party a "whites only" organization and used various devices, such as the "grandfather clause," to keep blacks and immigrants from voting. "Our mission was to establish the supremacy of the white race," the chairman of the judiciary committee bluntly declared. In the four years from 1896 to 1900, more than 120,000 black voters were removed from the rolls, their numbers dropping from 45 percent to 4 percent of eligible voters. By 1900 Louisiana did not have a single black representative in its Legislature. There would be none until 1967.

While legislation made things "separate," the "equal" treatment of the Supreme Court ruling seldom materialized. The greatest disaster would come in education. The South spent very little money on black schools. In New Orleans, the city school board did not open a public high school for blacks until 1917. Even then, black teachers were paid less than their white counterparts, and their pupils received second-hand books and supplies.

One by one the civil rights gains of Reconstruction vanished. So too did the principals in the Plessy v. Ferguson case. Judge Ferguson died in 1915 at age 77. In a front-page story, the *Times-Picayune* lauded him as one who "allied himself with the Democratic reform element" and "took part in the struggle for white supremacy." He was buried in the Lafayette Cemetery on Washington Avenue. In August 1925, some 50,000 white-robed members of the Ku Klux Klan marched in Washington, D.C.

Homer Plessy had died a few months earlier that year. His obituary in the *Times-Picayune* was simple: "Plessy—on Sunday, March 1, 1925, at 5:10 A.M., Homer A. Plessy, 63 years, beloved husband of Louise Bordenave." On the front page of the same paper was the headline "Supreme Court Puts Approval on Segregation," referring to a Louisiana Supreme Court ruling that upheld a segregated housing ordinance in New Orleans. Plessy lies with his mother's family in St. Louis Cemetery No. 1, at 200-year-old integrated Catholic graveyard in the Tremé area. Fifteen years after his death there were only 886 registered black voters in the state of Louisiana.

Nearly 15 more years would pass before NAACP attorney Thurgood Marshall obtained a rehearing of Plessy's cause in another landmark case, Brown v. Board of Education. In that instance, the Court overturned the 1896 ruling and declared "separate but equal" to be unconstitutional. That time, Homer Plessy won.

DOCUMENTS

The Atlanta Exposition Address, 1895

. . . A ship lost at sea for many days suddenly sighted a friendly vessel. From the mast of the unfortunate vessel was seen a signal, "Water, water; we die of thirst!" The answer from the friendly vessel at once came back, "Cast down your bucket where you are." A second time the signal, "Water, water; send us water!" ran up from the distressed vessel, and was answered, "Cast down your bucket where you are." And a third and fourth signal for water was answered, "Cast down your bucket where you are." The captain of the distressed vessel, at last heeding the injunction, cast down his bucket, and it came up full of fresh, sparkling water from the mouth of the Amazon River. To those of my race who depend on bettering their condition in a foreign land or who underestimate the importance of cultivating friendly relations with the Southern white man, who is their next-door neighbour, I would say: "Cast down your bucket where you are"—cast it down in making friends in every manly way of the people of all races by whom we are surrounded.

Cast it down in agriculture, mechanics, in commerce, in domestic service, and in the professions. And in this connection it is well to bear in mind that whatever other sins the South may be called to bear, when it comes to business, pure and simple, it is in the South that the Negro is given a man's chance in the commercial world, and in nothing is this Exposition more eloquent than in emphasizing this chance. Our greatest danger is that in the great leap from slavery to freedom we may overlook the fact that the masses of us are to live by the productions of our hands, and fail to keep in mind that we shall prosper in proportion as we learn to dignify and glorify common labour, and put brains and skill into the common occupations of life; shall prosper in proportion as we learn to draw the line between the superficial and the substantial, the ornamental gewgaws of life and the useful. No race can prosper till it learns that there is as much dignity in tilling a field as in writing a poem. It is at the bottom of life we must begin, and not at the top.

SOURCE: Booker T. Washington, *Up from Slavery: A Biography* (New York: Doubleday, Page and Co., 1901), 218–225.

Nor should we permit our grievances to overshadow our opportunities.

To those of the white race who look to the incoming of those of foreign birth and strange tongue and habits for the prosperity of the South, were I permitted I would repeat what I say to my own race, "Cast down your bucket where you are." Cast it down among the eight millions of Negroes whose habits you know, whose fidelity and love you have tested in days when to have proved treacherous meant the ruin of your firesides. Cast down your bucket among these people who have, without strikes and labour wars, tilled your fields, cleared your forests, built your railroads and cities, and brought forth treasures from the bowels of the earth, and helped make possible this magnificent representation of the progress of the South. Casting down your bucket among my people, helping and encouraging them as you are doing on these grounds, and to education of head, hand, and heart, you will find that they will buy your surplus land, make blossom the waste places in your fields, and run your factories. While doing this, you can be sure in the future, as in the past, that you and your families will be surrounded by the most patient, faithful, law-abiding, and unresentful people that the world has seen. As we have proved our loyalty to you in the past, in nursing your children, watching by the sick-bed of your mothers and fathers, and often following them with tear-dimmed eyes to their graves, so in the future, in our humble way, we shall stand by you with a devotion that no foreigner can approach, ready to lay down our lives, if need be, in defense of yours, interlacing our industrial, commercial, civil, and religious life with yours in a way that shall make the interests of both races one. In all things that are purely social we can be as separate as the fingers, yet one as the hand in all things essential to mutual progress. . . .

The wisest among my race understand that the agitation of questions of social equality is the extremest folly, and that progress in the enjoyment of all the privileges that will come to us must be the result of severe and constant struggle rather than of artificial forcing. No race that has anything to contribute to the markets of the world is long in any degree ostracized. It is important and right that all privileges of the law be ours, but it is vastly more important that we be prepared for the exercise of these privileges. The opportunity to earn a dollar in a factory just now is worth infinitely more than the opportunity to spend a dollar in an opera-house.

A Call for Equality, 1905

. . . We believe that [Negro] American citizens should protest emphatically and continually against the curtailment of their political rights. We believe in manhood suffrage: we believe that no man is so good, intelligent or wealthy as to be entrusted wholly with the welfare of his neighbor.

SOURCE: W. E. B. Du Bois, *Cleveland Gazette*, July 22, 1905.

We believe also in protest against the curtailment of our civil rights. All American citizens have the right to equal treatment in places of public entertainment according to their behavior and deserts.

We especially complain against the denial of equal opportunities to us in economic life; in the rural districts of the south this amounts to peonage and virtual slavery; all over the south it tends to crush labor and small business enterprises: and everywhere American prejudice, helped often by iniquitous laws is making it more difficult for Negro-Americans to earn a decent living.

Common school education should be free to all American children and compulsory. High school training should be adequately provided for all, and college training should be the monopoly of no class or race in any section of our common country. We believe that in defense of its own institutions, the United States should aid common school education, particularly in the south, and we especially recommend concerted agitation to this end. We urge an increase in public high school facilities in the south, where the Negro-Americans are almost wholly without such provisions. We favor well-equipped trade and technical schools for the training of artisans, and the need of adequate and liberal endowment for a few institutions of higher education must be patent to sincere well-wishers of the race.

We demand upright judges in courts, juries selected without discrimination on account of color and the same measure of punishment, and the same efforts at reformation for black as for white offenders. We need orphanages and farm schools for dependent children, juvenile reformatories for delinquents, and the abolition of the dehumanizing convict-lease system. . . .

We hold up for public execration the conduct of two opposite classes of men; the practice among employers of importing ignorant Negro-American laborers in emergencies, and then affording them neither protection nor permanent employment; and the practice of labor unions of proscribing and boycotting and oppressing thousands of their fellow-toilers, simply because they are black. These methods have accentuated and will accentuate the war of labor and capital, and they are disgraceful to both sides. . . .

We regret that this nation has never seen fit adequately to reward the black soldiers who in its five wars, have defended their country with their blood, and yet have been systematically denied the promotions which their abilities deserve. And we regard as unjust, the exclusion of black boys from the military and navy training schools. . . .

The Negro race in America, stolen, ravished and degraded, struggling up through difficulties and oppression, needs sympathy and receives criticism; needs help and is given hindrance, needs protection and is given mob-violence, needs justice and is given charity, needs leadership and is given cowardice and apology, needs bread and is given a stone. This nation will never stand justified before God until these things are changed.

Especially are we surprised and astonished at the recent attitude of the church of Christ—on the increase of a desire to bow to racial prejudice, to narrow the bounds of human brotherhood, and to segregate black men in some outer sanctuary. This is wrong, unchristian and disgraceful to twentieth century civilization. . . .

And while we are demanding, and ought to demand, and will continue to demand the rights enumerated above, God forbid that we should ever forget to urge corresponding duties upon our people.

> The duty to vote.
> The duty to respect the rights of others.
> The duty to work.
> The duty to obey the laws.
> The duty to be clean and orderly.
> The duty to send our children to school.
> The duty to respect ourselves, even as we respect others. . . .

"I Want to Come North," 1917

GRANVILLE, MISSISSIPPI, MAY 16, 1917

Dear Sir [editor of the *Defender*]: This letter is a letter of information of which you will find stamp envelop for reply. I want to come north some time soon but I do not want to leve here looking for a job where I would be in dorse all winter. Now the work I am doing here is running a guage edger in a saw mill. I know all about the grading of lumber. I have been working in lumber about 25 or 27 years. My wedges here is $3.00 a day 11 hours a day. I want to come North where I can educate my 3 little children also my wife. Now if you cannot fit me up at what I am doing down here I can learn anything any one els can. also there is a great deal of good women cooks here would leave any time all they want is to know where to go and some way to go. please write me at once just how I can get my people where they can get something for their work. There are women here cookeing for $1.50 and $2.00 a week. I would like to live in Chicago or Ohio or Philadelphia. Tell Mr. Abbott [owner of the *Defender*] that our pepel are tole that they can not get anything to do up there and they are being snatched off the trains here in Greenville and a rested but in spite of all this, they are leaving every day and every night 100 or more is expecting to leave this week. Let me here from you at once.

SOURCE: Emmett J. Scott, "Letters of Negro Migrants of 1916–1918," *Journal of Negro History,* 4 (July 1919): 435.

Chapter 7

War and Society, 1917–1918

In April 1917, after months of debate and disagreement on whether to join the war in Europe, the United States declared war on Germany. Unlike the major European powers embroiled in the conflict since 1914, America's participation in the war was brief—only about a year and a half. Nevertheless, the war exerted a tremendous impact on Americans, soldiers and civilians alike. For the first time, Americans fought on European soil, and they felt certain that their participation would play a crucial role in defeating the Germans and their allies.

The essay, drawn from David M. Kennedy's book Over Here: The First World War and American Society, describes the experiences and impressions of the American soldiers of World War I, the "doughboys." According to Kennedy, these soldiers held a highly romantic view of the war, seeing it in terms of heroism and adventure. The depictions of battle by Europeans during and after the conflict sharply contrast with the Americans' view: tales of destruction of towns and cities, the slaughter of hundreds of thousands of soldiers and civilians, and the misery of trench warfare. How do you account for the differences between the American soldiers' descriptions of the war and those of their European counterparts?

The Kennedy essay points out that actual combat could have a sobering effect on the doughboy, a conclusion supported by the first document—an excerpt from the diary of an unknown American flier, later shot down and killed over Germany.

Throughout the war, the federal government used propaganda to convince the public that the cause was noble, a clash between the forces of good and evil. Victory required the absolute loyalty and support of all citizens; any hint of questionable patriotism prompted great concern. For German Americans particularly, the patriotic near-hysteria of these times proved a terrible burden. In restaurants sauerkraut was renamed "liberty cabbage," and hamburger emerged as "liberty steak." Cincinnati's German Street was renamed English Street, and Pittsburgh banned the playing of Ludwig von Beethoven's music. German Americans were harassed and threatened with physical harm if they failed to demonstrate their commitment to the American war effort. The pressure on German Americans to declare their loyalty is vividly reflected in the second document, a statement by a German American distributed by the Committee on Public Information, an agency created by the federal government to generate public support for the war. How did the author's assessment of the war enable him to embrace the American cause without cutting his emotional ties to his native land?

Although a large segment of the population opposed entry into the war right up until 1917, support for the war effort flourished once the United States joined the conflict. Nevertheless, not all Americans supported the war; those who did not and refused to serve in the armed forces on the grounds of religion or conscience suffered condemnation. The final document reveals the experiences and convictions of Mennonites, who, despite their profound religious objections to the war, were drafted into the army. What relationship, if any, can you discern between the patriotic fervor of wartime society and intensified intolerance?

ESSAY

The Doughboys' War:
"An Extraordinary Interlude"

David M. Kennedy

It is easy to forget how vivid the Civil War seemed to Americans in the World War I era. Many men yet living had fought under Grant or Lee. More men still, especially those of an age to occupy influential positions in American life—including Theodore Roosevelt and Woodrow Wilson— had been impressionable boys when [General] Beauregard's batteries fired on Sumter. They were raised by hearthsides where fathers and uncles passed on the lore of Bull Run and Vicksburg, Chickamauga and the Wilderness, Cold Harbor and the Sunken Road, Antietam and the Bloody Angle. On registration day, June 5, 1917, Wilson addressed a convention of Confederate veterans, and spoke evocatively of "the old spirit of chivalric gallantry." That rhetoric and the attitude toward war it bespoke were comfortably familiar to two generations of Americans; but even while Wilson talked, both the language and the sentiment were as near to death as the graying men he faced.

Many of those aging veterans, and even more of their Union counterparts, remained powerful arbiters of popular values. Among the images they urged the young to regard reverently was that of war as an adventurous and romantic undertaking, a liberating release from the stultifying conventions of civilized society. No one had more eloquently articulated that sentiment than Oliver Wendell Holmes, Jr., a young Civil War officer in the 20th Massachusetts, veteran of Fredericksburg and Antietam, and for thirty years after 1902 a magisterial figure on the United States Supreme Court. Only in war, he told Harvard's graduating class in 1895, could men pursue "the divine folly of honor." From war "the ideals of the past for men have been drawn. . . . I doubt if we are ready to give up our inheritance." War might be terrible when you were in it, he said, but with time "you see that its message was divine." In the generation succeeding Holmes's, the charismatic Theodore Roosevelt whole-heartedly embraced those precepts and preached them to his countrymen with unflagging gusto. What American had not heard the account of the old Rough Rider waving his hat and charging up San Juan Hill, gleefully projecting an image of battle as a kind of pleasingly dangerous gentlemen's sport?

SOURCE: *Over Here: The First World War and American Society*, by David M. Kennedy. Copyright © 1980 by Oxford University Press. Reprinted by permission of Oxford University Press.

This irrepressibly positive and romantic view of war belonged particularly to an older elite, people like Holmes and Roosevelt: old-stock, Northeastern, often Anglophilic or Francophilic. In his study of prewar American culture, [historian] Henry May has called them "the beleaguered defenders of nineteenth-century tradition . . . the professional custodians of culture." From this quarter came some of the strongest pressure both for a permanent system of military training and for American intervention in the war. Almost unanimously, says May, "the leading men of letters, the college presidents, the old-line publishers, the editors of standard magazines, and their friends knew where they stood from the start" in 1914. "Instead of seeing the war as the doom of their culture, they believed it would bring about its revival: the war was a severe but necessary lesson in moral idealism." Thus did Princeton [University] President John Grier Hibben speak of the chastening and purifying effect of armed conflict. Thus did novelist Robert Herrick write of war's "resurrection of nobility. . . ." Everywhere, the venerable custodians of traditional culture spoke as if with a single voice: war was glorious, adventurous; it was manhood's destiny, a strenuous and virile antidote to the effete routine of modern life. And, as May has noted, it was the "young acquaintances of these elder idealists who were early in the field. The older colleges and the more exclusive prep schools contributed far more than their share to the volunteer units." Young men from the most prominent families and the most prestigious universities fought with the French or the English, joined the Lafayette Escadrille air unit, or the Norton-Harjes Ambulance Service.* It was, in short, the nation's most carefully cultivated youths, the privileged recipients of the finest education, steeped in the values of the genteel tradition, who most believed the archaic doctrines about war's noble and heroic possibilities.

Of all the young men who so believed, none did more passionately than Alan Seeger. A 1910 Harvard graduate given to writing florid and portentous verses, Seeger had gone to Paris in 1912, "in the spirit," says a sympathetic biographer, "of a romanticist of the eighteen-forties." Swelling with Byronic yearning for glory ("it is for glory alone that I am engaged," he wrote) and for a poetic death at an early age, in 1914 he joined the French Foreign Legion. For the next two years, huddled in billets in Champagne, he wrote of the war, in verse, in his diary, in letters to his

---

*Organized in March 1915 and privately financed by Americans, the Lafayette Escadrille was officered by French commanders and integrated into the French military service. The Escadrille was made up mostly of well-to-do young Americans. One famous "alumnus" was James R. Doolittle, who in 1942 led the first American airstrike of World War II against Tokyo. . . . Of the several volunteer ambulance units, the most publicized was founded in 1914 by Richard Norton, son of Harvard professor Charles Eliot Norton. Another unit, the American Ambulance Field Service, also attracted many volunteers. Among the later celebrated persons who served in one or another of the units were Ernest Hemingway, John Dos Passos, e. e. cummings, and Malcolm Cowley. Most volunteers were college graduates. . . .

family, and in articles sent to the New York *Sun* and the *New Republic*. He was, he said candidly, "of a sentimental and romantic nature." His writing alternated between lyrical tributes to the charms of the French countryside and awe-filled descriptions of the grandeur of war. "Will never forget the beauty of this winter landscape," he noted in his diary, "the delicate skies, the little villages under their smoking roofs. Am feeling perfectly happy and contented." He was no less happy to hear "the magnificent orchestra of war" in an artillery cannonade, and he wrote his mother: "You have no idea how beautiful it is to see the troops undulating along the road in front of one in *colonnes par quatre* as far as the eye can see with the captains and lieutenants on horseback at the head of their companies. . . ."

When Seeger was killed in 1916, the custodians of culture instantly transformed him into America's first genuine war hero. His uplifting descriptions of war, cast in the literary conventions of the medieval romance, admirably fitted their own views. Indeed, so admirably did Seeger suit the tastes of the traditional keepers of culture that in 1915 they were already calling him America's Rupert Brooke (the English poet killed in combat). They hastened to complete the comparison by prematurely announcing Seeger's heroic demise in October 1915. When he died in fact on July 23, 1916, some were so eager to invest his memory with all the symbolic freight it would bear that he was often erroneously said to have met his fate—that would have been the phrase—on the Fourth of July.

Seeger's poems were published soon after his death, to extravagant praise from established critics, and his *Letters and Diary* was released to the public the following summer. Theodore Roosevelt, the hero of "A Message to America" ("I would go through fire and shot and shell . . . if ROOSEVELT led"), eulogized him in appropriately archaic accents as "gallant, gifted young Seeger." A Wellesley [College] student surpassed even the medieval metaphors of the dead poet himself: "Had he lived in centuries past," she wrote, "he would have lived a knight, true to his 'idols—Love and Arms and Song.' In the twentieth century he still lived as true as was possible to those idols. So he will live in our hearts—Alan Seeger, Knight."

Seeger's was the authentic voice of late nineteenth-century American high culture, and it spoke powerfully of war's ennobling glory. Other writers couched a similar message in a more popular idiom. Robert W. Service, for example, in *Rhymes of a Red Cross Man*, sang of the

> . . . dream that War will never be ended;
> That men will perish like men, and valour be splendid;
>
> . . . .
>
> That though my eye may be dim and my beard be hoary,
> I'll die as a soldier dies on the Field of Glory.

When [Senator] Hiram Johnson read Service's poems to his family in the evenings, "all of us at times have been rather choked up." When he read them to his fellow Senators, he said, "you could have heard a pin drop."

Seeger's *Poems* and Service's *Rhymes* were both best sellers in 1917, as was Arthur Guy Empey's *"Over the Top,"* a runaway success that sold 350,000 copies in its first year of release and was later made into a movie. Empey became a featured speaker at countless Liberty bond rallies. Those developments no doubt pleased his publisher, George Haven Putnam of G. P. Putnam's Sons, a founder of the pro-preparedness National Security League. *"Over the Top"* was a go-get-'em confection in the Richard Harding Davis vein, a snappy autobiographical account of the New Jersey boy's adventures with the British Army in France. Disappointed that his own country had been "too proud to fight" after the sinking of the *Lusitania,* Empey went to England to become a "Tommy." Though his account of his exploits among the English was replete with condescending national comparisons—British trains had "matchbox" cars; Americans had "energy and push," the English mere "tenacity"—Empey clearly intended to convey affection for the British soldier and sympathy for the Allied cause. "Tommy Atkins," he said, "has proved himself to be the best of mates, a pal, . . . a man with a just cause who is willing to sacrifice everything but honor in the advancement of the same. It is my fondest hope," he added, "that Uncle Sam and John Bull, arms locked, as mates, good and true . . . will wend their way through the years to come, happy and contented in each other's company."

Empey provided the American public with a kind of primer on life at the front. In a bright, wisecracking style, liberally sprinkled with colorful British Army slang, Empey recounted his initiation into British Army ways, his arrival at the front, his first encounters with "Fritz" (the Germans), his wounding in a trench raid, and his trip back to "blighty" (home). The narrative was not without its accounts of horrors and of gut-grinding fears. In a grudging and stiffly jocular way, Empey even admitted to tears at the death of a mate: "I, like a great big boob, cried like a baby. I was losing my first friend of the trenches." But the tone of *"Over the Top"* was overwhelmingly positive. Even the scenes of terror and fright could not really terrify or frighten, so briskly were they related, and so swiftly did they sink beneath the glinting surface of Empey's quick-paced story. With unrelenting good humor, Empey portrayed the war as a kind of thrillful sporting adventure, where all the players, on his side at least, were good fellows who knew how to "die game." In the climactic battle scene, Empey was wounded, but his outfit "took the trench and the wood beyond, all right." The story faithfully followed the formula of the popular adventure tale: men expired with athletic grace, the hero proved his manhood by receiving a wound in virtual hand-to-hand combat, as convention required, and in the end his fellows triumphantly seized their objective. . . .

From accounts like these, many departing doughboys formed expectations of what awaited them in France. An affirmative and inspiring attitude toward war, preached by guardians of tradition like Holmes and

Roosevelt, nurtured by popular writers like Seeger and Empey, filled men's imaginations in 1917. That attitude was sufficiently strong to counter three years of news and propaganda about the atrocities of modern warfare; it was strong enough, even, to temper men's natural fear of death. Historian William L. Langer, for example, went to war as a young man in 1917, and later recalled with wonder "the eagerness of the men to get to France and above all to reach the front." . . .[Writer] John Dos Passos recollected similar sentiments from 1917: "We had spent our boyhood in the afterglow of the peaceful nineteenth century. . . . What was war like? We wanted to see with our own eyes. We flocked into the volunteer services. I respected the conscientious objectors, and occasionally felt I should take that course myself, but hell, I wanted to see the show."

Brimming with eagerness and enthusiasm, hundreds of thousands of young men embarked in 1917 and 1918 upon what Theodore Roosevelt alluringly called the "Great Adventure." Secretary [of War] Newton D. Baker consciously strove to model the stateside training camps on "the analogy of the American college," and countless contemporary observers noted the keen sense of schoolboyish anticipation and excitement that infected the fresh recruits. "As in similar encampments," said one trainee, "Fort Sheridan was alive with enthusiastic recruits, with an atmosphere somewhat like that of a college campus on the eve of a big game."

Even more than college boys, the young men in the Army were to be protected from wickedness and vice. Temperance crusaders, long devoted to changing the nation's drinking habits, were at war's outbreak riding a wave of recent successes. By 1917 nineteen states had adopted prohibition, and the increasingly powerful Anti-Saloon League was pressing for a prohibition amendment to the federal Constitution. Passionate "drys" shuddered at the opportunities for debauchery that army life might put in the path of the nation's manhood. Their political muscle helped convince the War Department to ban the sale of liquor in the vicinity of the training camps, and to forbid (on paper at least) any man in uniform from buying a drink. These measures imparted further momentum to the temperance cause, and contributed to the ratification of the Eighteenth Amendment in 1919.

The Army also undertook a campaign against sexual vice that had substantial influence on postwar life. The American Social Hygiene Association had urged as early as 1914 that the public be educated about venereal disease, though the Association cautioned that the effort should go forward "conservatively and gradually . . . without impairing modesty and becoming reticence in either young or old." Despite widespread concern about the debilitating effects of the "social disease," little had happened by 1917 to advance the Association's cause. Then the Army, determined to get the maximum number of "effectives" from the mass of inductees, and not troubled by questions of modesty, launched a great anti-VD campaign. It assigned the task to the Commission on Training Camp Activities (CTCA), a consortium of civilian service organizations, like the YMCA, Knights of Columbus, and Jewish Welfare Board, that worked under official Army auspices. Wanting results, the Army and the Commission cared little for reticence, and they minced no words about sexual matters. Speaking frankly of "balls" and "whores," one CTCA pamphlet carefully explained that wet dreams were normal and that masturbation, common folk wisdom notwithstanding, would not lead to insanity. The clear implication was that natural emission, or even masturbation, was greatly preferable to potentially infectious liaisons. In the same vein, the Commission placarded the camps with posters proclaiming: "A German Bullet is Cleaner than a Whore." Pamphlets urged sexual purity in the name of patriotism: "How could you look the flag in the face," asked one, "if you were dirty with gonorrhea?" "A Soldier who gets a dose," warned a poster, "is a Traitor!"

The campaign continued with the doughboys in France. The Commander in Chief gave special attention to the venereal report every morning, and venereal infection was made a matter for discipline. "Keeping our men clean," said [General John] Pershing, was a matter of the highest importance, "not only from the standpoint of effectives, but from that of morals." But, as elsewhere, Pershing's efforts in the battle for sexual purity were hampered by what the general daintily termed "the difference between the French attitude and our own." In February 1918, [French] Premier [Georges] Clemenceau magnanimously offered to help establish licensed houses of prostitution, customary in the French army, for what he obviously regarded as the long-suffering American troops. Pershing passed the letter containing the offer to Raymond Fosdick, head of the CTCA. Fosdick, in turn, showed Clemenceau's letter to Secretary Baker, who reportedly exclaimed: "For God's sake, Raymond, don't show this to the President or he'll stop the war." The Americans declined this bit of gracious Gallic generosity, and continued to mete out stern punishment to soldiers suffering from VD. The Army congratulated itself that the campaign drastically lowered the venereal infection rate among the doughboys. The educational drive had further import as well. For many young men, the Commission's pamphlets, films, and lectures no doubt constituted the first thorough sex education they had received. Surely very few had ever been exposed to such frank and open scientific discussion of matters about which the society had been notoriously mute. In its own blunt way, the Army contributed to the demythologizing of erotic life by bringing sexual matters into the arena of public discourse, which was to become a characteristic feature of twentieth-century American culture.

The Army cooperated less eagerly with another social experiment in 1917–18: intelligence testing and classification by mental ability of men who passed through the training camps. Testing people's intelligence was a novel procedure in the prewar era. First developed by French psychologist Alfred Binet in the early years of the century, the method was adopted and improved by Stanford University's Lewis Terman in 1916, and became known in the United States as the Stanford-Binet test. When America entered the war, the American Psychological Association pressured the War Department to use the tests to screen mental incompetents from the Army and to classify all inductees on the basis of their intelligence. Not incidentally, this plan would provide the professional psychologists with data-sets of previously undreamed-of size, the raw material for countless further studies.

The Army at first responded tepidly to these "mental meddlers," as one general called them. But by early 1918 trained psychological examiners were posted to all the camps. There they administered thousands of "alpha" tests to the literate inductees, and "beta" tests to the illiterate. The results were used to designate the recruits "superior," "average," or "inferior," so that personnel officers might then select potential officer trainees and distribute the remainder of the men proportionately, with reference to their tested intelligence, throughout the various units.

The testers were struck by the extent of illiteracy their examinations revealed—as many as 25 percent of the draftees could be so classified. Examiners were also unsettled by the meager educational backgrounds of the recruits. Most enlisted men had left school between the fifth and seventh grades. The median number of years of education ranged from 6.9 for native whites and 4.7 for immigrants to 2.6 for Southern blacks. In one large sample of native white draftees, fewer than 18 percent had attended high school, and most of those men had not graduated. The typical enlisted soldier, concludes one student, was "an ill-educated unsophisticated young man . . . the opposite of the Harvard boys who volunteered for ambulance duty before America entered the war."

The psychologists were less surprised by their correlation of test performances with racial and national backgrounds. Invariably, men from "native" or "old" immigrant stock scored heavily in the "superior" range, while draftees from "new" immigrant backgrounds fell disproportionately into the "inferior" category. More than half the Russian, Italian, and Polish draftees, for example, showed up as "inferior." Nearly 80 percent of the blacks who took the alpha test were labeled "inferior," and their illiteracy rates were significantly higher than those for whites.

The psychologists, striving for scientific objectivity, denied that their examinations were biased toward certain educational or cultural backgrounds, or toward a particular kind of scholastic skill. Yet it may be doubted whether the native intelligence of recent immigrants or poor rural blacks was fairly tested by questions about the authorship of "The Raven," the talents of the painter Rosa Bonheur, or the city in which the Overland car was manufactured—all standard queries on the alpha test. These examinations were the crudest devices of an infant psychological "science" that even in its maturity has not escaped criticism on grounds of cultural bias. The Army, to its credit, never lost its suspicion of the psychologists, and ended the testing program at the first opportunity, January 1919. But what the Army rejected, the nation's educational system eagerly adopted in the postwar era, as intelligence testing became a familiar procedure in the schools. And to many old-stock, white Americans, the widely publicized results of the wartime tests conveniently reinforced their already disparaging appraisal of the new immigrant groups and blacks.

Forewarned about disease, tested and labeled, introduced to the manual of arms, trained to drill, drill, drill, fitted out with a new-fangled safety razor (the war would change the shaving techniques of a generation), and saddled with packs, the doughboys marched out of the camps and up the ramps of the ships of the "Atlantic Ferry." Most left from Hoboken, [New Jersey], and nearly half sailed in British vessels. A lucky few cruised in some style on the *Leviathan*, the former Hamburg-American luxury liner *Vaterland*, impounded in New York harbor since 1914, and in 1917 seized and made to carry troops to battle against the men who built her. Others traveled on various Cunard [British] ships and American ocean liners, but a great many were shipped in converted freighters, hastily refitted, stark, and dirty. "Assigned quarters on lower deck," said a private put on board the British ship *Kashmir*; "the blackest, foulest, most congested hole that I ever set foot into." On arrival in France, the men were shoehorned into the notorious "40-and-8's"—diminutive French railway freightcars supposedly able to carry 40 men or 8 horses—and rumbled slowly away from the ports along the choked rail system to their forward training areas in the interior of France. Once off the train, the men began to walk, and for many it must have seemed that they walked forever. *Stars and Stripes* [the soldiers' newspaper in France] found no more fertile subjects for humor than the length of hikes and the weight of packs. Billeted in widely scattered areas that required lengthy walks to training facilities, and prodded by officers under orders not to let the troops become restless while Pershing's idle army grew to sufficient size, the men moved constantly—often, it seemed, just to be moving. As the diary of one reads:

> Sat. June 22, 1918: Left Colembert in A.M. and hiked with full packs about 7 kilos to Bellebrune.
> Wed. June 26, 1918: Hiked with full packs back to Colembert.
> Thur. June 27, 1918: Hiked back to Bellebrune.
> Sat. June 29, 1918: Hiked with light packs about 14 kilos to gas school.
> Wed. July 3: Hiked about 20 kilos to Bouinngues.

Thur. July 4: Hiked 10 kilos to rifle range.
Fri. July 5: Hiked 18 kilos to Buysschure.
Sat. July 6: Hiked 15 kilos to Oudezeele.

Two million men served in the AEF [American Expeditionary Force]. The experience struck nearly all of them as an extraordinary moment in their lives—while they passed through it, and when they later remembered it. That they considered it an extraordinary interlude at the time is evidenced by the diaries and journals and strikingly "literary" letters so many of them wrote during their period of service. Americans in 1917, especially those of the age and class who qualified for the AEF, were not the diary-keeping people they had once been. Yet thousands of men who had never before recorded in writing their daily doings, and never would again, faithfully kept journals while they were in the Army. Most of these records began with induction and ended with discharge, neatly delineating the time spent in uniform as a peculiar interval, a moment stolen from ordinary life and forever after sealed off in the memory as a bundle of images that sharply contrasted with "normal" experience. The reactions to France and to war were, of course, as varied as the men who recorded them. But even a modest sampling of the personal documents left behind—a few of them published, many deposited in libraries, more still passed down reverently as family heirlooms to later generations—reveals common responses to the shared enterprise, and common conventions of perception and language to which these men resorted in the effort to comprehend their experience and relate it to others.

They were, first of all, as much tourists as soldiers. Later reflections, governed by the masculine need to emphasize prowess at martial exploits, would tend to blot that fact from the record. But the average doughboy spent more peacetime than wartime in France. And, though as many as 1.3 million Americans came under enemy fire, few saw sustained or repeated battle. Virtually none was subjected to the horror and tedium of trench warfare for years on end, the typical lot of the European soldier. The Americans fought no major defensive battles. Their two chief engagements were relatively brief, mobile attacks in the closing weeks of the conflict.*

Hence, to a remarkable extent—remarkable at least when compared with the war writings of European combatants—the doughboys' accounts deal with topics other than war. It was AEF policy to rotate leave zones "in order to give all an equal chance to see as much of France as possible." Most coveted of all were the pink tickets that permitted a trip to Paris.

---

*In September 1918, the Americans at Saint Mihiel and Meuse-Argonne joined in the last great Allied offensive.

Stars and Stripes felt obliged to caution arriving troops against the "oo-la-la" idea of France as a great tourist playground. Too many men, said the journal, came over "expecting to find a sort of international Coney Island, a universal pleasure resort." "We have been all over France and seen and learn [*sic*] a lot," said one awe-struck New Yorker. After the Armistice [1918], the Army organized sporting events and provided educational opportunities for the idle troops. It also endlessly compelled them to solve "problems"—sham attacks against an imaginary enemy. Many men fought more of these mock battles than real ones. One long-suffering soldier reported in April 1919 that "every hill in this vicinity has been captured or lost at least ten times." But the same enlisted man spoke the sentiments of many when, describing his post-Armistice leave to Nice and Monte Carlo, he called it "the most important event in my life over here (from a social standpoint)."

Like previous generations of their traveling countrymen, the doughboys were impressed with the *age* of the Old World. "Its old cathedrals, chateaux and ancient towns have been quite wonderful to my eyes so accustomed to the look of the New World," said one. In countless diaries and letters the soldiers dwelt on the quaint antiquity of this town, or that church or chateau, their imaginations especially fired by the evocation of names from the history books. "The church here," wrote another doughboy, "is very, very old, probably built sometime in the 12th or 13th century. Saint Louis the Crusader, King of France, attended service there on three occasions and Jeanne d'Arc was there several times." "The architecture for the most part seems to represent a period several hundred years past," wrote another. "We are living, for the present, in barracks built about the time of Louis XIV, though no one here knows anything about them prior to Napoleon."

The France they described was rich with history, an old country inhabited by old people. No observation of French life was more common than remarking the elderly women in black who seemed to be the only residents of the ruined towns behind the front. A tired people in a blighted land, the French pursued antiquated ways. "My but the people are old fashioned," observed one enlisted man. "They still harvest with cradles and sickles. Once in a while you see a binder or mower. I've never saw [*sic*] a real wagon, they use carts." All signs, in short, confirmed the American myth of the Old World as an exhausted place, peopled by effete and even effeminate races. All this, of course, served as a useful foil for the image of American energy and "pep." "What an impression our boys are making on the French," enthused Raymond Fosdick, head of the Commission on Training Camp Activities. "They are the greatest lot of sheer boys you ever saw. . . . The French, who love to sit and meditate, are constantly gasping at the exuberance and tirelessness of our fellows." "Never was there such a spectacle in all history," exclaimed a *New York Times* correspondent, "as that of the fresh millions of free Americans flocking to the rescue of be-leaguered and exhausted Europe."

But if Europe was exhausted, it was still splendid to behold. Numerous accounts expressed rapt wonder at the sheer physical beauty of France. "Picturesque" was perhaps the most commonly used word in these de-scriptions. One is struck too by the frequency of panoramic portraits of nature, of efforts to translate a long sweep of the eye into a string of words. If sunrise and sunset were the characteristic themes in the writings of trench-bound British troops in Flanders, as Paul Fussell has observed in his study *The Great War and Modern Memory*, it was the panoramic landscape that most attracted the eye of Americans. . . .

Common to many Americans' perceptions of France was a sense of ceremony, which often had religious overtones. *Stars and Stripes* declared that France was "holy ground," and that more than once in history the French "at Chalons, at Tours, at the Marne—'saved the soul of the world.' " To many of the doughboys, the great war in which they were now engaged amounted to a ritual reenactment of those historic dramas. To the largely Protestant Americans, the exotic rites of French Catholicism fittingly ex-emplified the ceremonial attitude they deemed appropriate to the occasion. Alan Seeger had noted that "the Catholic religion with its idealization of the spirit of sacrifice makes an almost universal appeal in these times," and many members of the AEF agreed with him. The "Marseillaise" [French national anthem], too, had the power to "set you quivering." When French religion and patriotic music were combined, the effect was deeply moving. One American soldier attended high mass on Bastille Day, 1918, and a band at the flag-draped church played the "Marseillaise": "Rene, talk about throwing up your hat and shouting 'To Hell with the Kaiser.' The scene and music impressed me so much that I could hardly get my breath. I cannot describe how grand the whole thing was."

Time and again in the personal narratives of these touring provincials one suddenly hears a different voice. The rough and often wise-cracking American idiom abruptly gives way to a grandiloquent tone that speaks, for example, of the "red-tiled roofs resplendent in the sunlight, resembling huge cameos set conspicuously on the vine covered slopes." This strange diction was the language of the tourist brochures, or of the ubiquitous YMCA guides who shepherded the gawking troops about the various sights. It was not a natural voice. Those wondrous foreign scenes often exceeded the native American capacity for authentic speech, and the con-frontation with the unfamiliar was thus almost automatically rendered in clichés and highly stylized prose. To a significant degree, the same was true of descriptions of the war itself.

Reverence toward France and the "cause" was not carried over to the Army. Fellowship of arms gave certain consolation, but the physical con-ditions of life and the restrictions of the military regime were constant causes of complaint. Most pestiferous were the lice—"cooties"—that occasioned frequent trips to the delousing stations, and almost daily "shirt readings," or close inspections of clothing for nits. Equally wearing on men's bodies and spirits was army food—or lack of it. In vivid contrast with the wooden descriptions of tourist sights are the lively and lavish descriptions of those rare meals eaten somewhere—anywhere—other than the military mess. The careful recording of menus, indeed, took up a great deal of space in many soldiers' diaries and letters. Men frequently noted losses of more than ten percent of their body weight in the weeks after arrival in France. These accounts confirmed [British] Field Marshal [Douglas] Haig's observation that the Americans "hardly knew how to feed their troops." They also suggest that undernourishment may have dulled the fighting effectiveness of the AEF.

But the worst feature of military life was the discipline. Military hierarchy and subordination chafed against ingrained American values of equality and individualism. Anti-German propaganda harped on the supposedly slavish subservience of the "Hun" in order to enhance an image of the German soldier as an eminently bayonetable alien. The American resentment of martial authority could be found in all ranks, and sometimes manifested itself in striking ways. Even a pillar of traditional authority such as once and future Secretary of War Henry L. Stimson complained to his diary, while a staff officer in France, that "I am getting a little tired of kowtowing to regulars just because they are regulars." On the returning troop carriers in 1919, the doughboys enacted a ritual "funeral of Sam Browne." To the throaty cheers of the enlisted men, the officers solemnly marched to the ship's rail and threw their leather girth-and-shoulder "Sam Browne" belts, hated symbols of military caste, into the sea. Even the hierarchy of different services prompted resentment, as infantry officers often took potshots at airborne American pilots, the elite and haughty "Knights of the Air." "It is just a gesture of irritation at the air service," opined the commander of an observation balloon squadron, "something like boys throwing a rock at a limousine which is dashing by when they are having to work."

Long idle behind the lines, and then only briefly exposed to battle, the great mass of the American soldiers in France were spectators in the theater of war. They had come to see the "Big Show," and were not disappointed. Nothing in that show was more exciting than the aerial battles. Men approaching the front strained their eyes and ears for signs of aircraft, more out of curiosity than fear. Always they referred to aerial "duels," or "wonderful air battles," or "thrilling air fights." One balloonist described seeing "Richthofen's *circus*." The famed "Red Baron's" formation approached, "some of the planes with red bodies, and they fly along with some planes climbing and some dropping and give the effect of being on the rim of a giant wheel which is rolling thru the sky."

Artillery fire, too, provided visual spectacle on a colossal scale. In the rear training area, reported one young officer, "the most fun is going out to the artillery range." There, secure in a bomb-proof observation shelter near the target, "you can see the shot appear as a little black speck and follow it down to the earth when it bursts.". . .

But the big guns also brought death. Worse, they brought it without warning, from an unseen distance. In descriptions of shelling, one occasionally finds the faintly dawning realization that modern military combat was something quite different from what the eager troops had been led to expect. And its worst feature was its impersonality. Many men wrote of their sense of outraged helplessness while being shelled. Indeed, "shell shock" may have had as much to do with this feeling of impotence as it did with the physical effects of concussion. Even the irrepressible Alan Seeger found bombardment "distressing," because he was "being harried like this by an invisible enemy and standing up against all the dangers of battle without any of its exhilaration or enthusiasm." William Langer wrote that shellfire "has always seemed a bit unfair to me. Somehow it makes one feel so helpless, there is no chance of reprisal for the individual man. The advantage is all with the shell, and you have no comeback." Enduring shellfire often prompted fantasies of bloody personal reprisal. As one draftee wrote: "we cannot fight artillery. Jerry is a rotten sport. . . . Poor Frank Carr, he was hit with a shell and broken all up. I'll remember that and when it comes my time to run a bayonet into one of the skunks I'll look to heaven and cry out to Frank to watch me do the job up."

But negative notes in the contemporary reactions to the war were relatively rare. What most strikes the reader of these personal war records is their unflaggingly positive, even enthusiastic, tone. Seeger's sanguine reflection that war was affording him "the supreme experience" was re-iterated countless times by those who followed him to France. . . .

These expressions of exhilaration, wonder, and glory are notable not only for what they say but also for the way in which they say it. The sights of France elicited mostly tourist-brochure boilerplate from the doughboy writers. Similarly, the war itself seemed to overwhelm the power of the imagination to grasp directly, and of language to describe authentically. It is not especially surprising to find *Stars and Stripes* assuring a soldier-reader that he was the "spiritual successor" to "the Knights of King Arthur's Round Table." But it is to be remarked when countless common soldiers wrote privately of themselves in the same vein. American war narratives, with unembarrassed boldness, speak frequently of "feats of valor," of "the cause" and the "crusade." The memoirs and missives penned in France are shot through with images of knight-errantry and of grails thrillingly pursued. A truck driver in the aviation section of the AEF exclaimed that "war's great caldron of heroism, praise, glory, poetry, music, brains, energy, flashes and grows, rustles and roars, fills the heavens with its mighty being. . . .Oh! War as nothing else brings you back to the adventurous times of old." One of Lillian Wald's "boys" from the Henry Street Settlement proudly announced his enlistment in the "battle to throw down the shackles of Honensollern [sic] and Junkerism."

The ghost of Alan Seeger, and of the nineteenth-century literary conventions he exemplified, haunted these and innumerable similar passages. Faced with the unfamiliar reality of modern war, many young American soldiers tried to comprehend it in the comfortably familiar verbal formulae of their childhood storybooks. In the homeliest lines scribbled by the humblest privates, the war was frequently couched in language that appears to have been lifted verbatim from the pages of G. A. Henty or, more often, those of Sir Walter Scott. That language echoed, however pathetically, the epic posturings of George Creel* and the elaborately formal phrasing of [President] Woodrow Wilson. Those accents may ring strangely in the modern ear, but they flowed easily from the tongues and pens of the doughboys in 1918. The ubiquity of that idiom, from the White House to the trenches, suggested a widely made equation between the official and the personal definitions of the war's significance. If the war was to redeem Europe from barbarism, it would equally redeem individual soldiers from boredom; if the fighting in France was the "Great Adventure," the doughboys were the great adventurers; if Creel and Wilson could speak of the "Crusade," then it followed that American troops were crusaders. Not only did many doughboys accept without reflection the official definition of the war's meaning, but, perhaps more important, they translated that meaning into their understanding of their personal experiences, and described those experiences in language transported directly from the pious and inflated pronouncements of the spokesmen for traditional culture. That language pervaded all the vast "literature" produced during the war by members of the AEF. . . .

DOCUMENTS

Diary of an Unknown Aviator, 1918

We've lost a lot of good men. It's only a question of time until we all get it. I'm all shot to pieces. I only hope I can stick it. I don't want to quit. My nerves are all gone and I can't stop. I've lived beyond my time already.

It's not the fear of death that's done it. I'm still not afraid to die. It's this eternal flinching from it that's doing it and has made a coward out of

*Creel was Chairman of the U.S. Committee on Public Information.
SOURCE: *War Birds: Diary of an Unknown Aviator* (New York: George H. Doran Co., 1926), 267–71.

me. Few men live to know what real fear is. It's something that grows on you, day by day, that eats into your constitution and undermines your sanity. I have never been serious about anything in my life and now I know that I'll never be otherwise again. But my seriousness will be a burlesque for no one will recognize it. Here I am, twenty-four years old, I look forty and I feel ninety. I've lost all interest in life beyond the next patrol. No one Hun will ever get me and I'll never fall into a trap, but sooner or later I'll be forced to fight against odds that are too long or perhaps a stray shot from the ground will be lucky and I will have gone in vain. Or my motor will cut out when we are trench strafing or a wing will pull off in a dive. Oh, for a parachute! The Huns are using them now. I haven't a chance, I know, and it's this eternal waiting around that's killing me. I've even lost my taste for liquor. It doesn't seem to do me any good now. I guess I'm stale. Last week I actually got frightened in the air and lost my head. Then I found ten Huns and took them all on and I got one of them down out of control. I got my nerve back by that time and came back home and slept like a baby for the first time in two months. What a blessing sleep is! I know now why men go out and take such long chances and pull off such wild stunts. No discipline in the world could make them do what they do of their own accord. I know now what a brave man is. I know now how men laugh at death and welcome it. I know now why Ball went over and sat above a Hun airdrome and dared them to come up and fight with him. It takes a brave man to even experience real fear. A coward couldn't last long enough at the job to get to that stage. What price salvation now?

War is a horrible thing, a grotesque comedy. And it is so useless. This war won't prove anything. All we'll do when we win is to substitute one sort of Dictator for another. In the meantime we have destroyed our best resources. Human life, the most precious thing in the world, has become the cheapest. After we've won this war by drowning the Hun in our own blood, in five years' time the sentimental fools at home will be taking up a collection for these same Huns that are killing us now and our fool politicians will be cooking up another good war. Why shouldn't they? They have to keep the public stirred up to keep their jobs and they don't have to fight and they can get soft berths for their sons and their friends' sons. To me the most contemptible cur in the world is the man who lets political influence be used to keep him away from the front. For he lets another man die in his place.

The worst thing about this war is that it takes the best. If it lasts long enough the world will be populated by cowards and weaklings and their children. And the whole thing is so useless, so unnecessary, so terrible! . . .

The devastation of the country is too horrible to describe. It looks from the air as if the gods had made a gigantic steam roller, forty miles wide and run it from the coast to Switzerland, leaving its spike holes behind as it went. . . .

I've lost over a hundred friends, so they tell me—I've seen only seven or eight killed—but to me they aren't dead yet. They are just around the corner, I think, and I'm still expecting to run into them any time. I dream about them at night when I do sleep a little and sometimes I dream that some one is killed who really isn't. Then I don't know who is and who isn't. I saw a man in Boulogne the other day that I had dreamed I saw killed and I thought I was seeing a ghost. I can't realize that any of them are gone. Surely human life is not a candle to be snuffed out. . . .

German-American Loyalty, 1917

My emotions tell me one thing at this awful time, but my reason tells me another. As a German by birth it is a horrible calamity that I may have to fight Germans. That is natural, is it not? But as an American by preference, I can see no other course open. . . .

For 25 years Germany has shown dislike for the United States—the Samoan affair, the Hongkong contretemps, the Manila Bay incident, the unguarded words of the Kaiser himself, and, lastly, the Haitian controversy in 1914. . . . And it has not been from mere commercial or diplomatic friction. It is because their ideals of government are absolutely opposite. One or the other must go down. It is for us to say now which it shall be.

Because of my birth and feelings beyond my control I have no particular love for the French and less for the British. But by a strange irony of fate I see those nations giving their blood for principles which I hold dear, against the wrong principles of people I individually love. It is a very unhappy paradox, but one I can not escape. I do not want to see the allies triumph over the land of my birth. But I very much want to see the triumph of the ideas they fight for.

It sickens my soul to think of this Nation going forth to help destroy people many of whom are bound to me by ties of blood and friendship. But it must be so. It is like a dreadful surgical operation. The militaristic, undemocratic demon which rules Germany must be cast out. It is for us to do it—now. I have tried to tell myself that it is not our affair, that we should have contented ourselves with measures of defense and armed neutrality. But I know that is not so. The mailed fist has been shaken under our nose before. If Prussianism triumphs in this war the fist will continue

SOURCE: C. Kotzenabe, "German-American Loyalty," in Committee on Public Information, War Information Series, *American Loyalty* (Washington, D.C.: Government Printing Office, 1917), 5–6.

to shake. We shall be in real peril, and those ideas for which so much of the world's best blood has been spilled through the centuries will be in danger of extinction. It seems to me common sense that we begin our defense by immediate attack when the demon is occupied and when we can command assistance.

There is much talk of what people like me will do, and fear of the hyphen. No such thing exists. The German-American is as staunch as the American of adoption of any other land and perhaps more so. Let us make war upon Germany, not from revenge, not to uphold hairsplitting quibbles of international law, but let us make war with our whole heart and with all our strength, because Germany worships one god and we another and because the lion and the lamb can not lie down together. One or the other must perish.

Let us make war upon the Germany of the Junkerthum,* the Germany of frightfulness, the Germany of arrogance and selfishness, and let us swear not to make peace until the Imperial German Government is the sovereign German people.

Letters from Mennonite Draftees, 1918

DEAR BROTHER ———:

I went to Camp Cody, N. Mex., June 25, 1918. At first I drilled without a rifle, but later was asked to take one, explaining that the President's orders concerning the C. O.'s [conscientious objectors] required it, and I would get into noncombatant service in due time. I accepted it, and in two weeks was transferred to the infantry where, of course, I was asked again to take the rifle, and I saw that I had been deceived. I refused and explained why. Several nights after this, while I was in bed, some privates threw water into my bed, put a rope around my neck and jerked me out on the floor.

The next day two sergeants came to my tent and took me out, tied a gun on my shoulder and marched me down the street, one on each side of me, kicking me all the way. I was asked again whether I would take the rifle and drill. I refused and was taken to the bath-house, put under the shower bath where they turned on the water, alternating hot and cold, until I was so numb that I could scarcely rise. Just then one of the higher

---

Junkerthum refers to the Prussian military aristocracy.

SOURCE: J. S. Hartzler, *Mennonites in the World War or Nonresistance Under Test* (Scottdale, Pa.: Mennonite Publishing House, 1922), 124–27.

officers came in and asked what they were about. They explained that they were giving me a bath. The officer told me to dress and go to my tent, that he wanted to interview me himself. He asked if I would take a rifle and drill. I told him that I could not. He ordered my sergeant to put me on company street work until they got my transfer, and in three weeks I was given noncombatant service.

VERY TRULY YOURS,——

DEAR BROTHER:

I came home Wednesday evening, Feb. 5. To get home, receive a hearty welcome and many expressions of joy for the effort made to maintain the faith, was alone worth the hardships which we endured.

I had been gone a few days more than ten months, of which I spent twenty-four days in our company, ten days in detention camp, seventy-eight days in the guard-house, one night in the Kansas City Police "lock-up," one hundred ninety-seven days in the disciplinary barracks (Fort Leavenworth, Kans.) and two days on the way home. . . .

I do not approve of such practices as the world was engaged in, and will give them neither moral nor material support though it may mean imprisonment or even death for not doing so. If the army would never kill a man, I can not see how a person could become a part of it, giving moral and material support to its maintenance and still retain a Christian character. The standards it upholds and the injustices it practices are unbelievable to a man who never saw them. . . . The only part that I can have in the army is suffering its punishments. Its purposes and those of Christianity are as different as night and day. The aims of the army are coercion, terrorism, carnal force; the ideals of Christianity are love, meekness, gentleness, obedience to the will of God, etc. When these ideals are maintained to the best of our ability, by God's grace He will provide care and protection in ways not imagined by man.

As to noncombatant service: all branches of service have one purpose; viz., to make the whole system a stronger organization of terrorism, destruction, and death. While I would not have been directly killing any one, I would have been doing a man's part in helping another do the act, and lending encouragement to the same. To support a thing and refuse to do the thing supported is either ignorance or cowardice. To refuse to go to the trenches and still give individual assistance to another doing so, is either an improper knowledge of the issues at stake or downright fear to face the bullets. I have a greater conscientious objection against noncombatant than against combatant service. I feel that the principle is the same, and that both are equally wrong. I would feel guilty toward the other man to accept service where the danger was not so great. . . .

To an observer it may have seemed ridiculous to refuse to even plant flowers at the base hospital. In the first place, that was the duty of the working gang under the quartermaster's department. Technically I would not have been doing military duty for I had not "signed up;" virtually I would have been rendering service because I was at work. . . . The farther one went with the military officers the farther they demanded him to go. I felt that the farther I went the less reason I could give for stopping, so I concluded that the best place to stop was in the beginning. It was on the charge of refusing to plant flowers that I received my court-martial sentence of ten years of hard labor in the disciplinary barracks at Fort Leavenworth, Kans.

FRATERNALLY YOURS,——

Suggestions for Further Reading

On Southern black Americans after the Civil War, consult two works by Eric Foner: *Nothing but Freedom: Emancipation and Its Legacy* (1983) and his impressive *Reconstruction: America's Unfinished Revolution, 1863–1967* (1988). See also John Hope Franklin, *Reconstruction After the Civil War* (1961); Leon Litwack, *Been in the Storm So Long: The Aftermath of Slavery* (1979); and Howard Rabinowitz, *Race Relations in the Urban South, 1865–1890* (1980). On black poverty, see Jay R. Mandle, *The Roots of Black Poverty* (1978). C. Vann Woodward, *The Strange Career of Jim Crow* (1966), remains an important work. See also Edward Ayers, *The Promise of the New South: Life After Reconstruction* (1992), and Jacqueline Jones, *The Disposed: America's Underclass from the Civil War to the Present* (1992). Neil McMillen, *Dark Journey: Black Mississippi in the Age of Jim Crow* (1989) is especially good.

For settlement of the frontier, general works are Donald Worster, *Under Western Skies: Nature and History in the American West* (1992); Richard White *"It's Your Misfortune and None of My Own": A History of the American West* (1991); and Richard Bartell, *The New Country: Social History of the American Frontier, 1776–1890* (1974). An older book of value is Everett Dick, *Sod House Frontier: 1854–1890* (1937). See also W. Eugene Hollon, *The Great American Desert* (1966), and Joe B. Frantz and Julian E. Choate, Jr., *The American Cowboy: The Myth and the Reality* (1955). A comprehensive view of the West is presented in Rodman Paul, *The Far West and the Great Plains in Transition, 1859–1900* (1988), while a more controversial view is found in Patricia Nelson Limerick, *The Legacy of Conquest: The Unbroken Past of the American West* (1987).

On American Indians, consult Francis Paul Prucha, *The Great White Father: The United States Government and the American Indians* (1984); Angie Debo, *A History of the Indians of the United States* (1970); and Vine Deloria, Jr., *Custer Died for Your Sins: An Indian Manifesto* (1969). On reform and assimilation, see Robert W. Mardock, *Reformers and the American Indians* (1971), and Frederick E. Hoxie, *A Final Promise: The Campaign to Assimilate the Indians, 1880–1920* (1984). On the New Deal and the Indians, see Philip Kenneth, *John Collier's Crusade for Indian Reform, 1920–1954* (1977). On education, see Margarat Szasz, *Education and the American Indian: The Road to Self-Determination, 1928–1973* (1974). Rex Smith, *Moon of the Popping Trees: The Tragedy at Wounded Knee and the End of the Indian Wars* (1975), is a good book on cultural conflict.

For women after the Civil War, there are a number of useful works. General books are Peter Filene, *Him/Her Self: Sex Roles in Modern America* (1975), and Sheila M. Rothman, *Woman's Proper Place: A History of Changing Ideals and Practices, 1870 to the Present* (1978). On women and education, see Barbara Solomon, *In the Company of Educated Women* (1985). On women and work, see

David Katzman, *Seven Days a Week: Women and Domestic Service in Industrializing America* (1978); Leslie Tentler, *Wage-Earning Women: Industrial Work and Family in the United States, 1900–1930* (1979); Dee Garison, *Apostles of Culture: The Public Libraries and American Society, 1876–1920* (1979); Barbara Harris, *Beyond Her Sphere: Women and the Professions in American History* (1978); and Nancy Dye, *As Equals and Sisters: The Labor Movement and the Women's Trade Union League of New York* (1980). On changing attitudes and practices about birth control, see Linda Gordon, *Woman's Body, Woman's Right: A Social History of Birth Control in America* (1979), and James Reed, *From Private Vice to Public Virtue: The Birth Control Movement and American Society Since 1830* (1977). On feminism, the standard work is Eleanor Flexner, *Century of Struggle: The Women's Rights Movement in the United States* (1959). Also helpful are William O'Neill, *Everyone Was Brave: A History of Feminism in America* (1971), and William Leach, *True Love and Perfect Union: The Feminist Reform of Sex and Society* (1980). For feminism in the early twentieth century, Nancy Cott, *The Grounding of Modern Feminism* (1987), is also stimulating.

On immigration, Stephan Thernstrom (ed.), *The Harvard Encyclopedia of American Ethnic Groups* (1980), is outstanding. Two general works are Leonard Dinnerstein and David Reimers, *Ethnic Americans: A History of Immigration and Assimilation* (1987), and John Bodnar, *The Transplanted: A History of Immigrants in Urban America* (1985). John Higham, *Strangers in the Land: Patterns of Nativism, 1860–1925* (1955), is an especially good study of nativism. On the Italians, see Virginia Yans-McLaughlin, *Family and Community: Italian Immigrants in Buffalo, 1880–1930* (1977), and Humbert Nelli, *Italians in Chicago, 1880–1930: A Study in Ethnic Mobility* (1970). On Jews, see Moses Rischin, *The Promised City: New York's Jews, 1870–1914* (1962), and Irving Howe, *World of Our Fathers: The Journey of the East European Jews to America and the Life They Found and Made* (1976). For the Chinese, see Jack Chen, *The Chinese of America* (1981). Useful comparative studies are Thomas Kessner, *The Golden Door: Italian and Jewish Mobility in New York City, 1880–1915* (1977), and John Bodnar et al., *Lives of Their Own: Blacks, Italians and Poles in Pittsburgh, 1900–1960* (1982). On New York City, consult Nathan Glazer and Daniel Patrick Moynihan, *Beyond the Melting Pot: The Negroes, Puerto Ricans, Jews, Italians and Irish of New York City* (1963). For Jewish women, see Sydney Stahl Weinberg, *The World of Our Mothers: The Lives of Jewish Immigrant Women* (1988). Jewish women also are covered in Susan Glenn, *Daughters of the Shtetl* (1989), while Kathy Peis, *Cheap Amusements: Leisure in Turn-of-the-Century New York* (1985), explores the lives of working-class immigrant women in New York City. For Irish women see Hasia Diner, *Erin's Daughters in America: Irish Immigrant Women in the Nineteenth Century* (1983).

For industrialization and American workers, see Herbert Gutman, *Work, Culture and Society in Industrializing America* (1976); Stephan Thernstrom, *The Other Bostonians* (1973); and Melvyn Dubofsky, *Industrialism and the American Worker, 1865–1920* (1975). David Brody, *Steelworkers in America: The Non-*

Union Era (1976), is an excellent book. On workers in the Southern cotton mills, see Jacqueline Dowd Hall et al., *Like a Family: The Making of a Southern Cotton Mill World* (1987).

For the migration of blacks to the North, Forette Henri, *Black Migration: Movement North, 1900–1920* (1976), provides a general overview. For particular cities, see Gilbert Osofsky, *Harlem: The Making of a Ghetto, 1890–1930* (1968); David Katzman, *Before the Ghetto: Black Detroit in the Nineteenth Century* (1973); Allan Spear, *Black Chicago: The Making of a Ghetto, 1890–1920* (1967); Thomas Lee Philpott, *The Slum and the Ghetto: Neighborhood Deterioration and Middle Class Reform, Chicago, 1880–1930* (1976). Two excellent studies of white racism are George Frederickson, *The Black Image in the White Mind: The Debate on Afro-American Character and Destiny, 1817–1914* (1971), and Joel Williamson, *The Crucible of Race* (1984). An outstanding study of black culture is Lawrence Levine, *Black Culture and Black Consciousness: Afro-American Folk Thought from Slavery to Freedom* (1977). For a new view of the migration north, see James R. Grossman, *Land of Hope: Chicago, Black Southerners and the Great Migration* (1989).

On World War I, Frederick Luebke, *Bonds of Loyalty: German Americans and World War I* (1974), is informative. For the home front, see David Kennedy, *Over Here: The First World War and American Society* (1980). On women during the war, see Maurie W. Greenwald, *Women, War and Work: The Impact of World War I on Women Workers in the United States* (1980). For military aspects of the war, the standard treatment is Edward Coffman, *The War to End All Wars: The American Military Experience in World War I* (1968). On the economy see Ronald Schofer, *America in the Great War* (1991).

Part II

Modern American Society 1920–Present

WITH THE END OF WORLD WAR I, AMERICANS TURNED THEIR attention to affairs at home. The nation enjoyed a rising standard of living as the changes that marked post–Civil War America—urbanization, industrialization, immigration, the movement of women into the paid work force, and the rapid development of the West—continued unabated. Yet many were repelled by changes in American society wrought by these developments and looked back with nostalgia to the mid-nineteenth century. Some adopted ugly forms of protest and joined organizations like the revived Ku Klux Klan, while others attempted to outlaw behavior that they viewed as undesirable—for example, the consumption of alcoholic beverages. Although the Klan saw some of its goals (such as the restriction of immigration) achieved, by the late 1920s, its appeals to fear and bigotry had grown less attractive and a new social morality was emerging in the nation.

The collapse of the stock market in 1929 and the onslaught of the Great Depression of the 1930s forced Americans to face unemployment, bankruptcies, farm foreclosures, and a host of other economic problems. The New Deal tried many innovative methods of stimulating the ailing economy, but not until World War II did unemployment recede and a long period of economic growth, characterized by high consumption, begin. However, not everyone fared equally at home during the war; Japanese Americans on the West Coast were interned in dreary and isolated camps.

As the nation prospered in the years following World War II, many people sought a better life by buying homes in the mushrooming suburbs and by participating in the new consumerism. Yet postwar prosperity did not end social and economic injustice; beginning in the late 1960s blacks turned to protest to achieve their rights, as did American women. Although neither blacks nor women had achieved economic status equal to that of white males by the 1990s, they nonetheless had expanded their range of opportunities and roles in American society.

The essays and documents in the chapters that follow illuminate the major developments in American life since the end of World War I. They focus on the intolerance and the manners and morals of the 1920s, the impact of the Depression and World War II on American society, the internment of Japanese Americans during the war, the suburbanization of America during the 1950s and 1960s, the struggles of blacks and women for equality up to the present day, and the new immigration after 1945.

Chapter 8

Intolerance: A Bitter Legacy of Social Change

At the turn of the century, few issues sparked so much debate and concern as the large-scale immigration to the United States from southern and eastern Europe. To many native-born Americans, whose roots lay in northern and western Europe, these millions of newcomers came to symbolize the disappearance of an older, simpler American society. Native-born Americans feared that the new immigrants would not adapt to established ways and values, and that they would lower the standard of living by taking jobs from American citizens and by working for low wages. During World War I, several prominent leaders also expressed apprehension about the potential for divided loyalties on the part of immigrants. Such leaders as Theodore Roosevelt believed that immigants, especially German Americans, might retain allegiance to Germany, the nation's wartime enemy. Roosevelt wanted absolute patriotism—what he called "100 percent Americanism."

Fear and dread of foreigners intensified in the postwar years, with eastern European Jews and Roman Catholics being blamed for many of the nation's social problems. As one result of this mood, the Ku Klux Klan revived. This post–Civil

149

War vigilante group had first directed its hatred toward blacks, and later toward immigrants, whom it feared and despised. Within a few years of its reemergence in the early 1920s, the Klan spread its message of bigotry not only in the South, where it originated, but throughout the rest of the country as well. The Klan's growth and influence was imposing but brief. David Chalmers's essay "The Hooded Knights Revive Rule by Terror in the Twenties" examines the revival and eventual decline of the Klan during that decade. According to the essay, what attractions did the Klan hold for the thousands who joined it?

The first document comes from a 1926 article, "The Klan's Fight for Americanism," by Klan leader Hiram Evans. Notice how Evans's message combines bigotry and an alleged adherence to traditional American values. How does the document help to explain the Klan's appeal in sections of the country as different from each other in racial and ethnic makeup as Oregon, Georgia, and Massachusetts?

Although Evans's rantings seem outrageous to modern sensibilities, many people during this period, even in the highest levels of government, echoed the Klan philosophy. Evidence of this is found in the second document, an excerpt from congressional testimony in 1921 concerning U.S. immigration policy. Although those testifying do not refer to any specific countries of origin in their condemnation of immigrants, federal legislation passed in 1924 (the National Origins Act) makes it clear that legislators believed immigrants from some countries to be less desirable than those from others. The new approach, generally referred to as the "national-origins system," gave preference to immigrants from northern and western Europe; it severely limited immigration from the rest of the continent, and virtually barred Asians.

In 1952 Congress passed the McCarran-Walter Act, which was also based on the national-origins system. The final document reveals how the Senate subcommittee introducing the bill continued to defend this prejudicial system; both the Senate and the House demonstrated their concurrence through passage of the Act. In 1965 Congress finally replaced this law with a nondiscriminatory one.

ESSAY

The Hooded Knights Revive
Rule by Terror in the Twenties
David Chalmers

D. W. Griffith's 1915 melodrama, *The Birth of a Nation*, was a blockbuster of a motion picture, and it helped revive the Ku Klux Klan. The Kentucky-born Griffith created his pioneering film from a novel written by a North Carolinian named Thomas Dixon. Dixon's life was built on eloquence and passion. A fellow-student and friend of Woodrow Wilson at Johns Hopkins graduate school, Dixon had been a legislator, Baptist preacher, lecturer, novelist, playwright, and actor, always reaching out to a larger audience. Griffith gave him his biggest one.

Dixon's 1905 book, *The Clansman: An Historical Romance of the Ku Klux Klan*, was one of three that he wrote on the Invisible Empire which his uncle had helped lead in the Carolina piedmont. The story revolved around two star-crossed families, the Camerons and the Stonemans, one from the South and the other from the North. Their sons and daughters fell in love, but the War Between the States separated them and Reconstruction brought them disaster. Congressman Stoneman, copied from life after Radical Republican leader Thaddeus Stephens, was presented as a crippled, hate-filled villain, urged on by his mulatto mistress to degrade the captured South. With the murder of "The Great Soul," Abraham Lincoln, there was nothing to stop him. Black tyranny ruled the South, black corruption stained its legislative halls, and brutish black lust stalked its womanhood. However, at this darkest moment, the hooded knights of the Ku Klux Klan, led by young Ben Cameron, Civil War hero and beloved of Stoneman's daughter, rode forth to save the South and its downtrodden people.

D. W. Griffith took Dixon's story and made it into the movies' first colossal spectacular. In place of the usual fifteen-minute flicker, Griffith created a three-hour epic, dramatically restaging the war's battles, Sherman's March to the Sea, and Lincoln's assassination at Ford's Theater. Congressman Stoneman comes to the Southern town of Piedmont to oversee his schemes for melding the races. Cameron's "Little Sister," as he called her, and her mother, Mrs. Lenoir, leap from a cliff to their deaths after ravishment by a black renegade soldier. Cameron is arrested and sentenced to death for murder; Stoneman's son, in love with Cameron's sister, takes his place. Just in time, the Klan arrives to save the living, avenge the fallen, and reunite the lovers.

SOURCE: David Chalmers, "The Hooded Knights Revive Rule by Terror in the Twenties," *American History Illustrated* 14 (February, 1980): 28–37. Reprinted through courtesy of Cowles Magazines, publisher of *American History Illustrated*.

Breaking the former static role of the camera, using angles, movement, and changing focus, expanding irises, reaching in and out of close-ups, juxtaposing, and paralleling, Griffith created his masterpiece. As the bugle call rang out and the Klan rode to the rescue, theater orchestras pounded out themes from Wagner and "The Hall of the Mountain King." Audiences rose cheering in the South, and crowds demonstrated in protest in the North. The picture was seen by President Woodrow Wilson, members of Congress and the Supreme Court, and millions of spectators at $2 apiece, while William J. Simmons, a fraternal organizer, colonel in the Woodmen of the World, and failed Methodist minister, dreamed of a revival of the Klan itself.

"Colonel" Simmons's plan for the Klan was revealed in the words of the advertisement which he inserted in the December 7, 1915, Atlanta *Journal*. The "Knights of the Ku Klux Klan" was "A High Class Order for Men of Intelligence and Character." It was to be "The World's Greatest *Secret*, Social, Patriotic, Fraternal, Beneficiary Order." In other words, it was to be a lodge, a fraternity. The fact that it was to exclude all who were not white, native-born, or Protestant did not make it substantially different from other such organizations and most college fraternities. It was the chance factor of its Southern origin that provided the dynamic element— the name and legend of the Ku Klux Klan. In *The Birth of a Nation*, whose Atlanta advertisement shared the page with Simmons's hand-drawn announcement of the Klan, Thomas Dixon and D. W. Griffith had engraved an image of flowing robes and mystic, masked, night-riding, patriotic violence on the national imagination. While most fraternities guarded their lodge hall secrets against outsiders and aliens, the vigilante heritage of the Klan took it out into the cow-pastures and city streets to protect its version of American values.

Simmons's initial plans had been less extravagant. His specialty was lodge ritual. He had hoped for a mildly successful organization in the Southeast to which he could sell memberships, regalia, and insurance. World War I enabled the Klan to do a little public marching and patriotic snooping. After the war the Klan, with a small membership in Georgia and Alabama, emerged into a time of opportunity. The heightened emotions and restlessness that were not immediately stilled by an end to the fighting, the manly camaraderie of the war and the habit of violence, people going home and not going home, black men who had served in the Army or who had left the farms for the cities and Northern factories— all were unsettling elements.

There were race riots in Chicago, Omaha, and Knoxville, in Duluth, Springfield, and Tulsa, in Texas, Arkansas, Kansas, and Florida. Large numbers of immigrants were arriving from the Southern and Eastern European dwelling places of the Roman Catholic, Jew, Slav, and Bolshevik.

Life in the cities was confusing; the war to end war had turned sour, and the attempt to make society better by prohibition was either being flouted or downright corrupted. As with the original Ku Klux Klan, the unsettled times and the mysterious name (now potent with the legacy of its vigilante role during Reconstruction) undoubtedly shaped the direction the Klan would take for years to come.

Simmons engaged a pair of fund raisers, Edward Young Clarke and Mrs. Elizabeth Tyler, who were the Southern Publicity Association, to handle recruitment. Simmons was to receive $2 of the $10 initiation fee paid by each new member. The rest was to go to Clarke, Tyler, and their salesmen. The results were phenomenal. The Klan made good copy and the press rushed to spread reports of its doings. Within a year membership was nationwide and soared to almost 100,000.

The basic Southern emphasis on patriotism and white supremacy was expanded into the protection of basic morality and 100 percent Americanism. The American way of life and moral values were to be guarded not only against the Negroes, but from Roman Catholics, Jews, and Orientals, from aliens and immigrants, from bootleggers and road houses, from crime and corrupt politicians, from marital infidelity and sexual immorality, and from scoffers and unbelievers. Salesmen, or "kleagles," were selected from the Masonic and other lodges, touring lecturers from the evangelical ministry, and the country was divided and subdivided into sales districts. Local groups brought the Klan into town to combat bootlegging or corrupt city government, and Atlanta's usual advice to new chapters was to "clean up the town." Crosses burned on nearby hillsides, sheeted horsemen paraded down Main Street on Saturday night and the next morning marched down church aisles to make donations while choirs sang "The Old Rugged Cross" or "Onward Christian Soldiers."

Georgia . . . was the cradle for the reborn Klan. Colonel Simmons's blazing cross on Stone Mountain had been its first annunciation and Peachtree Street in Atlanta brought the robed faithful to its Imperial Palace. For fifty years Georgians would march in its parades and elect its candidates, as well as fight against its violence and intolerance. Nathan Bedford Forrest Klan No. 1 was the Imperial Empire's mother lodge, and in 1920 when Simmons triumphantly attended the annual reunion of the United Confederate Veterans in Houston, its Exalted Cyclops Nathan Bedford Forrest III rode beside him.

The Klan spread through the cities and small towns of Georgia. The mighty Robert E. Lee No. 1 of Birmingham was the heart of its strength in Alabama and Sam Houston No. 1 led the way in Texas, although probably outstripped in size and violence by Dallas's No. 66 and Beaumont's No. 7. Klan organizers did well in northern Louisiana and throughout Arkansas, but the Imperial Empire's earliest bastion of terror was in Texas and Oklahoma. Klan salesmen jumped across the continent to California, selling patriotism, fraternity, and moral enforcement. They spread out from Los Angeles, and moved northward across the border to power in Oregon, offering anti-Catholicism to the descendants of the New England and Midwestern Puritans. Its legions grew in Missouri and Kansas, and its salesmen worked their way up the Mississippi Valley, across the Great Plains, and into the mountain states. In 1924 Colorado became even a greater success story than Oregon, as the Klan helped elect the mayor of Denver, the governor, and both senators.

But in no realm did Klan political power become greater than in Indiana. Its ambitious Grand Dragon D. C. Stephenson built his organization on a bloc by bloc basis throughout the state, carrying in tow the governor and both senators, negotiating for the purchase of Valparaiso University, and working his own way toward the White House. The Klan's fraternal appeal to what its Ohio Grand Dragon described as "the submerged majority of Protestants" swelled the tide of its membership in Cincinnati, Columbus, Toledo, Akron, and the steel centers of the Mahoning Valley. The Klan did well in the small towns and industrial cities of central Michigan and among the anti-Catholic socialists of Wisconsin. It signed up its thousands in Chicago and the suburbs, battling against an anti-Klan city administration. In "Bloody Herrin" County down in fundamentalist southern Illinois, where the mountain people from Kentucky and Tennessee shared their country uneasily with French and Italian immigrant coal miners, labor conflict turned into a murderous Klan and anti-Klan war that brought in the National Guard some eight times in four years.

Nor was the East immune from the recruitments of the Invisible Empire. Torn from its past as an instrument by which the post–Civil War Reconstruction was undone, the Klan, which was mainly Democratic in the South, was Republican in the North. In both sections it represented the old moral values against the newcomers and social change. There was the same concern about foreigners, the Roman Catholic "threat" to the public schools, and the enforcement of prohibition. Klan marchers brought in by chartered trains "to give the micks something to think about" were attacked by mobs in the western Pennsylvania mill towns of Carnegie, Lilly, and Scottdale, but in the Philadelphia suburbs and down in Lancaster County, once the Klan got organized, it stayed organized.

While New York City was generally enemy territory, Klan weddings, christenings, church visits, volunteer fire departments, parades, rallies, county fair days, and local political victories marked the Klan as a leading organization in Long Island's Suffolk and Nassau counties. Upstate, Klan domain stretched from its Binghamton headquarters to Buffalo. It entered New Jersey from New York and Pennsylvania and despite denunciation at church conferences, it found a home among Methodist prohibitionists and along the seacoast from Atlantic City to Cape May. Portions of the Klan-infiltrated National Guard were disarmed in Rhode Island. Boston's Mayor [James] Michael Curley cracked down on Klan meetings with the same sternness he had shown to the birth control crusader Margaret Sanger (despite American Civil Liberties Union protest in both cases), and Klansmen and Irishmen fought on summer nights in central Massachusetts. On the other side of the ethnic line, the prominent Boston blue-blood author Lothrop Stoddard found no conflict between his Americanism and that of the Klan, which also helped elect *Mayflower* descendant William Owen Brewster governor of Maine.

Simmons's talents lay in the area of lodge ritual and florid oratory, and many of his rising territorial leaders felt that he was not fully capitalizing on the Klan's potential. Led by the Dallas dentist Hiram Wesley Evans, whom Simmons had brought to Atlanta to help run things at the Imperial Palace, they staged a coup on the eve of the first national Klonvokation in 1922. When Simmons realized that he had been pushed upstairs out of control of the Klan, he was furious. Evans only laughed and replied, "Let's get the money, colonel."

There has never been a reliable tally of the number who belonged to the Klan. Between its veil of secrecy and its public boastings, the estimates run from two to four million members. During its peak years in the early 'twenties, members were streaming in and out in such numbers that the Klan itself probably never knew its own size. The consensus of historians is that Indiana took the lead with perhaps several hundred thousand Klansmen, Klanswomen, Tri-K's, and Junior Klansmen, with Texas, Oklahoma, Illinois, Ohio, and Pennsylvania probably close to 100,000 each. At one time or another in the 1920s, perhaps at least one out of every ten white, native-born, Protestant adult males belonged to the Invisible Empire. While sheer size did not necessarily mean political domination or long life for a Klan realm, in communities all across the country its strength gave a sense of power and immunity from the law. The mayor of Enid, Oklahoma, explained to the American Civil Liberties Union that since the Klan had 1,500 members and he had ten policemen, there was no point in investigating a reported Klan flogging.

A part of the fraternal excitement of the Klan was violence, a heritage from its Reconstruction days and not out of keeping with the Klan's vigilante role as a fighter against crime and immorality. The Klan was secret, masked, decentralized, and righteous, often operating with community approval and police participation. Although some Northern realms such as Ohio and Pennsylvania had their "Night Riders" and "Triple S" ("Super-Secret-Society") squads, the Southwest particularly liked "a little rough stuff." In the early 'twenties there were regular whippings and tar-and-feather parties in the meadows along Dallas's Trinity River bottoms. The

Mer Rouge murders* brought a portion of Louisiana close to civil war, and Governor Jack Walton got himself impeached when he called out the National Guard and imposed martial law on much of Klan-ridden Oklahoma. Texas and Oklahoma led the way, but Klan floggers were also active in Georgia, Alabama, Florida, North Carolina, and Kern County, California, with scattered incidents elsewhere. In those areas where the Klan dominated, however, it was the fellow white, native-born, Anglo-Saxon, Protestant rather than the Negro, Roman Catholic, Jew, or alien who was on the receiving end—which may be a commentary on the extent of the alien danger against which the Klan warned.

What drew its scores of thousands to the Klan? Later generations have looked upon the hooded knights as sour, defensive, bigoted, and something of a joke. To their contemporaries, they were serious business. Famed juvenile court judge, Ben Lindsey, who fought the Klan in Denver, commented, "They paid ten dollars to hate somebody and they were determined to get their money's worth." Julian Harris, son of the creator of the Uncle Remus tales, won a Pulitzer Prize for the anti-Klan campaign of his Columbus, Georgia, *Enquirer-Sun*. Taking the popular booster slogan "It's Great To Be a Georgian," he asked, "Is it great to be a citizen of a state whose governor is a member of and subservient to that vicious masked gang?" New Jersey Methodist Bishop E. H. Hughes found it necessary to remind his fellow ministers that "It is not Anglo-Saxon blood but the blood of Jesus Christ that has made us what we are."

However, to the Klansmen, their purpose was a positive expression of good fellowship and what America was all about. The Klan was a reform movement, even as prohibition was. It was a means to protect society, to keep things good "the way they had been," to get rid of criminals and corrupt politicians, dangerous radicals and those who scoffed at or violated church and home, bought illegal alcohol, or threatened racial purity and the Anglo-Saxon heritage of America.

People prefer simple explanations and scapegoats. Presidents Warren Harding and Calvin Coolidge, the Congress, and the Supreme Court hardly seemed dangerous forces for change. The Klansman found a symbol that he enjoyed blaming: the outsider-alien, personified in the Roman Catholic Church and personalized in the Roman Pope. Ex-priests and "escaped" nuns were popular on the Klan lecture circuit where stories of papal intrigue, convent sin, guns hidden in church basements, and the menace of the Knights of Columbus were staples. From Maine to California, the Klan

---

*On August 24, 1922, in Mer Rouge, Louisiana, two white critics of the Ku Klux Klan were brutally tortured and then hanged by Klan members.

girded its emotional loins against the Roman menace. While no Episcopal, Methodist, or Baptist convention approved of the Klan and many church leaders denounced it, the Klan appeared to be taking a noisy leadership in protecting community morality. In short, it was doing what the churches talked about: the Klan spoke their language, made donations, and filled their benches. So it was very difficult for many ministers and parishioners to turn it down.

In addition to fraternalism, nativism, and the protection of basic moral Americanism, the Invisible Empire offered fellowship, excitement, and a sense of power—and advantage. The ritual and life of the Klan were those of the lodge, and the Ku Klux Klan was the fastest growing fraternity of the 1920s, far outdistancing the newly formed American Legion. Through the early years, Klansmen gathered at monster initiations, cross burnings and rallies, at Klan Day at the state fair in Dallas or the inauguration of Grand Dragon D. C. Stephenson at Kokomo. From the lodge halls of Birmingham's Robert E. Lee No. 1 to Phoenix's Kamelback Klan No. 6, from Shreveport and Grand Island, Portland, New Haven, Beaumont, Bangor, Billings, Binghamton, and Bakersfield, Klansmen felt that they were part of a full-throated, rising, powerful force in the nation.

Of course there was always the possibility of more than the psychological advantage of being in on it. Merchants put "TWK" (Trade With a Klansman) and "SYMWA" (Spend Your Money With Americans) stickers in their shop windows. Rising young politicians such as lawyer Hugo Black in Alabama joined, and county judge hopeful Harry Truman of Independence, Missouri, went through the first steps before he withdrew. With its soaring membership, the Klan seemed to have the votes.

Earle Mayfield in Texas was its first genuine U.S. Senator, and in Arkansas the Klan had its own primary first to decide which brother to support in the regular Democratic party one. Success whetted the appetites of the imperial potentates in Atlanta, and other eager hopefuls, from Maine to California. Altogether, the Klan substantially helped elect both senators from Colorado, Indiana, Oklahoma, and Alabama, and one each from Iowa, Oregon, Texas, Georgia, Tennessee, and Kentucky, as well as governors in Maine, Kansas, California, Wisconsin, Colorado, Indiana, Ohio, Tennessee, Alabama, Georgia, and Oregon. While some only accepted Klan support, at least five of the senators and four of the governors were Klan members.

In 1924, the Klan played a major role in presidential politics. The two candidates battling it out at the Democratic Convention in Madison Square Garden were the "wet," Catholic, New York governor, Al Smith, and the Georgia-born senator from California, William Gibbs McAdoo. McAdoo was not a bigot, but he had important support from Klan regions. The Platform Committee presented a plank opposing racial or religious discrimination, but the Smith supporters, and others, wanted the Klan denounced by name. As the Convention fought over the three crucial syllables, the supporters in the galleries chanted "Ku, Ku, McAdoo!" and "Booze! Booze! Booze!" at each other. The party's elder statesman and three times nominee, William Jennings Bryan, was hissed and booed when he asked for party unity and compassion, not condemnation, for those who belonged to the Klan. By an embittered 542 3/20 to 541 3/20 vote, the angry, shouting delegates failed to name the Klan. It was the climax of the Convention. Afterward it took nine days and 103 ballots to eventually send out John W. Davis as the compromise candidate to lose the election to Calvin Coolidge, who kept silent about it all.

In many communities, as the mayor of Enid, Oklahoma, had told the American Civil Liberties Union, the Klan held unchallenged power. That power, however, was unimaginative and soon squandered. The Klan was conservative, not revolutionary, and had little program other than to enjoy the spoils of office. Its members were a mixed bag of town and city blue- and white-collar workers, shopkeepers, and professional men. Although a potent force in politics, the Klan probably knew as little about economics as Warren G. Harding. Where it became involved, the Klan was pro-business and manipulated. Its leaders were friends to the electrical utilities in Oregon, and to the oil companies in Texas. In Kansas its top attorney also represented the anti-labor Associated Industries, and the Klan opposed street car regulation in Denver, public power ownership in Minneapolis, and the United Mine Workers in Kentucky. In the zones of emergence of the Northern cities, instead of organizing exclusionist neighborhood improvement associations, Klansmen spent their time at parades, church socials, fried chicken dinners, and lectures by Klan clergymen from Atlanta. The Klan's prime concern was fellowship and morality, not economics and urban dynamics.

On the national scene, the Klan supported immigration restriction, Federal aid to public education (as a counter to parochial schools), and non-participation in such "foreign" organizations as the League of Nations and the World Court. In state legislatures, Klansmen concentrated on protecting the flag, the Bible, racial purity, and the little red schoolhouse. This meant patriotic observances and readings from the King James Bible in the schools, and the exclusion of Roman Catholic teachers, or at least their wearing of religious garb. In Oregon the Klan combined with other fraternal lodges to pass a compulsory public school law, which the U.S. Supreme Court soon overruled.

But politics helped to undo the Klan's imperium. Leadership from Atlanta and in the state realms was remarkably inept. Conflict over which Klan candidate was going to be endorsed in Texas, Arkansas, and Oregon left bitter feelings. A jump to the Republican party did help produce a Klan senator from Oklahoma and a shift the other way elected a Democratic governor in Oregon, but the internal costs were high. State realms did not like being dictated to from Atlanta, and local Klansmen were no happier with the divisive, manipulative politics and authoritarian candidate-picking of their own Grand Dragons, who, in turn, had been imposed on the membership. Generally, the Klan was not successful in replacing other political associations and loyalties, and the men Klansmen elected, as well as those who told the Klansmen whom to elect, turned out to be of equally poor quality.

Although the Klan numbers and power often grew impressively, there was almost always someone to fight it, an editor such as Julian Harris or the Emporia, Kansas, *Gazette's* William Allen White to expose it, or a district attorney such as future Texas Governor Dan Moody, Denver's Philip Van Cise, or Alabama Attorney General Charles McCall to investigate and indict it. The New York *World*; Memphis *Commercial Appeal*; Columbus, Georgia, *Enquirer-Sun*; Montgomery, Alabama, *Advertiser*; and Indianapolis *Times* received Pulitzer Prizes for their anti-Klan campaigns.

Initially, all press coverage helped spread the Klan, and violence gave the Klan a "hell-of-a-fellow" sense of power. By the mid-1920s, almost everything the Klan did or that was reported about it revealed its ineptitude, immorality, corruption, and community destructiveness. When Indiana Grand Dragon D. C. Stephenson, the most powerful leader of the Northern Klan, went to prison for a sex murder, the Klan's reputation was further badly damaged. The more the Klan's linen was hung out in public, the dirtier it appeared for all to see, and the Invisible Empire was almost continually in court to settle internal disputes. Colonel Simmons and "Doc" Evans fought over who would be Imperial Wizard; Grand Dragons struggled against Imperial headquarters, and local klaverns against their state realms. The leadership on most levels ruled dictatorially and was out for the money. This struggle for the spoils and the exploitation of the membership wrecked the Klan in practically every state where it existed. By the latter half of the 1920s, membership was melting away. In 1926, when the Klan staged its second national parade down Pennsylvania Avenue in Washington, D.C., only half as many Klansmen and women came, and they marched in columns of four instead of sixteen and twenty abreast as they had done the year before.

During its years of glory, the Klan produced no statesmanlike leaders or social programs, but rather violence, local turmoil, and scandal. By the latter 1920s the country had settled down—even if the Klan had not—to enjoy Republican prosperity. The dangers of Rome or Russia seemed more distant and less real. The Klan's role in the American fraternal world had been irreparably damaged by its mismanagement and extremism. The self-confidence of the great early days had become a sour defensiveness laboring under a damaged reputation, which contrasted badly with a more dominant American optimism.

Even in 1928 when the Democrats picked the Irish Catholic Al Smith as [their] presidential candidate, Klan leaders could not produce a revival. With the crash and Great Depression of the 1930s, the Klan ranks thinned to even fewer thousands. Shrunken to the Southeastern United States, the Klan sometimes had friends in power and engaged in occasional night riding and anti-union violence. It denounced the New Deal as communistic, but offered no alternatives.

At the end of the 1930s, Imperial Wizard Hiram Evans sold the Klan's Peachtree Street Palace to the Roman Catholic Church and the Klan itself to a veterinarian, Jimmy Colescott, from Terre Haute in the once potent realm of Indiana. A joint meeting with the German-American bund, in New Jersey, drew bad publicity. World War II, gas rationing, and a lien from the Internal Revenue Service for back taxes temporarily put the Imperial Empire out of business.

It was brought back to life after the end of the greater war in Europe, and maintains a fragmented existence mainly in the Southeast today, unmasked by state and local laws and watched by the F.B.I. It failed as a resistance movement during the civil rights days of the 1950s and 1960s in the South. Despite the annual compulsion of the press, wire services, and television to rediscover the Klan and announce its "revival," the Klan endures but has not regained any of the unity, numbers, or influence it once had in the 1920s. It was still capable of violence, but at the end of the 1970s, the most serious Klan watcher, the Anti-Defamation League, computed the strength of the various contending Klans at no more than 10,000.

DOCUMENTS

The Klan's Fight for Americanism, 1926

The real indictment against the Roman Church is that it is, fundamentally and irredeemably, in its leadership, in politics, in thought, and largely in membership, actually and actively alien, un-American and usually anti-American. The old stock Americans, with the exception of the few such of Catholic faith—who are in a class by themselves, standing tragically torn

SOURCE: Reprinted from Hiram Evans, "Klan's Fight for Americanism," *North American Review* 123 (March–May 1926): 33–63, by permission of the University of Northern Iowa.

between their faith and their racial and national patriotism—see in the Roman Church today the chief leader of alienism, and the most dangerous alien power with a foothold inside our boundaries. It is this and nothing else that has revived hostility to Catholicism. By no stretch of the imagination can it fairly be called religious prejudice, though, now that the hostility has become active, it does derive some strength from the religious schism.

We Americans see many evidences of Catholic alienism. We believe that its official position and its dogma, its theocratic autocracy and its claim to full authority in temporal as well as spiritual matters, all make it impossible for it as a church, or for its members if they obey it, to coöperate in a free democracy in which Church and State have been separated. It is true that in this country the Roman Church speaks very softly on these points, so that many Catholics do not know them. It is also true that the Roman priests preach Americanism, subject to their own conception of Americanism, of course. But the Roman Church itself makes a point of the divine and unalterable character of its dogma, it has never seen fit to abandon officially any of these un-American attitudes, and it still teaches them in other countries. Until it does renounce them, we cannot believe anything except that they all remain in force, ready to be called into action whenever feasible, and temporarily hushed up only for expediency.

The hierarchical government of the Roman Church is equally at odds with Americanism. The Pope and the whole hierarchy have been for centuries almost wholly Italian. It is nonsense to suppose that a man, by entering a church, loses his race or national loyalties. The Roman Church today, therefore, is just what its name says—Roman; and it is impossible for its hierarchy or the policies they dictate to be in real sympathy with Americanism. Worse, the Italians have proven to be one of the least assimilable of people. The autocratic nature of the Catholic Church organization, and its suppression of free conscience or free decision, need not be discussed; they are unquestioned. Thus it is fundamental to the Roman Church to demand a supreme loyalty, overshadowing national or race loyalty, to a power that is inevitably alien, and which at the best must inevitably inculcate ideals un-American if not actively anti-American. . . .

The facts are that almost everywhere, and especially in the great industrial centers where the Catholics are strongest, they vote almost as a unit, under control of leaders of their own faith, always in support of the interests of the Catholic Church and of Catholic candidates without regard to other interests, and always also in support of alienism whenever there is an issue raised. They vote, in short, not as American citizens, but as aliens and Catholics! They form the biggest, strongest, most cohesive of all the alien *blocs*. On many occasions they form alliances with other alien *blocs* against American interests, as with the Jews in New York today, and with others in the case of the recent opposition to immigrant restriction. . . .

There are three of these great racial instincts, vital elements in both the historic and the present attempts to build an America which shall fulfill the aspirations and justify the heroism of the men who made the nation. These are the instincts of loyalty to the white race, to the traditions of America, and to the spirit of Protestantism, which has been an essential part of Americanism ever since the days of Roanoke and Plymouth Rock. They are condensed into the Klan slogan: "Native, white, Protestant supremacy."

First in the Klansman's mind is patriotism—America for Americans. He believes religiously that a betrayal of Americanism or the American race is treason to the most sacred of trusts, a trust from his fathers and a trust from God. He believes, too, that Americanism can only be achieved if the pioneer stock is kept pure. . . .

Americanism, to the Klansman, is a thing of the spirit, a purpose and a point of view, that can only come through instinctive racial understanding. It has, to be sure, certain defined principles, but he does not believe that many aliens understand those principles, even when they use our words in talking about them. Democracy is one, fairdealing, impartial justice, equal opportunity, religious liberty, independence, self-reliance, courage, endurance, acceptance of individual responsibility as well as individual rewards for effort, willingness to sacrifice for the good of his family, his nation and his race before anything else but God, dependence on enlightened conscience for guidance, the right to unhampered development— these are fundamental. But within the bounds they fix there must be the utmost freedom, tolerance, liberalism. In short, the Klansman believes in the greatest possible diversity and individualism within the limits of the American spirit. But he believes also that few aliens can understand that spirit, that fewer try to, and that there must be resistance, intolerance even, toward anything that threatens it, or the fundamental national unity based upon it.

The second word in the Klansman's trilogy is "white." The white race must be supreme, not only in America but in the world. This is equally undebatable, except on the ground that the races might live together, each with full regard for the rights and interests of others, and that those rights and interests would never conflict. Such an idea, of course, is absurd; the colored races today, such as Japan, are clamoring not for equality but for their supremacy. The whole history of the world, on its broader lines, has been one of race conflicts, wars, subjugation or extinction. This is not pretty, and certainly disagrees with the maudlin theories of cosmopolitanism, but it is truth. The world has been so made that each race must fight for its life, must conquer, accept slavery or die. The Klansman believes that the whites will not become slaves, and he does not intend to die before his time.

Moreover, the future of progress and civilization depends on the continued supremacy of the white race. The forward movement of the world for centuries has come entirely from it. Other races each had its chance and either failed or stuck fast, while white civilization shows no sign of having reached its limit. Until the whites falter, or some colored civilization has a miracle of awakening, there is not a single colored stock that can claim even equality with the white; much less supremacy.

The third of the Klan principles is that Protestantism must be supreme; that Rome shall not rule America. The Klansman believes this is not merely because he is a Protestant, nor even because the Colonies that are now our nation were settled for the purpose of wresting America from the control of Rome and establishing a land of free conscience. He believes it also because Protestantism is an essential part of Americanism; without it America could never have been created and without it she cannot go forward. Roman rule would kill it.

Congress Debates Immigration Restriction, 1921

HOUSE OF REPRESENTATIVES

Mr. [Lucian Walton] PARISH [D.-Tex.]. We should stop immigration entirely until such a time as we can amend our immigration laws and so write them that hereafter no one shall be admitted except he be in full sympathy with our Constitution and laws, willing to declare himself obedient to our flag, and willing to release himself from any obligations he may owe to the flag of the country from which he came.

It is time that we act now, because within a few short years the damage will have been done. The endless tide of immigration will have filled our country with a foreign and unsympathetic element. Those who are out of sympathy with our Constitution and the spirit of our Government will be here in large numbers, and the true spirit of Americanism left us by our fathers will gradually become poisoned by this uncertain element.

The time once was when we welcomed to our shores the oppressed and downtrodden people from all the world, but they came to us because of oppression at home and with the sincere purpose of making true and loyal American citizens, and in truth and in fact they did adapt themselves to our ways of thinking and contributed in a substantial sense to the progress and development that our civilization has made. But that time has passed now; new and strange conditions have arisen in the countries over there; new and strange doctrines are being taught. The Governments of

SOURCE: *Congressional Record*, April 20, 1921, 450, December 10, 1921, 177.

the Orient are being overturned and destroyed, and anarchy and bolshevism are threatening the very foundation of many of them, and no one can foretell what the future will bring to many of those countries of the Old World now struggling with these problems.

Our country is a self-sustaining country. It has taught the principles of real democracy to all the nations of the earth; its flag has been the synonym of progress, prosperity, and the preservation of the rights of the individual, and there can be nothing so dangerous as for us to allow the undesirable foreign element to poison our civilization and thereby threaten the safety of the institutions that our forefathers have established for us.

Now is the time to throw about this country the most stringent immigration laws and keep from our shores forever those who are not in sympathy with the American ideals. It is the time now for us to act and act quickly, because every month's delay increases the difficulty in which we find ourselves and renders the problems of government more difficult of solution. We must protect ourselves from the poisonous influences that are threatening the very foundation of the Governments of Europe; we must see to it that those who come here are loyal and true to our Nation and impress upon them that it means something to have the privileges of American citizenship. We must hold this country true to the American thought and the American ideals. . . .

Mr. [James V.] McCLINTIC [D.-Okla.]. Some time ago it was my privilege to visit Ellis Island, not as a member of the committee but as a private citizen interested in obtaining information relative to the situation which exists at that place. I stood at the end of a hall with three physicians, and I saw them examine each immigrant as they came down the line, rolling back the upper eyelid in order to gain some information as to the individual's physical condition. I saw them place the chalk marks on their clothing which indicated that they were in a diseased condition, so that they could be separated when they reached the place where they were to undergo certain examinations. Afterwards I went to a large assembly hall where immigrants came before the examiners to take the literacy test, and the one fact that impressed me more than anything else was that practically every single immigrant examined that day had less than $50 to his credit. . . .

Practically all of them were weak, small of stature, poorly clad, emaciated, and in a condition which showed that the environment surrounding them in their European homes was indeed very bad.

It is for this reason that I say the class of immigrants coming to the shores of the United States at this time are not the kind of people we want as citizens in this country. It is a well-known fact that the majority of immigrants coming to this country at the present time are going into the large industrial centers instead of the agricultural centers of the United States, and when it is taken into consideration that the large centers are already crowded to the extent that there was hardly sufficient living quarters to take care of the people, it can be readily seen that this class of people, instead of becoming of service to the communities where they go, they will become charges to be taken care of by charitable institutions. The week I visited Ellis Island I was told that 25,000 immigrants had been unloaded at that port. From their personal appearance they seemed to be the offcasts of the countries from which they came. . . .

National-Origins Formula Reaffirmed, 1951

The subcommittee [on immigration and naturalization] is cognizant of the facts existing at the time of the adoption of the national-origins formula and the bitter charges of discrimination hurled at the incorporation of the principle in our immigration laws. The formula is still subjected to such charges but they seem to have lost some of their force over the intervening period of years. Experience has demonstrated that the national-origins formula has been more of a numerically restrictive measure than a means of automatically selecting immigrants from the various nationalities in desired proportions.

Without giving credence to any theory of Nordic superiority, the subcommittee believes that the adoption of the national-origins formula was a rational and logical method of numerically restricting immigration in such a manner as to best preserve the sociological and cultural balance in the population of the United States. There is no doubt that it favored the peoples of the countries of northern and western Europe over those of southern and eastern Europe, but the subcommittee holds that the peoples who had made the greatest contribution to the development of this country were fully justified in determining that the country was no longer a field for further colonization, and henceforth, further immigration would not only be restricted but directed to admit immigrants considered to be more readily assimilable because of the similarity of their cultural background to those of the principal components of our population. . . .

SOURCE: U.S. Congress, Senate Committee on the Judiciary, *U.S. Immigration and Naturalization*, S. Rept. 1515, 82d Cong., 1st sess., 1951, 455.

Chapter 9

Morals and Manners in the 1920s

Following World War I, many Americans eagerly embraced what President Warren G. Harding called "a return to normalcy." The term conveyed a nostalgic vision of an America dotted with small towns and farms, with men and women pursuing traditional roles, oblivious to events in other parts of the world. But the clock could not be turned back. Indeed, this image of the "good old days" was not an accurate view of the nation even before the war. The sweeping urban-industrial revolution of post–Civil War America had stretched the social fabric, and would continue to do so.

The 1920 census provided dramatic evidence of the changes, revealing that for the first time a majority of Americans lived in urban areas. More Americans than ever before, including many women, now worked in factories and offices and saw their style of living affected by the automobile, the movies, a vast array of new consumer goods, and better housing, For much of the younger generation, the good days were not to be found in some distant past; they were to be enjoyed right now.

The essay by John D'Emilio and Estelle Friedman centers on the sexual revolution of the 1920s, particularly among American youth. How extensive were the post–World War I changes that the authors describe? How do D'Emilio and Friedman account for the revolution in sexual mores during the 1920s?

No one, as D'Emilio and Friedman indicate, was more prominently identified with the new morality than Margaret Sanger. In the first document, she strongly advocates family planning. What reasons does she give for families to control their size and the spacing of children? Does her argument have a contemporary quality in light of today's debates on abortion?

Many Americans were shocked by the ideas put forth by Sanger and alarmed by many of the societal changes that marked the decade. Some offered plans for countering these developments. In the second document, Senator Henry Myers of Montana singles out for criticism the movies (and the messages that they conveyed), to which millions—especially the young—flocked weekly. Could the movies have wielded as much influence as the senator claimed? What do you think his proposal of censorhip would have accomplished?

Criticism of the social climate in the United States did not originate in the 1920s; neither did attempts at reform. Nonetheless, in 1920 reformers had great hopes for a new age about to dawn. In that year the century-old battle against the consumption of alcoholic beverages appeared to have been won with the passage of the Eighteenth (Prohibition) Amendment to the Constitution. However, the third document—an excerpt from a statement issued in 1931 by a government commission established to investigate the effectiveness of the amendment and its accompanying legislation—provides findings to the contrary. Can you give any examples of illegal behavior widely practiced today? What are the difficulties in outlawing an activity that a large segment of the public deems acceptable?

ESSAY

The Sexual Revolution

John D'Emilio and Estelle Friedman

In the winter of 1924, the sociologists Robert and Helen Lynd arrived in Muncie, Indiana, to embark upon an intensive investigation of life in a small American city. The study that resulted, *Middletown*, became an American classic. Casting their net widely, the Lynds examined work, home, youth, leisure, religious beliefs, and civic institutions in an effort to draw a complex picture of life in the modern age. In the process, *Middletown* had much to say about the social context that was shaping sexuality in the 1920s and that would continue to affect American mores.

In order to emphasize the rapidly changing nature of social life in an industrial era, the Lynds offered 1890 as a counterpoint to the 1920s. Reflecting the small-town values that still survived at the turn of the century in parts of the country, males and females moved in different spheres; daughters remained at home with their mothers, and adolescent boys entered the public world of work which their fathers inhabited. Young men and women rarely mingled without the careful chaperonage of adults. Socializing continued to take place in public settings that brought families and community residents together. Once a couple had embarked upon a serious courtship, they gained the permission to be alone together, but most often in the family parlor or on the front porch, not far from parental supervision. A heavy taboo hung over sexual relations outside of marriage. Sex was an intensely private matter that came into public view only occasionally, when Muncie's small red-light district overstepped its boundaries, angering the citizenry.

Even as the Lynds described it, contemporary readers would have recognized this as the portrait of a world irrevocably lost. Indeed, the youth of Muncie, for whom change had been most dramatic, would not even have remembered what that earlier world was like. Instead, by the 1920s, adolescents moved in a youth-centered world, based in the high schools that most now attended. School had become, according to the Lynds, "a place from which they go home to eat and sleep." Males and females met in classes, at after-school activities and evening socials. Cars provided privacy, and marked the end of the "gentleman caller" who sat in the parlor. A majority of the students went out with friends four or more evenings a week. Youth patronized movies together, drove to nearby towns for weekend dances, and parked in lovers' lanes on the way home. Almost half of Muncie's male high school students, and a third of its female students, had participated in the recent vogue of the "petting" party; girls who did not were decidedly less popular. After graduation, boys and girls alike left home to work. Increasing economic independence led to less parental supervision over premarital behavior, at the same time that work allowed the young to continue to meet away from home.

This new autonomy and mobility of youth came at a time when Muncie society, through many of the items and activities of a consumer economy, was focused more and more on sexuality. The newspaper advice columns of Dorothy Dix and other syndicated writers instructed female readers in how to catch a man, the thrill and magic of love, and the nature of modern marriage at the same time that relationships were being redefined in romantic, erotic terms. Popular songs of the decade, such as "It Had to Be You," taught that love was a mysterious experience that occurred in a flash when the "chemistry" was right. Sex adventure magazines had become big sellers with stories titled "The Primitive Lover" ("She wanted a caveman husband") and "Indolent Kisses." Muncie's nine movie theaters, open daily and offering twenty-two programs a week, filled their houses by offering such fare as *Married Flirts, Rouged Lips,* and *Alimony*. One popular film of the decade, *Flaming Youth,* attracted audiences by promising images of "neckers, petters, white kisses, red kisses, pleasure-mad daughters, sensation-craving mothers."

The world that the Lynds described, of autonomous youth coming of age in a social environment where erotic images beckoned, has remained fixed in the popular view of the 1920s as a time of new sexual freedoms. Frederick Lewis Allen, in his best-selling account of the decade, *Only Yesterday,* looked at the cultural landscape and detected a "revolution in manners and morals." Images from the 1920s abound to sustain his assessment—flappers and jazz babies; rumble seats and raccoon coats; F. Scott Fitzgerald novels and speakeasies; petting parties and Hollywood sex symbols. And, in fact, despite the evidence of change in sexual mores in the years before World War I, the 1920s do stand out as a time when something in the sexual landscape decisively altered and new patterns clearly emerged. The decade was recognizably modern in a way that previous ones were not. The values, attitudes, and activities of the pre-Depression years unmistakably point to the future rather than the past.

One reason, perhaps, why the twenties have loomed so large as a critical turning point is that patterns of behavior and sexual norms formerly associated with other groups in the population had, by then, spread to the white middle class. The more lavish cabaret appropriated the music and dancing of black and white working-class youth. Movie palaces replaced storefront theaters, and Hollywood directors churned out feature-length films that attracted youths and adults of every class. Bohemian radicals relinquished their proprietorship over the work of modern sexual theorists such as Ellis and Freud, whose ideas received wide currency. Purity crusaders lost the momentum of the prewar years and found themselves rapidly left behind by a culture that scoffed at the sexual prudery of its ancestors. Although each of these developments had roots in the prewar era, not until the 1920s did they experience a full flowering.

The sexual issues that preoccupied the 1920s—the freedom of middle-class youth, the continuing agitation over birth control, debates about the future of marriage, the commercial manipulation of the erotic—suggest the direction in which American values were heading. Sexual expression was moving beyond the confines of marriage, not as the deviant behavior of prostitutes and their customers, but as the normative behavior of many Americans. The heterosocial world in which youth matured encouraged the trend, and the growing availability of contraceptives removed some of the danger attached to nonmarital heterosexuality. New ideas about the essential healthfulness of sexual expression reshaped marriage, too, as couples approached conjugal life with the expectation that erotic enjoyment, and not simply spiritual union, was an integral part of a successful marital relationship. To be sure, resistance to these modern norms surfaced. Some supporters of a new "companionate" marriage advocated it as a way of containing the excesses of youthful libido, while the new visibility of the erotic in popular culture antagonized some and spawned opposition. But, in general, American society was moving by the 1920s toward a view of erotic expression that can be defined as sexual liberalism—an overlapping set of beliefs that detached sexual activity from the instrumental goal of procreation, affirmed heterosexual pleasure as a value in itself, defined sexual satisfaction as a critical component of personal happiness and successful marriage, and weakened the connections between sexual expression and marriage by providing youth with room for some experimentation as preparation for adult status.

At times during the succeeding generation, the crises that punctuated mid-twentieth-century American life seemed to obscure this trend. Under the pressure of the Depression of the 1930s, for instance, the consumerism and commercialized amusements that gave play to sexual adventure temporarily withered. Sobriety and gloom replaced the buoyant exuberance of the previous decade. Dating became a simpler affair, while the anxieties of unemployment and hard times created sexual tensions in many marriages. Birth control became less an issue of freedom for women, and more a method of regulating the poor. After World War II, the impulse to conform and settle down after years of depression, war, and cold war encouraged a rush to early marriage and saw the birth rate zoom upward. Sexual experimentation appeared lost in a maze of suburban housing developments as a new generation took on family responsibilities and raised more children than their parents had. The erotic seemed to disappear under a wave of innocent domesticity, captured in television shows like *Father Knows Best* or the Hollywood comedies of Rock Hudson and Doris Day. A resurgent purity impulse attacked symbols of sexual permissiveness such as pornography and imposed penalties on those who deviated too sharply from family values.

Despite these appearances, however, the forces that fed sexual liberalism developed apace. The availability and accessibility of reliable contraceptives highlighted the divorce of sexual activity from the procreative consequences that inhibited erotic enthusiasm. Sexual imagery gradually became an integral feature of the public realm, legitimate and aboveground. A youth culture that encouraged heterosexual expressiveness became ubiquitous. Couples looked to marriage as a source of continuing erotic pleasures. By the mid-1960s, sexual liberalism had become the dominant ethic, as powerful in its way as was the civilized morality of the late nineteenth century. . . .

Birth control offers perhaps the most dramatic example of the change that occurred in American sexual mores during the middle of the twentieth century. At the start of the 1920s, it still bore the mark of radicalism, and the birth control movement appeared to many as a threat to moral order. The federal Comstock law, with its prohibition on the importation, mailing, and interstate shipment of contraceptive information and devices, remained in effect, and almost half of the states, including most of the populous ones of the Northeast and Midwest, had their own anti-contraceptive statutes. To agitate for birth control placed one outside the law. By the late 1960s, however, virtually all legal impediments to access had collapsed, and the federal government was actively promoting it. Advances in technology and shifts in values made reliable contraceptives an integral feature of married life as well as widely available to the unmarried.

For most of the 1920s and 1930s Margaret Sanger remained the key figure in the birth control movement and the individual most responsible for the changes that occurred. Though her leadership and visibility provided continuity with the pre–World War I agitation, the politics of the movement was undergoing an important shift. Government repression of radicalism and the decline of organized feminism after suffrage altered the context in which the fight for birth control was occurring. Sanger adapted to the new circumstances by detaching the question of contraception from larger social issues and movements. Throughout the twenties and thirties, she campaigned solely to make contraception freely available to women.

Even with a narrowed focus, however, Sanger remained a militant fighter, willing to use any means necessary to achieve her goals. She continued to risk arrest, believing as she did that "agitation through violation of the law was the key to the public." She also propagandized widely, through the pages of her journal (the *Birth Control Review*), through the books that she authored, and through her extensive speaking tours and public conferences. With the backing of her organization, the American Birth Control League, Sanger lobbied for legislative change and embarked once again on a venture in clinical services when she established the Clinical Research Bureau in 1923.

Sanger's lobbying efforts and the clinic that she supported point to an important way in which her strategy was evolving. In New York State in the 1920s, she campaigned for a "doctors only" bill, designed to allow physicians to provide contraceptives, but restricting that right to licensed practitioners. The Clinical Research Bureau, though it provided female clients with contraceptive devices, existed mainly to gather data that would persuade a science-conscious profession that safe, reliable methods of fertility control were available. Both initiatives aimed at enlisting the medical profession as allies in her cause, since its hostility to contraception constituted a major obstacle to success. In the process, however, the politics of birth control tilted in a more conservative direction. From a key issue in the struggle for female emancipation, contraception was gradually becoming a matter of professional health care. . . .

As one might expect, the contraceptive revolution moved hand in hand with changes in both sexual behavior and attitudes. Historians of twentieth-century mores have tended to underplay this shift, by emphasizing instead the stability of one important index of sexual behavior, the female premarital coital rate. For women coming of age in the 1920s, the incidence of premarital intercourse jumped sharply, to roughly fifty percent of the cohort, and thereafter remained relatively constant until the late 1960s. Yet hidden behind the stability of these figures lay a whole world of sexual change. Activity that provoked guilt in the 1920s had become integrated by the 1960s into a new code of sexual ethics that made it morally acceptable. What was daring and nonconformist in the earlier period appeared commonplace a generation later. And, as attitudes and ideals altered, so too did aspects of sexual activity. Dating, necking, and petting among peers became part and parcel of the experience of American youth, providing an initiatory stage, uncommon for their elders, leading to the coital experience of adulthood and marriage. To marriage itself, couples brought new expectations of pleasure, satisfaction, and mutual enjoyment, encouraged by a more explicit advice literature that emphasized the sexual component of conjugal life. The integration of contraception into middle-class married life also meant that the reproductive requirement for marital intimacy had receded far into the background. Though experience might not always live up to these new standards, men and women in the mid-twentieth century were approaching marriage with heightened anticipation of physical pleasure.

Evidence abounds of shifts in both standards and patterns of behavior among American youth in the decades after World War I. During the 1920s, white college youth captured the lion's share of attention of contemporaries seeking to chart the society's changing values. Although less than thirteen percent of the eighteen- to twenty-one-year-old population were enrolled in colleges at the end of the 1920s, the numbers had more than tripled since 1890. For the first time, a distinctive subculture took shape among the middle-class young, with values and activities that set them apart from their parents' generation.

Sexual innovation played a key role in this new world of youth. Particularly in coeducational institutions, heterosocial mixing became the norm. Young men and women mixed casually in classes, extracurricular activities, and social spaces, with a great deal of freedom from adult supervision. Dating in pairs, unlike the informal group socializing of the nineteenth century, permitted sexual liberties that formerly were sanctioned only for couples who were courting. College youth flaunted their new freedoms. As one male editor of a campus paper provocatively expressed it, "there are only two kinds of co-eds, those who have been kissed, and those who are sorry they haven't been kissed." Magazines debated the implications of "petting parties," an increasingly common feature of college life. One study of college youth during the 1920s found that ninety-two percent of coeds had engaged in petting, and that those "rejecting all sex play feel that they are on the defensive."

What a relatively small percentage of middle-class youth were experiencing in college, much larger numbers tasted in high school. By the 1920s, high school had become a mass experience, with almost three-quarters of the young enrolled. Here, too, adolescent boys and girls encountered one another daily, with casual interaction throughout the day that often continued into evening social activities. One observer of youthful mores estimated that a large majority of high school youth engaged in hugging and kissing and that a significant minority "do not restrict themselves to that, but go further, and indulge in other sex liberties which, by all the conventions, are outrageously improper." Automobiles allowed young people still living at home greater freedom of movement than ever before. Groups of teenagers might drive to the next town for a Saturday-night dance; on weeknights, too, it became easier to escape parental supervision. So quickly and widely did cars become an essential part of this heterosocial world of youth that one commentator labeled the auto "a house of prostitution on wheels." Assessing these changes, Ben Lindsey, a Colorado juvenile court judge who had dealt with the young for a generation, considered them to be reflective of a historic transformation in American life. "Not only is this revolt from the old standards of conduct taking place," he wrote, "but it is unlike any revolt that has ever taken place before. Youth has always been rebellious. . . . But this is different. It has the whole weight and momentum of a new scientific and economic order behind it."

Although the innovations in sexual behavior among middle-class youth were real, they nonetheless operated within certain peer-defined limits. Young men took liberties with women of their own class that their parents would have considered improper, but the sexual freedom of the 1920s was hardly a promiscuous one. The kissing and petting that occurred among couples who dated casually did not often progress beyond that. Surveys of sexual behavior among white middle-class women revealed that the generation coming of age in the 1920s had a significantly higher incidence of premarital intercourse than women born in the preceding decades. But the evidence also suggests that, for the most part, young women generally restricted coitus to a single partner, the man they expected to marry. "Going all the way" was permissible, but only in the context of love and commitment. For men, the changes in female sexual behavior had important implications. Beginning in the 1920s, the frequency of recourse

173

to prostitution began to decline. As Lindsey noted, "with the breaking up of those districts, [boys] turned to girls of their own class, a thing they had seldom done in the past."

As young people adopted the novel practice of dating, they shaped, learned, and refashioned its rules. Newspaper advice columns in the years after World War I printed letters from confused youth who wondered whether a good-night kiss was an appropriate ending for an evening date, and who searched for words to define the feelings aroused by the dating relationship. By the 1930s, the elaboration of this teenage ritual had produced words other than "love" to describe the emotions, and had differentiated "courting" and "keeping company" from the more casual, and common, practices of "going out" and "going steady." When the Lynds returned to Muncie in the 1930s, one young man reported to them that "the fellows regard necking as a taken-for-granted part of a date. We fellows used occasionally to get slapped for doing things, but the girls don't do that much any more. . . . Our high school students of both sexes . . . know everything and do everything—openly." Although he likely exaggerated in his claims about "everything," numerous surveys of American youth confirm the widening boundaries of permissible sexual activity. The rapid acceptance of this peer-directed system of dating, as well as the quick demise of its predecessor, can be inferred from changes in that reliable arbiter of social behavior, Emily Post's *Etiquette*. A chapter which, in the 1923 edition, was titled "Chaperons and Other Conventions" became "The Vanishing Chaperon and Other New Conventions" four years later; the passing of another decade brought the wistful heading "The Vanished Chaperon and Other Lost Conventions." One study of high school students in St. Louis on the eve of World War II found dating to be ubiquitous, with most couples returning home after one in the morning. Freed from parental supervision for long hours, boys and girls alike exhibited "a fairly general acceptance of the naturalness" of kisses and light petting as part of a date. Indeed, St. Louis's high school students proved far more tolerant about sexual matters than about other kinds of behavior such as smoking and drinking.

The system of dating, at least as it evolved between the two world wars, did not extend to all youth. Its adoption depended upon surplus income for clothes and entertainment, access to automobiles outside major cities, school attendance to enforce peer-based norms, and sufficient population density to sustain a range of commercialized amusements. Its contours thus mark it as a ritual of white middle-class youth in the cities and suburbs.

Among poor blacks in the rural South, for instance, older patterns of sociability persisted as young people experienced both traditional freedoms and constraints. With few sanctions against premarital intercourse, "sex play," according to one observer, "becomes matter-of-fact behavior for youth." As one young girl explained it, "I ain't never thought of there being anything wrong about it." Denied access because of segregation, poverty, and rural isolation from most of the places where formal dating took place, young rural blacks met at church, harvest festivals, picnics, and while working in the fields, much as they had in the past. Yet, an awareness of the world beyond the small rural community also generated a "longing for pleasures like those of the city." One young man expressed his discontent by telling an interviewer, "there ain't no decent place to take a girl. . . . If you ain't got a car, you just ain't nowhere." Meanwhile, black parents of moderate wealth and status, in an effort to differentiate themselves from the rural masses and to provide education and mobility for the next generation, socialized their children into strict moral codes. In his study of youth in the Black Belt before World War II, Charles Johnson found that among the elite, even young men accepted rigid standards of chastity. Parents kept close rein on their daughters, as the testimony of one North Carolina girl made clear: "Yes, I have a boy friend. He calls on me and takes me to socials. Sometimes mama lets me go to movies with him in the afternoon, but if he goes with me at night papa and mama go too."

For white youth as well, rural and small-town residence affected patterns of sexual interaction. In rural communities many young people lacked mobility. "I had no car," explained one youth who bemoaned his inability to date. "We lived 20 miles from town and to get to town I had to ride with my father or some other adult." Then, too, in smaller communities adults were able to watch the behavior of the young more closely. "I'll tell you, it's really tough getting it in a small town," one young man complained. "Everyone has their eyes on you and especially on the girl. You can hardly get away with anything." A young man who moved to the city when he was seventeen noted the difference it made. He had never felt much sexual desire during his years in the country, he commented, but city life with its abundant opportunities suddenly seemed to generate "much more interest in it."

Although urban working-class youth did not share in the sexual culture of the middle class, this by no means implied a sentence of chastity. In some cases it could translate into freedom from the constraints of peer-enforced norms. In cities and towns, white and black youth who dropped out of high school or who did not immediately marry after graduation found themselves earning wages, yet without the expense of maintaining a household. Removed from the web of daily gossip that shaped the behavior of high school and college students, they were more likely to move beyond petting in their sexual relationships. Dance halls, bowling alleys, skating rinks, and, after prohibition, bars provided settings for young men and women to meet; automobiles, bought with hard-earned wages, offered privacy. One high school dropout embarked upon her first sexual affair with a dance-hall partner. "I made up my mind at the dance Oscar could have it," she recalled. "Oh, it was wonderful. That night, I thought, 'I don't care if I have a baby.' " Several more relationships ensued before she married in her late teens. The thriving business in condoms that Malcolm X operated at a Boston dance hall suggests the ease with which sexual favors could be exchanged among working-class youth in the city. So, too, does evidence of prenuptial conceptions and illegitimacy among the poor and the working class. In one Illinois town, over half of the girls who did not graduate from high school gave birth within eight months of their wedding. And almost a quarter of the births in the lowest social class of whites occurred outside of marriage.

By accelerating the shift to city living, and by providing youth with more economic autonomy and freedom from adult supervision, World War II brought unprecedented opportunities for premarital experience. The war released millions of youth from the social environments that inhibited erotic expression, and threw them into circumstances that opened up new sexual possibilities. Millions of young men left home to join the military, while many young women migrated in search of employment. The demands of wartime drew teenagers into the paid labor force while weakening the influence that family and community held over their behavior.

Ample testimony from the war years confirms the sexual ex-pressiveness of youth. For many young women, men in uniform held erotic appeal. "When I was 16," one college student recalled,

> I let a sailor pick me up and go all the way with me. I had intercourse with him partly because he had a strong personal appeal for me, but mainly because I had a feeling of high adventure and because I wanted to please a member of the armed forces.

Another, rebuffed by a sailor boyfriend who felt she was too young, went on to have affairs with fifteen others by war's end. Civilian men, too, partook of the sexual freedom of the war years. One teenager described his life then as "a real sex paradise. The plant and the town were just full of working girls who were on the make. Where I was, a male war worker became the center of loose morality. It was a sex paradise." A high school student lost his virginity with a woman of thirty whose husband was overseas. "We weren't in love," he recalled, "although we were very fond of each other. The times were conducive for this sort of thing. Otherwise, nothing would ever have happened between us."

The response of moral reformers points to the changes that had occurred since the previous generation. Whereas those of the First World War focused on the dangers of prostitution, by the 1940s it was the behavior of "amateur girls"—popularly known as khaki-wackies, victory girls, and good-time Charlottes—that concerned moralists. "The old time prostitute in a house or formal prostitute on the street is sinking into second place," wrote one venereal-disease expert. "The new type is the young girl in her late teens and early twenties, the young woman in every field of life who is determined to have one fling or better." Efforts to scare GIs into continence by emphasizing the danger of disease had little impact on men who, according to one officer, "think as little of a gonorrheal infection as they do of the ordinary common cold." Or, as another phrased it, "the sex act cannot be made unpopular." Local law-enforcement officials worked overtime to contain the sexual behavior of young women, yet their efforts only seemed to confirm the perception that prostitution was not the issue. Arrests for selling sexual favors rose less than twenty percent during the war years, but charges of disorderly conduct increased almost two hundred percent, and those for other morals offenses, such as promiscuous behavior or patronizing bars too frequently, increased nearly as much. . . .

DOCUMENTS

Happiness in Marriage, 1926

Margaret H. Sanger

We must recognize that the whole position of womanhood has changed today. Not so many years ago it was assumed to be a just and natural state of affairs that marriage was considered as nothing but a preliminary to motherhood. A girl passed from the guardianship of her father or nearest male relative to that of her husband. She had no will, no wishes of her own. Hers not to question why, but merely to fulfil duties imposed upon her by the man into whose care she was given.

Marriage was synonymous with maternity. But the pain, the suffering, the wrecked lives of women and children that such a system caused, show us that it did not work successfully. Like all other professions, motherhood must serve its period of apprenticeship.

Today women are on the whole much more individual. They possess as strong likes and dislikes as men. They live more and more on the plane of social equality with men. They are better companions. We should be glad that there is more enjoyable companionship and real friendship between men and women.

This very fact, it is true, complicates the marriage relation, and at the same time ennobles it. Marriage no longer means the slavish subservience of the woman to the will of the man. It means, instead, the union of two strong

SOURCE: Margaret Sanger, *Happiness in Marriage* (Blue Ribbon Books, New York, 1926), 83–97.

and highly individualized natures. Their first problem is to find out just what the terms of this partnership are to be. Understanding full and complete cannot come all at once, in one revealing flash. It takes time to arrive at a full and sympathetic understanding of each other, and mutually to arrange lives to increase this understanding. Out of the mutual adjustments, harmony must grow and discords gradually disappear.

These results cannot be obtained if the problem of parenthood is thrust upon the young husband and wife before they are spiritually and economically prepared to meet it. For naturally the coming of the first baby means that all other problems must be thrust aside. That baby is a great fact, a reality that must be met. Preparations must be made for its coming. The layette must be prepared. The doctor must be consulted. The health of the wife may need consideration. The young mother will probably prefer to go to the hospital. All of these preparations are small compared to the regime after the coming of the infant.

Now there is a proper moment for every human activity, a proper season for every step in self-development. The period for cementing the bond of love is no exception to this great truth. For only by the full and glorious living through these years of early marriage are the foundations of an enduring and happy married life rendered possible. By this period the woman attains a spiritual freedom. Her womanhood has a chance to bloom. She wins a mastery over her destiny; she acquires self-reliance, poise, strength, a youthful maturity. She abolishes fear. Incidentally, few of us realize, since the world keeps no record of this fact, how many human beings are conceived in fear and even in repugnance by young mothers who are the victims of undesired maternity. Nor has science yet determined the possibilities of a generation conceived and born of conscious desire.

In the wife who has lived through a happy marriage, for whom the bonds of passionate love have been fully cemented, maternal desire is intensified and matured. Motherhood becomes for such a woman not a penalty or a punishment, but the road by which she travels onward toward completely rounded self-development. Motherhood thus helps her toward the unfolding and realization of her higher nature.

Her children are not mere accidents, the outcome of chance. When motherhood is a mere accident, as so often it is in the early years of careless or reckless marriages, a constant fear of pregnancy may poison the days and nights of the young mother. Her marriage is thus converted into a tragedy. Motherhood becomes for her a horror instead of a joyfully fulfilled function.

Millions of marriages have been blighted, not because of any lack of love between the young husband and wife, but because children have come too soon. Often these brides become mothers before they have reached even physical maturity, before they have completed the period of adolescence. This period in our race is as a rule complete around the age of twenty-three. Motherhood is possible after the first menstruation. But what is physically possible is very often from every other point of view inadvisable. A young woman should be fully matured from every point of view—physically, mentally and psychically—before maternity is thrust upon her. . . .

The problem of premature parenthood is intensified and aggravated when a second infant follows too rapidly the advent of the first, and inevitably husband and wife are made the slaves of this undreamed of situation, bravely trying to stave off poverty, whipped to desperation by the heavy hand of chance and involuntary parenthood. How can they then recapture their early love? It is not surprising that more often they do not even trouble themselves to conceal the contempt which is the bitter fruit of that young and romantic passion. . . .

Instead of being a self-determined and self-directing love, everything is henceforward determined by the sweet tyranny of the child. I have known of several young mothers, despite a great love for the child, to rebel against this intolerable situation. Vaguely feeling that this new maternity has rendered them unattractive to their husbands, slaves to a deadly routine of bottles, baths and washing, they have revolted. I know of innumerable marriages which have been wrecked by premature parenthood.

Love has ever been blighted by the coming of children before the real foundations of marriage have been established. Quite aside from the injustice done to the child who has been brought accidentally into the world, this lamentable fact sinks into insignificance when compared to the injustice inflicted by chance upon the young couple, and the irreparable blow to their love occasioned by premature or involuntary parenthood.

For these reasons, in order that harmonious and happy marriage may be established as the foundation for happy homes and the advent of healthy and desired children, premature parenthood must be avoided. Birth Control is the instrument by which this universal problem may be solved.

Moving Pictures Evoke Concern, 1922

Moving pictures, their educational influence for good or for bad, their growing importance as a factor in our civilization, the announced determination of those controlling the industry boldly to enter politics, and the desirability of regulation by law through censorship constitute a subject of acknowledged importance to the American people. . . .

The motion picture is a great invention, and it has become a powerful factor for good or bad in our civilization. It has great educational power for good or bad. It may educate young people in the ways of good citi-

SOURCE: A speech by Senator Henry Myers, *Congressional Record*, June 29, 1922, 9655–57.

zenship or in ways of dissoluteness, extravagance, wickedness, and crime. It furnishes recreation, diversion, and amusement at a cheap price to many millions of our people—largely the young. It is the only form of amusement within the means of millions. It possesses great potential possibilities for good. It may furnish not only amusement but education of a high order.

Through motion pictures the young and the old may see depicted every good motive, laudable ambition, commendable characteristic, ennobling trait of humanity. They may be taught that honesty is the best policy; that virtue and worth are rewarded; that industry leads to success. Those who live in the country or in small interior towns, and who never visit large cities, may see pictured the skyscrapers, the crowded streets, the rush and jam of metropolitan cities. Those who live in the interior, and never see the seacoast, may see on the screen the great docks and wharves of seaports and see the loading and unloading of giant ocean steamers. Those who live in crowded cities, and never see the country or get a glimpse of country life, may have depicted to them all the beauties of rural life and scenery. All may see scenes of the luxuriant Tropics, the grandeur of Alpine Mountains, polar conditions, life in the Orient. The cities, palaces, cathedrals, ports, rural life, daily routine, scenic attractions, mode of living of every country on the globe, may be brought to our doors and eyes for a small price. The industry may be made an education to the young.

However, from all accounts, the business has been conducted, generally speaking, upon a low plane and in a decidedly sordid manner. Those who own and control the industry seem to have been of the opinion that the sensual, the sordid, the prurient, the phases of fast life, the ways of extravagance, the risqué, the paths of shady life, drew the greatest attendance and coined for them the most money, and apparently they have been out to get the coin, no matter what the effect upon the public, young or old; and when thoughtful people have suggested or advocated official censorship, in the interest of good citizenship and wholesome morals, the owners of the industry have resented it and, in effect, declared that it was nobody's business other than theirs and concerned nobody other than them what kind of shows they produced; that if people did not like their shows they could stay away from them; that it was their business, and they would conduct it as they might please. At least they have vigorously fought all attempts at censorship and resented them. . . .

I have no doubt young criminals got their ideas of the romance of crime from moving pictures. I believe moving pictures are doing as much harm to-day as saloons did in the days of the open saloon—especially to the young. They are running day and night, Sunday and every other day, the year round, and in most jurisdictions without any regulation by censorship. I would not abolish them. They can be made a great force for good. I would close them on Sunday and regulate them week days by judicious censorship. Already some dozen or more States have censorship laws, with the right of appeal to the courts, and the movement is on in many other States.

When we look to the source of the moving pictures, the material for them, the personnel of those who pose for them, we need not wonder that many of the pictures are pernicious.

The pictures are largely furnished by such characters as Fatty Arbuckle, of unsavory fame, notorious for his scandalous debauchery and drunken orgies, one of which, attended by many "stars," resulted in the death of Virginia Rappe, a star artist; William Desmond Taylor, deceased, murdered for some mysterious cause; one Valentino, now figuring as the star character in rape and divorce sensations. Many others of like character might be mentioned.

At Hollywood, Calif., is a colony of these people, where debauchery, riotous living, drunkenness, ribaldry, dissipation, free love, seem to be conspicuous. Many of these "stars," it is reported, were formerly bartenders, butcher boys, sopers, swampers, variety actors and actresses, who may have earned $10 or $20 a week, and some of whom are now paid, it is said, salaries of something like $5,000 a month or more, and they do not know what to do with their wealth, extracted from poor people, in large part, in 25 or 50 cent admission fees, except to spend it in riotous living, dissipation, and "high rolling."

These are some of the characters from whom the young people of to-day are deriving a large part of their education, views of life, and character-forming habits. From these sources our young people gain much of their views of life, inspiration, and education. Rather a poor source is it not? Looks like there is some need for censorship, does it not? There could be some improvement, could there not? . . .

Prohibition Nonobserved, 1931

There is a mass of information before us as to a general prevalence of drinking in homes, in clubs, and in hotels; of drinking parties given and attended by persons of high standing and respectability; of drinking by tourists at winter and summer resorts; and of drinking in connection with public dinners and at conventions. In the nature of the case it is not easy to get at the exact facts in such a connection, and conditions differ somewhat in different parts of the country and even to some extent from year to year. This is true likewise with respect to drinking by women and drinking by youth, as to which also there is a great mass of evidence. In weighing this evidence much allowance must be made for the effect of new standards of independence and individual self-assertion, changed ideas as

source: U.S. Congress, House, U.S. National Commission on Law Enforcement, *Enforcement of the Prohibition Laws of the United States*, H. Doc. 722, 71st Cong., 3d sess., 1931, 21.

to conduct generally, and the greater emphasis on freedom and the quest for excitement since the war. As to drinking among youth, the evidence is conflicting. Votes in colleges show an attitude of hostility to or contempt for the law on the part of those who are not unlikely to be leaders in the next generation. It is safe to say that a significant change has taken place in the social attitude toward drinking. This may be seen in the views and conduct of social leaders, business and professional men in the average community. It may be seen in the tolerance of conduct at social gatherings which would not have been possible a generation ago. It is reflected in a different way of regarding drunken youth, in a change in the class of excessive drinkers, and in the increased use of distilled liquor in places and connections where formerly it was banned. It is evident that, taking the country as a whole, people of wealth, business men and professional men, and their families, and, perhaps, the higher paid workingmen and their families, are drinking in large numbers in quite frank disregard of the declared policy of the National Prohibition Act. . . .

Chapter 10

The Depression Years

The crusades against changing morals and manners during the 1920s seem trivial when compared to the challenges of the Great Depression of the 1930s. Although the United States had suffered economic declines before, the Great Depression was the worst ever: nearly a quarter of the work force was unemployed by 1933, banks failed, the stock market crashed, businesses declared bankruptcy, and families lost their homes and farms.

In the essay "America's Families Face the Great Depression," Steven Mintz and Susan Kellogg discuss how individual families coped with the disaster. Note that hard times devastated urban and rural families, blacks and whites, and Americans of all classes. What does the essay reveal about the strengths and weaknesses of families facing unemployment and other economic hardships?

When relief funds ran out, families suvived as best they could. The first document consists of excerpts from the testimony of Jacob Billikopf, executive director of the Federation of Jewish Charities in Philadelphia, before a Senate subcom-

mittee studying the issue. What light does the document shed on the reasons why millions of Americans responded so positively to President Franklin Roosevelt's message of hope and to his New Deal programs of relief and public employment?

Rural families, as the essay informs us, also suffered. Many landowning farmers did not possess sufficient acreage to support themselves. And almost half of all American farmers, sharecroppers trapped in the grip of a brutal poverty, did not even own the land that they worked. Some left for the cities, while others survived on earnings that scarcely provided a decent standard of living. Perhaps no other group caught the public eye so much as the Okies—farmers from Texas, Oklahoma, and elsewhere on the southern plains who migrated to California, driven from their homes by poverty and great clouds of dust. John Steinbeck's novel The Grapes of Wrath *brought the plight of these dust bowl refugees to the attention of the public, as did the writings of political activist Carey McWilliams. The second document, a statement by McWilliams before a Congressional committee, describes the conditions facing the Okies in California. That the Okies continued to flock to and remain in California reveals the desperate situation from which they fled. Why did they choose California as the place to rebuild their lives?*

The final document tells about the miseries of black families—especially women—in Depression-era New York City. How does the reading support claims that African Americans were the poorest and most disadvantaged Americans during the 1930s? What does the document suggest about racism?

The New Deal programs, particularly those directed toward relief and reform, helped businesses, farmers, and workers survive the worst ravages of the 1930s, but economic woes persisted until the boom of World War II finally vanquished the Great Depression.

ESSAY

America's Families Face the Great Depression

Steven Mintz and Susan Kellogg

Late in 1930 a crisis occurred in the life of five-year-old Russell Baker.* His thirty-three-year-old father died suddenly of an acute diabetic coma, leaving Russell, his mother, and two sisters with only an aging Model T Ford, a few dollars of insurance money, and several pieces of Sears-Roebuck furniture. Having no way of making a living and no prospects for the future, Russell's mother decided to leave her home in rural Morrisonville, Virginia, and move in with a younger brother who lived in Belleville, New Jersey, a commuter town on the outskirts of Newark. But before she packed up the family's meager belongings, she did something that would haunt Russell for the rest of his life. To make herself and her children less of a burden, she gave up her dimpled, blond-haired, ten-month-old baby Audrey to a childless aunt and uncle.

Stories like Russell Baker's were commonplace during the Great Depression. Many families were unable to protect themselves against adversity. In Pennsylvania, coal-mining families crowded three or four families together in one-room shacks and lived on wild weeds. In Arkansas, families were found living in caves. In St. Louis, adults and children dug through garbage dumps for rotten food. In Oakland, California, whole families inhabited sewer pipes. And in Harlan County, Kentucky, families subsisted on dandelions and blackberries. President Hoover declared, "Nobody is actually starving. The hoboes are better fed than they have ever been." But in New York City in 1933 at least twenty-nine people died of hunger, and in 1934 official statistics indicated 110 deaths caused by starvation.

After more than half a century, the images of the Great Depression remain etched in the American psyche—breadlines and soup kitchens, tin-can shanties known as "Hoovervilles," penniless men and women selling apples on street corners, and gray battalions of Arkies and Okies packed into Model A Fords heading to California. The depression confronted families with economic crisis and uncertainty, with loss of support and sustenance. The economic disaster caused a major revolution in the lives and welfare of families in America and the government's role in securing them. It produced a new recognition that the federal government had an

SOURCE: Steven Mintz and Susan M. Kellogg, *Domestic Revolutions: A Social History of American Life*, 133–45. Reprinted with permission of The Free Press, A Division of Simon & Schuster. Copyright © 1988 by The Free Press.

*Russell Baker is a Pulitzer Prize–winning columnist for the *New York Times*.

obligation to intervene to provide security against the risks of hunger and destitution. The economic collapse of the 1930s created a new and more threatening kind of poverty as well as a federal response that permanently changed the meaning and experience of poverty.

"Mass unemployment," a depression-era journalist observed, "is both a statistic and an empty feeling in the stomach. To fully comprehend it, you have to both see the figures and feel the emptiness." The economic collapse of the 1930s was terrifying in its scope and impact. By 1933, 50 percent of the labor force in Cleveland and 80 percent of the work force in Toledo were out of work. A million were jobless in New York. The unemployment rate was higher and the duration of high unemployment was longer in the United States than in Britain, France, or Germany. Unemployment jumped from less than three million in 1929 to four million in 1930, eight million in 1931, and twelve-and-a-half million in 1932. The unemployment rate climbed from just 3.2 percent in 1929 to 8.7 percent in 1930, 15.9 percent in 1931, and 23.6 percent in 1932, and before 1941 never fell below 14.3 percent. Worse yet, few of the jobless found new work quickly. A sixth of the unemployed were out of work for more than two years, and a third walked the streets looking for employment for at least one year.

The collapse was staggering in its dimensions. By 1933 Americans had only 54 percent as much income as they had had in 1929 to purchase food and clothing, pay taxes, or repay debts. Average family income tumbled 40 percent from $2,300 in 1929 to just $1,500 four years later. During 1932, the worst year of the depression, 28 percent of the nation's households, containing thirty-four million men, women, and children, did not have a single employed wage earner. But even those fortunate enough to hold jobs suffered drastic pay cuts and reductions in hours. Only one company in ten did [not] reduce wages, and by mid-1932, three-quarters of the nation's workers were on part-time schedules.

The depression not only created poverty, it also brought preexisting poverty to public notice. As the economy contracted, it revealed poverty that had been largely ignored during the boom years of the 1920s. In 1929 the Brookings Institution estimated that just 8 percent of American families had incomes of more than $5,000 a year, that more than 60 percent of the nation's families earned less than $2,000 a year, and that 42 percent lived on less than $1,500 annually. "At 1929 prices," the Brookings Institution calculated, "a family income of $2,000 may be regarded as sufficient to supply only basic necessities." Hence, prior to the depression, nearly 60 percent of American families lived at or below a basic subsistence level.

During the first few years of the twentieth century, a combination of social developments had contributed to an increase of poverty. Growth in the number of "broken" families—fractured by death, divorce, and desertion—had been under way throughout the 1920s. A rapid increase in the number of older Americans over the age of sixty-five, from 4.9 million to 6.6 million, also contributed to the growing incidence of poverty. Joblessness was on the rise even before the stock market crash, climbing from 1.5 million in 1926 to perhaps 2.86 million in 1929. Tenant farming had been climbing since the start of the century, and soil depletion, farm mechanization, boll weevils, and deflated crop prices pushed a million Americans off farms during the 1920s.

Economic hardship and physical want were not new. Immigrants, the unskilled, and female-headed families had long faced the threat of destitution. Before the 1930s the loss of employment for several months a year was a normal event for industrial and unskilled workers. In predepression Massachusetts 25 percent of workers were unemployed for three months a year in prosperous times, and more than 40 percent were jobless for periods of four months or more in bad years.

What was new after 1929 was that the trauma of joblessness and loss of property began to affect families that had previously felt immune from such fears. Families that had spent a lifetime accumulating a savings account or acquiring a farm or house suddenly found themselves penniless or unable to pay off mortgages. A fifth of the nation's commercial banks closed their doors, and nine million families lost their savings. By 1934 more than half of all homeowners in Indianapolis, Indiana, and Birmingham, Alabama, had defaulted on their loans, as had two-fifths of all homeowners in twenty other cities.

The spread of poverty to previously untouched families created two discernible groups of poor. There were the traditional poor, including the families of tenant farmers (numbering 8,500,000 in 1930), members of single-parent families (10,500,000), the disabled (1,000,000), and the elderly (6,500,000), whose economic insecurity predated the depression and whose numbers had been on the rise before 1929. And there were the "new" poor, comprising thousands of formerly middle-class and working-class families who had been thrown out of work or off farms by industrial shutdowns or bankruptcy, their savings accounts exhausted and hopes of being able to meet mortgages and automobile payments steadily diminishing.

The upsurge in unemployment and poverty after 1929 created new political pressures to force the federal government to assume an active role in alleviating the sufferings caused by unemployment, dependency, and old age. But even then, as bold as its initiatives were, the social safety net erected by Franklin Roosevelt's New Deal established a two-tiered system of social provision that would treat the "old" poor and the "new" poor differently.

To some Americans during the 1930s, the depression seemed to have a salutory effect on the family. It encouraged members of the family to turn "toward each other with greater, more intelligent interdependence."

Despite fears that the family would disintegrate, optimists noted, the depression sharply curtailed activities outside the home and forced families to pool their resources and find comfort in each other. Divorce rates actually declined during the depression, and in popular magazines a new emphasis on familial "comradeship, understanding, affection, sympathy, facilitation, accommodation, integration, [and] cooperation" was apparent. Families began to play new games like Monopoly together and to listen to the radio or go to the movies together. As a Muncie, Indiana, newspaper editorialized, "Many a family that has lost its car has found its soul."

Others, however, believed that the economic downturn had an essentially destructive impact on the family. Unemployment, part-time work, reduced pay, lowered living standards, and the demands of needy relatives tore at the fabric of family life, devastated men's self-esteem, and undermined a family's self-respect. The rate of increase in divorce declined, to be sure, but rates of desertion soared, and by 1940 there were over 1,500,000 married women living apart from their husbands. Family disintegration was dramatically evident in the facts that the number of children placed in custodial institutions rose 50 percent during the first two years of the depression and that more than 200,000 vagrant children wandered about the country as a result of the break-ups of their homes. The destructive impact of the depression was especially apparent in the growing numbers of children suffering acute undernourishment and contracting such diseases as pellagra and rickets, which indicated nutritional deficiencies. Many young people, reported the Children's Bureau, found themselves "going for days at a time without taking off their clothes to sleep at night, becoming dirty, unkempt, a host to vermin. They may go for days with nothing to eat but coffee, bread and beans."

The Great Depression would leave an indelible mark on American family life. Not only did it throw breadwinners out of jobs and impoverish families, it forced many Americans to share living quarters with relatives, delay marriages, put off having children, or tolerate unhappy marriages for financial reasons. In many cities, particularly in the South, as many as one-sixth of all families "doubled up" in apartments in order to cut expenses. As the economy contracted, the marriage rate declined. In 1932 there were 250,000 fewer marriages than in 1929, and altogether 800,000 marriages were postponed by the depression. The fall in the marriage rate was accompanied by a sharp decline in the birthrate, as economic uncertainty forced people to have fewer children than they wanted. For the first time in American history, the birthrate dropped below the replacement level, and Americans had nearly three million fewer babies than they would have had at the 1929 birthrate. The divorce rate also fell for the simple reason that fewer families could afford one. Between 1930 and 1935, there were 170,000 fewer divorces than would have occurred had predepression trends continued.

The gravest effects of the depression on family life were largely invisible to the casual observer. The most common response to its harsh disruptions was denial of economic realities. Many families sought desperately to maintain their social status by postponing payments on loans and mortgages, taking second mortgages on real estate, depleting savings accounts, or borrowing against insurance policies before being willing to pare luxuries or other expenditures. "Status" expenditures persisted as families sought to disguise their economic straits by painting the exteriors of their houses or purchasing new shutters in order to impress neighbors. Unable to confront the loss of income and the loss of social position it entailed, they tried to forestall disaster for as long as possible.

Other families sought to cope by adopting more labor-intensive household practices, including planting gardens, canning foods, making clothing, and doing their own household repairs. Sales of electric toasters, mixers, percolators, and washing machines slumped, as many families attempted to pickle, preserve, and cure food, bake bread, and dye cloth. In 1931 sales of glass jars reached an eleven-year high even though demand for store-bought bottled and canned foods declined. Falling back on their own resources, many Americans tried to return to an earlier state of self-sufficiency. Unemployed Massachusetts textile workers set up looms in their living rooms. Wives and mothers throughout the nation tried to earn supplementary income by taking in sewing or laundry or by dressmaking, performing manicures for a dollar, setting up parlor groceries, or feeding and housing boarders.

Pooling family incomes provided another buffer against loss of work. The 1930 census indicated that one-third of all American families had more than one wage earner and that a quarter had three or more income earners. Part-time jobs for children—running errands, mowing lawns, baby-sitting, and selling newspapers and magazines, shining shoes, carting groceries, or returning pop bottles for two cents apiece—supplemented their father's income. Altogether, half of the nation's unemployed lived in a household in which someone was working.

People turned to creative economies to meet the exigencies of the depression. They bought day-old bread, handed down old clothing, reused razor blades, used cardboard and cotton for shoe soles, and relined coats with old blankets. To cut expenses and avoid embarrassment, social interaction with friends and neighbors was sharply restricted. In New Haven, Connecticut, just 3 percent of the adults questioned said they still attended parties, and only 25 percent continued to visit neighbors. Club memberships and extracurricular school activities were also restricted, and fewer family members went to pool halls, bowling alleys, or boxing rings.

Given the inadequacy of public and private charity, individuals relied on kinship ties to provide financial support to relatives outside their immediate family, particularly elderly parents. Forty percent of the working wives in Cleveland, Ohio, and 50 percent of those in Utah contributed income to relatives living outside their home.

The economic dislocations caused by the depression had a powerful effect on the father's stature as economic provider and disciplinarian. Many fathers were overwhelmed by guilt because they were unable to support their families. One father told a *New York Daily News* reporter in 1932: "I haven't had a steady job in more than two years. Sometimes I feel like a murderer. What's wrong with me, that I can't protect my children?" And in truth, unemployment often significantly lowered the status of the husband within the family and undermined his role as primary decision maker. The inability to support their families proved to be psychologically debilitating for many men, who lost their sense of self-respect and were unable effectively to look for work. One wife commented, "they're not men anymore, if you know what I mean."

The father's diminished stature was mirrored by a great increase in the money-saving and -earning roles of mothers inside the family. Sociologists Robert and Helen Lynd were impressed by the profound changes that took place in women's roles during the depression in contrast to the fixity of men's roles. Despite widespread public hostility—evident in a Gallup poll indicating that 80 percent of men opposed employment for their wives under almost any circumstances—growing numbers of married women entered the paid labor force during the depression. Among families of high economic and educational attainment there was a marked relaxation in husbands' attitudes toward the employment of their wives. In Berkeley, California, nearly 40 percent of all wives worked at some point during the depression, and in rural Mississippi, two-thirds of all female textile workers were married.

In most cases women's occupational opportunities were narrowly circumscribed, hours exceedingly long, and pay low. In 1930 out of every ten working women, three were engaged in domestic service, two worked in textile or apparel factories, and one worked as a schoolteacher or nurse. In black families the economic contributions of married women were particularly great. Forty percent of black women were in the labor force at any time, against just 20 percent of white women.

Although economic loss and hardship visited all sections of the country, the effects of the depression varied widely according to region, class, race, gender, and age. All groups suffered. Between 1929 and 1933, doctors and lawyers saw their incomes fall as much as 40 percent; salaries of the most highly skilled New York stenographers tumbled from $40 a week to just $16; in Chicago, a majority of working women toiled for less than twenty-five cents an hour. Even among the privileged, some suffered. One-third of the Harvard class of 1911 confessed that they were hard up, on relief, or dependent on relatives. But the most severe economic hardship fell on those groups already trapped in poverty or in low-paid, unskilled jobs.

The plight of the elderly became increasingly desperate during these years. A Long Beach, California, physician looked out his window and saw three haggard old women bending over garbage cans, "clawing into the contents." Eighty-seven percent of older Americans had been self-supporting in 1910; this figure had declined to 67 percent in 1922 and 60 percent in 1930, even before the full impact of the depression had been felt. By 1940 two-thirds of all older Americans were dependent wholly or partly on public relief, private charity, or friends and relatives.

The depression also brought new hardships to the lives of younger Americans. Many families were so needy that their children went hungry. A fifth of New York City's children suffered from malnutrition, and in coal-mining areas of Illinois, Kentucky, Ohio, Pennsylvania, and West Virginia malnutrition was said to be over 90 percent. When a teacher told a young girl to go home to eat, the child replied, "I can't. This is my sister's day to eat."

Many children also lacked the opportunity to pursue an education. In 1932, a third of a million children could not attend school because their classrooms were closed for lack of funds. Schools in Dayton, Ohio, were open just three days a week, and more than three hundred Arkansas schools were shut for ten months or more.

To help their families make ends meet, many children were expected to find some sort of job. A Los Angeles family subsisted on a teenage daughter's earnings as a five-and-ten-cent-store clerk. Russell Baker was forced to go to work at the tender age of eight. In Oakland, California, 50 percent of all teenage boys and 25 percent of all teenage girls took up part-time jobs as baby-sitters, janitor's assistants, store clerks, and delivery boys.

Midwestern and Southern farmers were in particularly desperate straits. Take the example of the Gudgers, a white southern Alabama cotton share-cropping family of six. From their landlord, they received twenty acres of land, seed, an unpainted one-room house, a shed, a mule, and fertilizer as well as ration money of ten dollars a month. In return, they owed him half their corn and cotton crops, half their cottonseed, and 8 percent interest on their debts. By 1934, they were eighty dollars in debt; by 1935, their debts had risen another twelve dollars.

Few images have left a deeper imprint on the nation's historical memory than the picture of Midwestern or Southern farm families piling their meager possessions into an aging Ford jalopy and heading off to California. During the Great Depression, as many as a million Dust Bowl refugees and tenant farmers took to the nation's highways and railroads. Railroad officials in Kansas City counted 1,500 transients a day hitching rides on freight trains, and municipal officials in towns in Arizona, New Mexico, and Texas witnessed an influx of as many as 200 migrants a day. The Southern Pacific Railroad boasted that it threw 683,000 vagrants off its trains in 1931. Free public flophouses and missions in Los Angeles provided beds for 200,000 of the uprooted.

Many of the migrants were farmers and farm laborers, lured away from

191

debt-ridden farms by the hopes of jobs and a better life in the nation's cities but also pushed off the land by farm mechanization, shifts in consumer demand, and a drought that turned fertile land to dust. The trend toward mechanized farming was disastrous for small farmers and tenant farmers. Particularly in the South, draft animals were replaced by tractors, trucks, and combines, allowing a single farm family to perform the work formerly done by a dozen members of a threshing and harvest crew. Mechanization permitted many farmers to substitute their sons and daughters for hired help. As a result, 514,000 farm workers lost their jobs.

Displaced farmers and farm workers headed westward to California or northward to the industrial Midwest. Noted one observer: "They roll westward like a parade. In a single hour from a grassy meadow near an Idaho road I counted 34 automobiles with the license plates of states between Chicago and the mountains." Whole counties were depopulated. In 1936 seven counties in southeastern Colorado reported only 2,078 houses still occupied; 2,811 houses were abandoned and another 1,522 homes had disappeared.

Black Americans suffered during the depression with particular intensity. A year after the stock market crash, 32 percent of adult blacks were jobless in Baltimore, 38 percent in Pittsburgh, 70 percent in Charleston, and 75 percent in Memphis. In Chicago, 58 percent of black women were unemployed; in Detroit, 75 percent.

Hardship was particularly acute in the South, where three-fourths of the black population lived. In Macon County, Alabama, the site of Booker T. Washington's famous Tuskegee Institute, thirty miles east of Montgomery, black families lived in abysmal conditions of poverty. Their diet consisted almost entirely of salt pork, hominy grits, corn bread, and molasses. Red meat, fresh vegetables, fruit, and even milk were almost unknown luxuries. Most dwellings had dirt floors, no windows or screens, and almost no furniture. A fifth of the homes had no water; three-quarters had no sewage disposal. Privies were only constructed when underbrush was not nearby. Black income in Macon County averaged less than a dollar a day.

Before the depression, rural black Southerners suffered extreme poverty, but the economic crisis of the 1930s greatly worsened their position. Payment for picking a hundred pounds of cotton fell to twenty cents, a rate that amounted to sixty cents for a fourteen-hour day. Many sharecropping families were given cash advances of as little as ten dollars a month to support families of six or eight. Throughout the South the depression eliminated substantial numbers of jobs traditionally held by blacks in the building trades, street cleaning, garbage collecting, and domestic service.

Conditions were equally distressed in the North, where three million black Americans made their homes. In Chicago and in other large cities, the bulk of the black residents made their homes in what were euphemistically called "kitchenettes." Six-room apartments, previously rented for $50 a month, were divided into six kitchenettes renting for $8 a week, assuring landlords of a windfall of an extra $142 a month. Kitchenettes typically contained an icebox, a gas hot plate, and a single bed. A bathroom that once served a single family was now shared by six. A typical building that previously held sixty families now contained three hundred.

Northern blacks lived at the very bottom of the economic scale. During the depths of the depression, when the Works Progress Administration estimated that a family of four needed an income of $973 per year to support a minimum subsistence budget, more than 70 percent of Chicago's black families had annual incomes of less than $1000 and a third earned less than $500.

The dissolution of lower-class black family life was one of the most distressing consequences of the depression. In Chicago two out of every five adult black women were without husbands, mainly because of early widowhood. In one neighborhood on Chicago's west side, half of all households lacked a husband or father. The underlying causes of family instability were high mortality rates and the precarious economic status of black men. High rates of unemployment, lack of stable jobs, and low wages all made it difficult for lower-class black men to function effectively as breadwinners.

The full brunt of depression hardship was felt by black Americans, but the public response was woefully inadequate. Even though black unemployment rates were consistently one-and-a-half times higher than the rates for whites, just 3 million black Americans—one out of four—received any public relief during the depression. Even when relief was given, black families often received less than their white counterparts. In Texas rural black families received a quarter less aid than white families on relief. In Jacksonville, Florida, whites received thirty cents an hour on work relief; blacks, only twenty cents. In Harlem three-fourths of all jobless black families received no relief payments at all. To survive the depression the nation's black families had to rely largely on their own financial and emotional resources.

The nation's Mexican American families also suffered greatly during the depression. Their plight is illustrated by an incident that occurred in San Antonio, Texas, in February 1930. Approximately five thousand Mexican Americans gathered at the city's railroad station to depart the United States for resettlement in Mexico. In August of that year a special train carried another two thousand to central Mexico. Most Americans are now familiar with the forced relocation in 1942 of 112,000 Japanese Americans from the West Coast to internment camps. Far fewer are aware that during the Great Depression the Federal Bureau of Immigration (after 1933, the Immigration and Naturalization Service) and local authorities rounded up naturalized Mexican American citizens and shipped them to Mexico to relieve U.S. welfare rolls. In a shameful episode in U.S. history, more than 400,000 *repatriados*, many of them American citizens by birth, were sent across the Mexico–U.S. border from Arizona, California, and Texas.

Large-scale Mexican migration to the Southwest dates back to the 1880s when western railroads, construction companies, steel mills, mines, and canneries recruited Mexicans as manual laborers. Immigration increased still further early in the twentieth century as a result of rapid population growth in Mexico, the social upheaval caused by the Mexican revolution, and the growth of large-scale commercial agriculture in Arizona's Salt River valley, Texas's lower Rio Grande valley, and California's Imperial and San Joaquin valleys. Increasingly, during the 1920s, Mexican Americans moved into urban areas, where they established themselves in neighborhoods called *colonias*.

Typically, life in a *colonia* was divided into subunits of one or two blocks called *barrios*, made up largely of extended families. Customarily second-generation Mexican Americans tended to cluster around the home of the husband's father; children of the third generation, in contrast, increasingly lived adjacent to the wife's father. In other words the extended family remained important as an organizing principle even though individual households tended not to consist of three generations of a family.

Even before the stock market collapse, there was intense pressure, spearheaded by the American Federation of Labor and municipal governments, to reduce the number of Mexican immigrants. Opposition from local chambers of commerce, economic development associations, and state farm bureaus stymied efforts to impose an immigration quota, but rigid enforcement of existing laws slowed legal entry. After President Herbert Hoover appointed William N. Doak as Secretary of Labor in 1930, the Bureau of Immigration launched intensive raids designed to identify Mexican aliens liable for deportation. These were accompanied by city and county efforts to repatriate destitute Mexican American families. Altogether [during Doak's tenure] approximately 82,400 Mexican Americans were involuntarily deported by the federal government. Many more left because of the threat of unemployment, deportation, or loss of relief payments.

New Deal

The plight of the nation's families on March 4, 1933, the day Franklin Roosevelt assumed the presidency, was truly miserable. Philadelphia had exhausted all available funds for poor relief. Detroit had been forced to strike a third of the families receiving aid from its relief rolls; St. Louis dropped half its families from relief. New Orleans refused new applications for relief, and Dallas and Houston refused to aid black and Mexican American families. More than a hundred cities provided no relief at all.

The economic crisis of the 1930s called into question two key tenets of American political life. First, the depression threw into disrepute the nation's faith in limited government and generated a conviction that the federal government had a positive duty to intervene to rescue families from poverty. Second, it toppled the notion that public assistance could be left to private charity and local government and created a consensus that the federal government had a responsibility to support the aged, provide jobs for the unemployed, and protect families' savings. Debate still rages over how successful Franklin Roosevelt's programs were in dealing with the problems posed by the depression. But there can be no doubt that the New Deal was a critical watershed in the history of the American family, because for the first time the federal government became a major guarantor of family welfare.

During the Progressive Era, coalitions of reformers, progressive business associations, trade unions, and farmers had limited success in establishing a small number of social insurance schemes. Between 1911 and 1919, thirty-eight states adopted workers' compensation laws, and another thirty-nine instituted pensions for needy mothers with dependent children. In 1920 the federal government enacted a program of compulsory old age and disability insurance for its half-million civil servants. Six states followed suit before 1929, and most cities established limited pensions for police officers, fire fighters, and teachers. Private retirement plans remained extremely unusual, and private companies provided pensions to fewer than 50,000 beneficiaries.

The Great Depression revealed the total inadequacy of the nation's existing welfare programs. Local resources quickly proved inadequate to meet the growing need. In Chicago in 1931, 624,000 men and women—40 percent of the city's work force—walked the streets looking for jobs. Each day, these people lost $2 million in wages, but the city could provide only $100,000 in relief. In Philadelphia, private and public charities distributed $1 million a month in poor relief, providing families with only $1.50 to $2.00 a week for groceries. By June 1932 even these meager funds were exhausted. The same story was repeated throughout the nation. In south Texas the Salvation Army was forced to reduce its allocation for feeding each client to a penny a day. By early 1932, 20,000 children had been placed in institutions or foster homes because their parents could no longer support them. Total public and private expenditures on relief in 1932 amounted to only $317 million, less than $27 for each of the twelve million jobless.

Virtually every domestic government program enacted during the depression decade touched the nations' families. To reduce unemployment among the young, the Roosevelt administration created the Civilian Conservation Corps in April 1933. To fund state-run welfare programs, the New Deal established the Federal Emergency Relief Administration in May 1933. To provide jobs for 4 million jobless families, the Civil Works Administration was set up in November 1933, followed by the Works Progress Administration in May 1935.

Washington would enact several thousand pieces of legislation that would directly affect the welfare of the nation's families. . . .

DOCUMENTS

The Great Depression in Philadelphia, 1933

Relief stopped in Philadelphia on June 25 [1932]. For months previously 52,000 destitute families had been receiving modest grocery orders and a little milk.

The average allowance to a family at that time was about $4.35 per week, no provision being made for fuel, clothing, rent or any of the minimum accessories that go to make up the family budget.

Their rent was unpaid, their credit and their borrowing power exhausted. Most of them were absolutely dependent for existence on the food orders supplied through State funds administered by the Committee for Unemployment Relief. Then there were no more funds, and relief— except for a little milk for half-sick children, and a little Red Cross flour— was suddenly discontinued. And Philadelphia asked itself what was happening to these 52,000 families. There were no reports of people starving in the streets, and yet from what possible source were 52,000 families getting enough food to live on?

It was a fair question and the Community Council under the direction of Mr. Ewan Clague, a competent economist and in charge of its Research Bureau, set out to find the answer by a special study of 400 families who had been without relief for a period varying from 10 to 25 days. The families were not picked out as the worst cases, but as stated before were fairly typical of the 52,000.

According to Mr. Clague, and I am quoting him quite liberally, the count of the 400 families showed a total of 2,464 persons. The great majority ranged from five to eight persons per family.

In their effort to discover how these 2,464 human beings were keeping themselves alive the investigators inquired into the customary sources of family maintenance, earnings, savings, regular help from relatives, credit and, last but not least, the neighbors.

SOURCE: Jacob Billikopf, testimony from U.S. Congress, Senate Subcommittee of the Committee on Manufacturers, Hearings, *Federal Aid for Unemployment Relief*, 72d Cong., 2d sess., 1933, 8–11.

Some current income in the form of wages was reported by 128 families, though the amounts were generally small and irregular, two or three dollars a week perhaps, earned on odd jobs, by selling knickknacks on the street or by youngsters delivering papers or working nights. For the whole 128 the average wage income was $4.16 a week and 272 families of the 400 had no earnings whatsoever.

Savings were an even more slender resource. Only 54 families reported savings and most of these were nothing more than small industrial insurance policies with little or no cash surrender value, technically an asset, actually an item of expense. This does not mean that these families had not had savings—take for instance, the Baker family—father, mother, and four children. They had had $1,000 in a building and loan association which failed. They had had more than $2,000 in a savings bank, but the last cent had been withdrawn in January, 1931. They had had three insurance policies, which had been surrendered one by one. Both the father and the oldest son were tubercular, the former at the moment being an applicant for sanitarium care. This family—intelligent, clean, thrifty, and likable—one of thousands at the end of their rope—had had savings as a resource even a year ago, but not now.

The same situation, it was found, prevailed in regard to regular help from relatives. In the early stages of the depression a large proportion of relief families could count on this help in some form. But of our 400 families only 33 reported assistance from kinsfolk that could be counted on, and this assistance was slender indeed: A brother paid the rent to save eviction, a brother-in-law guaranteed the gas and electric bills, a grandmother, working as a scrubwoman, put in a small sum each week. Most of the relatives it was found were so hard pressed that it was all they could do to save themselves. As a matter of fact many relatives had moved in with the families and were recorded as members of the household.

In the absence of assets or income the next line of defense is credit. But most of the 400 families were bogged down in debt and retained only a vestige of credit. Take the item of rent or building and loan payments: Three hundred and forty-nine of the families were behind—some only a month or two, some for a year, a few for two or three years, with six months as the average for the group. . . .

Thus, then, the picture of the 400 families shaped itself. Generally no income, such as there was slight, irregular and undependable; shelter still available so long as landlords remained lenient; savings gone, credit exhausted.

But what of food, the never ending, ever pressing necessity for food? In this emergency the outstanding contribution has been made by neighbors. The poor are looking after the poor. In considerably more than a third of the 400 families the chief source of actual subsistence when grocery orders stopped was the neighbors. The supply was by no means regular or adequate but in the last analysis, when all other resources failed the neighbors rallied to tide the family over a few days. Usually it was leftovers, stale bread, meat bones for soup, a bowl of gravy. Sometimes the children are asked in for a meal. One neighbor sent two eggs a day regularly to a sick man threatened with tuberculosis. This help was the more striking since the neighbors themselves were often close to the line of destitution and could illy spare the food they shared. The primitive communism existing among these people was a constant surprise to the visitors. More than once a family lucky enough to get a good supply of food called in the entire block to share the feast. There is absolutely no doubt that entire neighborhoods were just living from day to day sharing what slight resources any one family chanced to have. Without this mutual help the situation of many of the families would have been desperate.

As a result of all these efforts, what did these families have? What meals did they get and of what did these meals consist? About 8 per cent of the total number were subsisting on one meal a day. Many more were getting only two meals a day, and still others were irregular, sometimes one meal, sometimes two, occasionally by great good fortune, three. Thirty-seven per cent of all families were not getting the normal three meals a day.

When the content of these meals is taken into consideration the facts are still more alarming. Four families had absolutely no solid food whatever—nothing but a drink, usually tea or coffee. Seventy-three others had only one food and one drink for all meals, the food in many cases being bread made from Red Cross flour. Even in the remaining cases, where there were two or three articles of food, the diets day after day and week after week consisted usually of bread, macaroni, spaghetti, potatoes, with milk for the children. Many families were getting no meat and very few vegetables. Fresh fruits were never mentioned, although it is possible that the family might pick these up in the streets occasionally.

These diets were exceedingly harmful in their immediate effects on some of the families where health problems are present. In a number of cases the children are definitely reported on a hospital diagnosis as anemic. Occasionally the adults are likewise affected. The MacIntyre family for instance: These two older people have an adopted child 8 years of age. The husband is a bricklayer by trade and the wife can do outside housework. They have had occasional odd jobs over the past year but have been very hard pressed. For the three meals immediately preceding the visit they reported the menus as follows: Dinner, previous day, bread and coffee; breakfast, bread and coffee; lunch, corn, fish, bread, and coffee; one quart of milk for the little girl for the entire three meals.

Also their health problems were serious. The wife has had several operations, the husband is a possible tuberculosis case, and the child is underweight. All three have also been receiving medical attention from a hospital for the past three years. The little girl has been nervous, has fainted at times, and is slightly deformed from rickets. Being undernourished, she needs cod-liver oil, milk, oranges, and the food which was possible only when the family was on relief. She went to camp for two weeks and returned up to weight and in good spirits. But relief was cut off while she was away, and she came back to meals of milk, coffee, and bread. In the short time at home she had become fretful and listless, refusing to take anything but milk. This whole family promised to be in serious health difficulties if their situation were long continued.

The Okies in California, 1939

The most characteristic of all housing in California in which migrants reside at the moment is the shacktown or cheap subdivision. Most of these settlements have come into existence since 1933 and the pattern which obtains is somewhat similar throughout the State. Finding it impossible to rent housing in incorporated communities on their meager incomes, migrants have created a market for a very cheap type of subdivision of which the following may be taken as being representative:

In Monterey County, according to a report of Dr. D. M. Bissell, county health officer, under date of November 28, 1939, there are approximately three well-established migrant settlements. One of these, the development around the environs of Salinas, is perhaps the oldest migrant settlement of its type in California. In connection with this development I quote a paragraph of the report of Dr. Bissell:

"This area is composed of all manners and forms of housing without a public sewer system. Roughly, 10,000 persons are renting or have established homes there. A chief element in this area is that of refugees from the Dust Bowl who inhabit a part of Alisal called Little Oklahoma. Work in lettuce harvesting and packing and sugar beet processing have attracted these people who, seeking homes in Salinas without success because they aren't available, have resorted to makeshift adobes outside the city limits. Complicating the picture is the impermeable substrata which makes septic tanks with leaching fields impractical. Sewer wells have resulted with the corresponding danger to adjacent water wells and to the water wells serving the Salinas public. Certain districts, for example, the Airport Tract and parts of Alisal, have grown into communities with quite satisfactory housing, but others as exemplified by the Graves district are characterized by shacks and lean-tos which are unfit for human habitation.". . .

source: Carey McWilliams, testimony from U.S. Congress, House Select Committee to Investigate the Interstate Migration of Destitute Citizens, *Hearings*, 76th Cong., 3d sess., 1941, 2543–44.

Typical of the shacktown problem are two such areas near the city limits of Sacramento, one on the east side of B Street, extending from Twelfth Street to the Sacramento city dump and incinerator; and the other so-called Hoovertown, adjacent to the Sacramento River and the city filtration plant. In these two areas there were on September 17, 1939, approximately 650 inhabitants living in structures that, with scarcely a single exception, were rated by the inspectors of this division as "unfit for human occupancy." The majority of the inhabitants were white Americans, with the exception of 50 or 60 Mexican families, a few single Mexican men, and a sprinkling of Negroes. For the most part they are seasonally employed in the canneries, the fruit ranches, and the hop fields of Sacramento County. Most of the occupants are at one time or another upon relief, and there are a large number of occupants in these shacktowns from the Dust Bowl area. Describing the housing, an inspector of this division reports:

"The dwellings are built of brush, rags, sacks, boxboard, odd bits of tin and galvanized iron, pieces of canvas and whatever other material was at hand at the time of construction."

Wood floors, where they exist, are placed directly upon the ground, which because of the location of the camps with respect to the Sacramento River, is damp most of the time. To quote again from the report:

"Entire families, men, women, and children, are crowded into hovels, cooking and eating in the same room. The majority of the shacks have no sinks or cesspools for the disposal of kitchen drainage, and this, together with garbage and other refuse, is thrown on the surface of the ground."

Because of the high-water table, cesspools, where they exist, do not function properly; there is a large overflow of drainage and sewage to the surface of the ground. Many filthy shack latrines are located within a few feet of living quarters. Rents for the houses in these shacktowns range from $3 to $20 a month. In one instance a landlord rents ground space for $1.50 to $5 a month, on which tenants are permitted to erect their own dugouts. The Hooverville section is composed primarily of tents and trailers, there being approximately 125 tent structures in this area on September 17, 1939. Both areas are located in unincorporated territory. They are not subject at the present time to any State or county building regulation. In Hooverville, at the date of the inspection, many families were found that did not have even a semblance of tents or shelters. They were cooking and sleeping on the ground in the open and one water tap at an adjoining industrial plant was found to be the source of the domestic water supply for the camp. . . .

The Bronx Slave Market, 1935

The Bronx Slave Market! What is it? Who are its dealers? Who are its victims? What are its causes? How far does its stench spread? What forces are at work to counteract it?

Any corner in the congested sections of New York City's Bronx is fertile soil for mushroom "slave marts." The two where the traffic is heaviest and the bidding is highest are located at 167th street and Jerome avenue and at Simpson and Westchester avenues. . . .

. . . Not only is human labor bartered and sold for slave wage, but human love also is a marketable commodity. But whether it is labor or love that is sold, economic necessity compels the sale. As early as 8 A.M. they come; as late as 1 P.M. they remain.

Rain or shine, cold or hot, you will find them there—Negro women, old and young—sometimes bedraggled, sometimes neatly dressed—but with the invariable paper bundle, waiting expectantly for Bronx housewives to buy their strength and energy for an hour, two hours, or even for a day at the munificent rate of fifteen, twenty, twenty-five, or, if luck be with them, thirty cents an hour. If not the wives themselves, maybe their husbands, their sons, or their brothers, under the subterfuge of work, offer worldly-wise girls higher bids for their time.

Who are these women? What brings them here? Why do they stay? In the boom days before the onslaught of the depression in 1929, many of these women who are now forced to bargain for day's work on street corners, were employed in grand homes in the rich Eighties, or in wealthier homes in Long Island and Westchester, at more than adequate wages. Some are former marginal industrial workers, forced by the slack in industry to seek other means of sustenance. In many instances there had been no necessity for work at all. But whatever their standing prior to the depression, none sought employment where they now seek it. They come to the Bronx, not because of what it promises, but largely in desperation.

Paradoxically, the crash of 1929 brought to the domestic labor market a new employer class. The lower middle-class housewife, who, having dreamed of the luxury of a maid, found opportunity staring her in the face in the form of Negro women pressed to the wall by poverty, starvation and discrimination.

Where once color was the "gilt edged" security for obtaining domestic and personal service jobs, here, even Negro women found themselves being displaced by whites. Hours of futile waiting in employment agencies, the fee that must be paid despite the lack of income, fraudulent agencies that sprung up during the depression, all forced the day worker to fend for herself or try the dubious and circuitous road to public relief.

SOURCE: Ella Baker and Marvel Cooke in *The Crisis* 42 (November 1935): 331.

As inadequate as emergency relief has been, it has proved somewhat of a boon to many of these women, for with its advent, actual starvation is no longer their ever-present slave driver and they have been able to demand twenty-five and even thirty cents an hour as against the old fifteen and twenty cent rate. In an effort to supplement the inadequate relief received, many seek this open market.

And what a market! She who is fortunate (?) enough to please Mrs. Simon Legree's* scrutinizing eye is led away to perform hours of multifarious household drudgeries. Under a rigid watch, she is permitted to scrub floors on her bended knees, to hang precariously from window sills, cleaning window after window, or to strain and sweat over steaming tubs of heavy blankets, spreads and furniture covers.

Fortunate, indeed, is she who gets the full hourly rate promised. Often, her day's slavery is rewarded with a single dollar bill or whatever her unscrupulous employer pleases to pay. More often, the clock is set back for an hour or more. Too often she is sent away without any pay at all.

---

*Mrs. Simon Legree is a reference to the wife of the villain of *Uncle Tom's Cabin.*

Chapter 11

World War II: The Home Front

The New Deal exerted an enormous impact on American society. For the embat-
tled farmers and workers and their families described in the previous chapter, the
federal government offered relief, mortgage aid, crop payments, and even employ-
ment—programs that helped to restore the nation's flagging morale and maintain
the people's faith in their government and economic system.

Yet as dramatic and innovative as the New Deal was, World War II brought
even more upheavals in the lives of Americans. Nearly 15 million men and
women found themselves serving in the armed forces, and the government inter-
vened in an unprecedented way in the economy. Rationing of such products as
butter, meat, sugar, and gasoline was introduced, and war contracts, initiated as
early as 1939, stimulated the manufacture of millions of uniforms and the pro-
duction of hundreds of thousands of ships, airplanes, tanks, and pieces of military

equipment. While millions served in the army, navy, air force, and marines, many civilians flocked to urban centers to work in the booming military economy.

William O'Neill's essay "The People Are Willing" describes numerous changes unfolding during this period, changes that enabled the United States to outproduce its enemies and win the war. But as O'Neill notes, innovations did not always come easily. What does he identify as the major challenges in uniting the American people and its economic system behind the war effort? How does he account for the many difficulties and government "bungling," especially in the early days of the war? Finally, how did the nation eventually achieve both full production and unity of purpose?

O'Neill's essay also discusses the impact of the war on particular groups. The first document is by a young man who joined the navy in 1939, nearly two years before America entered the conflict. Why did this young man leave his farm for the navy, and what does his choice indicate about the connection between the coming war and the eventual end of the Great Depression?

The essay also points to major changes in the lives of American women, among them the appearance of Rosie the Riveter, symbol of those who took wartime jobs formerly considered strictly for men. There were many Rosies, but recent studies reveal that the Rosie image may have been somewhat exaggerated: in many instances, women remained confined to a separate, limited sphere of opportunities. How does the second document, the recollections of a former defense worker, support this contention?

Although the nation achieved full employment during the war, the dislocations of those years spawned new problems. Children often fell victim to the disruptions of wartime society; at the height of the conflict, some localities reported increases of as much as 50 percent in the rate of juvenile delinquency. In the final document, Katherine Lenroot, chief of the Children's Bureau of the Department of Labor, discusses the forces driving juvenile delinquency and a relaxation of moral standards. Although many of these conditions were aggravated by the war and disappeared with the return of peace, can you identify some that persist today?

E S S A Y

The People Are Willing
William O'Neill

After Pearl Harbor a flood of volunteers overwhelmed recruiting offices, especially in the South. When the entire Lepanto, Arkansas football team joined the Navy, one member attempted suicide after failing to pass his physical. "I was afraid folks would think I was yellow because I didn't get into the service," he explained. Millions who were ineligible to serve wished to know what civilians could do to further the war effort. . . .

Most Americans believed that government did not need to be overly effective because the people themselves could manage. While they overstated its benefits, voluntarism was a fact of life, and Americans were capable—within limits—of doing what elsewhere were functions of government. This attribute manifested itself immediately after Pearl Harbor. Agencies like the Red Cross and local civilian defense offices were overwhelmed with offers to help. Because many commodities would soon be scarce, scrap drives were organized that collected not only rubber items but paper, fats, bones, a wide variety of metal goods, and other essential materials.

Towns convened meetings to discuss ways of aiding the war effort. Citizens' committees sprang up. Neighborhoods organized. When a Milwaukee air-raid warden could not afford a telephone, the other families on his block agreed to donate 10 cents a month apiece so he could subscribe to the service. In Chicago 23,000 block captains were sworn in at a mass ceremony by the head of the Office of Civilian Defense. West Coast hospitals reeled before waves of enthusiastic blood donors. The hottest literary property of 1942 was the Red Cross first aid manual, which, though not considered a book and therefore omitted from best seller lists, sold 8 million copies. Farmers began plowing at night in order to put their spring crops in early. Shipyard employees in San Francisco offered to work Sundays for free. That summer an event called The National Salvage Fair was held in New York as part of a campaign to establish Salvage Sewing Workrooms in which volunteers could use mill ends and scraps of cloth to make garments for the needy and establish a clothing reserve.

Though very much in the American grain, efforts such as these suffered from the limitations intrinsic to thousands of uncoordinated local schemes, often inspired by an excess of willing hands rather than any clear sense of purpose. By summer *Life* was overflowing with complaints. Congress was not doing a good job. Neither were the people. All the powerful interest

SOURCE: William O'Neill, *A Democracy at War: America's Fight at Home and Abroad in World War II*, The Free Press, 129–142, 247–250. Abridged and reprinted with the permission of The Free Press, a division of Simon & Schuster. Copyright © 1993 by William L. O'Neill.

groups continued to pursue their own agendas. Every scrap campaign had failed, the rubber drive most of all. People were still motoring frivolously. Washington was asking too little, and getting what it asked for. Everyone was living their dream of a "Hollywood war," instead of facing up to the real one in which sacrifices would have to be made.

These complaints were well founded. In 1941 when aluminum was in short supply, the call went out for housewives to turn in their pots and pans. Ten thousand tons of aluminum would build 4,000 fighter planes was what they were told. Obedient to duty's call, women stripped their kitchens and donated 70,000 tons of aluminum, apparently solving the problem. It transpired that only virgin aluminum was suitable for aircraft, so the donated cookware gathered dust until it was finally sold to scrap dealers. Then the stuff was turned into new pots and pans, women buying back what they had previously given.

More serious than bungling was government's reluctance to take full advantage of civilian support for the war effort, especially that of women. The public was encouraged to buy war bonds and practice conservation. Otherwise, it often seemed as if Washington did not want public participation in national defense, which had been the case before Pearl Harbor. In January 1941 one of Dr. Gallup's polls had revealed that 67 percent of those questioned were willing "to spend one hour each day training for home guard, nursing, first aid work, ambulance driving," and similar activities.

Though officials frequently remarked on the gravity of the world situation and the need to prepare for hardships, they seldom took their own advice. When asked what people could do, Frank Bane, Chief of the National Defense Advisory Commission's Division on State and Local Cooperation, suggested that it might be nice if women living near Army posts would help entertain the troops. They could also work as volunteers in the overburdened health and welfare programs of "war boom" towns, laudable suggestions, to be sure, but hardly a call to action.

In August the president of the General Federation of Women's Clubs—an old, large, and conservative body—complained that women were being discriminated against "intolerably" in the civil-defense program. The Office of Civilian Defense did not even have a women's division. There were only seven women in the entire federal government at the policymaking level. Women were excluded from serving in Civil Aeronautics Authority programs for training student pilots. The female Assistant National Civilian Defense Director had just resigned because Director Fiorello La Guardia disapproved of her effort to have the WPA survey and catalogue volunteer associations around the country, many of them women's groups, as possible contributors to civil defense.

Women were joining the Red Cross and other emergency related bodies in large numbers, but not because government was encouraging them to, or promising that if war came it would utilize their services. This lack of interest would not change very much after Pearl Harbor. In the age of total war the United States would make a semitotal effort, a limitation that was prefigured by government's earlier policy on civilian defense. This prejudice against women would seriously weaken the war effort.

It was obvious that vast numbers of men in uniform would be performing clerical tasks and other duties that were not gender-specific. Yet military leaders were slow to admit that women could do these jobs as well, if not better than, men, thereby freeing able-bodied males for combat. Early in 1942 the Army agreed to accept 10,000 volunteers for a Women's Army Auxiliary Corps only because a bill introduced in Congress by Representative Edith Nourse Rogers (R, MA) forced its hand. The Navy went on refusing to accept women in any capacity. There were plenty of men as yet undrafted, the military's reasoning went—which was true at the time, but this surplus did not last, forcing a change of heart. . . .

Lacking official outlets, women formed numerous paramilitary groups of their own, including the Powder Puff Platoon of Joplin, Missouri, the Green Guards of Washington, and the Women's Defense School of Boston, which taught a course in field cooking modeled on that of the Army. Some 25,000 women volunteered for the Women's Ambulance and Defense Corps of America, whose slogan was "The Hell We Can't." Its more than 50 chapters trained women to serve as air-raid wardens, security guards, and couriers for the armed forces. However, most who wished to contribute joined the Red Cross, which, with 3.5 million female volunteers, was by far the most important outlet for patriotic womanhood.

Some government agencies actually recognized opportunity when they saw it. The Office of Civilian Defense employed a number of female volunteers. The Office of Price Administration used 50,000 women in five states to conduct a three-day canvas in July 1942, during which they briefed 450,000 retailers on the new price regulations. For the most part, though, except for defense contractors who gradually warmed to the idea of hiring women workers, volunteer organizations remained the main outlets.

Of these latter groups, the most controversial was the American Women's Voluntary Services, founded by a group of Anglophile socialites in 1940 to prepare women for emergency work in a London-style blitz. It soon enrolled 350,000 members in almost every state. To refute mockers who accused them of being social butterflies out on a lark, AWVS cast a remarkably broad net for the times, organizing several units in Harlem, at least one Chinese chapter, a number of Hispanic units, and one affiliate consisting entirely of Taos tribeswomen. Defying local taboos, the New Orleans chapter bravely included Negro women. When it became evident that America was not going to be attacked by German bombers, the AWVS took on new assignments. In New York members sold $5 million worth of war bonds. In California there were AWVS "chuckwagons" that delivered food, including late-night snacks, to Coast Guard stations and remote military sites. In San

Francisco AWVS women taught Braille to blinded veterans. Others organized agricultural work camps in California and Colorado. Some New York suburbs had ambulances staffed entirely by AWVS members.

Though it was the biggest, AWVS was by no means the only volunteer women's organization that made a place for itself in the war effort. At least three other women's groups provided land and air ambulance services. There were also volunteer groups of working women, such as WIRES (Women in Radio and Electric Service), WAMS (Women Aircraft Mechanics), and WOWS (Women Ordnance Workers)—the latter of whom by 1943 had a membership of 33,000 in dozens of munitions plants. As part of an elaborate recruiting campaign, Oldsmobile created WINGS (also known as the "Keep 'Em Winning Girls"), workers who were given uniforms with a torch-and-wing insignia on the front pocket. So that housewives should not feel excluded, the *Ladies Home Journal* organized WINS (Women in National Service), saying that housewives were "the largest army in the nation fighting on the home front." The outpouring of female volunteers in a host of organizations enabled women to accomplish much, and suggested how much more they might have done had there been a system in place to take full advantage of their enthusiasm. Even as it was, when in April 1942 ten thousand women volunteers marched down Fifth Avenue in New York there were so many different uniforms that no one could identify them all. . . .

While the numerous complaints about government's incompetence and neglect were fully justified, it was important to keep in mind that the mills of American democracy were supposed to grind slowly. Though this was not apparent at first, the mess in Washington would improve. Private initiatives too would become more fruitful. Scrap drives got better, the rule seeming to be that behind every successful local drive there was one especially determined person. In Seattle, which had a very big one, that man was a local jeweler by the name of Leo Weisfield.

A landmark effort was the great Nebraska scrap drive of 1942, inspired by Henry Doorly, publisher of the state's biggest newspaper, the Omaha *World-Herald.* A unique feature of his plan was that prizes worth up to $2,000 in war bonds would be given to individuals and organizations who collected the most scrap, regardless of whether it was sold to dealers or donated gratis. This was a significant feature, not just because it meant that donors could mingle patriotism with profit, but because scrap dealers had the heavy equipment required to salvage large metal structures.

The drive collected 135 million tons of scrap, the equivalent of 103 pounds for every person in Nebraska. By comparison, the previous national scrap campaign collected only 213 million tons in its first two weeks, an average of barely more than a pound and a half for each American. Many Nebraska companies donated trucks, 40 a day on average, which were employed to transport scrap. The *World-Herald* itself contributed nine tons of old press parts which a frugal foreman had been stockpiling for 30 years. In the town of Oldrege a local department-store owner and a farm-implement dealer set up a nonprofit corporation that paid $10 a ton for salvage, a dollar and a half above the going rate. To finance it they borrowed money from the local bank, and with the aid of hundreds of volunteers ended up breaking even—a feat they accomplished by sorting the scrap, which enabled them to resell it to dealers for a premium that covered their overpayments.

Rural salvage was the most rewarding because of its scale. While towns-people were turning in old appliances, the countryside yielded up treasures in the form of disused iron bridges, farm machinery, and 537 tons of abandoned track donated by the Burlington Railroad. When the prizes were given out, the individual winner was a section hand for the Burlington who brought in 97,000 pounds of scrap. The winning business was a dinette in Norfolk whose owner hired two women to run the place while he collected 81,000 pounds of salvage. The junior prize went to the Omaha Future Farmers of America, who took time out from agricultural pursuits to amass a staggering 445,000 pounds.

The most successful state drive yet, the Nebraska model was widely copied, demonstrating that the will was there and could be mobilized with inventive planning. If the weakness of democracy was inefficient government, the strength was volunteerism, especially when it exploited the national love of competition.

An example of what could be done with official support was gasoline rationing, which went into effect on December 1, 1942—tardily, of course, but as so often happened, delay was needed to convince people that the rubber crisis really existed. Americans who hated rationing, complied with the rules as a whole, despite the inevitable chiseling and the rise of black marketeers and forgers of gas-ration permits. It helped that most people walked to work (40 percent) or took public transportation (23 percent). Even the 36 percent who commmuted by car accepted gasoline rationing after the Baruch Report came out. Though only 49 percent of all Americans saw a need for it when first proposed, by the end of 1942 the great majority of motorists (73 percent) supported gasoline rationing. The 35 mph speed limit won almost universal approval, 89 percent of car owners backing it. Fortunately, though the black market in gasoline eventually became a big business, it never grew so large as to jeopardize the war effort.

Rationing, an inconvenience to some, meant real sacrifice for others—such as small businesses that depended on the drive-in trade. Nine hundred restaurants in Los Angeles alone closed within the first two weeks after rationing took effect. Labor and other kinds of shortages would also devastate small businessmen and farmers. In Arkansas, 6,000 small businesses would fail by 1943 for lack of workers, while the state's farm population declined from 667,000 in 1940 to 292,000 by the spring of 1944.

In January 1943 pleasure driving was banned completely on the East

Coast, where a genuine gasoline shortage existed, virtually emptying the streets of major cities. Compliance was encouraged by police officers, who confiscated the gas-ration books of offending drivers. If after a court hearing the accused were found guilty of frivolous motoring, the fine was in gasoline coupons rather than cash—a powerful and effective deterrent. More important than stiff fines was patriotism, since experience would demonstrate that programs with which most Americans did not agree were ultimately unenforceable.

Conversely, programs that Americans believed in could not be stopped. Victory gardens were a case in point. Food production and conservation had been strongly encouraged in the First World War, and many families that did not ordinarily grow their own produce established kitchen gardens in response. People took it for granted that food would be short this time as well. They began planting vegetables in the spring, despite the Department of Agriculture, which initially dragged its feet. By April 1942, at least 6 million gardens were being cultivated, inspiring Secretary of Agriculture Claude Wickard to call for 18 million victory gardens—a goal that was easily reached. In 1943, more than 8 million tons of produce was grown on 20 million individual plots many of them very small. In cities with populations above 100,000, victory gardens averaged only 500 square feet in size—that is, about 20 by 25 feet—but nevertheless amounted collectively to 7 million acres, an area the size of Rhode Island.

Victory gardens appeared everywhere, not only on private lots but in parks, before the San Francisco City Hall, in the yards of schools and prisons, wherever there was arable soil, and hands to do the tilling. The Agriculture Department reported that the amount of vegetables grown in victory gardens exceeded "the total commercial production for fresh sale for civilian and non-civilian use." This was all the more impressive because, after being grown, much of this produce had to be canned—hence the slogan, "Eat what you can and can what you can't," no small thing, as a mistake could result in glass canisters exploding, or even bacterial growths that were potentially lethal.

Most of the conservation burden fell on women—and children, too, who were good collectors of scrap. In the fully mobilized household there were separate holders for tins, rags, bottles, paper, and bones. Tin cans were washed and flattened. Tinfoil and rubber bands were collected in balls. Bottle caps, chewing gum wrappers, and flashlight batteries were saved for later recycling. Because it was used to make munitions, schools had "Fat Parades," enabling children to make ceremonial deposits of accumulated kitchen grease. In rural areas they collected milkweeds, whose silken fibers would be stuffed into life jackets. . . .

Secretary of the Treasury Henry Morgenthau . . . wanted bonds sold widely and in such a way as to make Americans "war-minded." He believed this was even more important than helping finance defense purchases. To sell bonds was to sell the war, so bond drives were aimed at the average American rather than at wealthy investors—which meant, in turn, drawing heavily on the popular culture. Movie stars played important parts, with Hollywood organizing seven tours that played in 300 communities. Dorothy Lamour alone, the star of a series of "Road" pictures with Bob Hope and Bing Crosby, was credited with selling $350 million worth of bonds. Carole Lombard, a popular movie actress, gave her life to the cause, dying in a plane crash on her way home from a bond tour. In addition to bonds, "war stamps" costing only pennies were sold—mainly to children, though sometimes to adults, as when scantily-clad showgirls covered their flesh with 10¢ savings stamps for happy businessmen to peel off and purchase. Every form of hucksterism was employed in this cause, few managing to escape it. . . .

Despite occasional lapses, [President] Roosevelt did not truly believe in propaganda. In 1917, precisely because opinion was divided on the merits of intervention, Washington had cranked up a vast publicity machine to bolster the war effort. A Committee on Public Information was created to that end, which distributed 75 million pamphlets, issued 6,000 press releases, placed ads in leading magazines, enlisted a corps of "Four-Minute Men" who gave short, canned talks emphasizing German atrocities, and in other ways sought to promote war fever. The intellectual content of most of this is suggested by some of the war films endorsed by CPI, such as "The Prussian Cur" and "The Kaiser, the Beast of Berlin." . . .

After World War I many felt that the mixture of propaganda and intimidation had encouraged the violation of basic American rights, inflamed passions, contributed to vigilante action, stimulated xenophobia, oversimplified the issues, and aroused unrealistic expectations. FDR was not going to repeat the mistake. Public relations was one thing, a ministry of domestic propaganda another. Congress seconded his motion, conservatives fearing that government propaganda campaigns would glorify Roosevelt, the New Deal, and liberal internationalism—what Congresswoman Clare Boothe Luce referred to as "globaloney." . . .

Given Washington's lack of interest in propaganda, writers eager to aid the war effort were inspired to create their own. West Coast patriots formed the Hollywood Writer's Mobilization. Its counterpart on the East Coast was organized by Rex Stout, author of the popular Nero Wolfe detective novels, who launched the Writer's War Board two days after Pearl Harbor. Initially it helped sell war bonds, but soon grew "into a liaison office between writers and government departments, a kind of unpaid extension of the Office of War Information." Looking back, a former member described its purpose thusly. "The government was slow; we were fast. They were timid; we were bold. They used official gobbledygook; we had some wit. World War II was strangely unemotional and needed a WWB to stir things up." As this suggests, the mobilized wordsmiths put a high premium on ardor.

Members not only wrote advertising copy for war bonds, but used every known outlet to reach the public. The WWB itself might instigate a campaign; other times it responded to official requests. An example of the latter case occurred when the Air Force wanted to promote the enlistment of flight crew other than pilots. WWB's contribution included 12 short stories, 24 syndicated columns, three radio broadcasts, one novel, one handbook, and two popular songs—one of them entitled "I Wanna Marry a Bombardier." The campaign had to be terminated after it produced a surplus of volunteers. . . .

These were America's strengths, a lack of regimentation, the refusal to indoctrinate; and most of all the initiative of ordinary people organizing, conserving, collecting, recycling, buying war bonds—or if, like writers and entertainers, they had special skills, devoting them to public service. That government never found a way of fully exploiting their eagerness to help was its biggest wartime failure, and a curious one in light of the opinion polls showing a willingness to give beyond what was ever asked of civilians. . . .

Civilians contributed more to the winning of World War II than to any previous American conflict—on the homefront, but directly too in the battle against the U-boats. In this campaign the front lines were manned not just by sailors and fliers, but by civilian seamen of the U.S. merchant fleet, thousands of whom lost their lives to keep Britain and Russia going. Many more would have died had it not been for a handful of men in government and business who played key roles at critical points that were to make a tremendous difference. . . .

The war changed everything except human needs and desires. Many once ordinary tasks became fiendishly difficult to perform. Numerous goods previously taken for granted all but disappeared, were replaced by inferior substitutes, or disappeared altogether. People got by as best they could and some discovered in the war a welcome degree of excitement. Most found it possible, despite shortages and censorship, to amuse themselves, taking their pleasure in ways that tell us much about the American people and what they considered important.

It seems fair to say that life on the homefront was most difficult for married women. A 48-hour week and long commutes were the rule for all workers, regardless of gender. Because so many goods and services—including household appliances and supplies, certain foodstuffs, domestic help, and medical care—were in short supply, wives and mothers, whether employed or not, had to devote more time to such activities as housework and getting their children to doctors. Shopping was further complicated by ration books and the need to go from store to store looking for scarce products.

Like their husbands, service wives could "take it" and did not let fear for their absent loved ones keep them from shouldering what often were heavy burdens. One Illinois mother was left to care for three small boys when her tory, yet managed to run a Cub Scout troop, keep a victory garden, and put a hot meal on the table every night—if only tunafish casserole. When the fare prompted complaints she serenely replied, as every mother did in those years, "Think of the poor, starving children in Europe."

Consumers had to return used toothpaste tubes in order to buy new ones, while tinfoil and cellophane simply disappeared—as did bobby pins, which were replaced by wooden toothpicks and thread. Mostly a drain, shopping could be adventuresome if you had the right kind of luck. In April 1945, Audrey Davis triumphantly wrote to her husband at sea:

> Honey, I'm a success. I got sheets! Such a time—went to four of the biggest stores first and was turned down cold. Finally ended up in the basement of J. C. Penney's . . . and saw some bedding so on the off-chance, I asked. The girl said, shhh, and sneaked into a back room and brought out some carefully wrapped—didn't even know what I had brought, until I got home. I felt like someone buying hooch during Prohibition.

New clothes were devoid of elastic thread and webbing, metal buttons, zippers, hooks and eyes, silk, nylon, canvas, duck, and sometimes leather. Coats could not have pleats, gussets, bellows, yokes. A "victory suit," which carried economy to the point of eliminating lapels, was ruled out. To save wool, double-breasted suits could not be vested, and no suit could come with more than one pair of pants. Cloth could not go over cloth, eliminating trouser cuffs and patch pockets. Women's skirts were limited in length and circumference and certain dyes, especially greens and browns, were sometimes unavailable. Girdles, still everyday wear for women, had to be made of bone or piano wire instead of rubber. Shoes, when you could get them, came in six colors only, three of them shades of brown. Almost anything from coffee to canned goods, half the 1943 production went overseas, could run out without notice, cigarette shortages being a particular trial for a nation of smokers.

Irritation over rationing was continuous and so sharp that in 1943 Leon Henderson, one of the most brilliant New Dealers, had to resign as head of the Office of Price Administration even though he was, according to economist Kenneth Galbraith (who worked for him), one of the "unsung heroes of World War II". . . . Urban Americans grew used to queuing up. Not only were food and clothing rationed, but the number of ration "points" required for specific items fluctuated, obliging every housewife to update her calculations on a weekly, or even daily, basis. Black-marketeering, especially in meat, aggravated shortages. For some, getting meat was a major preoccupation. One mother seems never to have written her son abroad without addressing the problem, although in the mandatory positive voice, as when she told him of her discovery that "Spam fried in butter makes a very tasty Easter dinner."

*   *   *

A striking feature of the war effort, and a source of many problems, was the enormous increase in physical mobility. Including service personnel, 27.3 million people moved from their original county of residence. In the period 1935–40, an unusually active one, total civilian mobility had amounted to 2.8 million persons a year, but during each of the peak war years it averaged 4.7 million. With automobile use restricted, most long-distance travel was by train, putting enormous stress on the rail system and also the passengers—jammed into overcrowded and poorly maintained cars which were slow and often late due to breakdowns or from having been sidetracked for high-priority troop trains.

Difficult as travel became, starting over in strange places was worse. Adolescents were particularly affected, not only because relocation is emotionally most difficult at that age, but also because so many were going to work full-time or entering the services. In 1940 the number of employed persons between the ages of 14 and 17 was 1.7 million, whereas in 1944 it came to 4.61 million, of whom 1.43 million were part-time students. During World War II the decline in child labor was temporarily reversed, as also the trend toward longer periods of education. Total school attendance for the 14–19 age group in 1940 came to 9.159 million persons, whereas by 1944 it had fallen to 7.93 million. The number of boys and girls aged 14 to 18 who were employed rose from 1 million in 1940 to 2.9 million—the number of mill girls alone rising from 271,000 to 950,000.

By May 1943 some 1.8 million boys and girls under the age of 18 were employed by farms and factories. One Lockheed plant had 1,500 boys laboring as riveters and electricians and in metal fabrication and assembly work. According to the firm, two boys in four hours could accomplish more than an adult worker during a regular eight-hour shift. For those children who remained in school full-time, life was harder, too, as teacher quality declined and class sizes went up. In Arkansas by the 1945–46 school year half the prewar teachers were gone and 72 percent of their replacements had completed less than a semester of college. During 1942–43, out of 170,000 Arkansas youngsters between the ages of 13 and 18 about 100,000 failed to attend school, some taking jobs but many because teachers were not available.

As might be expected, crime rates were strongly influenced by the physical and social changes affecting such a large number of people. Since so many young males, the principal crime-committing group, were in uniform, most crimes declined—except possibly rapes, though as they were seldom reported, the statistics are not very useful. But the number of murders, a more reliable figure, fell from 8,329 in 1940 to a low of 6,675 in 1944. Auto thefts went up in 1942 when new cars became unavailable, but the total number of reported crimes followed the same curve as murders, falling after 1940 and rising again only in 1945 when veterans began reentering civilian life. Suicides declined by a third, from about 19,000 in 1940 to some 13,000 four years later. It is an all too human irony that life seemed more worth living in wartime, the suicide rate showing this even more than the rising birthrate.

All these figures are evidence that—not to make light of its hardships— the war was more interesting than the peace had been. The war put an end to Depression America and gave meaning to ordinary lives, since all citizens were to some degree participants in the national effort. Everything changed, not always for the better, to be sure, but change of itself was often welcome after the monotonous years of austerity that followed the stock market crash of 1929. Many people were given jobs they never expected to get, saw places they would otherwise not have known, and lived richer lives. . . .

DOCUMENTS

Joining the Navy (1939), c. 1991

Well, growing up on the farm in the thirties wasn't very pleasant. I re- member the banks going broke, the Depression, and then there were the dry years. I just didn't have a very good experience with living on a farm, and there weren't any jobs when I graduated out of high school, so I decided to join the navy. Part of their propaganda was "Join the navy, see the world, and learn a trade." The pay was $21.00 a month which sounded pretty good at that time. So I figured that would be a good opportunity to get off the farm.

John Zimola, Wahoo
U.S. Navy firecontrolman,
cruiser USS *Louisville*, Pacific Theater
(enlisted in 1939)

"Well, We Never Met Rosie" (1941–1945), c. 1991

You've probably heard stories about Rosie the Riveter. Well, we never met Rosie [at Lincoln Nebraska Steel Works]. There was just not very much involvement of women in what they used to refer to as a dirty industrial job. This was pretty rough work, handling heavy steel plates. We didn't do much riveting, but welding. We did have a young lady who came to work for us as a crane operator inside the shop. She was doing very well [until] one day she

SOURCE: *Nebraska History* 72, no. 4 (Winter 1991): 169. Testimony taken 1988–1991.
SOURCE: *Nebraska History* 72, no. 4.(Winter 1991): 188. Testimony taken 1988–1991.

started climbing the ladder to get in the cab of the overhead crane. . . . She fell and injured herself and she never came back. She was the only one there. I think that had something to do with it too. As a matter of fact, I'm relatively sure she's the only woman that ever applied at our place for employment during the war. Even after the war, we had very few women.

Earl Luff

Juvenile Delinquency During the War, 1944

Delinquency is a problem that is not readily susceptible to accurate and complete statistical measurement. Certain difficulties are readily apparent. It is not possible to determine the exact extent to which the increase in delinquency cases represents actual increase or to what extent it represents greater community concern, causing greater emphasis on finding cases and on taking measures that heretofore might not have been taken. It is unquestionable that emphasis placed on the control of venereal disease has resulted in the attention of the courts being called more frequently to problems of young girls than was formerly the case. Furthermore, from the standpoint of community concern about juvenile delinquency, the many unhappy, maladjusted, and neurotic children who fail to come to the attention of agencies and courts, yet who make up a large group of individuals who are potential delinquents, easily precipitated into delinquency by unfavorable environment, are of importance equal to those already delinquent in the legal sense.

Although we may lack the means of comprehensive measurement of the problem of delinquent behavior, evidence of increases during the past few years is apparent in recent reports from varied and reliable sources. Field reports of representatives of the Children's Bureau of the United States Department of Labor and other public and private agencies, and special studies and reports of particular communities indicate that the problem is of sufficient proportions to warrant concern.

SOURCE: Testimony of Katherine Lenroot in U.S. Congress, Senate Subcommittee of the Committee on Education and Labor, Hearings, *Wartime Health and Recreation*, 78th Cong., 2nd Sess., 1944, 103–104.

Chapter 12

The Internment of Japanese Americans: Executive Order 9066

During World War II, the United States government removed from their homes 110,000 West Coast immigrant and native-born Japanese and interned them in stark, isolated "relocation centers." The essay in this chapter is excerpted from "Personal Justice Denied," a 1984 report written by a group of scholars for the federal Commission on Wartime Relocation and Internment of Civilians. It examines the events and arguments leading up to President Roosevelt's signing of

Executive Order 9066, under which Japanese Americans were ordered from their homes and housed in government camps. The report also details the conditions that prevailed in the relocation centers. As you read the essay, consider why the internment occurred and what roles wartime hysteria, greed, and racism may have played in it.

The first two documents illustrate the mood and attitudes prevalent at the time of the internment. The first comes from the testimony presented by Earl Warren before a congressional committee meeting in San Francisco in 1942. Today Warren is best remembered as Chief Justice of the U.S. Supreme Court from 1953 to 1969, and a staunch defender of civil rights. In 1942, however, he was California's attorney general and a future candidate for governor. In response to questioning regarding the civil rights of Japanese Americans, he replied, "I believe, sir, that in time of war every citizen must give up some of his normal rights." Even if one accepts such a belief, does it excuse the treatment of Japanese Americans during the war?

The second document is from Supreme Court Justice Hugo Black's majority opinion in the case of Korematsu v. United States *(1944). After reading the accounts of removal and relocation in the essay, evaluate Justice Black's statement that it is "unjustifiable to call [the relocation centers] . . . concentration camps" and his assertion that "to cast this case into outlines of racial prejudice, without reference to the real military dangers which were present, merely confuses the issue."*

Since the end of the war, racial attitudes toward Japanese Americans, as well as other minorities, have considerably improved in the United States. In the case of Japanese Americans, their outstanding military service during the war no doubt aided their acceptance by other Americans. The 442d Regimental Combat Team, composed almost entirely of Japanese Americans, suffered enormous casualties in Italy and was the most decorated unit in the war.

The final document, remarks by President Ronald Reagan on signing a bill authorizing monetary restitution for those interned, expresses the nation's regret over that wartime act.* Do you believe that racial attitudes have improved to the point that Americans would never again commit or permit such a miscarriage of justice? Explain the reasons for your answer.

---

*In October 1990, Japanese Americans began to receive restitution checks.

ESSAY

Personal Justice Denied

Commission on Wartime Relocation and

Internment of Civilians

At dawn on December 7, 1941, Japan began bombing American ships and planes at Pearl Harbor. The attack took our forces by surprise. Japanese aircraft carriers and warships had left the Kurile Islands for Pearl Harbor on November 26, 1941, and Washington had sent a war warning message indicating the possibility of attack upon Pearl Harbor, the Philippines, Thailand or the Malay Peninsula. Nevertheless, the Navy and Army were unprepared and unsuspecting. After a few hours of bombing, Japan had killed or wounded over 3,500 Americans. Two battleships were destroyed, four others sunk or run aground; a number of other vessels were destroyed or badly damaged. One hundred forty-nine American airplanes had been destroyed. Japan lost only 29 planes and pilots.

That night President Roosevelt informed his Cabinet and Congressional leaders that he would seek a declaration of war. On December 8 the President addressed a joint session of Congress and expressed the nation's outraged shock at the damage which the Japanese had done on that day of infamy. The declaration of war passed with one dissenting vote. Germany and Italy followed Japan into the war on December 11.

At home in the first weeks of war the division between isolationists and America Firsters, and supporters of the western democracies, was set aside, and the country united in its determination to defeat the Axis powers. Abroad, the first weeks of war sounded a steady drumbeat of defeat, particularly as the Allies retreated before Japanese forces in the Far East. On the same day as Pearl Harbor, the Japanese struck the Malay Peninsula, Hong Kong, Wake and Midway Islands, and attacked the Philippines, destroying substantial numbers of American aircraft on the ground near Manila. The next day Thailand was invaded and within days two British battleships were sunk off Malaysia. On December 13 Guam fell, and on Christmas the Japanese captured Wake Island and occupied Hong Kong. In the previous seventeen days, Japan had made nine amphibious landings in the Philippines. General Douglas MacArthur, commanding Army forces in the islands, evacuated Manila on December 27, withdrew to the Bataan Peninsula, and set up headquarters on Corregidor. With Japan controlling all sea and air approaches to Bataan and Corregidor, after three months the troops isolated there were forced

SOURCE: Commission on Wartime Relocation and Internment of Civilians, *Personal Justice Denied* (Washington, D.C.: Government Printing Offices, 1984), 47–50, 83–89, 156–63, 176–78.

to surrender unconditionally in the worst American defeat since the Civil War. On February 27 the battle of the Java Sea resulted in another American naval defeat with the loss of thirteen Allied ships. In January and February 1942, the military position of the United States in the Pacific was bleak indeed. Reports of American battlefield deaths gave painful personal emphasis to the war news.

Pearl Harbor was a surprise. The outbreak of war was not. In December 1941 the United States was not in the state of war-readiness which those who anticipated conflict with the Axis would have wished, but it was by no means unaware of the intentions of Japan and Germany. The President had worked for some time for Lend-Lease and other measures to support the western democracies and prepare for war. In 1940, he had broadened the political base of his Cabinet, bringing in as Secretary of the Navy Frank Knox, the publisher of the Chicago *Daily News* who had been Alfred M. Landon's vice-presidential candidate in 1936. Roosevelt drafted as Secretary of War one of the most distinguished Republican public servants of his time, Henry L. Stimson, who had served as Secretary of War under Taft and Secretary of State under Hoover. Stimson, who brought with him the standing and prestige of half a century of active service to his country, carried a particularly impressive weight of principled tradition. He brought into the War Department other, younger easterners, many of whom were fellow lawyers and Republicans. John J. McCloy came from a prominent New York law firm to become first a Special Assistant and then Assistant Secretary for War, and after the outbreak of war he was the civilian aide to Stimson responsible for Japanese American questions. Roosevelt later named Francis Biddle, a Philadelphian who was a firm defender of civil rights, as Attorney General when Robert Jackson was appointed to the Supreme Court.

Ten weeks after the outbreak of war, on February 19, 1942, President Roosevelt signed Executive Order 9066, which gave to the Secretary of War and the military commanders to whom he delegated authority the power to exclude any persons from designated areas in order to secure national defense objectives against sabotage and espionage. The order was used, as the President, his responsible Cabinet officers and the West Coast Congressional delegation knew it would be, to exclude persons of Japanese ancestry, both American citizens and resident aliens, from the West Coast. Over the following months more than 100,000 people were ordered to leave their homes and farms and businesses. "Voluntary" resettlement of people who had been branded as potentially disloyal by the War Department and who were recognizable by their facial features was not feasible. Not surprisingly, the politicians and citizens of Wyoming or Idaho believed that their war industries, railroad lines and hydroelectric dams deserved as much protection from possible sabotage as did those on the Pacific Coast, and they opposed accepting the ethnic Japanese. Most of the evacuees were reduced to abandoning their homes and livelihoods and being transported by the government to "relocation centers" in desolate interior regions of the west.

As the Executive Order made plain, these actions were based upon "military necessity." The government has never fundamentally reviewed whether this massive eviction of an entire ethnic group was justified. In three cases the Supreme Court reviewed the Executive Order in the context of convictions for violations of military orders issued pursuant to it, but the Court chose not to review the factual basis for military decisions in wartime, accepting without close scrutiny the government's representation that exclusion and evacuation were militarily necessary. Forty years later, the nation is sufficiently concerned about the rights and liberties of its citizens and residents, that it has undertaken to examine the facts and pose to itself the question of whether, in the heat of the moment, beset by defeat and fearful of the future, it justly took the proper course for its own protection, or made an original mistake of very substantial proportion. "Peace hath her victories/No less renowned than war."

Was a policy of exclusion militarily justified as a *precautionary* measure? This is a core initial question because the government has conceded at every point that there was no evidence of actual sabotage, espionage or fifth column* activity among people of Japanese descent on the West Coast in February 1942. The Commanding General of the Western Defense Command, John L. DeWitt, put the point plainly, conceding in his recommendation to the War Department "[t]he very fact that no sabotage has taken place to date." The Justice Department, defending the exclusion before the Supreme Court, made no claim that there was identifiable subversive activity. The Congress, in passing the Japanese-American Evacuation Claims Act in 1948, reiterated the point:

> [D]espite the hardships visited upon this unfortunate racial group by an act of the Government brought about by the then prevailing military necessity, there was recorded during the recent war not one act of sabotage or espionage attributable to those who were the victims of the forced relocation.

Finally, the two witnesses before the Commission [on Wartime Relocation and Internment of Civilians] who were most involved in the evacuation decision, John J. McCloy and Karl R. Bendetsen, who was first liaison between the War Department and the Western Defense Command and later General DeWitt's chief aide for the evacuation, testified that the decision was not taken on the basis of actual incidents of espionage, sabotage or fifth column activity.

*The term *fifth column* refers to a group of saboteurs and derives from rebel activity in Madrid during the Spanish Civil War.

One may begin, then, by examining the competent estimates of possible future danger from the ethnic Japanese, citizen and alien, on the West Coast in early 1942. This is not to suggest that a well-grounded suspicion is or should be sufficient to require an American citizen or resident alien to give up his house and farm or business to move hundreds of miles inland, bearing the stigma of being a potential danger to his fellow citizens—nor that such suspicion would justify condemnation of a racial group rather than individual review—but it does address the analysis that should be made by the War Department charged with our continental defenses. . . .

The intelligence services have the task of alerting and informing the President, the military and those charged with maintaining security about whether, where and when disruptive acts directed by an enemy may be expected. Intelligence work consists predominantly of analytical estimate, not demonstrably comprehensive knowledge—there may always be another, undiscovered ring of spies or a completely covert plan of sabotage. Caution and prudence require that intelligence agencies throw the net of suspicion wide, and take measures to protect vital information or militarily important installations. At the same time, if intelligence is to serve the ends of a society which places central value on personal liberty, even in time of war, it must not be overwhelmed by rumors and flights of fancy which grip a fearful, jittery public. Above all, effective intelligence work demands sound judgment which is immune to the paranoia that treats everyone as a hostile suspect until his loyalty is proven. In 1942, what credible threat did Japan pose to the internal peace and security of the United States?

It was common wisdom that the Nazi invasions of Norway and Western Europe had been aided by agents and sympathizers within the country under attack—the so-called fifth column—and that the same approach should be anticipated from Japan. For this reason intelligence was developed on Axis saboteurs and potential fifth columnists as well as espionage agents. This work had been assigned to the Federal Bureau of Investigation and the Navy Department but not to the War Department. The President had developed his own informal intelligence system through John Franklin Carter, a journalist, who helped Roosevelt obtain information and estimates by exploiting sources outside the government. None of these organizations operated with the thoroughness of, say, the modern CIA, but they were the best and calmest eyes and ears the government had.

Each of these sources saw only a very limited security risk from the ethnic Japanese; none recommended a mass exclusion or detention of all people of Japanese ancestry. . . .

Under General DeWitt's guidance from the Presidio [of San Francisco, Army Headquarters on the West Coast], the War Department moved toward the momentous exclusion of American citizens from the West Coast without any thoughtful, thorough analysis of the problems, if any, of sabotage and espionage on the West Coast or of realistic solutions to those problems. In part there was an easy elision between excluding Issei* and Nisei.** The legal basis for excluding aliens was essentially unquestioned; no rigorous analysis of military necessity was needed because there were no recognized interests or rights to weigh against the interest in military security that was served by moving enemy aliens. The very word "Japanese," sometimes used to denote nationality and at other times to indicate ethnicity, allowed obvious ambiguities in discussing citizens and resident aliens. The War Department came toward the problem with a few major facts: the Japanese were winning an incredible string of victories in the Far East; the West Coast was lightly armed and defended, but now appeared far more vulnerable to Japanese raid or attack than it had been before Pearl Harbor—although General Staff estimates were that the Japanese could not make a sustained invasion on the West Coast. But after the surprise of Pearl Harbor, laymen, at least, doubted the reliability of military predictions: it was better to be safe than sorry. And laymen had a great deal to say about what the Army should do on the West Coast. . . .

It was the voices of organized interests, politicians and the press on the West Coast that DeWitt heard most clearly—and the War Department too. The first weeks after Pearl Harbor saw no extensive attacks on the ethnic Japanese, but through January and early February the storm gathered and broke. The latent anti-Japanese virus of the West Coast was brought to life by the fear and anger engendered by Pearl Harbor, stories of sabotage in Hawaii and Japan's victories in Asia. Among private groups the lead was typically taken by people with a long history of anti-Japanese agitation and by those who feared economic competition. It is difficult . . . to recreate the fear and uncertainty about the country's safety which was generally felt after Pearl Harbor; it is equally impossible to convey . . . the virulence and breadth of anti-Japanese feeling which erupted on the West Coast in January and February of 1942.

On January 2 the Joint Immigration Committee sent a manifesto to California newspapers which summed up the historical catalogue of charges against the ethnic Japanese. It put them in the new context of reported fifth column activity in Hawaii and the Philippines and a war that turned the Japanese into a problem for the nation, not California alone. Repeating the fundamental claim that the ethnic Japanese are "totally unassimilable," the manifesto declared that "those born in this country are American citizens by right of birth, but they are also Japanese citizens,

*Issei were first-generation Japanese Americans.
**Nisei were second-generation Japanese Americans.

223

liable . . . to be called to bear arms for their Emperor, either in front of, or behind, enemy lines." Japanese language schools were attacked as "a blind to cover instruction similar to that received by a young student in Japan— that his is a superior race, the divinity of the Japanese Emperor, the loyalty that every Japanese, wherever born, or residing, owes his Emperor and Japan." In these attacks the Joint Immigration Committee had the support of the Native Sons and Daughters of the Golden West and the California Department of the American Legion, which in January began to demand that "all Japanese who are known to hold dual citizenship . . . be placed in concentration camps." By early February, Earl Warren, then Attorney General of California, and U. S. Webb, a former Attorney General and coauthor of the Alien Land Law, were actively advising the Joint Immigration Committee how to persuade the federal government that all ethnic Japanese should be removed from the West Coast. . . .

These traditional voices of anti-Japanese agitation were joined by economic competitors of the Nikkei [Japanese Americans]. The Grower-Shipper Vegetable Association was beginning to find a voice in January, although its bluntest statement can be found in a *Saturday Evening Post* article in May:

> We're charged with wanting to get rid of the Japs for selfish reasons. We might as well be honest. We do. It's a question of whether the white man lives on the Pacific Coast or the brown man. They came into this valley to work, and they stayed to take over. . . . If all the Japs were removed tomorrow, we'd never miss them in two weeks, because the white farmers can take over and produce everything the Jap grows. And we don't want them back when the war ends, either.

Through January and early February, the Western Growers Protective Association, the Grower-Shippers, and the California Farm Bureau Federation all demanded stern measures against the ethnic Japanese. All assured the newspapers and politicians to whom they wrote that the removal of the ethnic Japanese would in no way harm or diminish agricultural production.

This wave of self-assured demands for a firm solution to the "Japanese problem" encountered no vigorous, widespread defense of the Issei and Nisei. Those concerned with civil liberties and civil rights were silent. For instance, a poll of the Northern California Civil Liberties Union in the spring of 1942 showed a majority in favor of the evacuation orders.

West Coast politicians were not slow to demand action against ethnic Japanese. Fletcher Bowron, reform mayor of Los Angeles, went to Washington in mid-January to discuss with Attorney General Biddle the general protection of Los Angeles as well as the removal of all ethnic Japanese from Terminal Island in Los Angeles Harbor. By February 5, in a radio address, the Mayor was unequivocally supporting mass evacuation. In the meantime, all Nisei had been removed from the city payrolls. The Los Angeles County Board of Supervisors fired all its Nisei employees and adopted a resolution urging the federal government to transport all Japanese aliens from the coast. Following Los Angeles, 16 other California counties passed formal resolutions urging evacuation; Imperial County required the fingerprinting, registration and abandoning of farming by all enemy aliens; San Francisco demanded suppression of all Japanese language newspapers. Portland, Oregon, revoked the licenses of all Japanese nationals doing business in the city. The California State Personnel Board ordered all "descendants" of enemy aliens barred from civil service positions, and Governor Olson authorized the State Department of Agriculture to revoke the produce-handling licenses of enemy aliens. Attorney General Warren found these measures unlawful, but he sympathized with their basic aim, laboring to persuade federal officials that the military should remove ethnic Japanese from what Warren thought sensitive areas on the West Coast.

In Washington, most West Coast Congressmen and Senators began to express similar views, Congressman Leland Ford of Los Angeles taking the early lead. On January 16, 1942, he wrote the Secretaries of War and Navy and the FBI Director informing them that his California mail was running heavily in favor of evacuation and internment:

> I know that there will be some complications in connection with a matter like this, particularly where there are native born Japanese, who are citizens. My suggestions in connection with this are as follows:
>
> 1. That these native born Japanese either are or are not loyal to the United States.
>
> 2. That all Japanese, whether citizens or not, be placed in inland concentration camps. As justification for this, I submit that if an American born Japanese, who is a citizen, is really patriotic and wishes to make his contribution to the safety and welfare of this country, right here is his opportunity to do so, namely, that by permitting himself to be placed in a concentration camp, he would be making his sacrifice and he should be willing to do it if he is patriotic and is working for us. As against his sacrifice, millions of other native born citizens are willing to lay down their lives, which is a far greater sacrifice, of course, than being placed in a concentration camp. . . .

This clamor for swift, comprehensive measures against the ethnic Japanese both reflected and was stimulated by the press. In December the West Coast press had been comparatively tolerant on the issue of the Nikkei, but by January more strident commentators were heard. John B.

Hughes, who had a regular Mutual Broadcasting Company program, began a month-long series from Los Angeles which steadily attacked the ethnic Japanese, spreading rumors of espionage and fifth column activity and even suggesting that Japanese dominance of produce production was part of a master war plan.

Nurtured by fear and anger at Japanese victories in the Far East and by eagerness to strike at the enemy with whom the Nisei were now identified, calls for radical government action began to fill letters to the editor and newspaper commentary. Private employers threw many ethnic Japanese out of their jobs, while many others refused to deal with them commercially. Old stereotypes of the "yellow peril" and other forms of anti-Japanese agitation provided a ready body of lore to bolster this pseudopatriotic cause. By the end of January the clamor for exclusion fired by race hatred and war hysteria was prominent in California newspapers. Henry McLemore, a Hearst syndicated columnist, published a vicious diatribe:

> I am for immediate removal of every Japanese on the West Coast to a point deep in the interior. I don't mean a nice part of the interior either. Herd 'em up, pack 'em off and give 'em the inside room in the badlands. Let 'em be pinched, hurt, hungry and dead up against it. . . .
>
> Personally, I hate the Japanese. And that goes for all of them.

By the end of January the western Congressional delegation and many voices in the press and organized interest groups were pressing for evacuation or internment of aliens and citizens. The Presidio at San Francisco listened, and by January 31, General DeWitt had embraced the Representatives' view that all enemy aliens and dual citizens should be evacuated and interned; action should be taken at the earliest possible date "even if they [the aliens and dual citizens] were temporarily inconvenienced." . . .

In the face of . . . demands for evacuation and the recommendation of his Secretary of War, Roosevelt was not likely to reconsider his decision. Nevertheless, on February 17 Attorney General Biddle sent a memorandum to the President in the guise of a briefing paper for a press conference. . . . :

> For several weeks there have been increasing demands for evacuation of all Japanese, aliens and citizens alike, from the West Coast states. A great many of the West Coast people distrust the Japanese, various special interests would welcome their removal from good farm land and the elimination of their competition, some of the local California radio and press have demanded evacuation, the West Coast Congressional Delegation are asking the same thing and finally, Walter Lippman [*sic*] and Westbrook Pegler recently

have taken up the evacuation cry on the ground that attack on the West Coast and widespread sabotage is imminent. My last advice from the War Department is that there is no evidence of imminent attack and from the F.B.I. that there is no evidence of planned sabotage.

I have designated as a prohibited area every area recommended to me by the Secretary of War, through whom the Navy recommendations are also made. . . .

We are proceeding as fast as possible. To evacuate the 93,000 Japanese in California overnight would materially disrupt agricultural production in which they play a large part and the farm labor now is so limited that they could not be quickly replaced. Their hurried evacuation would require thousands of troops, tie up transportation and raise very difficult questions of resettlement. Under the Constitution 60,000 of these Japanese are American citizens. If complete confusion and lowering of morale is to be avoided, so large a job must be done after careful planning. The Army has not yet advised me of its conclusion in the matter.

There is no dispute between the War, Navy, and Justice Departments. The practical and legal limits of this Department's authority which is restricted to alien enemies are clearly understood. The Army is considering what further steps it wishes to recommend.

It is extremely dangerous for the columnists, acting as "Armchair Strategists and Junior G-Men," to suggest that an attack on the West Coast and planned sabotage is imminent when the military authorities and the F.B.I. have indicated that this is not the fact. It comes close to shouting FIRE! in the theater; and if race riots occur, these writers will bear a heavy responsibility. Either Lippman [*sic*] has information which the War Department and the F.B.I. apparently do not have, or is acting with dangerous irresponsibility.

No minds were changed, and by this time the Attorney General was taking coarse and threatening abuse for his unwillingness to join the stampede to mass evacuation. . . .

On February 17 [Secretary of War] Stimson recorded meeting with War Department officials to outline a proposed executive order; General Gullion undertook to have the order drafted that night: "War Department orders will fill in the application of this Presidential order. These were outlined and Gullion is also to draft them." Further, Stimson said, "It will involve the tremendous task of moving between fifty and one hundred thousand people from their homes and finding temporary support and sustenance for them in the meanwhile, and ultimately locating them in new places away from the coast." In short, whatever his views during discussion with the President a few days before, Stimson now contemplated a mass move.

On February 18, 1942, Stimson met about the executive order with Biddle, Ennis, Rowe, and Tom Clark of the Department of Justice; and Robert Patterson, Under Secretary of War; McCloy; Gullion; and Bendetsen from the War Department. Stimson wrote:

> Biddle, McCloy and Gullion had done a good piece of work in breaking down the issues between the Departments the night before, and a draft of a presidential executive order had been drawn by Biddle based upon that conference and the preceding conference I had had yesterday. We went over them. I made a few suggestions and then approved it. This marks a long step forward towards a solution of a very dangerous and vexing problem. But I have no illusions as to the magnitude of the task that lies before us and the wails which will go up in relation to some of the actions which will be taken under it.

The Attorney General remembered the tenor of the meeting somewhat differently, but, writing in his autobiography, agreed about the result:

> Rowe and Ennis argued strongly against [the Executive Order]. But the decision had been made by the President. It was, he said, a matter of military judgment. I did not think I should oppose it any further. The Department of Justice, as I had made it clear to him from the beginning, was opposed to and would have nothing to do with the evacuation.

In Los Angeles on the night of February 19, the United Citizens Federation, representing a wide range of pro-Nisei interests, held its first meeting of more than a thousand people. Plans were laid to persuade the press, the politicians and the government that their attacks upon the ethnic Japanese were unfounded. It was too late.

Earlier in the day, President Roosevelt had signed Executive Order 9066. The Order directed the Secretary of War and military commanders designated by him, whenever it was deemed necessary or desirable, to prescribe military areas "with respect to which, the right of any person to enter, remain in, or leave shall be subject to whatever restrictions the Secretary of War or the appropriate Military Commander may impose in his discretion." There was no direct mention of American citizens of Japanese descent, but unquestionably the Order was directed squarely at those Americans. A few months later, when there was talk of the War Department using the Executive Order to move Germans and Italians on the East Coast, the President wrote Stimson that he considered enemy alien control to be "primarily a civilian matter except of course in the case of the Japanese mass evacuation on the Pacific Coast."

The next day, to underscore the government's new-found unity on this decision, Attorney General Biddle sent to the President's personal attention a memorandum justifying the Executive Order and its broad grant of powers to the military. . . . :

> This authority gives very broad powers to the Secretary of War and the Military Commanders. These powers are broad enough to permit them to exclude any particular individual from military areas. They could also evacuate groups of persons based on a reasonable classification. The order is not limited to aliens but includes citizens so that it can be exercised with respect to Japanese, irrespective of their citizenship.
>
> The decision of safety of the nation in time of war is necessarily for the Military authorities. Authority over the movement of persons, whether citizens or noncitizens, may be exercised in time of war. . . . This authority is no more than declaratory of the power of the President, in time of war, with reference to all areas, sea or land.
>
> The President is authorized in acting under his general war powers without further legislation. The exercise of the power can meet the specific situation and, of course, cannot be considered as any punitive measure against any particular nationalities. It is rather a precautionary measure to protect the national safety. It is not based on any legal theory but on the facts that the unrestricted movement of certain racial classes, whether American citizens or aliens, in specified defense areas may lead to serious disturbances. These disturbances cannot be controlled by police protection and have the threat of injury to our war effort. A condition and not a theory confronts the nation.

After the decision, there was no further dissent at the highest levels of the federal government. The War Department stood behind the facts and the Justice Department stood behind the law which were the foundation of the Executive Order. . . .

WRA [the War Relocation Authority] had to move quickly in finding centers to house 120,000 people and in developing policies and procedures for handling the evacuees soon to come under its jurisdiction. The President had stressed the need for immediate action; both the War Department and the WRA were anxious to remove the evacuees from the primitive, make-shift assembly centers.

Selecting the sites for the relocation centers proved complicated. Two sites had been chosen by military authorities before the WRA was born. Eight more locations were needed—designed to be "areas where the evacuees might settle down to a more stable kind of life until plans could be developed for their permanent relocation in communities outside the evacuated areas." Site selection required the War Department and the WRA to agree, although each had different interests. The WRA retained the portion of its early plan that called for large-scale agricultural programs in which evacuees would clear, develop and cultivate the land. Thus, the centers had to be on federal land so that improvements would become a public benefit. The Army, now face-to-face with the actual movement of people, no longer advocated freedom of movement outside the Western Defense Command. It became concerned about security and insisted that sites be located at a safe distance from "strategic installations," a term that included power lines and reservoirs. The Army also wanted each camp to have a population of at least 5,000 so that the number of guards could be minimized. To be habitable, the centers had to have suitable transportation, power and water facilities. By June 5, after considering 300 proposed sites and negotiating with many potentially affected state and local government officials, the WRA chose the final eight sites.

More than any other single factor, the requirement for large tracts of land virtually guaranteed that the sites would be inhospitable. As [historian] Roger Daniels explained it: "That these areas were still vacant land in 1942, land that the ever-voracious pioneers and developers had either passed by or abandoned, speaks volumes about their attractiveness."

The sites were indeed unattractive. Manzanar [California] and Poston [Arizona], selected by the Army, were in the desert. Although both could eventually produce crops, extensive irrigation would be needed, and Poston's climate was particularly harsh. Six other sites were also arid desert. Gila River, near Phoenix, suffered almost as severely from the heat. Minidoka [Idaho] and Heart Mountain [Wyoming], the two northernmost centers, were known for hard winters and severe dust storms. Tule Lake [California] was the most developed site; located in a dry lake bed, much of it was ready for planting. Topaz [Utah] was covered in greasewood brush. Granada [Colorado] was little better, although there was some provision for irrigation. The last two centers—Rohwer and Jerome in Arkansas—were entirely different. Located in swampland, the sites were heavily wooded, with severe drainage problems. . . .

Having selected the sites, the WRA's second job was to develop the policies and procedures that would control the lives of evacuees. This was begun almost immediately, with help from the JACL.* In his April 6 letter to Eisenhower,** Masaoka set forth a long list of recommendations for regulating life in the camps and stressed, among other things, the importance of respecting the citizenship of the Nisei, protecting the health of elderly Issei, providing educational opportunities, and recognizing that the

---

*The Japanese-American Citizens League (JACL) was headed by Bill Masaoka.
**Milton Eisenhower was in charge of the camps during their early operation.

evacuees were "American" in their outlook and wanted to make a contribution to the war effort. The first set of policies issued May 29 were labeled by the Director "tentative, still fairly crude, and subject to immediate change." Further, they did not reach the centers until three weeks after the first groups had arrived. They were not clarified until August, when over half the evacuee population had been transferred to the centers. Given the limited time available and the novelty of WRA's task as both jailer and advocate for the evacuees, it is not surprising that the agency was not fully prepared. Still, the fact that WRA was not able to provide dependable answers to basic questions about how the centers would be managed probably fed the disaffection that increasingly characterized reactions to the relocation centers.

The confluence of diverse political interests had again conspired against the evacuees. The new centers at which they were arriving were barely an improvement over the assembly centers they had left. The increased freedom and possible resettlement they had anticipated had been reversed in favor of confinement. And the rules that would govern their lives were uncertain or non-existent. . . .

Except at Manzanar, which was built as an assembly center and transferred to the WRA for use as a relocation center, all the relocation camps were built from scratch. Thus, the design and facilities were relatively standard. By agreement with the WRA, the camps were built by the War Department according to its own specifications. Barbed-wire fences, watchtowers, and armed guards surrounded the residential and administrative areas of most camps.

The military police and administrative personnel had separate quarters, more spacious and better furnished. At most centers, evacuees built the administrative housing, which had not been included in the original construction contracts. At Topaz, Gladys Bell and her family, who were with the administrative staff, had an entire four-room barrack complete with piano. At Manzanar, staff houses were painted and had residential cooling systems, refrigerators, indoor toilets and baths.

Arrangements for the evacuees were not comparable. The basic organizational unit was once again the "block," consisting of about 12 to 14 barracks, a mess hall, baths, showers, toilets, a laundry and a recreation hall. Each barrack was about 20 by 100 to 120 feet, divided into four or six rooms, each from 20 by 16 to 20 by 25 feet. Each room housed at least one family, even if the family was very large. Even at the end of 1942, in 928 cases, two families shared a 20-by-25-foot room.

Construction was of the kind used to house soldiers overseas—the so-called "theatre of operations" type, modified somewhat to accommodate women and children. The barracks were built of planks nailed to studs and covered with tarpaper. In some places the green wood warped quickly, cracking walls and floors. Congressman Leland Ford said of the Manzanar barrack that "on dusty days, one might just as well be outside as inside." "So much of our work was done sloppily," Dean Meeker testified of Heart Mountain:

> I can remember the foreman's comment when he found cracks in the building. He said, "Well, I guess those Japs will be stuffing their underwear in there to keep the wind out."
>
> In my defense, I will say I applied a bit more diligence and care to my work when I realized people would actually have to survive a Wyoming winter in this housing. We all knew that there was no way anyone accustomed to California weather could possibly survive a Wyoming winter in those barracks. If they were from California, they probably didn't even own the proper clothing for a winter in Cody.

No inside walls or ceilings were included in the original plans. As part of a winterization program, however, evacuee construction crews eventually added firboard ceilings and inside walls in many of the centers.

A visiting reporter from *The San Francisco Chronicle* described quarters at Tule Lake:

> Room size—about 15 by 25, considered too big for two reporters. Condition—dirty.
>
> Contents—two Army cots, each with two Army blankets, one pillow, some sheets and pillow cases (these came as a courtesy from the management), and a coal-burning stove (no coal). There were no dishes, rugs, curtains, or housekeeping equipment of any kind. (We had in addition one sawhorse and three pieces of wood, which the management did not explain.)

The furnishings at other camps were similar. At Minidoka, arriving evacuees found two stacked canvas cots, a pot-bellied stove and a light bulb hanging from the ceiling; at Topaz, cots, two blankets, a pot-bellied stove and some cotton mattresses. Rooms had no running water, which had to be carried from community facilities. Running back and forth from the laundry room to rinse and launder soiled diapers was a particular inconvenience. . . .

Others, however, found not even the minimal comforts that had been planned for them. An unrealistic schedule combined with wartime shortages of labor and materials meant that the WRA had difficulty meeting its construction schedule. In most cases, the barracks were completed, but at some centers evacuees lived without electric light, adequate toilets or laundry facilities. . . .

Mess halls planned for about 300 people had to handle 600 or 900 for short periods. Three months after the project opened, Manzanar still lacked equipment for 16 of 36 messhalls. At Gila:

There were 7,700 people crowded into space designed for 5,000. They were housed in messhalls, recreation halls, and even latrines. As many as 25 persons lived in a space intended for four.

As at the assembly centers, one result was that evacuees were often denied privacy in even the most intimate aspects of their lives. . . . Even when families had separate quarters, the partitions between rooms failed to give much privacy. Gladys Bell described the situation at Topaz:

[T]he evacuees . . . had only one room, unless there were around ten in the family. Their rooms had a pot-bellied stove, a single electric light hanging from the ceiling, an Army cot for each person and a blanket for the bed. Each barrack had six rooms with only three flues. This meant that a hole had to be cut through the wall of one room for the stovepipe to join the chimney of the next room. The hole was large so that the wall would not burn. As a result, everything said and some things whispered were easily heard by people living in the next room. Sometimes the family would be a couple with four children living next to an older couple, perhaps of a different religion, older ideas and with a difference in all ways of life—such as music.

Despite these wretched conditions the evacuees again began to rebuild their lives. Several evacuees recall "foraging for bits of wallboard and wood" and dodging guards to get materials from the scrap lumber piles to build shelves and furniture. . . . Eventually, rooms were partitioned and shelves, tables, chairs and other furniture appeared. Paint and cloth for curtains and spreads came from mail order houses at evacuee expense. Flowers bloomed and rock gardens emerged; trees and shrubs were planted. Many evacuees grew victory gardens. One described the change:

[W]hen we entered camp, it was a barren desert. When we left camp, it was a garden that had been built up without tools, it was green around the camp with vegetation, flowers, and also with artificial lakes, and that's how we left it.

The success of evacuees' efforts to improve their surroundings, however, was always tempered by the harsh climate. In the western camps, particularly Heart Mountain, Poston, Topaz and Minidoka, dust was a principal problem. Monica Sone described her first day at Minidoka:

[W]e were given a rousing welcome by a dust storm. . . . We felt as if we were standing in a gigantic sand-mixing machine as the sixty-mile gale lifted the loose earth up into the sky, obliterating everything. Sand filled our mouths and nostrils and stung our faces and hands like a thousand darting needles. Henry and Father pushed on ahead while Mother, Sumi and I followed, hanging onto their jackets, banging suitcases into each other. At last we staggered into our room, gasping and blinded. We sat on our suitcases to rest, peeling off our jackets and scarves. The window panels rattled madly, and the dust poured through the cracks like smoke. Now and then when the wind subsided, I saw other evacuees, hanging on to their suitcases, heads bent against the stinging dust. The wind whipped their scarves and towels from their heads and zipped them out of sight.

In desert camps, the evacuees met severe extremes of temperature as well. In winter it reached 35 degrees below zero and summers brought temperature as high as 115°. Because the desert did not cool off at night, evacuees would splash water on their cots to be cool enough to sleep. Rattlesnakes and desert wildlife added danger to discomfort.

The Arkansas camps had equally unpleasant weather. Winters were cold and snowy while summers were unbearably hot and humid, heavy with chiggers and clouds of mosquitos. . . .

The WRA walked a fine line in providing for evacuees' basic needs. On the one hand was their genuine sympathy for the excluded people. On the other was a well-founded apprehension that the press and the politicians would seek out and denounce any evidence that evacuees were being treated generously. WRA's compromise was to strive for a system that would provide a healthy but Spartan environment. They did not always succeed, and it was usually the evacuees who suffered when they failed.

The meal system was institutional—food served in messhalls at designated times. Lines were long and tables crowded. Special arrangements were made for infants, the sick or elderly, but, as in most institutions, they were developed from necessity, not convenience. There were formula kitchens for the babies, to which their mothers brought them at designated times; some mothers walked many "blocks" as often as six times a day to get their infants fed when the camps first opened. Others bought hot plates to make formula, but without running water this system was almost as unsatisfactory. The arrangements for those on restricted diets were difficult. The diet kitchens were often located in the administration complex, far from the residential area; the sick and the elderly had to walk as much as a mile three times a day to get their special food.

Food quality and quantity varied among centers, generally improving in the later months as evacuees began to produce it themselves. The WRA's expressed policy was that evacuees were entitled to the same treatment as other American citizens: WRA was to provide an adequate diet; foods rationed to the public would be available to evacuees in the same quantities.

The reality, however, was very different. Weiners, dry fish, rice, macaroni and pickled vegetables are among the foods evacuees recall eating most frequently. Meatless days were regular at some centers—two or three times a week, and many items were unavailable. Continuing dairy shortages meant that, at most centers, fluid milk was served only to those with special needs, while at others, there was watery skim milk. In fact, no really appetizing meals could be produced regularly under a requirement that feeding the evacuees could not cost more than rations for the Army, which were set at 50 cents per person per day. Actual costs per evacuee were approximately 45 cents per person per day; sometimes they fell as low as 31 cents.

In January 1943, after accusations that evacuees were being coddled, the WRA adopted new policies which showed that their fear of adverse publicity had overcome any humanitarian impulse. "At no time would evacuees' food have higher specifications than or exceed in quantity what the civil population may obtain in the open market." Centers were ordered to submit their planned menus for each 30-day period to Washington for advance approval to make sure that the public was adequately informed of WRA feeding policies and procedures. Perhaps the best that can be said of the meal system is that no one starved.

No one froze either. As winter approached, many evacuees were unprepared, either because they had brought no warm clothing due to baggage limitations or because they did not own such clothing, never having needed it at home. In response, the WRA provided monthly clothing allowances and distributed surplus clothing. Each employed evacuee and his or her dependents were supposed to receive from $2 to $3.75 each month, depending on the evacuee's age and the climate of the center. The system, however, did not work well because the shorthanded WRA assigned it to an inexperienced, overworked staff, which was unable to handle the additional workload, and delays continually frustrated evacuees at the mercy of the WRA for their survival. The surplus distribution became the principal source of warm clothing during the first winter, when need was greatest. The clothes were old GI peajackets and uniforms, sizes 38 to 44. However unattractive, they were warm and a source of great amusement. . . .

Discontent over camp living conditions was inevitable. Housing and food were poor. Suspicion that staff was stealing and selling food was widespread. Wages and clothing allowances were delayed. For many older residents, there were no jobs. WRA had promised that household goods would be brought to evacuees as soon as they arrived; months later, none had come. There were continual shortages of equipment and material for education and recreation. WRA had promised that one of its first jobs would be to build schools and furnish school equipment, but priority often went instead to improving quarters for WRA personnel.

Fear, uncertainty and the monotony of enforced idleness aggravated tension. At the older centers, WRA policies had not been set when evacuees arrived, and there were no answers to many of their questions. They feared the future—not only what would happen after the war, but also whether there would be enough food or quality medical care at the centers. Many had lost income and property, which left them few resources to fall back on. They feared the "outside." Relations with outside communities were poor, and evacuees knew that some towns had passed resolutions against the free movement of evacuees. Local communities and politicians had investigated the camps for evidence of "coddling."

Evacuees feared and resented the changes forced by life in the centers, particularly the breakdown of family authority, created in part by a situation in which children no longer depended so heavily on their parents. Family separation was common, and mass living discouraged normal communication and family activity. Perhaps most difficult, the position of the head of the family had been weakened. No longer the breadwinner providing food and shelter, he had been supplanted by the government; his authority over the family and his ability to lead and discipline were diminished. Children unsettlingly found their parents as helpless as they.

At the root of it all, evacuees resented being prisoners against whom no crime was charged and for whom there was no recourse. Armed guards patrolled their community and searched their packages. No evacuee could have a camera. Even beer was prohibited. For a long time, no evacuee could leave the center, except for emergency reasons, and then only in the company of someone who was not of Japanese ancestry. Evacuee positions were subordinate to WRA personnel, regardless of ability, and wages were low. At some centers, project officials actively tried to maintain class and role distinctions, forbidding WRA personnel and evacuees to eat in the same messhall, for example. . . .

DOCUMENTS

In Support of Evacuation, 1942

[CALIFORNIA STATE] ATTORNEY GENERAL WARREN. For some time I have been of the opinion that the solution of our alien enemy problem with all its ramifications, which include the descendants of aliens, is not only a Federal problem but is a military problem. We believe that all of the decisions in that regard must be made by the military command that is charged with

SOURCE: Testimony of Earl Warren, U.S. Congress, House Select Committee Investigating National Defense, *San Francisco Hearing,* 77th Cong., 2d sess., 11009–11019.

the security of this area. I am convinced that the fifth column activities of our enemy call for the participation of people who are in fact American citizens, and that if we are to deal realistically with the problem we must realize that we will be obliged in time of stress to deal with subversive elements of our own citizenry. . . .

A wave of organized sabotage in California accompanied by an actual air raid or even by a prolonged black-out could not only be more destructive to life and property but could result in retarding the entire war effort of this Nation far more than the treacherous bombing of Pearl Harbor.

I hesitate to think what the result would be of the destruction of any of our airplane factories in this State. It will interest you to know that some of our airplane factories in this State are entirely surrounded by Japanese land ownership or occupancy. It is a situation that is fraught with the greatest danger and under no circumstances should it ever be permitted to exist. . . .

Unfortunately, however, many of our people and some of our authorities and, I am afraid, many of our people in other parts of the country are of the opinion that because we have had no sabotage and no fifth column activities in this State since the beginning of the war, that means that none have been planned for us. But I take the view that that is the most ominous sign in our whole situation. It convinces me more than perhaps any other factor that the sabotage that we are to get, the fifth column activities that we are to get, are timed just like Pearl Harbor was timed and just like the invasion of France, and of Denmark, and of Norway, and all of those other countries. . . .

I want to say that the consensus of opinion among the law-enforcement officers of this State is that there is more potential danger among the group of Japanese who are born in this country than from the alien Japanese who were born in Japan. That might seem an anomaly to some people, but the fact is that, in the first place, there are twice as many of them. There are 33,000 aliens and there are 66,000 born in this country.

In the second place, most of the Japanese who were born in Japan are over 55 years of age. There has been practically no migration to this country since 1924. But in some instances the children of those people have been sent to Japan for their education, either in whole or in part, and while they are over there they are indoctrinated with the idea of Japanese imperialism. They receive their religious instruction which ties up their religion with their Emperor, and they come back here imbued with the ideas and the policies of Imperial Japan. . . .

We believe that when we are dealing with the Caucasian race we have methods that will test the loyalty of them, and we believe that we can, in dealing with the Germans and the Italians, arrive at some fairly sound conclusions because of our knowledge of the way they live in the community and have lived for many years. But when we deal with the Japanese we are in an entirely different field and we cannot form any opinion that we believe to be sound. . . .

MR. [JOHN] SPARKMAN. I have noticed suggestions in newspaper stories. I noticed a telegram this morning with reference to the civil rights of these people. What do you have to say about that?

ATTORNEY GENERAL WARREN. I believe, sir, that in time of war every citizen must give up some of his normal rights.

Exclusion and Internment Upheld, 1944

The petitioner, an American citizen of Japanese descent, was convicted in a federal district court for remaining in San Leandro, California, a "Military Area," contrary to Civilian Exclusion Order No. 34 of the Commanding General of the Western Command, U.S. Army, which directed that after May 9, 1942, all persons of Japanese ancestry should be excluded from that area. No question was raised as to the petitioner's loyalty to the United States. . . .

Like curfew, exclusion of those of Japanese origin was deemed necessary because of the presence of an unascertained number of disloyal members of the group, most of whom we have no doubt were loyal to this country. It was because we could not reject the finding of the military authorities that it was impossible to bring about an immediate segregation of the disloyal from the loyal that we sustained the validity of the curfew order as applying to the whole group. In the instant case, temporary exclusion of the entire group was rested by the military on the ground. The judgment that exclusion of the whole group was for the same reason a military imperative answers the contention that the exclusion was in the nature of group punishment based on antagonism to those of Japanese origin. That there were members of the group who retained loyalties to Japan has been confirmed by investigations made subsequent to the exclusion. Approximately five thousand American citizens of Japanese ancestry refused to swear unqualified allegiance to the United States and to renounce allegiance to the Japanese Emperor, and several thousand evacuees requested repatriation to Japan. . . .

It is said that we are dealing here with the case of imprisonment of a citizen in a concentration camp solely because of his ancestry, without evidence or inquiry concerning his loyalty and good disposition towards the United States. Our task would be simple, our duty clear, were this a

SOURCE: Justice Hugo Black's majority opinion in *Korematsu* v. *United States*, 323 U.S. 214 (1944).

case involving the imprisonment of a loyal citizen in a concentration camp because of racial prejudice. Regardless of the true nature of the assembly and relocation centers—and we deem it unjustifiable to call them concentration camps with all the ugly connotations that term implies—we are dealing specifically with nothing but an exclusion order. To cast this case into outlines of racial prejudice, without reference to the real military dangers which were presented, merely confuses the issue. Korematsu was not excluded from the Military Area because of hostility to him or his race. He was excluded because we are at war with the Japanese Empire, because the properly constituted military authorities feared an invasion of our West Coast and felt constrained to take proper security measures, because they decided that the military urgency of the situation demanded that all citizens of Japanese ancestry be segregated from the West Coast temporarily, and finally, because Congress, reposing its confidence in this time of war in our military leaders—as inevitably it must—determined that they should have the power to do just this. There was some evidence of disloyalty on the part of some, the military authorities considered that the need for action was great, and time was short. We cannot—by availing ourselves of the calm perspective of hindsight—now say that at that time these actions were unjustified.

President Ronald Reagan's Apology, 1988

The Members of Congress and distinguished guests, my fellow Americans, we gather here today to right a grave wrong. More than 40 years ago, shortly after the bombing of Pearl Harbor, 120,000 persons of Japanese ancestry living in the United States were forcibly removed from their homes and placed in makeshift internment camps. This action was taken without trial, without jury. It was based solely on race, for these 120,000 were Americans of Japanese descent.

Yes, the Nation was then at war, struggling for its survival, and it's not for us today to pass judgment upon those who may have made mistakes while engaged in that great struggle. Yet we must recognize that the internment of Japanese-Americans was just that: a mistake. For throughout the war, Japanese-Americans in the tens of thousands remained utterly loyal to the United States. Indeed, scores of Japanese-Americans volunteered for our Armed Forces, many stepping forward in the internment camps themselves. The 442d Regimental Combat Team, made up entirely of Japanese-Americans, served with immense distinction to defend this

SOURCE: *Weekly Compilation of Presidential Documents,* Ronald Reagan, August 10, 1988.

nation, their nation. Yet back at home, the soldiers' families were being denied the very freedom for which so many of the soldiers themselves were laying down their lives.

Congressman Norman Mineta, with us today, was 10 years old when his family was interned. In the Congressman's words: "My own family was sent first to Santa Anita Racetrack. We showered in the horse paddocks. Some families lived in converted stables, others in hastily thrown together barracks. We were then moved to Heart Mountain, Wyoming, where our entire family lived in one small room of a rude tar paper barrack." Like so many tens of thousands of others, the members of the Mineta family lived in those conditions not for a matter of weeks or months but for 3 long years.

The legislation that I am about to sign provides for a restitution payment to each of the 60,000 surviving Japanese-Americans of the 120,000 who were relocated or detained. Yet no payment can make up for those lost years. So, what is more important in this bill has less to do with property than with honor. For here we admit a wrong. Here we reaffirm our commitment as a nation to equal justice under the law.

I'd like to note that the bill I'm about to sign also provides funds for members of the Aleut community who were evacuated from the Aleutian and Pribilof Islands after a Japanese attack in 1942. This action was taken for the Aleuts' own protection, but property was lost or damaged that has never been replaced.

And now in closing, I wonder whether you'd permit me one personal reminiscence, one prompted by an old newspaper report sent to me by Rose Ochi, a former internee. The clipping comes from the *Pacific Citizen* and is dated December 1945.

"Arriving by plane from Washington," the article begins, "General Joseph W. Stilwell pinned the Distinguished Service Cross on Mary Masuda in a simple ceremony on the porch of her small frame shack near Talbert, Orange County. She was one of the first Americans of Japanese ancestry to return from relocation centers to California's farmlands." "Vinegar Joe" Stilwell was there that day to honor Kazuo Masuda, Mary's brother. You see, while Mary and her parents were in an internment camp, Kazuo served as staff sergeant to the 442d Regimental Combat Team. In one action, Kazuo ordered his men back and advanced through heavy fire, hauling a mortar. For 12 hours, he engaged in a singlehanded barrage of Nazi positions. Several weeks later at Cassino, Kazuo staged another lone advance. This time it cost him his life.

The newspaper clipping notes that her two surviving brothers were with Mary and her parents on the little porch that morning. These two brothers, like the heroic Kazuo, had served in the United States Army. After General Stilwell made the award, the motion picture actress Louise Allbritton, a Texas girl, told how a Texas battalion had been saved by the

442d. Other show business personalities paid tribute—Robert Young, Will Rogers, Jr. And one young actor said: "Blood that has soaked into the sands of a beach is all of one color. America stands unique in the world: the only country not founded on race but on a way, an ideal. Not in spite of but because of our polyglot background, we have had all the strength in the world. That is the American way." The name of that young actor— I hope I pronounce this right—was Ronald Reagan. And, yes, the ideal of liberty and justice for all—that is still the American way.

Thank you, and God bless you. And now let me sign H.R. 442, so fittingly named in honor of the 442d.

Thank you all again, and God bless you all. I think this is a fine day.

Chapter 13

Moving to Suburbia: Dreams and Discontents

World War II set off an economic boom marked by the steady growth of family and individual incomes that lasted, with few interruptions, until 1973. Never before had the nation experienced such prosperity. Never before had material products that Americans associated with "the good life"—automobiles, dishwashers, stereos, televisions, and more—become so readily available to large segments of the population.

The keystone of the middle-class dream was home ownership. During the 1930s and 1940s, the lyrics of popular ballads like "My Blue Heaven" had expressed the desire for a bungalow in the suburbs, in which husband, wife, and children would live an idyllic life. But wartime demands for the construction of military bases and for defense industries had brought private home building, already slowed by the Depression, to a virtual halt. Within a few years of the war's end, however, the building boom was under way. Kenneth Jackson's essay "The Baby Boom and the Age of the Subdivision" describes how the postwar demand for suburban housing, fueled by veterans and their growing families, was served by government assistance and enterprising builders. Among the latter, William

Levitt was possibly the most ingenious; the housing tracts that he built, called Levittowns, came to symbolize post–World War II construction. Which innovations in home construction and community planning were most likely responsible for establishing Levitt's reputation?

Jackson describes not only the birth of postwar suburbs but also the lifestyles that characterized those communities. Although large numbers of people voted their approval of suburban life by deciding to relocate their families, the movement was not without critics. The homogeneity and conformity of housing developments were frequent targets, as illustrated by the first document, Malvina Reynolds's popular song of the early 1960s, "Little Boxes." Do the lyrics give a fair picture of the suburbs?

The second document, from the best-selling book The Feminine Mystique *by feminist Betty Friedan, singles out for attack another aspect of suburban life, which the author calls "The Problem That Has No Name." What did Friedan see as the impact of suburbanization on the American housewife? Did the problem she discusses arise because of suburban development, or because of larger cultural changes that took place in cities as well as in suburbs?*

Whether suburban life was as bleak for white women as "Little Boxes" and Betty Friedan imply is debatable. Nevertheless, white families at least had a choice, if they had the means, to live where they chose. For black Americans, suburban housing opportunities were limited. The last document, a summary of residential patterns, points to a factor to which Kenneth Jackson alludes: racial segregation. What does this report tell us about race relations in suburban America? Keep housing in mind later, when you asssess the impact of the civil-rights movement.

ESSAY

The Baby Boom and the Age of the Subdivision

Kenneth Jackson

What the Blandings wanted . . . was simple enough: a two-story house in quiet, modern good taste, . . . a good-sized living room with a fire place, a dining room, pantry, and kitchen, a small lavatory, four bedrooms and accompanying baths, . . . a roomy cellar . . . plenty of closets.

—Eric Hodgins,
Mr. Blandings Builds His Dream House (1939)

No man who owns his own house and lot can be a Communist. He has too much to do.

—William J. Levitt, 1948

At 7 P.M. (Eastern time) on August 14, 1945, radio stations across the nation interrupted normal programming for President Harry S Truman's announcement of the surrender of Japan. It was a moment in time that those who experienced it will never forget. World War II was over. Across the nation, Americans gathered to celebrate their victory. In New York City two million people converged on Times Square as though it were New Year's Eve. In smaller cities and towns, the response was no less tumultuous, as spontaneous cheers, horns, sirens, and church bells telegraphed the news to every household and hamlet, convincing even small children that it was a very special day. To the average person, the most important consequence of victory was not the end of shortages, not the restructuring of international boundaries or reparations payments or big power politics, but the survival of husbands and sons. Some women regretted that their first decent-paying, responsible jobs would be taken away by returning veterans. Most, however, felt a collective sigh of relief. Normal family life could resume. The long vigil was over. Their men would be coming home.

In truth, the United States was no better prepared for peace than it had been for war when the German *Wehrmacht* crossed the Polish frontier in the predawn hours of September 1, 1939. For more than five years military necessity had taken priority over consumer goods, and by 1945 almost everyone had a long list of unfilled material wants.

SOURCE: From *Crabgrass Frontier: The Suburbanization of the United States* by Kenneth T. Jackson. Copyright © 1985 by Oxford University Press, Inc. Reprinted by permission.

Housing was the area of most pressing need. Through sixteen years of depression and war, the residential construction industry had been dormant, with new home starts averaging less than 100,000 per year. Almost one million people had migrated to defense areas in the early 1940s, but new housing for them was designated as "temporary," in part as an economy move and in part because the real-estate lobby did not want emergency housing converted to permanent use after the war. Meanwhile, the marriage rate, after a decade of decline, had begun a steep rise in 1940, as war became increasingly likely and the possibility of separation added a spur to decision making. In addition, married servicemen received an additional fifty dollars per month allotment, which went directly to the wives. Soon thereafter, the birth rate began to climb, reaching 22 per 1,000 in 1943, the highest in two decades. Many of the newcomers were "good-bye babies," conceived just before the husbands shipped out, partly because of an absence of birth control, partly because the wife's allotment check would be increased with each child, and partly as a tangible reminder of a father who could not know when, or if, he would return. During the war, government and industry both played up the suburban house to the families of absent servicemen, and between 1941 and 1946 some of the nation's most promising architects published their "dream houses" in a series in the *Ladies' Home Journal*.

After the war, both the marriage and the birth rates continued at a high level. In individual terms, this rise in family formation coupled with the decline in housing starts meant that there were virtually no homes for sale or apartments for rent at war's end. Continuing a trend begun during the Great Depression, six million families were doubling up with relatives or friends by 1947, and another 500,000 were occupying quonset huts or temporary quarters. Neither figure included families living in substandard dwellings or those in desperate need of more room. In Chicago, 250 former trolley cars were sold as homes. In New York City a newly wed couple set up housekeeping for two days in a department store window in hopes that the publicity would help them find an apartment. In Omaha a newspaper advertisement proposed: "Big Ice Box, 7 × 17 feet, could be fixed up to live in." In Atlanta the city bought 100 trailers for veterans. In North Dakota surplus grain bins were turned into apartments. In brief, the demand for housing was unprecedented.

The federal government responded to an immediate need for five million new homes by underwriting a vast new construction program. In the decade after the war Congress regularly approved billions of dollars worth of additional mortgage insurance for the Federal Housing Administration. Even more important was the Servicemen's Readjustment Act of 1944, which created a Veterans Administration mortgage program similar to that of FHA. This law gave official endorsement and support to the view that the 16 million GI's of World War II should return to civilian life with a home of their own. Also, it accepted the builders' contention that they needed an end to government controls but not to government insurance on their investments in residential construction. According to novelist John Keats, "The real estate boys read the Bill, looked at one another in happy amazement, and the dry, rasping noise they made rubbing their hands together could have been heard as far away as Tawi Tawi."

It is not recorded how far the noise carried, but anyone in the residential construction business had ample reason to rub their hands. The assurance of federal mortgage guarantees—at whatever price the builder set—stimulated an unprecedented building boom. Single-family housing starts spurted from only 114,000 in 1944, to 937,000 in 1946, to 1,183,000 in 1948, and to 1,692,000 in 1950, an all-time high. However, . . . what distinguished the period was an increase in the number, importance, and size of large builders. Residential construction in the United States had always been highly fragmented in comparison with other industries, and dominated by small and poorly organized house builders who had to subcontract much of the work because their low volume did not justify the hiring of all the craftsmen needed to put up a dwelling. In housing, as in other areas of the economy, World War II was beneficial to large businesses. Whereas before 1945, the typical contractor had put up fewer than five houses per year, by 1959, the median single-family builder put up twenty-two structures. As early as 1949, fully 70 percent of new homes were constructed by only 10 percent of the firms (a percentage that would remain roughly stable for the next three decades), and by 1955 subdivisions accounted for more than three-quarters of all new housing in metropolitan areas.

Viewed from an international perspective, however, the building of homes in the United States remained a small-scale enterprise. In 1969, for example, the percentage of all new units built by builders of more than 500 units per year was only 8.1 percent in the United States, compared with 24 percent in Great Britain and 33 percent in France. World War II, therefore, did not transform the American housing industry as radically as it did that of Europe.

The family that had the greatest impact on postwar housing in the United States was Abraham Levitt and his sons, William and Alfred, who ultimately built more than 140,000 houses and turned a cottage industry into a major manufacturing process. They began on a small scale on Long Island in 1929 and concentrated for years on substantial houses in Rockville Center. Increasing their pace in 1934 with a 200-unit subdivision called "Strathmore" in Manhasset, the Levitts continued to focus on the upper-middle class and marketed their tudor-style houses at between $9,100 and $18,500. Private commissions and smaller subdivisions carried the firm through the remainder of the prewar period.

In 1941 Levitt and Sons received a government contract for 1,600 (later increased to 2,350) war workers' homes in Norfolk, Virginia. The effort was a nightmare, but the brothers learned how to lay dozens of concrete foundations in a single day and to preassemble uniform walls and roofs. Additional contracts for more federal housing in Portsmouth, Virginia, and for barracks for shipyard workers at Pearl Harbor provided supplemental experience, as did William's service with the Navy Seabees from 1943 to 1945. Thus, the Levitts were among the nation's largest home builders even before construction of the first Levittown.

Returning to Long Island after the war, the Levitts built 2,250 houses in Roslyn in 1946 in the $17,500 to $23,500 price range, well beyond the means of the average veteran. In that same year, however, they began the acquisition of 4,000 acres of potato farms in the Town of Hempstead, where they planned the biggest private housing project in American history.

The formula for Island Trees, soon renamed Levittown, was simple. After bulldozing the land and removing the trees, trucks carefully dropped off building materials at precise 60-foot intervals. Each house was built on a concrete slab (no cellar); the floors were of asphalt and the walls of composition rock-board. Plywood replaced ¾-inch strip lap, ¾-inch double lap was changed to ⅜-inch for roofing, and the horse and scoop were replaced by the bulldozer. New power hand tools like saws, routers, and nailers helped increase worker productivity. Freight cars loaded with lumber went directly into a cutting yard where one man cut parts for ten houses in one day.

The construction process itself was divided into twenty-seven distinct steps—beginning with laying the foundation and ending with a clean sweep of the new home. Crews were trained to do one job—one day the white-paint men, then the red-paint men, then the tile layers. Every possible part, and especially the most difficult ones, were preassembled in central shops, whereas most builders did it on site. Thus, the Levitts reduced the skilled component to 20–40 percent. The five-day work week was standard, but they were the five days during which building was possible; Saturday and Sunday were considered to be the days when it rained. In the process, the Levitts defied unions and union work rules (against spray painting, for example) and insisted that subcontractors work only for them. Vertical integration also meant that the firm made its own concrete, grew its own timber, and cut its own lumber. It also bought all appliances from wholly owned subsidiaries. More than thirty houses went up each day at the peak of production.

Initially limited to veterans, this first "Levittown" was twenty-five miles east of Manhattan and particularly attractive to new families that had been formed during and just after the war. Squashed in with their in-laws or in tiny apartments where landlords frowned on children, the GI's looked upon Levittown as the answer to their most pressing need. Months before the first three hundred Levitt houses were occupied in October 1947, customers stood in line for the four-room Cape Cod box renting at sixty dollars per month. The first eighteen hundred houses were initially available only for rental, with an option to buy after a year's residence. Because the total for mortgage, interest, principal, and taxes was *less* than the rent, almost everyone bought; after 1949 all units were for sale only. So many of the purchasers were young families that the first issue of *Island Trees*, the community newspaper, opined that "our lives are held closely together because most of us are within the same age bracket, in similar income groups, live in almost identical houses and have common problems." And so many babies were born to them that the suburb came to be known as "Fertility Valley" and "The Rabbit Hutch."

Ultimately encompassing more than 17,400 separate houses and 82,000 residents, Levittown was the largest housing development ever put up by a single builder, and it served the American dream-house market at close to the lowest prices the industry could attain. The typical Cape Cod was down-to-earth and unpretentious; the intention was not to stir the imagination, but to provide the best shelter at the least price. Each dwelling included a twelve-by-sixteen-foot living-room with a fireplace, one bath, and two bedrooms (about 750 square feet), with easy expansion possibilities upstairs in the unfinished attic or outward into the yard. Most importantly, the floor plan was practical and well-designed, with the kitchen moved to the front of the house near the entrance so that mothers could watch their children from kitchen windows and do their washing and cooking with a minimum of movement. Similarly, the living room was placed in the rear and given a picture window overlooking the back yard. This early Levitt house was as basic to post–World War II suburban development as the Model T had been to the automobile. In each case, the actual design features were less important than the fact that they were mass-produced and thus priced within the reach of the middle class.

William Jaird Levitt, who assumed primary operating responsibility for the firm soon after the war, disposed of houses as quickly as other men disposed of cars. Pricing his Cape Cods at $7,990 (the earliest models went for $6,990) and his ranches at $9,500, he promised no down payment, no closing costs, and "no hidden extras." With FHA and VA "production advances," Levitt boasted the largest line of credit ever offered a private home builder. He simplified the paperwork required for purchase and reduced the entire financing and titling transaction to two half-hour steps. His full-page advertisements offered a sweetener to eliminate lingering resistance—a Bendix washer was included in the purchase price. Other inducements included an eight-inch television set (for which the family would pay for the next thirty years). So efficient was the operation that *Harper's Magazine* reported in 1948 that Levitt undersold his nearest competition by $1,500 and still made a $1,000 profit on each house. As *New York Times* architecture critic Paul Goldberger has noted, "Levittown houses were social creations more than architectural ones—they turned the detached, single-family house from a distant dream to a real possibility for thousands of middle-class American families."

Buyers received more than shelter for their money. When the initial families arrived with their baby strollers and play pens, there were no trees, schools, churches, or private telephones. Grocery shopping was a planned adventure, and picking up the mail required sloshing through the mud to Hicksville. The Levitts planted apple, cherry, and evergreen trees on each plot, however, and the development ultimately assumed a more parklike appearance. To facilitate development as a garden community, streets were curvilinear (and invariably called "roads" or "lanes"), and through traffic was shunted to peripheral thoroughfares. Nine swimming pools, sixty playgrounds, ten baseball diamonds, and seven "village greens" provided open space and recreational opportunities. The Levitts forbade fences (a practice later ignored) and permitted outdoor clothes drying only on specially designed, collapsible racks. They even supervised lawn-cutting for the first few years—doing the jobs themselves if necessary and sending the laggard families the bill.

Architectural critics, many of whom were unaccustomed to the tastes or resources of moderate-income people, were generally unimpressed by the repetitious houses on 60-by-100-foot "cookie cutter lots" and referred to Levittown as "degraded in conception and impoverished in form." From the Wantagh Parkway, the town stretched away to the east as far as the eye could see, house after identical house, a horizon broken only by telephone poles. Paul Goldberger, who admired the individual designs, thought that the whole was "an urban planning disaster," while [social critic] Lewis Mumford complained that Levittown's narrow range of house type and income range resulted in a one-class community and a backward design. He noted that the Levitts used "new-fashioned methods to compound old-fashioned mistakes."

But Levittown was a huge popular success where it counted—in the marketplace. On a single day in March 1949, fourteen hundred contracts were drawn, some with families that had been in line for four days. "I truly loved it," recalled one early resident. "When they built the Village Green, our big event was walking down there for ice cream."

In the 1950s the Levitts shifted their attention from Long Island to an equally large project near Philadelphia. Located on former broccoli and spinach farms in lower Bucks County, Pennsylvania, this new Levittown was built within a few miles of the new Fairless Works of the United States Steel Corporation, where the largest percentage of the community's residents were employed. It was composed on eight master blocks, each of about one square mile and focusing on its own recreational facilities. Totaling about 16,000 homes when completed late in the decade, the town included light industry and a big, 55-acre shopping center. According to Levitt, "We planned every foot of it—every store, filling station, school, house, apartment, church, color, tree, and shrub."

In the 1960s, the Levitt forces shifted once again, this time to Willing-

249

boro, New Jersey, where a third Levittown was constructed within distant commuting range of Philadelphia. This last town was the focus of Herbert Gans's well-known account of *The Levittowners.* The Cape Cod remained the basic style, but Levitt improved the older models to resemble more closely the pseudo-colonial design that was so popular in the Northeast.

If imitation is the sincerest form of flattery, then William Levitt has been much honored in the past forty years. His replacement of basement foundations with the radiantly heated concrete slab was being widely copied as early as 1950. Levitt did not actually pioneer many of the mass-production techniques—the use of plywood, particle board, and gypsum board, as well as power hand tools like saws, routers, and nailers, for example—but his developments were so widely publicized that in every large metropolitan area, large builders appeared who adopted similar methods. . . .

FHA and VA programs made possible the financing of their immense developments. Title VI of the National Housing Act of 1934 allowed a builder to insure 90 percent of the mortgage of a house costing up to nine thousand dollars. Most importantly, an ambitious entrepreneur could get an FHA "commitment" to insure the mortgage, and then use that "commitment" to sign himself up as a temporary mortgagor. The mortgage lender (a bank or savings and loan institution) would then make "production advances" to the contractor as the work progressed, so that the builder needed to invest very little of his own hard cash. Previously, even the largest builders could not bring together the capital to undertake thousand-house developments. FHA alone insured three thousand houses in Henry J. Kaiser's Panorama City, California; five thousand in Frank Sharp's Oak Forest; and eight thousand in Klutznick's Park Forest project.

However financed and by whomever built, the new subdivisions that were typical of American urban development between 1945 and 1973 tended to share five common characteristics. The first was peripheral location. A Bureau of Labor Statistics survey of home building in 1946–1947 in six metropolitan regions determined that the suburbs accounted for at least 62 percent of construction. By 1950 the national suburban growth rate was ten times that of central cities, and in 1954 the editors of *Fortune* estimated that 9 million people had moved to the suburbs in the previous decade. The inner cities did have some empty lots—serviced by sewers, electrical connections, gas lines, and streets—available for development. But the filling-in process was not amenable to mass production techniques, and it satisfied neither the economic nor the psychological temper of the times.

The few new neighborhoods that were located within the boundaries of major cities tended also to be on the open land at the edges of the built-up sections. In New York City, the only area in the 1946–1947 study where city construction was greater than that of the suburbs, the big growth was on the outer edges of Queens, a borough that had been largely undeveloped in 1945. In Memphis new development moved east out Summer, Poplar, Walnut Grove, and Park Avenues, where FHA and VA subdivisions advertised "No Down Payment" or "One Dollar Down" on giant billboards. In Los Angeles, the fastest-growing American city in the immediate postwar period, the area of rapid building focused on the San Fernando Valley, a vast space that had remained largely vacant since its annexation to the city in 1915. In Philadelphia thousands of new houses were put up in farming areas that had legally been part of the city since 1854, but which in fact had functioned as agricultural settlements for generations.

The second major characteristic of the postwar suburbs was their relatively low density. In all except the most isolated instances, the row house completely lost favor; between 1946 and 1956, about 97 percent of all new single-family dwellings were completely detached, surrounded on every side by their own plots. Typical lot sizes were relatively uniform around the country, averaging between ⅕ (80 by 100 feet) and ⅒ (40 by 100 feet) of an acre and varying more with distance from the center than by region. Moreover, the new subdivisions allotted a higher proportion of their land area to streets and open spaces. Levittown, Long Island, for example, was settled at a density of 10,500 per square mile, which was about average for postwar suburbs but less than half as dense as the streetcar suburbs of a half-century earlier. This design of new neighborhoods on the assumption that residents would have automobiles meant that those without cars faced severe handicaps in access to jobs and shopping facilities.

This low-density pattern was in marked contrast with Europe. In war-ravaged countries east of the Rhine River, the concentration upon apartment buildings can be explained by the overriding necessity to provide shelter quickly for masses of displaced and homeless people. But in comparatively unscathed France, Denmark, and Spain, the single-family house was also a rarity. In Sweden, Stockholm committed itself to a suburban pattern along subway lines, a decision that implied a high-density residential pattern. Nowhere in Europe was there the land, the money, or the tradition for single-family home construction.

The third major characteristic of the postwar suburbs was their architectural similarity. A few custom homes were built for the rich, and mobile homes gained popularity with the poor and the transient, but for most American families in search of a new place to live some form of tract house was the most likely option. In order to simplify their production methods and reduce design fees, most of the larger developers offered no more than a half-dozen basic house plans, and some offered half that number. The result was a monotony and repetition that was especially stark in the early years of the subdivision, before the individual owners had transformed their homes and yards according to personal taste.

251

But the architectural similarity extended beyond the particular tract to the nation as a whole. Historically, each region of the country had developed an indigenous residential style—the colonial-style homes of New England, the row houses of Atlantic coastal cities, the famous Charleston town houses with their ends to the street, the raised plantation homes of the damp bayou country of Louisiana, and the encircled patios and massive walls of the Southwest. This regionalism of design extended to relatively small areas; early in the twentieth century a house on the South Carolina coast looked quite different from a house in the Piedmont a few hundred miles away.

This tradition began eroding after World War I, when the American dream house became . . . the Cape Cod cottage, a quaint one-and-a-half-story dwelling. This design remained popular into the post–World War II years, when Levittown featured it as a bargain for veterans. In subsequent years, one fad after another became the rage. First, it was the split-level, then the ranch, then the modified colonial. In each case, the style tended to find support throughout the continent, so that by the 1960s the casual suburban visitor would have a difficult time deciphering whether she was in the environs of Boston or Dallas.

The ranch style, in particular, was evocative of the expansive mood of the post–World War II suburbs and of the disappearing regionality of style. It was almost as popular in Westchester County as in Los Angeles County. Remotely derived from the adobe dwellings of the Spanish colonial tradition and more directly derived from the famed prairie houses of [architect] Frank Lloyd Wright, with their low-pitched roofs, deep eaves, and pronounced horizontal lines, the typical ranch style houses of the 1950s were no larger than the average home a generation earlier. But the one-level ranch house suggested spacious living and an easy relationship with the outdoors. Mothers with small children did not have to contend with stairs. Most importantly, the postwar ranch home represented newness. In 1945 the publisher of the *Saturday Evening Post* reported that only 14 percent of the population wanted to live in an apartment or a "used" house. Whatever the style, the post–World War II house, in contrast to its turn-of-the-century predecessor, had no hall, no parlor, no stairs, and no porch. And the portion of the structure that projected farthest toward the street was the garage.

The fourth characteristic of post–World War II housing was its easy availability and thus its reduced suggestion of wealth. To be sure, upper-income suburbs and developments sprouted across the land, and some set high standards of style and design. Typically, they offered expansive lots, spacious and individualized designs, and affluent neighbors. But the most important income development of the period was the lowering of the threshold of purchase. At every previous time in American history, and indeed for the 1980s as well, the successful acquisition of a family home required savings and effort of a major order. After World War II, however, because of mass-production techniques, government financing, high wages, and low interest rates, it was quite simply cheaper to buy new housing in the suburbs than it was to reinvest in central city properties or to rent at the market price.

The fifth and perhaps most important characteristic of the postwar suburb was economic and racial homogeneity. The sorting out of families by income and color began even before the Civil War and was stimulated by the growth of the factory system. This pattern was noticeable in both the exclusive Main Line suburbs of Philadelphia and New York and in the more bourgeois streetcar developments which were part of every city. The automobile accentuated this discriminatory "Jim Crow" pattern. In Atlanta where large numbers of whites flocked to the fast-growing and wealthy suburbs north of the city in the 1920s, [it was] reported that: "By 1930, if racism could be measured in miles and minutes, blacks and whites were more segregated in the city of Atlanta than ever before." But many pre-1930 suburbs—places like Greenwich, Connecticut; Englewood, New Jersey; Evanston, Illinois; and Chestnut Hill, Massachusetts—maintained an exclusive image despite the presence of low-income or minority groups living in slums near or within the community.

The post-1945 developments took place against a background of the decline of factory-dominated cities. What was unusual in the new circumstances was not the presence of discrimination—Jews and Catholics as well as blacks had been excluded from certain neighborhoods for generations—but the thoroughness of the physical separation which it entailed. The Levitt organization, which was no more culpable in this regard than any other urban or suburban firm, publicly and officially refused to sell to blacks for two decades after the war. Nor did resellers deal with minorities. As William Levitt explained, "We can solve a housing problem, or we can try to solve a racial problem. But we cannot combine the two." Not surprisingly, in 1960 not a single one of the Long Island Levittown's 82,000 residents was black.

The economic and age homogeneity of large subdivisions and sometimes entire suburbs was almost as complete as the racial distinction. Although this tendency had been present even in the nineteenth century, the introduction of zoning—beginning with a New York City ordinance in 1916—served the general purpose of preserving residential class segregation and property values. In theory zoning was designed to protect the interests of all citizens by limiting land speculation and congestion. And it was popular. Although it represented an extraordinary growth of municipal power, nearly everyone supported zoning. By 1926 seventy-six cities had adopted ordinances similar to that of New York. By 1936, 1,322 cities (85 percent of the total) had them, and zoning laws were affecting more property than all national laws relating to business.

In actuality zoning was a device to keep poor people and obnoxious industries out of affluent areas. And in time, it also became a cudgel used by suburban areas to whack the central city. Advocates of land-use restrictions in overwhelming proportion were residents of the fringe. They sought through minimum lot and set-back requirements to insure that only members of acceptable social classes could settle in their privileged sanctuaries. Southern cities even used zoning to enforce racial segregation. And in suburbs everywhere, North and South, zoning was used by the people who already lived within the arbitrary boundaries of a community as a method of keeping everyone else out. Apartments, factories, and "blight," euphemisms for blacks and people of limited means, were rigidly excluded.

While zoning provided a way for suburban areas to become secure enclaves for the well-to-do, it forced the city to provide economic facilities for the whole area and homes for people the suburbs refused to admit. Simply put, land-use restrictions tended to protect residential interests in the suburbs and commercial interests in the cities because the residents of the core usually lived on land owned by absentee landlords who were more interested in financial returns than neighborhood preferences. For the man who owned land but did not live on it, the ideal situation was to have his parcel of earth zoned for commercial or industrial use. With more options, the property often gained in value. In Chicago, for example, three times as much land was zoned for commercial use as could ever have been profitably employed for such purposes. This overzoning prevented inner-city residents from receiving the same protection from commercial incursions as was afforded suburbanites. Instead of becoming a useful tool for the rational ordering of land in metropolitan areas, zoning became a way for suburbs to pirate from the city only its desirable functions and residents. Suburban governments became like so many residential hotels, fighting for the upper-income trade while trying to force the deadbeats to go elsewhere.

Because zoning restrictions typically excluded all apartments and houses and lots of less than a certain number of square feet, new home purchasers were often from a similar income and social group. In this regard, the postwar suburbs were no different from many nineteenth-century neighborhoods when they were first built. Moreover, Levittown was originally a mix of young professionals and lower-middle-class blue-collar workers.

As the aspiring professionals moved out, however, Levittown became a community of the most class-stratifying sort possible. This phenomenon was the subject of one of the most important books of the 1950s. Focusing on a 2,400-acre project put up by the former Public Housing Administrator Phillip Klutznick, William H. Whyte's *The Organization Man* sent shudders through armchair sociologists. Although Whyte found that Park Forest, Illinois, offered its residents "leadership training" and an "ability to chew on real problems," the basic portrait was unflattering. Reporting excessive conformity and a mindless conservatism, he showed Park Foresters to be almost interchangeable as they fought their way up the corporate ladder, and his "organization man" stereotype unfortunately became the norm for judging similar communities throughout the nation.

By 1961, when President John F. Kennedy proclaimed his New Frontier and challenged Americans to send a man to the moon within the decade, his countrymen had already remade the nation's metropolitan areas in the short space of sixteen years. From Boston to Los Angeles, vast new subdivisions and virtually new towns sprawled where a generation earlier nature had held sway. In an era of low inflation, plentiful energy, federal subsidies, and expansive optimism, Americans showed the way to a more abundant and more perfect lifestyle. Almost every contractor-built, post–World War II home had central heating, indoor plumbing, telephones, automatic stoves, refrigerators, and washing machines.

There was a darker side to the outward movement. By making it possible for young couples to have separate households of their own, abundance further weakened the extended family in America and ordained that most children would grow up in intimate contact only with their parents and siblings. The housing arrangements of the new prosperity were evident as early as 1950. In that year there were 45,983,000 dwelling units to accommodate the 38,310,000 families in the United States and 84 percent of American households reported less than one person per room.

Critics regarded the peripheral environment as devastating particularly to women and children. The suburban world was a female world, especially during the day. Betty Friedan's 1963 classic *The Feminine Mystique* challenged the notion that the American dream home was emotionally fulfilling for women. As Gwendolyn Wright has observed, their isolation from work opportunities and from contact with employed adults led to stifled frustration and deep psychological problems. Similarly, Sidonie M. Gruenberg warned in the *New York Times Magazine* that "Mass produced, standardized housing breeds standardized individuals, too—especially among youngsters." Offering neither the urbanity and sophistication of the city nor the tranquility and repose of the farm, the suburb came to be regarded less as an intelligent compromise than a cultural, economic, and emotional wasteland. No observer was more critical than Lewis Mumford, however. In his 1961 analysis of *The City in History*, which covered the entire sweep of civilization, the famed author reiterated sentiments he had first expressed more than four decades earlier and scorned the new developments which were surrounding every American city:

In the mass movement into suburban areas a new kind of community was produced, which caricatured both the historic city and

the archetypal suburban refuge: a multitude of uniform, uniden-
tifiable houses, lined up inflexibly, at uniform distances, on uniform roads, in a treeless communal waste, inhabited by people of
the same class, the same income, the same age group, witnessing
the same television performances, eating the same tasteless pre-
fabricated foods, from the same freezers, conforming in every outward and inward respect to a common mold, manufactured in the
central metropolis. Thus, the ultimate effect of the suburban escape
in our own time is, ironically, a low-grade uniform environment
from which escape is impossible.

Secondly, because the federally supported home-building boom was
of such enormous proportions, the new houses of the suburbs were a major
cause of the decline of central cities. Because FHA and VA terms for new
construction were so favorable as to make the suburbs accessible to almost
all white, middle-income families, the inner-city housing market was deprived of the purchasers who could perhaps have supplied an appropriate
demand for the evacuated neighborhoods.

The young families who joyously moved into the new homes of the
suburbs were not terribly concerned about the problems of the inner-city
housing market or the snobbish views of Lewis Mumford and other social
critics. They were concerned about their hopes and their dreams. They
were looking for good schools, private space, and personal safety, and
places like Levittown could provide those amenities on a scale and at a
price that crowded city neighborhoods, both in the Old World and in the
New, could not match. The single-family tract house—post–World War II
style—whatever its aesthetic failings, offered growing families a private
haven in a heartless world. If the dream did not include minorities or the
elderly, if it was accompanied by the isolation of nuclear families, by the
decline of public transportation, and by the deterioration of urban neighborhoods, the creation of good, inexpensive suburban housing on an unprecedented scale was a unique achievement in the world.

DOCUMENTS

Little Boxes, 1962

Little boxes on the hillside, little boxes made of ticky tacky,
Little boxes on the hillside, little boxes all the same.
There's a green one and a pink one and a blue one and a yellow
   one,
And they're all made out of ticky tacky and they all look just the
   same.

And the people in the houses all went to the university
Where they were put in boxes and they came out all the same;
And there's doctors, and there's lawyers and there's business
   executives
And they're all made out of ticky tacky and they all look just the
   same.

And they all play on the golf course and drink their martini dry
And they all have pretty children and the children go to school
And the children go to summer camp and then to the university
Where they are all put in boxes and they come out all the same.

Coda (retard like a music box running down)

The Problem That Has No Name, 1963

The suburban housewife—she was the dream image of the young American women and the envy, it was said, of women all over the world. The American housewife—freed by science and labor-saving appliances from the drudgery, the dangers of childbirth and the illnesses of her grandmother. She was healthy, beautiful, educated, concerned only about her husband, her children, her home. She had found true feminine fulfillment. As a housewife and mother, she was respected as a full and equal partner to man in his world. She was free to choose automobiles, clothes, appliances, supermarkets; she had everything that women ever dreamed of.

In the fifteen years after World War II, this mystique of feminine fulfillment became the cherished and self-perpetuating core of contemporary American culture. Millions of women lived their lives in the image of those pretty pictures of the American suburban housewife, kissing their husbands goodbye in front of the picture window, depositing their station wagonsful of children at school, and smiling as they ran the new electric waxer over the spotless kitchen floor. They baked their own bread, sewed their own and their children's clothes, kept their new washing machines and dryers running all day. They changed the sheets on the beds twice a week instead of once, took the rug-hooking class in adult education, and pitied their poor frustrated mothers, who had dreamed of having a career. Their only dream was to be perfect wives and mothers; their highest ambition to have five children and a beautiful house, their only fight to get and keep their husbands. They had no thought for the unfeminine prob-

SOURCE: Reprinted from *The Feminine Mystique* by Betty Friedan, by permission of W. W. Norton & Co., Inc. Copyright © 1983, 1974, 1973, 1963 by Betty Friedan.

lems of the world outside the home; they wanted the men to make the major decisions. They gloried in their role as women, and wrote proudly on the census blank: "Occupation: housewife."

For over fifteen years, the words written for women, and the words women used when they talked to each other, while their husbands sat on the other side of the room and talked shop or politics or septic tanks, were about problems with their children, or how to keep their husbands happy, or improve their children's school, or cook chicken or make slipcovers. Nobody argued whether women were inferior or superior to men; they were simply different. Words like "emancipation" and "career" sounded strange and embarrassing; no one had used them for years. When a French-woman named Simone de Beauvoir wrote a book called *The Second Sex*, an American critic commented that she obviously "didn't know what life was all about," and besides, she was talking about French women. The "woman problem" in America no longer existed.

If a woman had a problem in the 1950s and 1960s, she knew that something must be wrong with her marriage, or with herself. Other women were satisfied with their lives, she thought. What kind of a woman was she if she did not feel this mysterious fulfillment waxing the kitchen floor? She was so ashamed to admit her dissatisfaction that she never knew how many other women shared it. If she tried to tell her husband, he didn't understand what she was talking about. She did not really understand it herself. For over fifteen years women in America found it harder to talk about this problem than about sex. Even the psychoanalysts had no name for it. When a woman went to a psychiatrist for help, as many women did, she would say, "I'm so ashamed," or "I must be hopelessly neurotic." "I don't know what's wrong with women today," a suburban psychiatrist said uneasily. "I only know something is wrong because most of my patients happen to be women. And their problem isn't sexual." Most women with this problem did not go to see a psychoanalyst, however. "There's nothing wrong really," they kept telling themselves. "There isn't any problem."

But on an April morning in 1959, I heard a mother of four, having coffee with four other mothers in a suburban development fifteen miles from New York, say in a tone of quiet desperation, "the problem." And the others knew, without words, that she was not talking about a problem with her husband, or her children, or her home. Suddenly they realized they all shared the same problem, the problem that has no name. They began, hesitantly, to talk about it. Later, after they had picked up their children at nursery school and taken them home to nap, two of the women cried, in sheer relief, just to know they were not alone.

Gradually I came to realize that the problem that has no name was shared by countless women in America. As a magazine writer I often interviewed women about problems with their children, or their marriages, or their houses, or their communities. But after a while I began to recognize the telltale signs of this other problem. I saw the same signs in suburban ranch houses and split-levels on Long Island and in New Jersey and West-chester County; in colonial houses in a small Massachusetts town; on patios in Memphis; in suburban and city apartments; in living rooms in the Mid-west. Sometimes I sensed the problem, not as a reporter, but as a suburban housewife, for during this time I was also bringing up my own three children in Rockland County, New York. I heard echoes of the problem in college dormitories and semiprivate maternity wards, at PTA meetings and luncheons of the League of Women voters, at suburban cocktail par-ties, in station wagons waiting for trains, and in snatches of conversation overheard at Schrafft's. The groping words I heard from other women, on quiet afternoons when children were at school or on quiet evenings when husbands worked late, I think I understood first as a woman long before I understood their larger social and psychological implications. . . .

If I am right, the problem that has no name stirring in the minds of so many American women today is not a matter of loss of femininity or too much education, or the demands of domesticity. It is far more important than anyone recognizes. It is the key to these other new and old problems which have been torturing women and their husbands and children, and puzzling their doctors and educators for years. It may well be the key to our future as a nation and a culture. We can no longer ignore that voice within women that says: "I want something more than my husband and my children and my home."

Segregation in the Suburbs, 1994

Roosevelt, L.I.—When Marshella Atkinson's parents decided to leave Brooklyn for Long Island, the enthusiasm of friends and teachers made her smile with anticipation.

Perhaps they pictured the swimming pools of nearby Levittown, or the shopping centers of Garden City, or the well-stocked library and spot-less corridors of Plainview-Old Bethpage High School. Ms. Atkinson is not sure.

But four years later, the 16-year old does know one thing: they could not have meant Roosevelt, where boarded-up houses dot the walk home from high school and people complain that their streets are last to be plowed by the town of Hempstead, where Roosevelt is the most troubled section.

SOURCE: Diane Jean Schemo, "Existent Racial Segregation Mars Suburbs' Green Dream," *The New York Times*, March 17, 1994. Copyright © 1994 by *The New York Times* Company. Reprinted by permission.

"I think they set it up so that when a black family moves here, it ends up in Roosevelt," said Ms. Atkinson, a junior at Roosevelt High School. She glanced at a hole in her classroom ceiling where tiles had been ripped away. Graffiti scarred the walls. "I thought it was going to be a dream place," she said.

Drawn by the promise of escape from inner-city congestion and violence, more and more families like the Atkinsons are moving to America's suburbs. Like the white middle class before them, they come for a home of their own, good schools, open spaces and relative safety, everything that the suburbs symbolize in the American narrative.

But segregation is not declining as black and Hispanic people move to the suburbs, according to John R. Logan, a sociologist at the State University of New York at Albany, who has studied segregation around 10 major cities. Nationally, 1 black person in 3 now lives in the suburbs, but even those with middle-classe incomes usually end up in middle-class pockets of poorer neighborhoods.

Lily-white communities tend not to become integrated but to remain largely lily-white, with the addition of well-defined minority precincts. On long Island, 95 percent of black residents are concentrated in 5 percent of the census tracts. According to census data, the average white person in Nassau County lives in a census tract in which only 8 percent of the residents are black or Hispanic. The average white child attends a school that is just 9 percent black. . . .

"Both within cities and suburbs, Hispanics and blacks are segregated, and they're forced to locate in the least desirable communities," Professor Logan said. "And I see no evidence that any change in civil rights laws or fair housing legislation is having any effect."

Of course, some blacks choose to live in black neighborhoods. Others opted for integrated areas that white flight has since rendered mostly black. Still others can afford only the cheapest suburban housing. But a great many blacks complain they are never shown the full range of housing choices or are discouraged from buying in predominantly white communities.

Once they arrive, blacks find that the suburban landscape and the suburban way of life increase racial isolation: The tendency to restrict parks, libraries and other amenities to local residents; to rely on cars rather than on mass transit, and to emphasize home rule in government promote a segregated existence, no matter what the intent.

While the Long Island suburbs, in their postwar expansion, were providing the blueprint for an America of the automobile age, the plan accepted white prejudices of the day, typically restricting the emerging communities to "members of the Caucasian race."

Federal laws now bar discrimination, but mechanisms of segregation endure. James Thomas landed in the Suffolk County hamlet of Bellport after a thwarted attempt to buy a house in white Port Jefferson 33 years ago. Mr.

Thomas's mailman, who was white, offered to sell Mr. Thomas his Cape Cod in Bellport for $10,500. "You have to take where you can get," the retired factory supervisor said.

For 20 years, Bellport remained a "solid, good community." But what he thought was steady integration turned out to be a white hemorrhage. A decade ago, Mr. Thomas realized that the people moving in were no longer working class or middle class but getting by on government aid. Bellport became as blighted as any city neighborhood, its streets lined with prostitutes and certain corners given over to drug dealing.

Mr. Thomas looked across the hedges at a house that had burned down several months before: a jungle of exposed wires and half-fallen floors. For him, the delay in razing the house, since removed, was sure proof of the Town of Brookhaven's disregard for blacks. "You can't tell me that this would be left to stand this way in a white neighborhood," he said.

Services Dwindle

Whites who bought homes in the suburbs typically began a lifelong climb up the social and economic ladder. Many blacks are forced to watch their investment decline as whites flee, poorer minorities move in and services dwindle. Homeowners like Ed Larson of the North Amityville Taxpayers Association meet to enlist police against drug peddlers, prostitutes and street crime, problems that seldom preoccupy their white counterparts.

"If the America dream is to buy a house in the suburbs, send your kid to a good school and have some grass, yes, it's the American dream," said Hugh A. Wilson, director of the Institute for Suburban Studies at Adelphi University. "If it's also to do that in an integrated setting, then for blacks, it's not fulfilling the dream."

Some blacks complain that isolation feeds a quiet acceptance of racism. Alton Williams, first vice president of the Nassau County Guardians, which represents black police officers, said he was shocked to see a white supremacist flyer on another officer's bulletin board. It showed a smiling blond child with the caption "MISSING: A future for white children in America."

Chapter 14

The Black Struggle for Equality

Not all groups shared in the economic boom after World War II. Blacks who had migrated to the North in search of a better life were often sorely disappointed at what they found. Many of those who remained in the South as sharecroppers and tenants were forced off the land by federal government programs that encouraged farmers to leave their fields fallow and by new machinery that replaced human labor. In addition, blacks in both the North and South encountered discrimination in employment, housing, schools, and public facilities. Segregation and dis-

263

franchisement proved most severe in the South, however, where local and state governments imposed and enforced them as policies.

In the mid-1950s, a struggle for racial equality and civil rights emerged. Jane Stevenson's essay "Rosa Parks Wouldn't Budge" brings to life the story of the 1955 bus boycott in Montgomery, Alabama, the event generally credited with launching the renewed crusade and the career of its great leader, Martin Luther King Jr. What factors made Montgomery's bus system an "appropriate target for the integration movement"? In what ways did the tactics employed by the boycotters illustrate King's philosophy of militant nonviolence?

Stevenson points out that plans for concerted black action against racial discrimination followed the U.S. Supreme Court's antisegregation ruling of May 1954 in Brown *v.* Board of Education. *The first document presents excerpts from Chief Justice Earl Warren's statement of the unanimous opinion. What were the key points in the Court's sweeping condemnation of school segregation?*

Although the Supreme Court's decision in Brown, *and later the Montgomery bus boycott cases, won widespread support among whites as well as blacks, many white Americans, particularly in the South, were determined to maintain segregation and to deny blacks political and social equality. As the civil rights movement grew, segregationist opposition became more intense and turbulent. Ironically, as television brought this violence and the contrasting peaceful resistance of the civil rights activists into homes throughout the nation, popular support for black demands strengthened. Congress finally responded, passing the Civil Rights Act of 1964 and the Voting Rights Act of 1965. The speech by Congressman Jamie Whitten of Mississippi comprising the second document expresses sentiments typical of those who opposed the 1964 Civil Rights Act. Compare Whitten's arguments with those of Justice Warren in the* Brown *decision.*

The final document, an account of growing up black in America, is by Hosea Williams, an African-American civil rights leader. As you read his story, compare the description of black life in the South to Congressman Whitten's speech. How do Whitten's remarks strike you in light of the racism encountered by Williams and other black Americans?

ESSAY

Rosa Parks Wouldn't Budge
Jane Stevenson

A neatly dressed, middle-aged black woman was riding home on a Montgomery, Alabama, bus on the evening of Thursday, December 1, 1955. Her lap was full of groceries, which she was going to have to carry home from the bus stop, and her feet were tired from a long day's work.

Mrs. Rosa Parks was sitting in the first row of seats behind the section marked "Whites Only." When she chose this seat, there had been plenty of empty ones both in front of and behind the "Great Divide." Now they were all occupied, and black passengers were standing in the aisle at the rear.

Then two white men got aboard. They dropped their dimes into the fare box. The driver called over his shoulder, "Niggers move back." Three of the passengers obediently rose from their seats in the black section and stood in the aisle. Rosa Parks did not.

Even when the driver repeated his order and heads turned to see who was "making trouble," she sat as if she hadn't heard. The driver swore under his breath, pulled over to the curb, put on the brakes, and came to stand above her.

"I said to move back. You hear?"

All conversation stopped. No one dared move. Mrs. Parks continued to stare out the window at the darkness. The driver waited. Sounds of other traffic dramatized the silence in the bus.

It was a historic moment: the birth of a movement that was to challenge and ultimately change the social patterns that had established themselves in most Americans' minds as a way of life which was traditional and deeply rooted in the South.

Actually, that tradition of racial segregation—loosely nicknamed Jim Crow—was not as venerable as most of its adherents believed. Many segregation laws—especially those concerned with public transportation—only dated from the turn of the twentieth century, and at the start had been resisted, through boycotts, by southern blacks, sometimes successfully. But by 1906 resistance had worn itself out. And in the intervening fifty years the memory had also worn itself out. E. D. Nixon, the man who proposed the Montgomery bus boycott of 1955–56, had never heard of the successful Montgomery bus boycott of 1900–1902. In fact he did not even

SOURCE: Jane Stevenson, "Rosa Parks Wouldn't Budge," *American Heritage* XXIII, 2 (February 1972): 56–64, 85. Copyright © 1972 by *American Heritage*, a division of Forbes Inc.

know that boycotts were again being tried—without much success—in a few southern cities; for example, Baton Rouge.

Nixon was a leader of the Brotherhood of Sleeping Car Porters and one of the founders of both the Alabama state and the Montgomery city branches of the National Association for the Advancement of Colored People [NAACP]. For almost a year before the night of Mrs. Parks's refusal to give up her seat, he had been trying to persuade Montgomery's black community that "the only way to make the power structure do away with segregation on the buses was to take some money out of their pockets."

Few aspects of Jim Crow life were as galling to Montgomery blacks as travel on the city's bus line, which most of them had to use to get to and from work, school, and the central shopping district. There were runs on which a white passenger was a curiosity. Yet the first four rows of seats (ten places) were permanently reserved for whites. And blacks sitting behind those rows could be told to vacate their seats if whites got on after the reserved section was filled.

Blacks also had to endure discourtesy and sometimes hostility from many drivers, all of whom were white. Some used insulting language; others picked quarrels and put blacks off the bus for real or imagined offenses. Some played a peculiarly tormenting practical joke. Since all fares had to be deposited in the box beside the driver, every passenger had to get on by the front door. Blacks then had to get off the bus and board from the rear. The game was to wait until a black passenger got outside, slam the two doors, and drive off, leaving him standing on the curb without his dime.

Resentment was wide and deep in the black community. Some whites, too, were known to disapprove of the bus drivers' harassments. And even among the die-hard segregationists, the mixing of races on a public bus was hardly the emotionally charged issue that integrated schools, or parks, or swimming pools, were. For all these reasons, in the months following the United States Supreme Court ruling of May, 1954, against segregated schools in *Brown* v. *Board of Education*, black leaders all over the South had been arguing that city bus lines were the next appropriate target for the integration movement.

In Montgomery three individual blacks, all women, had refused to give up their seats when ordered. In each case Nixon and the Montgomery NAACP had vainly tried to rally the black community to some sort of effective protest.

The most nearly successful attempt had been organized in March, 1955, after one of these three, a fifteen-year-old high school girl named Claudette Colvin, had been arrested and removed in handcuffs. An *ad hoc* committee of prominent Negro leaders had called on the manager of the bus company and on the City Commission, which governed Montgomery, to protest the way she had been treated and the whole system that led to such acts of spontaneous defiance. Three demands had been formulated: a guarantee of courtesy by drivers; a first-come first-served seating policy; and the hiring of Negro drivers on runs predominantly in Negro areas.

The proposed seating plan would not have ended segregation on the buses. It only required that when all seats were filled (blacks having seated themselves from the back forward and whites from the front backward), the next passengers to board would have to stand, no matter what the color of their skins. Such plans were in use in other southern cities, and the manager of the Montgomery City Lines was willing to go along with the idea until he consulted the company's attorney, Jack Crenshaw, who declared that the company was obligated to abide by the law, which was "clear on the principle of segregated seating."

In fact, it was not at all clear. Alabama state law did require clearly segregated white and black sections, but the Montgomery city code had a provision that no passenger could be required to give up his seat if another was not available. And there was sound legal opinion to the effect that within the city's limits the Montgomery statute took precedence over state law.

Nevertheless, Crenshaw's ruling stiffened the company's resistance. Hope of a legal challenge died when Claudette Colvin's parents refused to let her appear in court. Then community interest cooled to such a degree that the next woman who refused to move back received no organized support at all.

No one knew this background better than Mrs. Parks, who had worked with Nixon on many projects in the NAACP. She could hardly have hoped that her gesture was going to work any profound change in the status quo. She didn't move—as she explained later—because she was "bone weary" and suddenly fed up with being imposed upon. Yet circumstances would render her arrest the spark that lit the fires of resistance.

When E. D. Nixon got home that evening, his wife told him that Mrs. Parks had called from the city jail. Nixon telephoned the desk sergeant to ask about the charges and bail, and was refused the information, as an "unauthorized person." Ordinarily his next step would have been to call a young black Montgomery lawyer named Fred Gray, with whom he had worked on some NAACP cases. But Gray happened to be out of town. So Nixon turned instead to Clifford Durr, a distinguished white Alabamian who had recently returned to private law practice after twenty years in Washington, D.C. Durr had been on the legal staff of the Reconstruction Finance Corporation in the early New Deal years; later he had served as general counsel for the Defense Plant Corporation; and finally he had been a member of the Federal Communications Commission. He and his wife Virginia were part of a small group of southern white liberals who met, with black counterparts, under the aegis of the Alabama Council on Human

Relations, to find ways of improving the South's racial picture. Nixon had come to know and trust them both.

"I called Mr. Durr," Nixon remembered later, "and he called down to the jail and they told him what the charge was. Bail was about $50, so I could make that all right." Then Nixon drove the attorney and his wife (who was a friend of Rosa Parks's) down to the jail. "I made the bond," Nixon told an interviewer, "and we got Mrs. Parks out. We carried her on home, and had coffee and talked."

Over coffee, Durr explained the legal alternatives as he saw them: Mrs. Parks could be defended "on the facts." She had not violated the Montgomery city code because there was no other seat available. He thought such a case could be won, but no challenge to segregation was involved. On the other hand, her attorney could challenge the constitutionality of the Alabama state law. That would mean a protracted and expensive battle, with no possible hope of victory short of a successsful appeal to the United States Supreme Court. But a victory there would strike a major blow against Jim Crow.

Such a fight would need the backing of some national organization like the NAACP. Above all, it would take all the community support that Montgomery's blacks could mobilize.

Fired by the prospect Durr outlined, Nixon went home and told his wife, "I think we got us our test case at last." As he saw it, Fred Gray would take Rosa Parks's case and "do like Mr. Durr said. Go up all the way!" Meantime, he added, "What we got to do now is see about getting folks to stay off those buses Monday when Mrs. Parks comes up in Recorder's Court."

Mrs. Nixon told her husband he was "just plain crazy." "If headaches was selling for a dollar a dozen," she said, "you'd be the guy who'd go into a drug store and ask the man to put some in a bag." She didn't believe sympathy for Mrs. Parks was going to keep people off the buses "when it's as cold as this, and Christmas coming on."

There was some cause for pessimism. Montgomery's black community of fifty thousand persons was, in one observer's phrase, "as caste-ridden as any country in the world except India." No issue and no leader had yet managed to bring anything resembling unity out of its political, religious, economic, and cultural diversity. There might be strong support for Mrs. Parks in the professional group (made up in the main of faculty members from Alabama State College), but those people did not use public transportation. The working people, who did, depended on the buses to get to their jobs and on their jobs to feed and shelter their families. The risk of losing even a single day's pay was too much to ask of the head of a household already living on the edge of poverty.

But Nixon was determined to ask just that and more. Before he went to bed that night he planned a meeting of some forty people for the next day at the Dexter Avenue Baptist Church, a leaflet calling for a one-day bus boycott, and a Monday evening mass meeting to organize further action. He hoped to find a leader to carry on while he was out of town on his job.

Among the local blacks whom Nixon summoned was the Reverend Ralph Abernathy, a militant young Baptist preacher wholeheartedly in agreement with the plan and eager to get to work. There was also the Reverend H. H. Hubbard, head of the Baptist Ministerial Alliance. The Baptists were the largest denomination in the black community, so Hubbard's promise to cooperate in notifying his associates was crucial, and Nixon was elated to get it. Thus encouraged, he called young Dr. Martin Luther King, Jr., the new pastor of the Dexter Avenue church.

It was a fateful contact. Neither man could foresee that it would put young Dr. King on the road to national and historic importance, a Nobel Prize, and, ultimately, death at an assassin's hand. The future leader was then merely a recently arrived young minister of a fashionable Negro church in a southern town, well educated in the North, with a doctorate from Boston University, but with no other distinctions or activist record. Busy with his new duties, in fact, and the responsibilities to a young baby at home, he had only recently turned down the presidency of the local NAACP, and he told Nixon that while the protest organizers were welcome to meet in his church, he was not sure of his own participation. But he soon changed his mind and, with it, his destiny.

The meeting of more than forty people that afternoon quickly agreed to a one-day boycott of the city buses on the day of Mrs. Parks's trial. When it came to agreeing on demands, however, the initial unity was threatening to dissolve until someone pointed out that demands were unimportant compared to the practical problem of spreading the word quickly. There was no black "ghetto" in Montgomery. Negroes lived everywhere in and around the city. A volunteer phone committee could start work at once, but many black families were without phones—and radios or TV sets—and did not take newspapers. Leaflets, which Abernathy had wanted mimeographed immediately on hearing from Nixon, could be passed out at stores where Saturday shoppers congregated. Announcements could be made from church pulpits on Sunday, provided that every minister in town could be persuaded that the notice was important enough not to be ignored.

Transportation was a more serious problem. The first draft of the leaflet said: " . . . *take a car, or share a ride, or walk.*" But thousands lived too far from their jobs to walk, had no car, and knew no one with whom to share. For them some alternative way of getting to work on Monday had to be found, or the protest would not achieve the 50 per cent cut in company revenues that was the agreed target.

Someone suggested appealing to the Negro cab companies, asking them to pick up pedestrians and carry them to their destination for the ten-cent bus fare. (Segregation was so complete in Montgomery that only cabs driven by blacks and marked "Colored" were permitted to carry black passengers. The eighteen such companies and their 210 black drivers would prove a strong help in the first days of the boycott.)

By the time the meeting adjourned, assignments for phoning, distributing leaflets, and reaching ministers and the cab companies had been handed out, and morale was high. Some optimist even suggested that the passenger load of the bus lines might be cut as much as 60 or 65 per cent! Then, two events took place on Sunday that increased the chances of such success. The first was the result of a Friday encounter between E. D. Nixon and a reporter from the Montgomery *Advertiser* named Joe Azbell. The *Advertiser*, Montgomery's major journal, was seen by everyone, white and black, who read the papers in the city. It was by chance that Nixon ran into the white reporter, whom he knew to be friendly. Nixon told him he would give him a hot tip, but warned: "I don't expect to cooperate with anybody who's going to write some sort of degrading story about Negroes."

Azbell promised to write a useful story, if any. Then Nixon told him about Mrs. Parks's action and the planned boycott. Both men agreed that the story should not be attributed to Nixon, but that Azbell should "find" one of the leaflets on some city sidewalk. Sure enough, Sunday morning's *Advertiser* carried a two-column, front-page story, presumably given to the paper by an indignant white woman who had got it from her illiterate maid. The tone was properly disapproving ("Just listen to what the Negroes are up to now!"). But Azbell had kept the bargain, and as Nixon had anticipated, "every preacher in town saw it before he went into his pulpit that morning," and found it important enough to announce.

The other helpful event was a radio announcement by Montgomery's police commissioner that two motorcycle policemen would be assigned to follow every bus on Monday, "to protect anyone who wished to ride from harassment by goon squads." This, it was believed, had the effect of frightening some waverers away from the bus stops.

It was dark when the first buses began to roll on Monday, December 5. Dr. King and his wife, Coretta, who lived a few yards from a stop on one of the predominantly Negro runs, were up at dawn to see how the prospects for a 60 per cent reduction looked.

The early buses were usually crowded with black domestic workers on their way to make breakfast in white kitchens. Today, the first bus was empty. The Kings stayed at the window until the next bus passed. It, too, was empty. The third had two passengers, both white.

As the sky brightened, those of the planning committee with cars cruised the streets in different parts of town. What they saw was amazing. Sidewalks were crowded with black pedestrians. College and high school students were thumbing rides. Cars driven by blacks were overloaded with ride-sharers. There were a few old-fashioned horse-drawn buggies on the street, and one man was seen riding a mule. Youngsters waved in derisive humor at motorcycle policemen behind most of the buses. Some walkers—with up to six miles to go—sang as they trudged along. As King later wrote in his book, *Stride Toward Freedom*: "A miracle had taken place. The once dormant and quiescent Negro community was now fully awake."

At 9:30 A.M. the drama shifted to the courtroom, as Mrs. Parks's case was called. Fred Gray adhered to the line Durr had suggested. He ignored the conflict of state and local laws, and argued instead that segregation on public transportation was a violation of the spirit and letter of the United States Constitution. Without comment on Gray's argument, the judge found Mrs. Parks guilty and fined her ten dollars and court costs, which brought the total to something like fourteen dollars. Gray announced that his client would appeal the verdict, and she was released on bail. Now it was time for a third act: the mass meeting scheduled for 7 P.M. at the Holt Street Baptist Church.

But first, Nixon and Abernathy talked over the needs of the future. These included long-term plans and a permanent organization to carry out the fight. Nixon proposed to call it the Montgomery Citizens' Council, but Abernathy thought that sounded like the White Citizens' Councils that were springing up in opposition to school desegregation. His own suggestion was the Montgomery Improvement Association, and Nixon agreed to go along. They also agreed to ask the meeting to approve of repeating the demands made in Claudette Colvin's case—which fell short of total integration. And then, Abernathy raised the potentially touchy issue of leadership. "Brother Nixon, you're going to serve as president, aren't you?"

"Not unless you all turn down the man I have in mind. That's this young reverend, Martin Luther King, Jr."

Abernathy was surprised. King was not only young—not quite twenty-seven years old—but very new to the area. To nominate him would be to pass over a number of other, older ministers, many of whom had good qualifications.

"I'll tell you my reasons," Nixon said. "First, there's the way he talks. Day I first heard him preach, I turned to the fellow sitting next to me and I said, 'I don't know just how I'm going to do it, but one day I'm going to hook him to the stars!' "

King's education equipped him to talk to Montgomery's white leaders in their own terms. King had a reputation for courage, too. As Nixon said, "You knew he wasn't any white man's nigger." And he had not been in Montgomery long enough to become entangled in any of the factional struggles that divided the black community.

Abernathy agreed that King was a good choice, but thought he would decline. So it was decided to nominate him without warning at a session of the "planning committee"—which would frame resolutions to present to the mass meeting. King was so astonished by the very fact of his election—it was unanimous—that he put up no resistance, confessing later that if he had had time to think, he would have almost certainly refused. Immediately afterward he received a tough assignment: presenting to the crowd not merely the routine matters of choosing a name and officers but the hard choice of whether to continue the boycott or merely threaten to renew it if demands were not met. That decision, clearly, had to be made by those who would carry it out: the thousands of humble people who had walked on this cold, gray morning. Many of them would be present at the Holt Street Baptist Church, and they would there be asked to vote on whether they could sustain their incredible initial momentum by approving a recommendation to continue.

By the seven o'clock meeting time there was not a seat empty in the Holt Street church. Loudspeakers had been installed on the roof to accommodate latecomers who might not find room inside. It took Dr. King fifteen minutes to work his way through the crowd from his car, and ten more to get to the platform after he was inside. The audience was singing "Onward, Christian Soldiers" when he joined Nixon, Abernathy, a number of other ministers, Mrs. Parks, and Fred Gray. After the ritual of prayer and scripture reading—with which all such meetings open in the South—and an ovation for Mrs. Parks, E. D. Nixon rose, glancing at Montgomery's police commissioner, whom he saw seated in one of the pews.

"Before you brothers and sisters get comfortable in your seats," Nixon began, "I want to say if anybody here is afraid, he better take his hat and go home. This is going to be a long, drawn-out affair, and before it's over, somebody's going to die."

There were loud amens, but no one reached for his hat. Nixon then delivered a rouser in favor of continuing the boycott, ending with the challenge: "We've worn aprons long enough. It's time for us to take them off!"

The next speaker was Martin Luther King, Jr. He came to the rostrum almost completely unprepared for what he knew by now would be one of the most important addresses of his life. There had hardly been time in the two hours since he had been given this task to think through the basic purpose of his speech. His analysis had gone as far as dividing it into two possibly contradictory aims: the first, to drain off the anger of those who were "tired of being kicked about by the brutal feet of oppression"—anger that might lead to violence of which he disapproved; and a second, to "keep them courageous and prepared for action." Or, as he put it in another place, the problem was to be militant and moderate at the same time. To make things more difficult, he would have to face the microphones and lights of television crews, for news of the morning's action had focused national attention on Montgomery.

King rose to the moment. Pulpit oratory, once a typical American art, is obsolete in most parts of the country today. But it lingers on in the black

South, and King's sermon was a classic production. Stating the Christian case for nonviolent protest, he said: "We have been amazingly patient . . . but we come here tonight to be saved from that patience that makes us patient with anything less than freedom and justice." Though he roused his audience at first by shouting, "We are tired. Tired of being segregated and humiliated," he brought them down to calmness again by declaring, "Once again we must hear the words of Jesus. 'Love your enemies. Bless them that curse you. Pray for them that despitefully use you.' If we fail to do this, our protest will end up as a meaningless drama on the stage of history. . . . We must not become bitter and end up by hating our white brothers." And in a final chord, he wooed them to their better selves.

"If you will protest courageously, and yet with dignity and Christian love, future historians will say, 'There lived a great people—a black people—who injected new meaning and dignity into the veins of civilization.' This is our challenge and our overwhelming responsibility."

The audience rose, cheering, and one elderly woman remembered afterward the feeling that she "saw angels standing all around him when he finished, and they were lifting him up on their wings!"

Even before Ralph Abernathy read the recommendation, the verdict was in. It was, in Clifford Durr's recollection, "a grass roots verdict if there ever was one. Some of the [black] middle-class professionals were saying, 'Well, we showed them this morning.' But the maids and the cooks, the ones who had done the walking, were saying, 'We haven't showed them a thing yet! But we're going to stay off those buses until they make up their minds to treat us decently.' "

For the first few days this unanimous determination created a euphoric optimism. In view of the unprecedented effectiveness of the boycott and the willingness of the Montgomery Improvement Association [M.I.A.] to settle for a partial victory such as first-come first-served seating through separate doors, it was generally believed that there would be a negotiated settlement. But on Thursday, December 8, when Abernathy's committee met with the City Commission, the bus company attorney, Jack Crenshaw, once more insisted that the Alabama law required continued total segregation. City officials were taking a hard line, too. It was clear that they did not want a Negro victory to stimulate further challenges. And a hint was dropped of strong action to come. The city code set a minimum cab fare of forty-five cents per passenger. Negro taxi companies might soon be forbidden to take passengers at ten cents per trip. The next day that threat did materialize. But fortunately, on Thursday evening there had been one of the twice-weekly meetings planned for the boycott's duration as a way of exchanging information, squelching rumors, boosting morale, and ratifying decisions. Anticipating the city's action, the chairman had appealed for volunteer drivers. One hundred and fifty names were handed in. Next, Rufus Lewis's Transportation Committee sat up all night, working out the details of a system which utilized the whole intricate network of black institutions that had grown up under the hothouse conditions of total segregation.

On Tuesday, just a week after the first day of the boycott, thousands of leaflets were ready for distribution, showing on a map of the city the location of forty-eight dispatch and forty-two pick-up stations, with the hours at which each would be operative. There were plenty of problems still. Dispatch stations for sending people off to work were easy to locate in Negro neighborhoods, and churches could shelter riders who had to wait in bad weather. But after-hours pick-up stations had to be in less friendly territory. Without the intimate knowledge of Montgomery's white neighborhoods supplied by black mail carriers, this part of the plan would have been impossible to design. There were never quite enough volunteer dispatchers at rush hours. Cars sometimes broke down, and so, occasionally, did the tempers of passengers and drivers. But overall, the car pools worked as well as, if not better than, the old bus system. And their impact as a unifying force in the black community was incalculable.

It was expensive, but help came from two unexpected sources. As the "Montgomery Story" was spread throughout the country by the news media, contributions began coming in to the M.I.A. from cities in the North and West. Black churches took up collections to buy station wagons, which were presented to Montgomery churches of the same denominations for car-pool use.

The load was also lightened by some white Montgomery housewives, who entered into a sort of conspiracy with their black domestics. Accepting the police commissioner's fiction about "goon squads," these women began to drive their maids and cooks to and from work, "to protect them from harassment." When the mayor protested that this gave aid and comfort to the boycott, ladies wrote letters to the newspaper suggesting that he provide them with other help before telling them how to run their households.

As weeks went by without the blacks yielding, threats of violence began to be directed against the leadership of the M.I.A. King, Abernathy, Nixon, and other officers started to receive hate mail and phone calls warning them to "get out of town or else. . . . " Then, on January 30, the ugliness erupted.

On that night, while Dr. King was attending one of the regular mass meetings, a bomb tossed onto the porch of his house exploded seconds later with a shattering roar. Having heard the thud as the missile landed, Mrs. King and a visiting friend had moved quickly toward the rear of the house. They and the Kings' infant daughter escaped injury. But it looked for a time as if the chief casualty of the night would be the concept of nonviolence to which the Negroes had so far been held by their leaders.

Rushing home, King found an angry crowd milling on his lawn. As he stepped from his car, he heard one black man offer to shoot it out with a white policeman who was trying to push him back. Mayor W. A. "Jackie" Gayle and Police Commissioner Clyde Sellers were on hand, along with white reporters and the police. The mood of the crowd was so hostile that all of them later reported having felt that a race riot was a distinct and immediate possibility.

Dr. King went into his house, assured himself that his family was all right, and then came back to speak to the crowd. His voice was unusually quiet, and everyone else stopped speaking or moving, to listen.

"My wife and baby are all right," he told them. "I want you to go home and put down your weapons. We cannot solve this problem through retaliatory violence. . . . We must love our white brothers no matter what they do to us. We must make them know that we love them. Jesus still cries out across the centuries, 'Love your enemies.' This is what we must live by." Then, his voice swelling with emotion, he added: "Remember, if I am stopped, this movement will not stop, because God is with this movement."

It was another miracle of oratory, in a different style from his Holt Street speech. This time there was no applause. Simply, at his request, the crowd began to melt away, and with it, the tension. King even got them to listen quietly as the mayor promised a reward for information leading to the arrest of the bombers. But it had been a close thing. A small incident could have brought bloodshed. Calm returned, although two nights later a bomb landed—harmlessly—in the Nixons' yard.

After that climactic moment, there was a year-long struggle marked by court actions, by feats of improvisation that kept the M.I.A.'s transportation system rolling, and finally by fresh bombings.

Perhaps the most significant and least publicized action on the legal front was the petition on behalf of the M.I.A. for a hearing on the constitutionality of the Alabama segregation law before a three-judge federal court. This tactic was first suggested by Clifford Durr. About mid-April he realized that something more would be needed than Mrs. Parks's appeal, which was before the Alabama court of appeals, to carry the case to the top. The Supreme Court could not render a decision "on the merits" until the Alabama court had spoken—almost certainly against Rosa Parks. . . .

Durr therefore suggested to Fred Gray that he petition for a special three-judge federal court and ask it for an injunction against discrimination in seating, on the grounds that it was a violation of rights guaranteed in the Constitution. Such a panel was allowable in a federal action challenging a state law. And its rulings could be appealed directly to the Supreme Court.

Gray went to work at once, made contact with the New York and Washington branches of the NAACP, got some high-powered co-counsel, and filed his petition. The hearing was set for early in May. The court was composed of Richard T. Rives, at the time judge of the United States Circuit Court for the district including Alabama, who was the presiding justice; Judge Frank Johnson, an indigenous "Andrew Jackson Republican" (in Durr's words) from the northern part of Alabama; and Judge Seybourne Lynn of Birmingham.

Within three weeks, two of the three white southern judges—Johnson and Rives—outvoted their colleague and ruled in favor of Gray's petition. Rives, who wrote the majority opinion, was threatened, obliged to listen to sermons attacking the federal judiciary in the Montgomery church he attended, and had garbage dumped on his son's grave in a local cemetery. Johnson took similar abuse. But the strategem was successful.

The federal question was raised at last. For the city of Montgomery appealed the ruling "on the merits," and the state of Alabama joined in the appeal; the matter now went onto the Supreme Court's docket. . . .

Montgomery authorities were meanwhile harassing the car pools. A car full of riders would be flagged down; the inspecting officer would find one or more violations of the state safety standards—weak brakes, poorly aligned headlights, or something else. The driver would be forced to abandon his vehicle, and a city wrecker would be called to tow it away (at the owner's expense) for repairs (also at his expense) in a city-approved shop. A similar tactic was the arbitrary cancellation of black auto-owners' insurance.

But all this was only prelude to the main attack. On October 30 Mayor Gayle directed the city's legal department to request an injunction "to stop the operation of the car pools or transportation systems growing out of the bus boycott," and to collect damages of fifteen thousand dollars for loss of tax revenues. Fred Gray's counterpetition to prevent the city's interference on behalf of the bus company was denied. A hearing was set for November 13.

There was no question in the minds of the M.I.A. leaders that this was, as King confessed to a mass meeting on the second of November, a bad moment. The city was certain to get its injunction, and to end the car pools would hopelessly undercut the boycott. He tried to rally confidence by saying, "This may well be the darkest hour before dawn. We have moved all these months with . . . daring faith. . . . We must go on with that same faith. . . . "

November 13 found the main contestants on both sides in court for the injunction hearing. The same judge who had tried Mrs. Parks a year earlier was listening to the arguments when, some time around noon, there was an interruption.

The two attorneys for the city, the mayor, and the police commissioner were all called out of the court, and there was an excited buzzing at the press table. One of the reporters brought over to the defense table a copy of a message just received over the wire service teletype machine:

The United States Supreme Court today affirmed a decision of a special three-judge U.S. District Court declaring Alabama's state and local laws requiring segregation on buses unconstitutional. The Supreme Court acted without listening to any argument; it simply said, "the motion to affirm is granted and the Judgment is affirmed."

Legally, the struggle was over. The black-led and black-supported boycott, rising out of Mrs. Parks's spontaneous act, had resulted in the highest court's driving another nail in the coffin of legalized segregation. But life follows law slowly. It took a month more for the judicial mandate actually to reach Montgomery. In that time the injunction against the car pools was granted. So blacks, still staying off the buses, walked many extra miles when no alternative arrangements were possible.

The interval was used to prepare the black community for the first day of the new dispensation. Sheets of suggestions on how to behave "in a loving manner" were distributed. Role-playing sessions were held in black churches. Among whites reactions varied. The City Commission received front-page coverage to proclaim its "determination [to] do all in its power to oppose the integration of the Negro race with the white race in Montgomery . . . [and] stand like a rock against social equality, intermarriage and mixing of the races under God's creation and plan." But the fateful December 21, the day of official desegregation, came and went with what the Montgomery *Advertiser* called "a calm but cautious acceptance of this significant change in Montgomery's way of life." Black and white ministers sat together undisturbed in what had been the "Whites Only" section. Drivers were uniformly courteous. Most white passengers chose to ignore the innovation; those who made nasty remarks were in turn ignored by the blacks. . . .

Ahead lay many events [in the struggle for civil rights]: sit-ins, freedom rides, gunfire on the campus of the University of Mississippi, the March on Washington, the Civil Rights and Voting Rights acts of 1964 and 1965, the summers of rioting in northern cities—and then, the murder of Martin Luther King, Jr., in a Memphis motel. Perhaps it would take the decade of the seventies to discover the full meaning of the record that began with the Montgomery boycott. But in that January of 1957, as integrated buses rolled down the streets of the Confederacy's first capital, over which the Stars and Bars still flew, almost everyone must have sensed that a new page in the history of black (and white) Americans had been turned.

DOCUMENTS

School Segregation
Ruled Unconstitutional, 1954

Today, education is perhaps the most important function of state and local governments. Compulsory school attendance laws and the great expenditures for education both demonstrate our recognition of the importance of education to our democratic society. It is required in the performance of our most basic public responsibilities, even service in the armed forces. It is the very foundation of good citizenship. Today it is a principal instrument in awakening the child to cultural values, in preparing him for later professional training, and in helping him to adjust normally to his environment. In these days, it is doubtful that any child may reasonably be expected to succeed in life if he is denied the opportunity of an education. Such an opportunity, where the state has undertaken to provide it, is a right which must be made available to all on equal terms.

We come then to the question presented: Does segregation of children in public schools solely on the basis of race, even though the physical facilities and other "tangible" factors may be equal, deprive the children of the minority group of equal education opportunities? We believe that it does.

In *Sweatt* v. *Painter*, . . . in finding that segregated law school for Negroes could not provide them equal educational opportunities, this Court relied in large part on "those qualities which are incapable of objective measurement but which make for greatness in a law school." In *McLaurin* v. *Oklahoma State Regents*, . . . the Court, in requiring that a Negro admitted to a white graduate school be treated like all other students, again resorted to intangible considerations: " . . . his ability to study, to engage in discussions and exchange views with other students, and, in general, to learn his profession." Such considerations apply with added force to children in grade and high schools. To separate them from others of similar age and qualifications solely because of their race generates a feeling of inferiority as to their status in the community that may affect their hearts and minds in a way unlikely ever to be undone. The effect of this separation on their educational opportunities was well stated by a finding in the Kansas case by a court which nevertheless felt compelled to rule against the Negro plaintiffs:

> Segregation of white and colored children in public schools has a detrimental effect upon the colored children. The impact is greater

SOURCE: Chief Justice Earl Warren's majority opinion in *Brown* v. *Board of Education of Topeka*, 347 U.S. 483 (1954).

when it has the sanction of the law; for the policy of separating the races is usually interpreted as denoting the inferiority of the Negro group. A sense of inferiority affects the motivation of the child to learn. Segregation with the sanction of law, therefore, has a tendency to [retard] the educational and mental development of Negro children and to deprive them of some of the benefits they would receive in a racial[ly] integrated school system.

. . . We conclude that in the field of public education the doctrine of "separate but equal" has no place. Separate educational facilities are inherently unequal. Therefore, we hold that the plaintiffs and others similarly situated for whom the actions have been brought are, by reason of the segregation complained of, deprived of the equal protection of the laws guaranteed by the Fourteenth Amendment. . . .

Opposition to the Civil Rights Bill, 1964

Truly . . . this is a sad day. As a student of law, and a practicing lawyer, I never dreamed that the day would ever come when more than two-thirds of the Congress—Senate and House—would virtually destroy the Constitution, violating every intent of the founders of our Republic.

For 10 years the executive and judiciary departments have had a virtual partnership to set up a dictatorship. Here, today the Congress gets in on the act, says, "Me, too," and ratifies the unconstitutional acts which have gone before.

Present conditions are so similar to the days just preceding the Civil War, we should pause to remember that heart-breaking conflict, which pitted brother against brother, and father against son—today, it is section against section, and those who need to straighten out their own sections, cover up by going to mine.

As we look back upon those troubled times we can see that sound leaders of both sides deplored any effort to settle the issue by armed conflict. Unfortunately, the radicals of that day prevented a peaceful solution. Then, as now, they were not satisfied to run their own local affairs, but insisted that all other sections conform to their pattern. A terrible war resulted. . . .

Instead of forcing integration upon the Southern States, truly it would be well for the rest of the country to learn from the States of the South

SOURCE: Speech of Congressman James Whitten in *Congressional Record*, July 2, 1964, 15886–87.

that the way for peace and harmony is to provide for separate but equal facilities and protect each race in the enjoyment of its own way of life. . . .

You may well ask why the Supreme Court rendered the unanimous decision in the Brown integration case. It was probably argued that if we do not bring about integration in the United States, we will lose the contest with Russia throughout the world; and if we do not do this, Russia will eventually conquer the world. It was said by the press, "If Russia takes over here, the first thing they will do is set up a dictatorship. If Russia takes over," they charged, "they will do away with the right to trial by jury." "Yes," they said, "if we do not integrate, Russia will force on us a system similar to Hitler's in Germany or Stalin's in Russia."

What did they do in Germany and Russia? What was the source of their absolute control of those nations? Why, they had the courts issue decrees, then they used troops and government officers to enforce the decrees.

Have we not done that here? We have seen the Supreme Court, unwilling to wait for constitutional amendment in the regular process, change the Constitution. We have seen the President send troops and Federal officials to enforce such decrees. Our Government does itself what we feared Russia might do.

We were told we have to integrate all the races of the United States or we cannot hold the friendship of the people of India, China, Japan, Africa, and all the rest. If that be true, why have China and Japan been at dagger's point throughout history? Talk about India—in spite of what you read, we know in many areas people of the same color cannot even touch each other.

The agitation is right here at home. People are using the threat of Russia here in the United States to accomplish their personal desires and actually to impose the Russian system of required conformity upon us.

My friends, history clearly shows an individual must have pride or he makes no real progress. A family must have pride or it goes down the scale. So it is with countries. So it is with race. Any race, whatever it may be, which feels it must be intermixed with another acknowledges its own lack. Such a race will not serve itself well, nor that with which it wishes to intermix.

Integration, where it has taken place, has only led to great turmoil. We all know that if you go into some sections of New York City at night you take your life in your hands; and you may be in danger there in the daytime. You can not go to certain areas of Chicago without danger to life and limb. The same is true of most of our major cities. Rape, murder, and robbery are commonplace in some areas of Washington. . . .

In recent weeks we have seen agitators deliberately go into areas of the South for the admitted purpose of violating laws of the States which have never been held to be beyond the power of such States, but rather

280

have been held to be within the power; and then we have seen the Federal Government move its force in to protect such individuals in their avowed purpose of testing existing laws.

What if it were the law against murder they wished to test, or rape, or treason? Is there one rule in the Federal Government for laws the executive or the judiciary likes and another for the laws they do not like? . . .

I am proud that the people of my section are showing real self-restraint under trying circumstances. I hope time will show you who support this bill, that you are wrong; that those on the Supreme Court who have led this Nation down the road to state socialism are wrong; and that the present judicial dictatorship of the Supreme Court, supported by the executive branch, and here affirmed by this Congress, is all wrong and that this act will be repealed; that the rights of individuals to accumulate and control one's own property, the right to choose one's own customers, one's own companions and one's friends, regardless of color, will be reestablished. Only then . . . will our Nation endure.

Growing Up Black in the South: A Remembrance, 1977

I was born in poverty. My mother was never married to my father, which was a stigma in the American society. . . . I was reared up in Decatur County, Georgia . . . that's southwest Georgia, and the racism of segregation was so prevalent until it was something that you had to notice, like black farmers couldn't plant tobacco. They didn't allow black men to plant tobacco, 'cause there's a lot of money in it. White people virtually owned black people . . . they'd concoct debts, like you get in jail, all the white man had to do, to come there, and the sheriff would let you out, and the white man tell the sheriff to tell you he paid a hundred dollars for you, but you didn't have to worry 'bout that hundred dollars long as you stay on his farm and work. If you ever left to go to Florida, he'd come get you, arrest you and bring you back. . . . There's a white man down there named Wonnie Miller. On the Wonnie Miller farm, all the blacks were born and worked and lived and died in poverty, and they worked like slaves from "cain't to cain't"—say, "Ya cain't see your hand before your face when you go out in the field, and ya cain't see your hand when you come in from the field," because it was dark each time. And Mr. Wonnie used to ride a big horse and never really worked, and he died a millionaire. All his children are rich. . . .

SOURCE: Reprinted by permission of The Putnam Publishing Group from *My Soul Is Rested: Movement Days in the Deep South Remembered* by Howell Raines, 437–38. Copyright © 1977 by Howell Raines.

We used to walk two and a half miles to school . . . the white kids always had a bus. No black kids were allowed to ride the bus, and I guess every day of my life—it looked like to me every day, probably just my imagination—those white kids would spit on us or throw rocks at us, holler, and call us "niggers." *Every* day. Pick at us, and I just knew that was not right.

In my early life once whites tried to lynch me about a little white girl that was from a very poor family that lived up there. Her father was a bum, wouldn't work; all he did was fish and hunt all the time, just like some of the black families. The word got around that I was havin' affair with the girl. This was a rumor, and they came to the house to lynch me . . . and my grandfather stood 'em off with a gun. We went over to white man's house, Mr. Wonnie Miller, who took the thing up and stopped the whites. . . .

The vast majority of blacks was reared in the same circumstances I was reared in. It's just hard for me to see how they can go along and take it. Then I educated myself and became a professional person. I thought you could escape black America by being educated and professional and being rich, and you just cain't do it.* . . .

I was paid well. I went right up, straight up the ladder. I was accepted, *I thought*, but what I really finally decided, I had hit that "nigger ceiling." They wasn't gonna let me go no higher. . . . I had more publication than all the white guys put together, except an old Ph.D. who had thirty years in the lab. So the assistant chief's job became open, and I thought sure they'd make me the assistant chief, because I thought they had accepted me as a scientist. And they gave the job to a white girl who knew very little chemistry, and that was a very hard pill for me to swallow. But you know the old thing 'bout how Jackie Robinson made it in baseball, the old poem, "Life Ain't Been No Christmas Day," and all this jazz, so I bought it and buckled my bed up: "After all, I'm black and she's white. My day comin'."

I remember one time after I bought this new home and new car. . . . You know, I was a social climbin', middle-class Negro. I guess I was the first black person in Savannah to have a zoysia lawn. I remember buying this grass from Sears and Roebuck, and had sodded my lawn, and I was out there one day tryin' to water it, and my hose would not stretch to sprinkle across the whole lawn. I had a big lot there. And I went back up to this new drugstore . . . gonna buy some hose connectors, an extension to a hose. . . . And I carried my two sons with me. They wasn't but

---

*Williams became a chemist with the U.S. Department of Agriculture Bureau of Entomology in Savannah.

about six and seven, six and eight years old then, and as we walked into this drugstore, it had a long lunch counter and these white kids were sittin' on these stools, spinnin' around, eatin' hot dogs and drinkin' Co-cola.

And my boys started askin' me, "Daddy, let's get a sandwich and a Coke." But I always will believe what they wanted to do was play on those stools, and I said, "Naw, you cain't have a Coke and sandwich." And one of 'em started cryin'. And I said, "Well, you know, I'm gonna take you back home and Momma'll fix you a hot dog and give you a Coke," and then both of 'em started cryin'. And both of them just fell out in the floor, which was very unusual for my kids to do me like that. And I remember stoopin' down and I started cryin', because I realized I couldn't tell 'em the truth. The truth was they was black and they didn't 'low black people to use them lunch counters. So I picked the two kids up and went back to the car and I guess I made 'em a promise that I'd bring 'em back someday. So that really got me involved.

Chapter 15

The Revival of Feminism

When women gained the vote in 1920, the women's movement that had long sought this goal—dating back to the mid-nineteenth century—became dormant for several decades. Yet that victory by no means marked the end of the struggle for equality of opportunity and treatment for women. The franchise gained women entry to the voting booth, but few won elective office. Women still found most of their employment opportunities in the traditional, low-paying, "feminine" occupations, and their wages typically ranged lower than those of men with similar experience, education, skill, and responsibility. Moreover, during the Great Depression, married women discovered that many employers hesitated to hire them, insisting that men be given preference for available jobs.

In 1923 a group of women led by Alice Paul proposed an equal rights amendment (ERA) to the Constitution designed to ensure sexual equality. The idea lay quiescent for nearly half a century until the resurgence of the women's movement in the 1960s, detailed in William H. Chafe's essay "The Rivival of Feminism." How does Chafe account for the renewed strength of the movment at that time? What, in addition to adoption of the amendment, does the essay identify as key objectives of the "new feminism"?

By 1970 the ERA had again become a live issue. The first document is a state-

ment in support of the amendment before a Senate committee by the well-known feminist writer and editor Gloria Steinem. To what extent and in what ways might the ERA affect the conditions that Steinem describes?

In 1972 Congress approved the ERA by the necessary two-thirds margin, and opinion polls indicated support for the amendment by a vast majority of the American public. Nevertheless, the amendment failed to receive ratification by the required three-quarters of the states. Opposition centered in the South, several western states, Missouri, and Illinois.

The defeat of the ERA, although a major setback, did not fatally injure the women's movement. A growing number of women ran for and were elected to office after 1970. And in 1984, for the first time, a woman, Geraldine Ferraro, was selected as a vice-presidential candidate. Encouraged by the spirit of feminism, and aided by civil rights legislation, favorable court decisions, and government-directed affirmative action programs, increasing numbers of women have entered traditional male occupations. In 1960 only 3.5 percent of lawyers were women, compared to 14 percent in 1982. Among physicians, 6.8 percent were women in 1960; by 1982 the figure had risen to 14.3 percent.

In addition to the ERA, abortion became a highly controversial issue after 1973. The Supreme Court in Roe v. Wade (1973), parts of which are included in the second document, paved the way for the legalization of abortion in many states that had formerly imposed severe limits on the procedure. What did the justices say about the right to privacy and how it affected abortion? Did the Court suggest that abortion was an absolute right? The last document is a statement by President George Bush to a group of prolife (antiabortion) marchers in the nation's capital. What possibilities for compromise, if any, do you see on this issue?

E S S A Y

The Revival of Feminism
William H. Chafe

HELMER: Before all else, you are a wife and mother.
NORA: That I no longer believe. I believe that before all
else, I am a human being, just as much as you are—or at
least that I should try to become one.

Henrik Ibsen, *A Doll's House* (1879)

In the fall of 1962, the editors of *Harper's* observed a curious phenomenon. An extraordinary number of women seemed "ardently determined to extend their vocation beyond the bedroom, kitchen and nursery," but very few showed any interest in feminism. Both observations were essentially correct. In the years during and after World War II, millions of women had left the home to take jobs, but the expansion of their "sphere" occurred without fanfare and was not accompanied by any organized effort to challenge traditional definitions of woman's place. If many women were dissatisfied with what one housewife called the endless routine of "dishwashing, picking up, ironing, and folding diapers," they kept their frustration to themselves. Women examined their futures privately and with an unmilitant air. They had not yet developed a sense of collective grievance.

Eight years later, feminism competed with the Vietnam war, student revolts, and inflation for headlines in the daily press. Female activists picketed the Miss America contest, stormed meetings of professional associations to demand equal employment opportunities, and forced their way into male bars and restaurants in New York. They called a national strike, wrote about the oppression of a "sexual politics," and sat in at editorial offices of *Newsweek* and *Ladies' Home Journal*. At times, it seemed that the media had been taken over by women's liberation, so often did female activists appear on network television and in national magazines. In an era punctuated by protest, feminism had once again come into its own. If not all women subscribed to the new fight for equality, an energetic minority nevertheless believed that the time had come to finish the task of gaining for women the same rights that men had.

The evolution of any protest movement is a complicated phenomenon. In general, however, at least three preconditions are required: first, a point of view around which to organize; second, a positive response by a portion of the aggrieved group; and third, a social atmosphere which is conducive

SOURCE: From *The American Woman: Her Changing Social, Economic, and Political Roles, 1920–1970* by William Henry Chafe. Copyright © 1972 by Oxford University Press, Inc. Reprinted by permission.

to reform. To an extent unmatched since the last days of the suffrage fight, all three elements came together in the American woman's movement during the 1960s. Articulate feminists presented a cogent indictment of society's treatment of women. A substantial number of females who had already experienced profound change in their lives were responsive to the call to end discrimination. And the society at large was peculiarly attuned to the need for guaranteeing equality to all its citizens. No one development by itself could have explained the rebirth of the woman's movement, but all three together created a context in which, for the first time in half a century, feminism became a force to be reckoned with in American society.

The ideological keynote of the feminist revival was sounded in 1963 by Betty Friedan. In the years after World War II, she charged, American women had been victimized by a set of ideas—a "feminine mystique"—which permeated society and defined female happiness as total involvement in the roles of wife and mother. Advertisers manipulated women into believing that they could achieve fulfillment by using the latest model vacuum cleaner or bleaching their clothes a purer white. Women's magazines romanticized domesticity and presented an image of woman as "gaily content in a world of bedroom, kitchen, sex, babies and home." And psychiatrists like Marynia Farnham and Helene Deutsch popularized the notion that any woman dissatisfied with a full-time occupation as housewife was somehow emotionally maladjusted. As a result, Friedan declared, a woman's horizons were circumscribed from childhood on by the assumption that her highest function in life was to care for her husband and rear their children. In effect, the home had become a "comfortable concentration camp" which infantilized its female inhabitants and forced them to "give up their adult frame of reference." Just as Victorian culture had repressed the need of women to express themselves sexually, modern culture denied them the opportunity to use their minds.

Despite some exaggerations, Friedan articulated a point of view which struck a responsive chord, and within a year others presented a similar position. Adopting a more academic perspective, Ellen and Kenneth Keniston placed particular emphasis on the fact that young girls had no positive models of career women to emulate. "The most effective forms of oppression are those with which the victim covertly cooperates," they declared, and women provided a case in point. Denied any culturally approved alternative to homemaking, most females internalized society's view of their place and accepted a "voluntary servitude" in the home rather than risk losing their femininity. Alice Rossi made the same point. "There are few Noras in contemporary society," she observed, "because women have deluded themselves that a doll's house is large enough to find complete fulfillment within it."

All the feminists agreed that the limitations placed on women's activities had a profoundly destructive effect. When a woman's sole focus of interest was the home, they claimed, she was forced to overcompensate for her lack of power in other areas by establishing an emotional tyranny over her husband and children. Females who made a full-time occupation of motherhood, Alice Rossi declared, treated their children "like hothouse plants" and tried to live vicariously "in and through them." Consequently, youngsters were stifled and prevented from growing into autonomous personalities. At the same time, the conditions of suburban living made it difficult for a wife to achieve the marital fulfillment which the "mystique" led her to expect. Husbands were away 80 per cent of the time, and it was almost impossible for a wife to derive the same measure of satisfaction from the few hours a couple spent together that a man found in the full variety of his occupational and social experiences. The family thus became a breeding ground of discontent and unhappiness. Female neurosis skyrocketed, divorces multiplied, and a generation of children grew up spoiled and dependent.

Ultimately, however, the feminists traced the "woman problem" to the fact that females were denied the same opportunity as men to develop an identity of their own. The success of any interpersonal relationship depended on the autonomy and strength of each participant. Yet in many cases, cultural conditioning had prevented women from achieving a sense of themselves as persons. While men were encouraged to fashion their own destinies, females were confined to those roles which were rooted in their biological functions. Assigned to a place solely on the basis of sex, women were kept from seeing themselves as unique human beings, distinct from others. All females participated equally in the undifferentiated roles of housewife and mother, but many lacked a more precise image of themselves as individuals. As one young mother wrote:

> I've tried everything women are supposed to do—hobbies, gardening, pickling, canning, and being very social with my neighbors. . . . I can do it all, and I like it, but it doesn't leave you anything to think about—any feeling of who you are. . . . I love the kids and Bob and my home. . . . But I'm desperate. I begin to feel that I have no personality. I'm a server of food and putter-on of pants and a bedmaker, somebody who can be called on when you want something. But who am I?

To the feminists, the question struck at the core of the alienation of modern women and could be answered only if wives and mothers rejected cultural stereotypes and developed a life of their own outside the home. A career, the feminists claimed, had two advantages. First, it would allow women to realize their potential as individuals in the wider society. And second, it was the only way by which they could achieve the personal recognition and identity essential to a healthy family life. A study of Vassar students had shown that women with professional aspirations experienced fewer problems of personal adjustment and enjoyed a greater degree of self-fulfillment than those who rejected a career and opted for a life in the home. Another survey by Abraham H. Maslow disclosed that "high dominance" women—those who were aggressive and assertive—had a better sex life and less neurosis than "low dominance" women who more closely conformed to cultural stereotypes. Wives and mothers with careers, Alice Rossi declared, would demand less of their husbands, provide a "living model" of independence and responsibility to their children, and regain a sense of their own worth as persons. With an independent existence outside the home, they would cease to be parasites living off the activities of those around them and instead become full and equal partners in the family community.

To a remarkable extent, the new feminists presented a uniform analysis of women's position in contemporary society. They all believed that the women's rights movement had suffered a grievous setback in the years after 1945, that the "feminine mystique" had forced females to accept a "voluntary servitude" in the home, and that women could break out of their "prison" only if they developed outside interests and rectified the imbalance of social and family relationships. To that end, they urged a radical modification of cultural stereotypes, the creation of new community institutions like child-care centers, and a concerted campaign by women to develop a "lifelong commitment" to the professions or business.

Unfortunately, the feminists also shared in common several misconceptions. To begin with, they assumed that all homemakers secretly resented their position and if given a chance would automatically decide to pursue a career. While such an assumption might describe some women, it certainly did not apply to all. The challenges of a full social life, volunteer work, good cooking, and enlightened child care provided many women with a diverse and rewarding existence—one which they would not choose to sacrifice even if the opportunity presented itself. Such women may have "voluntarily" accepted a life in the home, but their condition was not that of servitude nor could they honestly be described as oppressed. A 1962 Gallup Poll, for example, showed that three out of five women were "fairly satisfied" with their achievements, and believed that they were happier than their mothers.

Second, the feminist analysis betrayed the same middle-class bias which had characterized the women's rights movement from its inception. Even if many housewives were discontented, very few had either the training or motivation to follow a career in business or the professions. Such an option existed only for the best educated and most dedicated segment of the female population; it did not represent a realistic alternative for most women. Furthermore, Friedan and the other feminists concentrated their attention on suburban, college graduates who by definition had been exposed at least briefly to the possibility of a different way of life. Millions of lower-class women, on the other hand, lacked both the sophistication and experience to envision the possibility of an alternative life-style. Such women agreed without hesitation that their husbands' sphere of responsibility should remain separate from their own. The wife of the blue-collar worker rarely asked the question "Who am I?" first, because it never occurred to her, and, second, because she already knew the answer. Brought up to be a wife and mother, she accepted her ascribed status as both natural and right.

Finally, contemporary feminists often showed an appalling ignorance of history in their contention that the "feminine mystique" represented a post–World War II phenomenon. The "cult of true womanhood" pervaded nineteenth-century culture, and the ideology of the "mystique" dominated the editorial policy of women's magazines in the twentieth century long before 1945. Indeed, the consistency of anti-feminist arguments constitutes one of the most striking facts of the entire debate in America over woman's place. When Adlai Stevenson told the graduates of Smith in 1955 that their political task was to "influence man and boy" through the "humble role of housewife," he was essentially repeating a point of view which had been expressed for centuries. Similarly, women had been told for over a hundred years that equality would lead to the destruction of the home and the family. There was nothing necessarily new about the feminine mystique, nor could it be said that women in the 1950s were more "victimized" than they had been at other times in history. The feminists had simply given fresh expression to an old problem.

Nevertheless, the fact that the problem was discovered anew represented a development of critical importance. As a result of the feminists' contribution, a cogent if controversial viewpoint emerged around which to build a movement of popular protest. Talk about female discontent had been rife for years, but for the first time in a generation dissatisfied women had a focus for their anger. Friedan, in particular, exerted a significant influence. With eloquence and passion, she dramatized through case studies the boredom and alienation of those afflicted by "the problem that has no name." In addition, she was able to take her readers behind the scenes to editorial offices and advertising firms where they could see firsthand the way in which the image of the feminine mystique was formed. It was hard not to be outraged after reading how advertising men—who themselves viewed housework as menial—tried to sell cleaning products as an answer to drudgery and as a means of expressing creativity. If, as Friedan claimed, the women frustrated by such manipulation were legion, her book helped to crystallize a sense of grievance and to provide an ideological position with which the discontented could identify. *The Feminine Mystique* sold more than a million copies, and, if not all its readers agreed with the conclusions, they could not help but re-examine their own lives in light of the questions it raised.

No protest movement occurs in a vacuum, however, and it is unlikely that feminism could have gained the energy it did during the 1960s had not Americans been preoccupied with the demand to eliminate prejudice and discrimination. Historically, women's rights advocates had succeeded in focusing attention on their grievances only at a time of generalized social reform. The feminist movement began when abolitionism provided female activists with an opportunity to organize and exposed them directly to the physical and psychological reality of discrimination based on sex. For nearly forty years after the Civil War, the movement was stagnant and isolated. The advent of Progressivism offered another vehicle for advance, and in a generation dedicated to ending social injustice women's rights leaders succeeded in placing suffrage on the agenda of reform and in building a national coalition sufficient to win enactment of the Nineteenth Amendment. On both occasions, women themselves played an important part in creating the atmosphere of reform, but their own cause benefited most from the climate of opinion which resulted.

It was not surprising, therefore, that the revival of the woman's movement in the 1960s coincided with another national crusade to redress the grievances of oppressed minority groups. The civil rights revolution dramatized the immorality of discriminating against any group of people on the basis of physical characteristics. It provided a model of moral indignation and tactical action which women (as well as Indians and Mexican-Americans) quickly adopted as their own. And it spawned a generation of young female leaders who determined to remove the stumbling block of discrimination from their own path at the same time that they fought for the liberation of their black brothers and sisters. Like their abolitionist ancestors, many latent feminists fully realized the extent of their own oppression only through the "sexism" of their male civil rights colleagues. Forced to do menial women's work, and denied an equal voice in policy-making councils ("the position of women in our movement should be prone," black leader Stokely Carmichael said), they rapidly concluded that their own freedom was also on the line, and set out to win it. Whenever America became sensitive to the issue of human rights, it seemed, the woman's movement acquired new support in one way or another, and the 1960s proved no exception to the rule. The civil rights movement did not cause the revival of feminism, but it did help to create a set of favorable circumstances.

The most important precondition for the resurgence of the woman's movement, however, was the amount of change which had already occurred among American females. If women had been as oppressed as the feminists claimed, no amount of rhetoric could have aroused them from their captivity. Social scientists have pointed out that rebellions almost never occur among people enslaved in a "closed system," especially in a concentration camp. Rather, revolutions begin in response to "rising expectations," after a group has started on the road to improvement and become aware of its relative deprivation. It is reasonable to assume, therefore, that, unless substantial shifts had already taken place in women's lives, the ideology of the feminists would have fallen on barren ground. There was little in the writings of Friedan or Rossi which had not been anticipated in one form or another by Charlotte Perkins Gilman.* Yet Gilman never received the enthusiastic reception accorded her latter day successors. One explanation, it would seem, is that Gilman spoke to an audience which, by virtue of the social structure of the time, was incapable of hearing her message, while Friedan and her colleagues addressed a society which was more prepared to listen. It would be an exaggeration to say that the ideology of the feminists was simply catching up with reality. But if reality had not already altered considerably—if women had not already departed in such great numbers from their traditional sphere—it is doubtful that the feminists' call for further change would have met with the response it did.

In fact, a strong case could be made that the changes which had occurred directly set the stage for the possibility of feminist success. To begin with, over 40 per cent of all women—including wives—held jobs by the end of the 1960s. Included in that number were a substantial number of middle-class women (41 per cent of those whose husbands earned from $8,000–10,000) and approximately 50 per cent of all mothers with children six to eighteen years old. For the first time in the nation's history, almost half the adolescent girls in the country were growing up with examples in their own homes of women who combined outside employment with marriage. To be sure, very few of these women occupied positions which could be described as executive, but they did have interests outside the home and clearly contradicted the image of the captive housewife.

In addition, the evidence suggested that many working mothers already provided a positive model to their children. Repeated surveys of elementary and high school students showed that children of mothers who held jobs approved of maternal employment and that the girls intended to work after they married and had children. Significantly, adolescent females were more likely to name their mother as the person they most admired if she worked than if she did not work. "The [employed] mother," Lois Hoffman has written, "may represent to her daughter a person who has achieved success in areas that are, in some respects, more salient to a growing girl than household skills." Alice Rossi noted that, if a woman had a career, she "might finally provide her children with . . . a healthy dose of inattention, and a chance for adolescence to be a period of fruitful immaturity and growth." But surveys by social scientists indicated that many working mothers were already imparting lessons of self-reliance to

*Gilman was a militant feminist of the early twentieth century.

their teenage children and that part-time and voluntary employment in particular seemed to foster a heathier child-mother relationship. The family, in the eyes of many experts, was becoming less child-centered and more person-centered, largely as a result of the growing interest of mothers in activities outside the home.

Not surprisingly, maternal employment also exerted considerable influence on the female child's self-image. Most sociologists agree that children learn their future sex roles by observing their parents. Since mothers who worked presented a different role model than most housewives, their children grew up with a substantially revised image of what it meant to be a woman. On a battery of tests administered to female students, daughters of working mothers scored lower on scales of traditional femininity, viewed the female role as less restricted to the home, and believed that both men *and* women participated in and enjoyed a variety of work, household, and recreational experiences. To some extent, the results of maternal employment differed according to the age and sex of the child and the social class of the mother. Women with pre-school children, for example, often felt guilty about not fulfilling their maternal responsibilities and tended to compensate by overprotecting their children. Similarly, in lower-class households where mothers were forced to work because of economic need, maternal employment sometimes reflected negatively on the father's ability as a provider, causing male children to become more dependent, withdrawn, and passive. The evidence indicated, however, that, in most families where both spouses worked, the presence of a working mother had no deleterious effect on the emotional or mental development of children, but instead encouraged young girls in particular to perceive sexual spheres as overlapping. It was likely that, as more and more mothers took jobs, a new generation of daughters would appear, with a commitment to function just as fully in the world outside the home as their brothers.

Finally, female employment seemed to have a salutary effect on the attitudes of both men and women toward equality. Not only did female workers themselves increasingly value their jobs as an opportunity for self-expression and personal recognition, but, in addition, their husbands gave signs of shifting their philosophy on issues involving women's rights. A survey of households in a Western city showed that husbands of working wives were more likely than husbands of non-working wives to favor equal pay (62 per cent versus 49 per cent), to believe that sexual intercourse should occur only when both partners desired it (68 per cent versus 50 per cent), to think that men should help around the house "all the time" (29 per cent versus 13 per cent), and to indicate a willingness to make sacrifices for a wife's career (20 per cent versus 8 per cent). The figures were not overwhelming, and it was possible that a husband's attitudes either preceded or were independent of a wife's working pattern. But together with other data which showed a close relationship between women's work and the companionate family the survey results gave support to the suggestion that female employment, in its own way, was causing a profound modification in relationships between the sexes.

On balance, then, it appeared that the ground was well prepared for a revival of the woman's movement. If the feminists had been correct in their analysis, almost all women might have been expected to cling to their traditional roles, afraid to leave the hearth because of the oppobrium attached to any vocation other than homemaking. The evidence indicated, however, that, despite the popularity of the feminine mystique, a dramatic change in the content of women's sphere had already taken place. Women's rights advocates were correct in claiming that little progress had occurred in areas such as professional opportunities, community services, and fair pay. But they vastly exaggerated the degree of women's servitude. As [sociologist] David Reisman noted in 1964, "there is much less resignation and inhibition among women [today than in my mother's generation]. . . . Instead, there is an effort to lead a multi-dimensional life." If the barriers to equality had not been eliminated, women nevertheless enjoyed more freedom than ever before, and the extent to which ideas and expectations were shifting—especially among the young—created the context in which a renewed drive for equality was possible.

In response to such developments, the woman's movement came to life in the mid-1960s. At first slowly, then with growing confidence and strength, feminist leaders established new organizations to carry on the battle for equal rights. Like most social movements, the new feminism was comprised of different constituencies. On the "right" wing was the National Organization for Women (NOW) formed in 1966 by Betty Friedan. Supported primarily by well-educated professional women, NOW represented a reformist approach to equality and acted on the assumption that the social structure could be changed from within through legislation and persuasion. Women's liberation groups, in contrast, were made up mostly of younger, more radical women, many of whom had been involved in the peace, civil rights, and student movements, and who were convinced that revolutionary change offered the only answer to sexual inequality. Through such mechanisms as "consciousness-raising"—a process in which small groups of women share their common experiences—members of women's liberation sought to understand the depth of what it means to be female and to explore ways of overcoming the sources of oppression in their lives.

Although the diffuse structure of the movement encouraged division and controversy, most feminists subscribed to a core set of demands which constituted the essence of their program. All insisted on an end to job discrimination, all supported the repeal of abortion laws, and all urged the creation of twenty-four-hour-a-day child-care centers. Most important, all wanted an end to class treatment, to the idea that women, because of their sex, should automatically be expected to do the housework, act as secretaries at meetings, or rear children. Women were individuals, they claimed, not sex objects or servants, and wherever a female was assigned a place on the basis of sex alone, whether at a news magazine where women were "researchers" rather than "reporters," or in the home where husbands expected wives to get up with the baby at night, discrimination existed and had to be rooted out. Critics of the movement frequently dismissed women's liberation as a middle-class fad which was irrelevant to the real problems of society, but, in fact, feminist proposals spoke to all women and, if implemented, were more likely to benefit the ghetto-dweller than the affluent resident of the suburb.

Perhaps the most notable characteristic of the movement was its ability to make news. In an era dominated by the mass media, the feminists displayed consummate skill in drawing public attention to themselves and "raising" America's consciousness to the inequalities from which women suffered. Television might spotlight the more spectacular tactics of the movement such as sit-ins or boycotts, but it also dealt seriously with more substantive concerns. Every network (and most magazines) devoted special programs to the reasons for the feminist protest, and enterprising reporters ferreted out impressive documentation to support charges of sex discrimination. Unequal pay, the tragedy of unwanted pregnancies which could not legally be terminated, and the frustration of many women with domesticity—all were given nationwide exposure. The success of the feminists in attracting publicity alerted millions of uninvolved women to the possibility that they too might be victims of discrimination. Many females might have rejected the idea that they were an "oppressed class," but, as they talked about the effort by feminists to "liberate" them, the likelihood increased that they would discern examples of inequality and prejudice in their own lives and develop a heightened sense of sex solidarity.

Significantly, the resurgence of feminism coincided with other signs of independence among American women. The *New York Times* reported that a "new breed of middle class women" was emerging and that suburban housewives who had previously stayed at home all day were seeking jobs, going back to school, and engaging in volunteer work. Both the Protestant and Catholic churches were confronted by an increasing militancy among women who demanded equal recognition. A leader of American Baptist women threatened a floor fight if a female was not included in the top hierarchy of the Baptist convention, and angry nuns insisted on an end to supervision by priests. The feminist message also met with an enthusiastic response among the young women of "middle America." Representatives of the Future Homemakers of America declared that women's liberation had exerted a "definite influence" on their 600,000 members. Teenage girls still wanted to marry and have children, FHA leaders noted, but they now believed that fulfillment as women could come only if they also worked in a gainful occupation. Although such reports were obviously impressionistic, two studies of teenage girls in Georgia and Washington state showed that a sizable majority planned to hold jobs after they married and that less than 25 per cent definitely anticipated *not* being employed.

A 1970 Gallup Poll confirmed that many women—especially the well educated—were developing greater sensitivity to their rights. Although 65 per cent of the respondents believed that women were generally given an even break with men, a majority also declared that females were discriminated against in business and in the professions. Eight years earlier, in a similar poll, less than 30 per cent felt that females suffered from job discrimination, and only 39 per cent said that women were underpaid. More important, the level of discontent in 1970 rose appreciably among women with a college education. Almost half the college respondents (47 per cent) asserted that women did not receive an even break with men, and 75 per cent declared that women were discriminated against in gaining executive positions (significantly, 70 per cent of women with college degrees were in the labor force by the end of the decade). In a parallel finding, [social scientist] Mirra Komarovsky discovered that women who were married to blue-collar workers and who had a high school diploma were far more likely to demand that their husbands share in domestic and child-rearing responsibilities than those with only elementary schooling. Education thus appeared to be another critical variable in fostering self-awareness among females and correlated directly with perceptions of inequality.

Perhaps the greatest evidence that the woman's movement had made an impact was the increased attention it received from politicians. For more than four decades after passage of the suffrage, feminist demands had largely been ignored by government leaders. By the late 1960s, however, a change in attitude began to appear. After having been bottled up in committee for forty-seven years, the Equal Rights Amendment to the Constitution was brought before the House of Representatives where it received enthusiastic support. James Hodgson, Richard Nixon's Secretary of Labor, announced in 1970 that federal contracts would henceforth contain a clause mandating the employment of a certain quota of women. Attorney General John Mitchell initiated federal suits under Title VII of the 1964 Civil Rights Act to end job discrimination against women in such large corporations as Libby-Corning Glass and American Telephone and Telegraph. And under feminist pressure, the Nixon Administration required 2,000 colleges and universities to turn over their personnel files to the federal government so that it could determine whether females were victims of prejudice in hiring and wages.

The same effort to respond to the demands of the woman's movement occurred at other levels of government. Despite the vigorous opposition of the Catholic Church, abortion reform laws were passed in seventeen states. By 1970, over 200,000 women were receiving legal abortions annually—a 1,000 per cent increase over two years earlier. Candidates for public office made support of women's rights a major plank of their platforms. Municipal leaders instructed department chiefs to seek out qualified women for executive posts. And school boards began to change their rules on such things as who could take home economics and shop courses, and who could play on athletic squads. If women's liberationists scorned some of the actions as corrupt tokenism, the fact remained that their movement had become big enough in the eyes of political leaders to merit co-opting.

Nevertheless, there was little reason to be over-optimistic. Although some progress had been made on laws involving job discrimination, resistance to change mounted as the stakes became higher and more deeply entrenched social values were challenged. Once again, the child-care issue symbolized the difficulties faced by women's rights advocates. When Congress enacted a massive day-care program designed to make child-care facilities available to every working mother in the country, President Nixon vetoed the measure, declaring that it would commit "the vast moral authority of the national Government to the side of communal approaches to child-rearing. . . . " The family, Nixon insisted, was "the keystone of our civilization," and enlightened public policy required that it be strengthened rather than weakened. On a second controversial issue, Nixon issued an emotional statement opposing abortion reform and defending the rights of unborn fetuses, thereby lending his support to those in the various states who were striving to overturn liberalized abortion statutes. Thus, while feminists and their sympathizers could draw some encouragement from the progress which had taken place, opposition to change remained both strong and effective.

In most ways, then, the fight had just begun. Radical feminists would not be satisfied with halfway measures or limited legislative reforms. They desired drastic change, the end of a system which assumed that men were powerful and women weak, males aggressive and females passive. American culture, [feminist] Kate Millett wrote, was permeated by an oppressive ideology in which all that could "be described as distinctly human . . . [was] reserved for the male." If politics meant power, then women were still disenfranchised. Even in "liberal" households, they were expected to do the dirtiest chores, take primary responsibility for rearing the children, and put their aspirations behind those of their husbands. For Millett and her allies, the answer had to be revolution—the abolition of patriarchy, an end to the family as presently constituted, and replacement of the traditional socialization process. Emancipation could be achieved only when every vestige of sexual stereotyping had been eliminated, when "masculine" and "feminine" spheres disappeared, and members of each sex were free to develop as individuals.

In a very real sense, the woman's movement had gone full cycle. The women who started feminism in the nineteenth century had ideas which were similar in substance, if not in tone, to those of their successors. They too wanted an end to the notion that women should occupy a separate sphere, and they too insisted on every person's right to be a human being first and a man or a woman second. "Whatsoever it is morally right for a man to do it is morally right for a woman to do," [abolitionist] Sarah Grimké wrote in 1838. And Margaret Fuller* added: "What Woman needs . . . is as a nature to grow, as an intellect to discern, as a soul to live freely. . . . We would have every arbitrary barrier thrown down. We would have every path laid open to Woman as well as to Man." More than a century later, the same plea echoed across the country. Sometimes raucous, often bitter, it nevertheless had the strength of appealing to the basic principle that every human being is unique and sacred and has an inalienable right to determine his or her own destiny.

Whether the new feminism could succeed where its predecessors had failed was an open question. It seemed unlikely that the vast majority of Americans were yet ready to accept the ramifications of complete sexual equality. The nuclear family, the concept of maternal responsibility for child-rearing, the importance of privatism—all were cherished values and all to some extent stood in the way of the revolution envisioned by women's rights advocates. On the other hand, the signs of change were manifold. The number of three- and four-year-olds in nursery schools or kindergartens doubled between 1965 and 1970. Nearly 70 per cent of all women approved in principle the idea of day-care centers. And most young people gave at least verbal allegiance to the values associated with sexual equality. The proportion of women living alone or with roommates rose 50 per cent during the 1960s, and the increase was 109 per cent for those in the crucial marrying range of twenty to thirty-four years old. A Barnard senior, the *New York Times* reported, was introduced to friends "as the only girl at Barnard who's getting married," and applications by women students to professional schools mounted. If such facts were any index, it seemed that fewer women saw marriage and motherhood as their only vocation, and that young mothers were increasingly prepared to utilize day-care facilities so that they could resume careers in the world outside the home.

Whatever the case, there could be little question at the end of the 1960s that feminism had once again become a vital force in American society. Women's liberation groups spread from the city to the suburbs. Groups of welfare mothers, airline stewardesses, and female soldiers all asserted their right to equal treatment with men. And officials in government and business went out of their way to give at least the appearance of meeting feminist demands. America might not be ready for the revolutionary ideas of the more extreme feminists, but more and more women were demonstrating an acute consciousness of the need to end discrimination based

*Margaret Fuller, 1810–1850, was a feminist, critic, and journalist.

on sex. The future was uncertain, but as the nation entered a new decade, feminism exhibited a strength, vitality, and appeal which had not been seen in the United States for half a century.

DOCUMENTS

In Support of ERA, 1970

My name is Gloria Steinem. I am a writer and editor. I have worked in several political campaigns, and am currently a member of the Policy Council of the Democratic National Committee.

During twelve years of working for a living, I've experienced much of the legal and social discrimination reserved for women in this country. I have been refused service in public restaurants, ordered out of public gathering places, and turned away from apartment rentals; all for the clearly-stated sole reason that I am a woman. And all without the legal remedies available to blacks and other minorities. I have been excluded from professional groups, writing assignments on so-called "unfeminine" subjects such as politics, full participation in the Democratic Party, jury duty, and even from such small male privileges as discounts on airline fares. Most important to me, I have been denied a society in which women are encouraged, or even allowed, to think of themselves as first-class citizens and responsible human beings.

However, after two years of researching the status of American women, I have discovered that I am very, very lucky. Most women, both wage-earners and housewives, routinely suffer more humiliation and injustice than I do.

As a freelance writer, I don't work in the male-dominated hierarchy of an office. (Women, like blacks and other visibly-different minorities, do better in individual professions such as the arts, sports, or domestic work; anything in which they don't have authority over white males.) I am not one of the millions of women who must support a family. Therefore, I haven't had to go on welfare because there are no day care centers for my children while I work, and I haven't had to submit to the humiliating welfare inquiries about my private and sexual life, inquiries from which men are exempt. I haven't had to brave the sex bias of labor unions and employers, only to see my family subsist on a median salary 40 percent less than the male median salary.

SOURCE: Testimony of Gloria Steinem, U.S. Congress, Senate Committee on the Judiciary, Subcommittee on Constitutional Amendments, Hearings, *The "Equal Rights" Amendment*, 91st Cong., 2d sess., 1970, 335–37.

I hope this committee will hear the personal, daily injustices suffered by many women—professionals and day laborers, women housebound by welfare as well as suburbia. We have all been silent for too long. We won't be silent anymore.

The truth is that all our problems stem from the same sex-based myths. We may appear before you as white radicals or the middle-aged middle class or black soul sisters, but we are *all* sisters in fighting against these outdated myths. Like racial myths, they have been reflected in our laws. Let me list a few:

That Women Are Biologically Inferior to Men

In fact, an equally good case can be made for the reverse. Women live longer than men, even when the men are not subject to business pressures. Women survived Nazi concentration camps better, keep cooler heads in emergencies currently studied by disaster-researchers, are protected against heart attacks by their female sex hormones, and are so much more durable at every stage of life that nature must conceive 20 to 50 percent more males in order to keep some balance going.

Man's hunting activities are forever being pointed to as tribal proof of superiority. But while he was hunting, women built houses, tilled the fields, developed animal husbandry, and perfected language. Men, being all alone in the bush, often developed into a creature [*sic*] as strong as women, fleeter of foot, but not very bright.

However, I don't want to prove the superiority of one sex to another. That would only be repeating a male mistake. English scientists once definitively proved, after all, that the English were descended from the angels, while the Irish were descended from the apes: it was the rationale for England's domination of Ireland for more than a century. The point is that science is used to support current myth and economics almost as much as the church was.

What we do know is that the difference *between* two races or two sexes is much smaller than the differences to be found *within* each group. Therefore, in spite of the slide show on female inferiorities that I understand was shown to you yesterday, the law makes much more sense when it treats individuals, not groups bundled together by some condition of birth.

A word should be said about Dr. Freud, the great ninteenth-century perpetuator of female inferiority. Many of the differences he assumed to be biological, and therefore changeless, have turned out to be societal, and have already changed. . . .

That Women Are Already Treated Equally in This Society

I'm sure there has been ample testimony to prove that equal pay for equal work, equal chance for advancement, and equal training or encouragement is obscenely scarce in every field, even those—like food and fashion industries—that are supposedly "feminine."

300

A deeper result of social and legal injustice, however, is what sociologists refer to as "Internalized Aggression." Victims of aggression absorb the myth of their own inferiority, and come to believe that their group is in fact second-class.

Women suffer this second-class treatment from the moment they are born. They are expected to be rather than achieve, to function biologically rather than learn. A brother, whatever his intellect, is more likely to get the family's encouragement and education money, while girls are often pressured to conceal ambition and intelligence, to "Uncle Tom."

I interviewed a New York public school teacher who told me about a black teenager's desire to be a doctor. With all the barriers in mind, she suggested he be a veterinarian instead.

The same day, a high school teacher mentioned a girl who wanted to be a doctor. The teacher said, "How about a nurse—"

Teachers, parents, and the Supreme Court may exude a protective, well-meaning rationale, but limiting the individual's ambition is doing no one a favor. Certainly not this country. It needs all the talent it can get.

That American Women Hold Great Economic Power

Fifty-one percent of all shareholders in this country are women. That's a favorite male-chauvinist statistic. However, the number of shares they hold is so small that the total is only 18 percent of all shares. Even those holdings are often controlled by men.

Similarly, only 5 percent of all the people in the country who receive $10,000 a year or more, earned or otherwise, are women. And that includes all the famous rich widows.

The constantly-repeated myth of our economic power seems less testimony to our real power than to the resentment of what little power we do have.

That Children Must Have Full-Time Mothers

American mothers spend more time with their homes and children than those of any other society we know about. In the past, joint families, servants, a prevalent system in which grandparents raised the children, or family field work in the agrarian systems—all these factors contributed more to child care than the labor-saving devices of which we are so proud.

The truth is that most American children seem to be suffering from too much Mother, and too little Father. Part of the program of Women's Liberation is a return of fathers to their children. If laws permit women equal work and pay opportunities, men will then be relieved of their role as sole breadwinner. Fewer ulcers, fewer hours of meaningless work, equal responsibility for his own children: these are a few of the reasons that Women's Liberation is Men's Liberation, too.

As for the psychic health of the children, studies show that the quality of time spent by parents is more important than the quantity. The most damaged children were not those whose mothers worked, but those whose mothers preferred to work but stayed home out of role-playing desire to be a "good mother."

That the Women's Movement Is Not Political, Won't Last, or Is Somehow Not "Serious"

When black people leave their nineteenth-century roles, they are feared. When women dare to leave theirs, they are ridiculed. We understand this, and accept the burden of ridicule. It won't keep us quiet anymore.

Similarly, it shouldn't deceive male observers into thinking this is somehow a joke. We are 51 percent of the population, we are essentially united on these issues across boundaries of class or race or age, and we may well end by changing this society more than the civil rights movement. That is an apt parallel. We, too, have our right wing and left wing, our separatists, gradualists, and Uncle Toms. But we are changing our own consciousness, and that of the country. [Friedrich] Engels noted the relationship of the authoritarian, nuclear family to capitalism: the father as capitalist, the mother as means of production, and the children as labor. He said the family would change as the economic system did, and that seems to have happened, whether we want to admit it or not. Women's bodies will no longer be owned by the state for the production of workers and soldiers: birth control and abortion are facts of everyday life. The new family is an egalitarian family.

Gunnar Myrdal noted thirty years ago the parallel between women and Negroes in this country. Both suffered from such restricting social myths as: smaller brains, passive natures, inability to govern themselves (and certainly not white men), sex objects only, childlike natures, special skills and the like. When evaluating a general statement about women, it might be valuable to substitute "black people" for "women"—just to test the prejudice at work.

And it might be valuable to do this Constitutionally as well. Neither group is going to be content as a cheap labor pool anymore. And neither is going to be content without full Constitutional rights.

Finally, I would like to say one thing about this time in which I am testifying.

I had deep misgivings about discussing this topic when National Guardsmen are occupying our campuses, the country is being turned against itself in a terrible polarization, and America is enlarging an already inhuman and unjustifiable war.* But it seems to me that much of the trouble this country is in has to do with the Masculine Mystique; with the myth

---

*In 1970, many colleges were centers of the struggle for civil rights for women and minorities and the anti-Vietnam War movement.

that masculinity somehow depends on the subjugation of other people. It is a bipartisan problem: both our past and current Presidents seem to be victims of this myth, and to behave accordingly.

Women are not more moral than men. We are only uncorrupted by power. But we do not want to imitate men, to join this country as it is, and I think our very participation will change it. Perhaps women elected leaders—and there will be many more of them—will not be so likely to dominate black people or yellow people or men; anybody who looks different from us.

After all, we won't have our masculinity to prove.

A Woman's Right to Abortion, 1973

We forthwith acknowledge our awareness of the sensitive and emotional nature of the abortion controversy, of the vigorous opposing views, even among physicians, and of the deep and seemingly absolute convictions that the subject inspires. One's philosophy, one's experiences, one's exposure to the raw edges of human existence, one's religious training, one's attitudes toward life and family and their values, and the moral standards one establishes and seeks to observe, are all likely to influence and to color one's thinking and conclusions about abortion.

In addition, population growth, pollution, poverty, and racial overtones tend to complicate and not to simplify the problem.

Our task, of course, is to resolve the issue by constitutional measurement, free of emotion and of predilection. We seek earnestly to do this, and, because we do, we have inquired into, and in this opinion place some emphasis upon, medical and medical-legal history and what that history reveals about man's attitudes toward the abortion procedure over the centuries. . . .

It perhaps is not generally appreciated that the restrictive criminal abortion laws in effect in a majority of States today are of relatively recent vintage. Those laws, generally proscribing abortion or its attempt at any time during pregnancy except when necessary to preserve the pregnant woman's life, are not of ancient or even of common-law origin. Instead, they derive from statutory changes effected, for the most part, in the latter half of the nineteenth century. . . .

The Constitution does not explicitly mention any right of privacy. In a line of decisions, however, the Court has recognized that a right of personal privacy, or a guarantee of certain areas or zones of privacy, does exist under the Constitution. . . .

SOURCE: *Roe* v. *Wade* (1973).

This right of privacy, whether it be founded in the Fourteenth Amendment's concept of personal liberty and restrictions upon state action, as we feel it is, or, as the District Court determined, in the Ninth Amendment's reservation of rights to the people, is broad enough to encompass a woman's decision whether or not to terminate her pregnancy. The detriment that the State would impose upon the pregnant woman by denying this choice altogether is apparent. Specific and direct harm medically diagnosable even in early pregnancy may be involved. Maternity, or additional offspring, may force upon the woman a distressful life and future. Psychological harm may be imminent. Mental and physical health may be taxed by child care. There is also the distress, for all concerned, associated with the unwanted child, and there is the problem of bringing a child into a family already unable, psychologically and otherwise, to care for it. In other cases, as in this one, the additional difficulties and continuing stigma of unwed motherhood may be involved. All these are factors the woman and her responsible physician necessarily will consider in consultation.

On the basis of elements such as these, appellant and some amici argue that the woman's right is absolute and that she is entitled to terminate her pregnancy at whatever time, in whatever way, and for whatever reason she alone chooses. With this we do not agree. Appellant's arguments that Texas either has no valid interest at all in regulating the abortion decision, or no interest strong enough to support any limitation upon the woman's sole determination, is unpersuasive. The Court's decisions recognizing a right of privacy also acknowledge that some state regulation in areas protected by that right is appropriate. [A] State may properly assert important interests in safeguarding health, in maintaining medical standards, and in protecting potential life. At some point in pregnancy, these respective interests become sufficiently compelling to sustain regulation of the factors that govern the abortion decision. The privacy right involved, therefore, cannot be said to be absolute. . . .

We, therefore, conclude that the right of personal privacy includes the abortion decision, but that this right is not unqualified and must be considered against important state interests in regulation. . . .

The appellee and certain amici argue that the fetus is a "person" within the language and meaning of the Fourteenth Amendment. In support of this, they outline at length and in detail the well-known facts of fetal development. If this suggestion of personhood is established, the appellant's case, of course, collapses, for the fetus's right to life is then guaranteed specifically by the Amendment. The appellant conceded as much on reargument. On the other hand, the appellee conceded on reargument that no case could be cited that holds that a fetus is a person within the meaning of the Fourteenth Amendment.

The Constitution does not define "person" in so many words. Section 1 of the Fourteenth Amendment contains three references to "person."

The first, in defining "citizens," speaks of "persons born or naturalized in the United States." The word also appears both in the Due Process Clause and in the Equal Protection Clause. "Person" is used in other places in the Constitution. . . . But in nearly all these instances, the use of the word is such that it has application only postnatally. None indicates, with any assurance, that it has any possible prenatal application.

All this, together with our observation, supra, that throughout the major portion of the nineteenth century prevailing legal abortion practices were far freer than they are today, persuades us that the word "person," as used in the Fourteenth Amendment, does not include the unborn. . . .

President George Bush Opposes Abortion, 1989

Good afternoon, ladies and gentlemen. This is George Bush in the Oval Office.* And before you begin your march today, on this first Monday of my Presidency, I wanted to take just a few brief moments to restate my firm support of our cause and to share with you my deep personal concern about our American tragedy of abortion on demand.

We are concerned about abortion because it deals with the lives of two human beings, mother and child. I know there are people of good will who disagree, but after years of sober and serious reflection on the issue, this is what I think. I think the Supreme Court's decision in *Roe* versus *Wade* was wrong and should be overturned. I think America needs a human life amendment. And I think when it comes to abortion there's a better way: the way of adoption, the way of life.

I know that this morning several of your leaders had a meeting in the White House with Vice President Quayle. I know, too, that you and hundreds of thousands with you across the country have raised a voice of moral gravity about abortion, a voice of principle, a voice of faith, a full voice that properly asserts and affirms the basic dignity of human life. I'm confident that more and more Americans every year—every day—are hearing your message and taking it to heart.

And, ladies and gentlemen—and, yes, young people as well—I promise you that the President hears you now and stands with you in a cause that must be won.

God bless you all, and God bless life.

SOURCE: *Weekly Compilation of Presidential Documents*, George Bush, January 23, 1989.

*The President spoke at 12:05 P.M. from the Oval Office at the White House via an electronic communications link with the rally site. Participants had gathered on the Ellipse for a march to the Supreme Court on the occasion of the sixteenth anniversary of the Court's decision of *Roe* v. *Wade*, which legalized abortion.

Chapter 16

America's Latest Immigrants

The United States, as everyone knows, is a nation of immigrants; however, at different times, the newcomers have come from various lands. Until recently most hailed from Europe, with Germany, Great Britain, Italy, Ireland, and Poland sending the greatest numbers. Fewer entered from Mexico, Asia, and the Caribbean. Since the sweeping immigration reforms of 1965, these latter areas have replaced Europe as the major source of immigration. In the 1980s and early 1990s, Europeans amounted to only about 10 percent of new immigrants, while Mexico, China, the Philippines, Jamaica, India, Korea, the Dominican Republic, and Iran have topped the immigrant figures.

Among the post–World War II newcomers were over two million refugees, at first Europeans, then Cubans in the 1960s, and Indochinese after 1975. When the United States–backed regime in Saigon fell to the communists in April 1975, the long and futile American involvement in Vietnam finally ended. During 1961–1973, the time of active U.S. military participation, our nation divided deeply over the war—its origins, purposes, tactics, and morality. The communist victory did not heal all these divisions, however, and American scholars, politicians, and the public drew different "lessons" about the Vietnam War.

The continuing public disagreement about foreign policy was not the only *legacy of the bitter and bloody Vietnam War. The essay by Stanley Karnow points to another result: the flight of nearly one million refugees from Southeast Asia and their subsequent settlement in the United States. Many underwent harrowing trials during the journey. The first group was airlifted by American helicopters from Saigon in the last days of the war, and hundreds of thousands of others later fled across the Thai border or escaped by sea (the "boat people"). Karnow's essay focuses on a Vietnamese community in Orange County, California, where a considerable number of these immigrants settled. What special problems did these people face? Have they adjusted to life in America? How do their experiences compare to those of earlier waves of immigrants?*

As dramatic as the arrivals of war refugees have been, neighboring Mexico has sent the largest number of immigrants to the United States since the 1950s. Most Mexicans entered the United States with proper immigration papers, but some, like Miguel Torres, came illegally, repeatedly crossing the 1,900-mile border between the two nations. Torres's story is told in the first document. How does the lack of a visa affect his life? How do the experiences of such immigrants compare with those of the Vietnamese refugees?

Americans have always felt ambivalent about newcomers, and beginning in the 1880s, they began to restrict the numbers allowed to enter the United States. The restrictions culminated in the National Origins Quotas of the 1920s, which drastically limited the number of people who could obtain a visa. After World War II, Congress and the president once again liberalized immigration policy. But the new laws did not eliminate all anxiety about newcomers, and immigration, especially undocumented immigration, has become controversial in states like California and Florida. People currently worried about immigrants have insisted that newcomers take jobs from Americans and cost taxpayers by draining social services. In the second document, a 1981 letter to the Washington Post, *U.S. senator Alan Simpson suggests another source of opposition to recent immigration. What does Senator Simpson see as a problem with the current flow of immigration? Have similar things been said about prior waves of immigrants?*

ESSAY

Orange County's Little Saigon: Bridging Two Worlds
Stanley Karnow

"Americans go to bank for loan, Vietnamese go to friends," Gi is saying. "I ask this guy for a thousand, another for two thousand, soon I have eighteen thousand. We trust each other, so no interest. He know I do the same for him one day."

Nguyen Huu Gi, a slender and amiable man, is explaining how he was able to start the little computer store that he runs with his family in a part of California that, for his visitor, resonates with echoes of another time and another country.

When I left Vietnam after years of covering the war, I never expected to see Saigon again. But I am back there now, at least in spirit. For the Vietnamese refugees who have streamed into California since the Communists conquered their country in 1975 have created a facsimile Saigon in Orange County, an hour's drive south of Los Angeles. To commemorate its antecedents—and in hopes of diverting tourists from nearby Disneyland—the local authorities have formally recognized the area's character in a freeway sign: "Little Saigon."

SURVIVORS WITH A NEED TO CLUSTER

Insecure on alien soil, newcomers have historically clung together during their early years in America. Irish congregated in Boston, Germans in Milwaukee, the Jews and Italians in New York City. But the Vietnamese feel an even stronger urge to cluster. Unlike immigrants, who uprooted themselves by choice, they are refugees from war, devastation and political repression, and many continue to be traumatized by their perilous escapes. They are also tormented by an almost obsessive nostalgia for a native land that, many fear, they may never see again. Though most have shown extraordinary resilience, others have failed to adjust fully to America, and their problems are straining their mental stability as well as their family ties. As a Vietnamese social worker explained to me, "We are survivors, grasping each other for support. A place like Little Saigon provides that support."

The U.S. Government, striving to avert a repetition of the massive Cuban impact on Miami, originally attempted to disperse the first Vietnamese arrivals around the country. The policy miscarried.

Seeking to be with their relatives and friends, and lured by a warm climate reminiscent of home, more than a quarter of the one million Vietnamese

SOURCE: Stanley Karnow, "In Orange County's Little Saigon, Vietnamese Try to Bridge Two Worlds," from *Smithsonian* August 1992, 28–39.

refugees who poured into America after 1975 eventually migrated to California. At least 70,000 settled in Orange County, making it the biggest concentration of Vietnamese outside Vietnam.

If Vietnam meets America in Little Saigon, it is also where the two cultures collide. Scanning the Orange County telephone directory, for example, I encounter pages of Nguyens and Phams, the Vietnamese parallels of Smith and Jones. But many have adopted such American first names as Harry and Pat. Those who have kept their Vietnamese names often reverse them in Western fashion, so that a friend of mine, formerly Tran Nghia, is now Nghia Tran. East and West blend in enterprises like the Eurasian Mortgage Company.

Little Saigon is devoted to commerce, as its prototype was before the Communists curbed capitalism. But while the refugees have transplanted their own brand of business in this foreign setting, they have embraced the most American of consumer institutions—the shopping center.

The towns of Garden Grove, Westminster and Santa Ana, which form the core of the Orange County Vietnamese community, bustle with malls like the Asian Village and the Le Loi Center, the latter named for a 15th-century Vietnamese emperor, and they rival one another in vitality. Westminster's business district is the area formally known as Little Saigon. There one afternoon, cruising down Bolsa Avenue, a main artery, I stop at the Asian Garden, an ornate two-story arcade whose curved tile roof and lacquered pillars were designed to evoke the Orient. At its entrance sits a mammoth Buddha flanked by the gods of prosperity, longevity and happiness, a quartet presumably convened to inspire confidence in its merchandise. Stepping inside, I am propelled into what the real Saigon might be today had America and its South Vietnamese clients won the war.

Blaring from audiocassette stores is a cacophony of music ranging from hard rock to syrupy sentimental, all in Vietnamese. Peering into one, I see tapes made in Vietnam, legal through an amendment to the U.S. embargo on trading with the former enemy. There are travel agencies that primarily ticket Vietnamese, who are increasingly returning to Vietnam on visits. "Homesickness," a Vietnamese editor told me, "is reaching epidemic proportions here."

DRIED LIZARD AND STARFISH FLAKES

The arcade abounds in jewelers, testimony to the Vietnamese propensity to convert savings into gems or gold rather than trust the banks. A pharmacy contains, instead of aspirin and cold pills, drawers of such esoteric items as ground antler, dried lizard, starfish flakes and assorted grades of ginseng, a prized restorative that can cost as much as $2,000 a pound. I browse through bookshops stocked with novels, political tracts and girlie magazines, all published locally in Vietnamese. As in old Saigon, there are custom tailors surrounded by bolts of cloth, and dressmakers prepared to run up *ao dais*, the flowing silk tunic-and-pants ensembles worn by Vietnamese women at cere-monies. Cafés are crowded with Vietnamese men chatting over glasses of café au lait, just as they did in the real Saigon, where conversation was a cottage industry. The malls are also information hubs, where refugees ex-change news and gossip, mainly about Vietnam.

Eating, a Vietnamese addiction, accounts for Little Saigon's diversity of restaurants. They come in nearly every size, from holes in the wall to garish palaces adorned with dragons and colored lanterns. Reflecting Vietnam's re-gionalism, some serve robust southern dishes while others offer simpler northern fare. The most popular are bistros dedicated to *pho*, the national Vietnamese noodle soup, a melange of cabbage, parsley, coriander and soy-bean sprouts topped with shrimp, squid, beef, pork or chicken. At one I enter to sample a bowl, the waiter cannot understand English, and we negotiate in sign language, as I often did in Vietnam. A Vietnamese acquaintance who lives in Chicago remarked to me following a visit to Little Saigon: "After 15 years in America, it was the first time I spent a week without speaking a word of English."

A delight of old Saigon were street markets, with their mounds of fruit, vegetables, spices, herbs and meats. The equivalent in Orange County are American-style supermarkets, complete with carts and checkouts manned by brisk, bilingual sales personnel. Their lavish inventories make the Saigon markets of my memory seem bare by comparison.

I stroll into one whose vegetable bins overflow with vast varieties of Chi-nese cabbage, snow peas and sweet pea leaves, string beans and soybeans, tofu, bamboo shoots, white radishes, hot and sweet peppers, water chest-nuts, fresh and dried mushrooms, garlic, ginger and other roots I cannot identify. The fruit counter is crammed with Asian pears, persimmons, man-goes, papayas, litchis and Malaysian durians, whose putrid smell belies their sweetness. There are shelves of bottled oils and sauces—sesame, soybean, oyster, shrimp paste and above all *nuoc mam*, a singular Vietnamese concoc-tion made from fermented fish. Piled high in yet another section are sacks of rice from almost every land in Asia, whose distinctive textures can be dis-cerned by connoisseurs.

The seafood department is an aquarium of giant tanks filled with live lobsters and crayfish, crabs, squid and baby octopuses, carp, catfish, bass, flounder, grouper and other species. There are dried jellyfish, smoked eels, preserved shark fins, crispy seaweed and sea cucumber—a gelatinous ma-rine grub that reputedly possesses medicinal properties.

Unlike old Saigon, a raucous wartime tenderloin of bars and nightclubs, Orange County is quiet—except on Saturday nights, when the action can be found at such discos as the Ritz, where I am taken by friends.

The spacious hall is vintage Travolta as beams of light pierce clouds of dry-ice smoke. A Vietnamese combo called the Shotguns switches from waltzes to tangos to rock as Vietnamese couples of every age pack the floor—

the women in black tights, designer jeans or frilly frocks, the men in blue denims, flashy suits or cowboy outfits. The star attraction is Lynda Trang Dai, a 24-year-old beauty billed as the "Vietnamese Madonna," who struts in a sequined bra and hot pants as she belts out rock tunes in Vietnamese. I later learn from a newspaper interview with her that she escaped from Saigon with her family in 1978, and started singing at a California high school. Her sexy image is just a pose, she says. "I don't smoke, I don't drink. I'm just your typical Vietnamese girl." But there are no "typical" Vietnamese refugees. Many have thrived, many have lagged behind—and many languish in poverty. According to Walter Barnes, a California refugee and immigration official, "There are some tremendous successes and tremendous failures. In the middle is a bunch of people trying to do their best."

Their backgrounds in Vietnam, coupled with when and how they fled, have shaped their lives in America.

The first wave to arrive in 1975 was largely composed of Saigon government officials and army officers, doctors, lawyers and businessmen, and employees of the U.S. mission in Vietnam. Almost half had college degrees, and most were more or less proficient in English. Many had studied in the United States and knew Americans who helped them to get settled. Though Vietnamese refugees faced racial hatred elsewhere—and do to this day—they were warmly welcomed as victims of Communism in Orange County, a conservative bastion. Most important, nearly all arrived with their families, a source of their strength.

Initially many were forced to take menial jobs, but they were motivated, diligent and enterprising. Eventually they prospered—so that, by the early '80s, their household income equaled the U.S. average.

Horatio Alger would have been proud of Frank Jao, one of the prime developers of Little Saigon. An ethnic Chinese from Vietnam, he is a soft-spoken bantamweight in his 40s, whose only displays of wealth are tailored suits and a Mercedes sedan. He tells me his story over dinner in a local French restaurant.

Saigon was booming during the late 1960s as the United States pumped billions into the war, and Jao found a solid job with a private American firm. Fleeing the Communists, he and his wife landed at Camp Pendleton, the U.S. Marine base in California, where some of the first refugees were greeted. Jao had only $50 in his pocket. He earned another fifty—his American debut as an entrepreneur—by selling his Vietnamese jacket to a souvenir hunter.

Jao started over as a door-to-door vacuum cleaner salesman, but rejections depressed him. Going from one job to another, he began to study real estate, and earned his sales license at a propitious moment. Light industrial plants were moving into Orange County, and Jao was soon selling houses to their employees.

Observing that there were then only a few Asian stores in the area to serve the Vietnamese influx, Jao persuaded a Chinese friend to open a grocery in Westminster, arranged the deal and went on to others. To aid destitute relatives in Vietnam, the refugees mailed them articles that could be sold on the free market—a practice that still continues. The preferred articles were pharmaceutical products that fetched high prices in Saigon, and Jao induced Vietnamese druggists to set up outlets in Orange County. He formed investment syndicates and, borrowing heavily to finance the venture, completed his first shopping center by 1980. His firm, Bridgecreek Development, has since built 14 shopping centers. He has sometimes consulted a geomancer to be sure that the shopping centers are auspiciously situated, and once a year has firework displays—partly a publicity gimmick but also a time-honored Asian device to ward off evil spirits.

"I don't know anything about politics," Jao protests to me with an aw-shucks shrug. In fact, he is close to the local power elite, which assures him official favors. He contributes to the Republican Party, a force in Orange County, as well as such key groups as the fire and police departments. He was a principle force behind the legislation to give Westminster's business district its official designation, but he lost his battle against titling the area Little Saigon—a label, he tells me, that recalls "bad memories of the war."

The next surge of refugees gathered momentum during the late 1970s, bringing in a different breed of Vietnamese—peasants and fisherfolk fleeing poverty, young men evading conscription in Vietnam's new wars against China and in Cambodia, or Chinese expelled by the Communists as suspected surrogates of China. Escaping by sea, often aboard rickety, overcrowded craft, the boat people were lashed by savage storms or ran out of food and water, and many were robbed, raped, even murdered by pirates. Those who reached Thailand or Malaysia were frequently turned away or confined to refugee camps, sometimes for years. And those lucky enough to get to America arrived amid the severest inflation in a generation, followed by the worst recession in a half-century.

Many adapted through remarkable fortitude and hard work. One such was Nguyen Huu Gi, who had started his computer store with loans from his friends. When I visit him, his wife is at the counter, his teenage daughter is toting up accounts, and two of his sons, college students, are repairing a computer.

A former math teacher who remained in Vietnam for five years under the Communists, Gi fled for the sake of his children. "They come home from school singing Communist songs, but cannot add numbers," he recalls. "All Communists care about is politics, not science or math, just politics. So I decide to escape, even if my family die at sea."

SAILING INTO A STORM FOR SECURITY

Gi and friends pooled their money, bought a small boat and secretly left Vietnam with 55 people aboard. Heading into stormy weather to elude pursuit, they made it to Singapore. Four months later, he landed in Houston with his wife and four children, sponsored by his brother, who had settled there earlier. There a new challenge awaited them. Unable to hold a job, Gi realized that he had to learn English and acquire a skill. He moved to California, which offers liberal social services, and his family lived on welfare while he studied English and computer science. A computer company later engaged him, and eventually he had saved $8,000. He opened his store in 1985, having proceeded in Vietnamese style. As he explains:

"Americans make big investment, hire manager, technicians. Vietnamese cannot afford that, but wife and children all work hard. At first I keep old job while wife and friend take care of store; later I quit to run business full time. Until last year we are here seven days a week, sometimes until 2 in the morning. Now we're doing OK, so we take Sunday off."

Not all Vietnamese families are so cohesive. Though they are purportedly models of harmony, many are frustrated by the pressures of America. Numbers of refugee couples brought their difficulties from Vietnam, where wartime tensions strained marriages, and the pace of America has aggravated their troubles. Divorce among them, while rare by American standards, is rising. Husbands reduced to menial jobs or welfare often lose status in their wives' eyes. Women have also discovered freedom in America. Many are working and, to their spouses' dismay, rejecting their traditional submissive role. Marriages are further threatened as Vietnamese women turn toward white American men, whom they assume to be rich and able to rescue them from hardship—and who are often charmed by their grace and beauty. As one Vietnamese tells me, "Not a week passes that an American doesn't flirt with my wife."

Meanwhile, parents preoccupied with earning a living often lack the time and energy to pay attention to their children. Or children who have adapted rapidly to America feel estranged from parents unable to adjust as quickly. Frequently kids who have become fluent in English no longer communicate easily with parents who are comfortable only in Vietnamese. "What we're seeing," a counselor at an Orange County school observed, "is the classic immigrant experience of families drifting apart because their members can't keep up with each other in a new society."

America is especially tough on the elderly. In Vietnam they were respected in accordance with Confucian tenets, and they could mingle with contemporaries in villages or urban districts. But many, particularly in California, suffer from what Dr. Ton That Niem, an Orange County psychiatrist, terms "adjustment disorder." Unable to drive, they cannot shop or visit friends, and they sit alone at home watching television in English, which they cannot understand. Their sons and daughters are too busy to see them regularly, while their Americanized grandchildren, who often cannot speak Vietnamese, frequently snub them. Many dream of returning to Vietnam—at least to die. Or, as they euphemistically put it, "I want to go back to retire."

Equally serious are the problems facing the political prisoners released

by the Communists. The United States has agreed to take most of the estimated 200,000 originally detained if they want to come, and some 22,000,
including families, have arrived during the past two years. The thousands
more to come will badly need help.

Like the first wave of refugees, most are onetime professionals who, for
one reason or another, failed to flee when the Communists took over. Many
are skilled, but their age is against them. I talk with one who, still jittery after
his ordeal, requests anonymity. Call him Linh.

A former South Vietnamese Air Force major trained in Illinois, he was
aboard a helicopter poised to take off from Saigon as the Communists entered the city. Suddenly he jumped out of the chopper. "I couldn't leave my
wife and four children behind," he recalls.

Ordered to report for "re-education," Linh complied—and spent seven
years at hard labor in the jungle. He and his fellow prisoners were fed meager rations of cassava and rice, and many died of malnutrition or malaria. A
political pariah after his release in 1982, he subsisted in Saigon as a private
tutor until he could emigrate with his family.

Knowing America, he expected to adjust easily. But jobs were scarce
even for Americans in their 50s, and before he was hired by a relief agency
his family relied on welfare, which he considered humiliating. His wife is
now a seamstress, and his children solder circuit boards in an electronics
plant while studying English at night. Though they barely make ends meet,
Linh hopes that his three sons and a daughter, ages 18 to 23, will shortly enter
college. "I'm too old to start again," he says. "The future belongs to my children. That is why we're here."

Vietnamese refugee children are often depicted as whiz kids, and while
the image is exaggerated, many are indeed overachievers. Like other Asians,
who traditionally revere scholars, they value learning. They also see education as both the path to success and, consistent with their sense of filial piety,
the way to bring esteem to their family.

One of the liveliest days I spend in Orange County is at Saddleback High
School in Santa Ana. Though Vietnamese represent only about 15 percent of
the student body of some 2,800, most of it Hispanic, they are invariably the
valedictorians. At the 1992 commencement, 26 of the top 33 students were
Vietnamese.

Sitting in on an advanced-placement English class, I am amazed by the
verve of the students, most of them Vietnamese. Led by a bouncy teacher
named Chris Lammers, they read aloud from Sophocles' *Oedipus Rex*, ana-
lyzing the tragedy with eloquence and even digressing into a discussion of
the Freudian Oedipus complex. Later I chat with Minh Le Tran and Kieu
Oanh Nguyen Ha, both straight-A students who had fled from Vietnam with
their families in the late '70s.

Minh, who hopes to become a businessman, speaks of his parents' aspirations for him. "They're really proud of me," he says. "so I have to keep improving, even if there's no room for improvement. I also feel their pressure. Just study, they say. I can't wash the dishes, mow the lawn or take a summer job. Their entire goal is to see me succeed." Similarly, Kieu Oanh says, "I know that my success is a big thing for my parents, and I sense that pressure. But it's also important to me. For example, I'm in speech contests. People look at me funny when I begin, since I'm a refugee and they expect my accent to be horrible. So I feel good when they're surprised that my English is fluent."

When I raise the question of identity, Kieu Oanh replies, "My parents made me learn to read and write Vietnamese—or at least tried to. At home we speak Vietnamese and English, but my Vietnamese isn't that great. I'm more comfortable in English. I think in English. So I guess I'm not really Vietnamese but more American—maybe a kind of transitional Vietnamese."

Striving to preserve their heritage, a Buddhist center in Orange County conducts courses for Vietnamese children on Sunday mornings. About 200 kids in gray shirts and blue jeans, ages 7 to 18, sit attentively around tables in the courtyard as Vietnamese instructors lecture them. The youngest are practicing tones, a basic of the Vietnamese language, while teenagers listen to talks on Vietnamese culture. However, I notice they speak English among themselves. Standing over one girl, I also observe that her loose-leaf binder contains, besides her notes in Vietnamese, a picture of Vanilla Ice, the American rap star.

By contrast, many young Vietnamese are dropouts, and some belong to criminal gangs. They owe their delinquency to the war or years in refugee camps. Many came to America without one or both parents, and miss the restraints imposed by tight kinship ties. Often they lack respect for their fathers, who they feel have forfeited their traditional authority by their failure to adapt to the United States. And many, carried away by the permissiveness of America, rebuff hard work and discipline.

Little Saigon is prey to teenage Vietnamese gangs like the "Santa Ana Boys" and "Cheap Boys," or the "Wally Girls" and "Pomona Girls," their female counterparts. Armed with knives, pistols and even semiautomatic weapons, they steal cars, rob stores and extort from merchants. They specialize in "home invasions," breaking into the homes of affluent Vietnamese and forcing them to hand over their concealed valuables by torturing children, raping women in front of husbands or killing a family member. Some graduate into nationwide Asian crime syndicates engaged in big-time rackets like prostitution, illegal gambling, check scams and narcotics.

One morning I tour Garden Grove with Thien Cao, a community service officer with the Garden Grove Police Department. Nodding at youngsters in punk haircuts and expensive tennis shoes in cafés and pool halls, he identifies them as gang members. "Our biggest problem," he goes on, "is persuading the Vietnamese to report crimes. Their instinct if they witness a crime is to run away. It's a hangover from the war, when they tried to stay out of the crossfire. In Vietnam the cops were often corrupt, so they distrust the police here. They're also afraid to testify, since the courts usually release gang members on bail or recognizance, and victims fear being attacked again—which often happens. Another headache is getting suspects to talk. The prospect of a juvenile home doesn't scare a kid who has risked escape and spent years in a refugee camp."

Civic duty in Little Saigon is organized but very separate from the larger community. While few Vietnamese merchants belong to the Westminster Chamber of Commerce, the Vietnamese Chamber of Commerce is thriving. Chiefly concerned with their own interests, they are also split into various factions, a division reflected in the dozens of flimsy Vietnamese-language journals that represent one group or another. As refugees, many are depressed as well by the burdens of survival, and they tend to focus on personal problems rather than on community affairs. Not a single Vietnamese sits on any of the Orange County's town councils. But many indulge in "exile politics," mainly through impassioned anticommunist movements that maintain that they can promote change in Vietnam. Several Vietnamese critics of these movements have been murdered by extremists. Dr. Ton That Niem explains the appeal of these groups for numbers of refugees. "Just as someone whose leg has been amputated insists that he can still feel his foot, they cannot accept the fact that they are cut off from their native land."

I drive to the town of Costa Mesa one afternoon for a meeting of the National United Front for the Liberation of Vietnam, whose well-dressed supporters resemble innocuous Rotarians as they listen to idealistic speeches. But the group did try to live up to its name in 1987, when its founder, Hoang Co Minh, attempted to infiltrate a platoon of commandos into Vietnam from adjacent Laos. Minh, a former South Vietnamese admiral who had worked as a house painter in Washington, reportedly died, and the unit was wiped out in the action. Five front members have since been indicted by a federal grand jury for tax evasion and for conspiring to divert donations into a chain of noodle soup restaurants.

Little Saigon's future partly hinges on the future of Vietnam. Should the Communist regime crumble, as Communist regimes are doing everywhere, many older refugees may be tempted to return. Anticipating that prospect, some have already been investing in Saigon businesses under recent reforms that permit private ownership. But younger Vietnamese seem to be too directed toward mainstream America to go back to Vietnam, except on visits. The most ardent exponent of assimilation I hear is Minh Le Tran, the Saddleback High School student—whose views, I am told, are shared by many in his generation. "I feel shackled in Little Saigon," he says. "When I grow up, I want to live in some place like Maine, where it's not all Vietnamese, and I can play bridge with my neighbors on Thursday night."

DOCUMENTS

An Undocumented Mexican Immigrant: Miguel Torres, 1977

Miguel Torres is a slight, shy youth of twenty with a pale skin and El Greco features. He works in a mushroom plant in California. He has entered the United States illegally four times in the past year, and he has been caught three times. He told his story through a trusted interpreter.

I was born in a small town in the state of Michoacán in Mexico. When I was fifteen, I went to Mexico City with my grandmother and my mother. I worked in a parking lot, a big car lot. People would come in and they'd say, "Well, park my car." and I'd give them a ticket and I'd park the car and I'd be there, you know, watching the cars. I got paid in tips.

But I wanted to come to the United States to work and to earn more money. My uncle was here, and I thought if I could come to him, I could live with him and work and he would help me.

It's not possible to get papers to come over now. So when I decided to come, I went to Tijuana in Mexico. There's a person there that will get in contact with you. They call him the Coyote. He walks around town, and if he sees someone wandering around alone, he says, "Hello, do you have relatives in the United States?" And if you say yes, he says, "Do you want to visit them?" And if you say yes, he says he can arrange it through a friend. It costs $250 or $300.

The Coyote rounded up me and five other guys, and then he got in contact with a guide to take us across the border. We had to go through the hills and the desert, and we had to swim through a river. I was a little scared. Then we come to a highway and a man was there with a van, pretending to fix his motor. Our guide said hello, and the man jumped into the car and we ran and jumped in, too. He began to drive down the highway fast and we knew we were safe in the United States. He took us to San Isidro that night, and the next day he took us all the way here to Watsonville. I had to pay him $250 and then, after I'd been here a month, he came back and I had to give him $50 more. He said I owed him that.

I was here for two months before I started working, and then my uncle got me a job, first in the celery fields picking celery, washing it, packing it, and later picking prunes. Then, all of a sudden, one day the Immigration showed up, and I ran and I hid in a river that was next to the orchard. The man saw me and he questioned me, and he saw I didn't have any papers. So

SOURCE: Joan Morrison and Charlotte Fox Zabusky. *American Mosaic: The Immigrant Experience in the Words of Those Who Lived It,* 347–49. Copyright © 1980 by Joan Morrison and Charlotte Fox Zabusky. Reprinted by permission of the publisher, Dutton, an imprint of New American Library, a division of Penguin Books USA Inc.

317

they put me in a van and took me to Salinas, and there was some more illegals there and they put us in buses and took us all the way to Mexicali near the border. We were under guard; the driver and another one that sleeps while one drives. The seats are like hard boards. We'd get up from one side and rub, you know, that side a little bit and then sit on the other side for a while and then rub that side because it's so hard. It was a long trip.

When we arrived in Mexicali, they let us go. We caught a bus to Tijuana, and then at Tijuana, that night, we found the Coyote again and we paid him and we came back the next day. I had to pay $250 again, but this time he knew me and he let me pay $30 then and $30 each week. Because he knew me, you know. He trusted me.

We came through the mountains that time. We had to walk through a train tunnel. It all lasted maybe about three hours, through the tunnel. It was short; for me it was short. We're used to walking, you know. Over in Mexico we have to walk like ten miles to go to work or to go home or to go to school, so we're used to walking. To me it was a short distance to walk for three hours. And after we got out of the tunnel, we got into a car; and from there, from the tunnel, we came all the way into Los Angeles. That was the second time. We didn't see any border patrol either time.

The second time I was here for three months. My uncle managed to get me a job in the mushroom plant. I was working there when the Immigration came. There's this place where they blow air between the walls to make it cool and I hid there. And I was watching. The Immigration was looking around the plant everywhere. There was another illegal there, and he just kept on picking the mushrooms. He'd only been back a couple of days himself. The Immigration walked over there, and that kid turned around and looked at the Immigration and said, "What's the matter? What happened?" And the Immigration looked at him and said, "Oh, nothing," and the kid kept right on picking mushrooms. Yet he was an illegal! He knew how to act, play it cool. If you just sit tight they don't know you're illegal.

Well, the Immigration looked between the walls then and he caught me again. That was the second time. They put handcuffs on me with another guy and we were handcuffed together all the way from California to Mexicali.

Altogether I've been caught three times this year and made the trip over here four times. It's cost me one thousand dollars but it's still better than what I was making in Mexico City.

It's the money. When you come back here you get more money here than you do over there. Right now, the most that I'd be getting in Mexico would be from 25 to 30 pesos a day, which is maybe $2.00, $2.50. And here, with overtime, sometimes I make $150 a week. Things are expensive here, but it's expensive over there, too. And I like the way people live here. All the—what do you call it—all the facilities that you have here, all the things you can get and everything.

The boss at the mushroom factory doesn't ask for papers. He doesn't say anything about it. The last time, he hired me back as soon as I got back here, without any questions.

I learned to hide my money when the Immigration catch me. You know, if you have a lot on you, they take you fifteen or twenty miles from the border in Mexico. But if you have just two dollars or so, they let you go right in Tijuana. Then it's easier to come back. You can just walk right down the street and find the Coyote or someone like him. A man I know was hitchhiking along the road near San Diego and someone picked him up and it was the Immigration man who had just brought him back to Mexico! The Immigration laughed and said, "You got back faster than I did." Of course, he took him back to Mexico again then. But that man is back in Watsonville now, working in the brussels sprouts. It takes a longer time for the Immigration to catch us than it does for us to come back. [*Laughs.*]

I'd like to be able to stay here, to live here and work; but the only way now is to find someone that'll say, "Well, I'll marry you, I'll fix your papers for you." There's a lot of them who do that. I'd be willing to if I could find someone that would do it for me. You pay them, you know. You don't sleep together or even live in the same house, but they marry you. A long time ago you could fix up papers for your nephew or brother, a friend, a cousin. It was real easy then. But now it has to be close relations: mother, father, wife, son, or daughter. My uncle can't do it for me. The only way I could do it would be if I could marry an American citizen.

I'd like to learn English because it would be easier for me. There is a night school here, but I don't like to go because after work I like to go out and mess around and goof off. [*Laughs.*] Maybe I'll go later. If I could just learn a tiny bit of English, you know, I could turn around and tell the Immigration, "What's the matter with you? What do you want?" and I wouldn't be recognized as an illegal.

Senator Simpson on Immigration, 1981

The current flow of immigrants and refugees to the United States is out of control. Existing law allows total legal admissions to grow continuously, sometimes without regard to the needs of this country. Refugees are being admitted in numbers four times the 50,000 level, which was specified as being the "normal" flow in the Refugee Act of 1980. The United States today is taking in more legal immigrants and refugees for permanent resettlement than the rest of the world combined. In addition, hundreds of thousands of *illegal* immigrants cross our borders every year. . . .

The fundamental obligation of the government of any nation—indeed,

SOURCE: "Senator Simpson on Immigration" from The *Washington Post*, April 28, 1981. © The Washington Post Company. Reprinted with permission.

the very reason for its existence—is to promote the national interest; that may be defined as the long-term welfare of the majority of its citizens and their descendants. Accordingly, I believe that U.S. immigration policy should consider first the well-being of the American people. . . .

If immigration is continued at a high level and yet a substantial portion of these new persons and their descendants do not assimilate satisfactorily into our society, they may well create in America some of the same social, political and economic problems that exist in the countries from which they have chosen to depart. Furthermore, if language and cultural separation rise above a certain level, the unity and political stability of our nation will—in time—be seriously eroded.

Immigration and refugee policy reform is a perilous minefield of emotionally charged issues, but it is imperative that needed reforms be accomplished in an atmosphere of calm, compassionate and careful deliberation.

ALAN K. SIMPSON,
U.S. Senator (R-Wyo.)

Washington

Suggestions for Further Reading

Some of the changes in American society during the 1920s are covered in Lois Banner, *The American Beauty: A Social History Through Two Centuries of the American Idea, Ideal, and Image of the Beautiful Woman* (1983), and William Leuchtenburg, *Perils of Prosperity, 1914–1932* (1958). A good study on Prohibition is Andrew Sinclair, *Era of Excess: A Social History of the Prohibition Movement* (1964). On the Ku Klux Klan, see Kenneth Jackson, *The Ku Klux Klan in the Cities, 1915–1930* (1967), and David Chalmers, *Hooded Americanism: The First Century of the Ku Klux Klan* (1965). Information about the Klan and bigotry can also be found in David Bennett, *The Party of Fear: From Nativist Movements to the New Right in American History* (1988). Paula Fass, *The Damned and the Beautiful: American Youth in the 1920s* (1977), is valuable, as is J. Stanley Lemons, *The Woman Citizen: Social Feminism in the 1920s* (1973). A classic study of that era is Helen Merrill Lynd and Robert S. Lynd, *Middletown: A Study of Contemporary American Culture* (1929). On gay and lesbian history, see George Chauncey, *Gay New York: Gender, Urban Culture, and the Making of the Gay Male World, 1890–1940* (1994), and Lillian Faderman, *Odd Girls and Twilight Lovers: A History of Lesbian Life in Twentieth-Century America* (1991).

On the Great Depression, a good introduction is Robert S. McElvaine, *The Great Depression: America, 1929–1941* (1984). Also of use are Caroline Bird, *The Invisible Scar: The Great Depression and What It Did to American Life, From Then Until Now* (1966); Donald Worster, *Dust Bowl: The South Plains in the 1930s* (1979); and William Leuchtenburg, *Franklin Roosevelt and the New Deal* (1963). For women during the 1930s, see Susan Wave, *Holding Their Own: American Women in the 1930s* (1982). On blacks, see Nancy Weiss, *Farewell to the Party of Lincoln: Black Politics in the Age of FDR* (1983). A good picture of life in one American community can be found in Robert Lynd and Helen Lynd, *Middletown in Transition: A Study in Cultural Conflict* (1937). Information on workers during the Great Depression and after can be found in Robert H. Zieger, *American Workers, American Unions, 1920–1985* (1986). Other good books on the Great Depression are Lizabeth Cohen, *Making a New Deal* (1990), and James Goodman, *Stories of Scottsboro: The Rape Case That Shocked 1930s America and Revived the Struggle for Equality* (1994).

America during World War II has received increasing attention. For introductions see William O'Neill, *A Democracy at War* (1993), and Peter Lingeman, *Don't You Know There Is a War On?* (1970). Another general work is Richard Polenberg, *War and Society* (1972). On Japanese Americans, see Peter Irons, *Justice at War* (1983), and Roger Daniels, *Concentration Camps, U.S.A.* (1970). On women during the war, see D'Ann Campbell, *Women at War with America: Private Lives in a Patriotic Cause* (1984); Maureen Honey, *Creating Rosie the Riveter: Class, Gender and Propaganda During World War II* (1984); and

Ruth Milkman, *Gender at Work: The Dynamics of Job Segregation During World War II* (1987). The experience of gay men and women is told by Allan Berube, *Coming Out Under Fire: The History of Gay Men and Women in World War II* (1990).

For changes during the war and after, see Kenneth Jackson, *Crabgrass Frontier: The Suburbanization of the United States* (1985), and Gavin Wright, *Old South, New South: Revolutions in the Southern Economy Since the Civil War* (1986). On suburbs, see Herbert J. Gans, *Levittowners: Ways of Life and Politics in a New Suburban Community* (1982); Gwendolyn Wright, *Building the Dream: A Social History of Housing in America* (1981); and William Dobriner, *Class in Suburbia* (1963). Elaine May, *Homeward Bound: American Families in the Cold War* (1988), attempts to trace the impact of the Cold War on families. Also useful are Arlene Skolnick, *Embattled Paradise: The American Family in an Age of Uncertainty* (1991), and Donald Katz, *Home Fires: An Intimate Portrait of One Middle-Class Family in Postwar America* (1992).

The civil rights movement is covered in Harry Ashmore, *Civil Rights and Wrongs: A Memoir of Race and Politics, 1944–1994* (1994). Another overall view is Harvard Sitkoff, *The Struggle for Black Equality, 1954–1992* (1993). On the background of the *Brown v. Board of Education* decision, see Richard Kruger, *Simple Justice: The History of Brown vs. Board of Education: Black America's Struggle for Equality* (1976). A moving biography of Martin Luther King Jr. is Stephen Oates, *Let the Trumpet Sound: The Life of Martin Luther King* (1982). The process of ghettoization is discussed in Nicholas Lemann, *The Promised Land: The Great Black Migration and How It Changed America* (1991), and Arnold Hirsch, *Making the Second Ghetto: Race and Housing in Chicago, 1940–1960* (1983). A controversial book about black progress is William Wilson, *The Declining Significance of Race: Blacks and Changing American Institutions* (1978). Wilson's *The Truly Disadvantaged: The Inner City, the Underclass, and Public Policy* (1987) centers on poverty. An attempt to look at black progress is Reynolds Farley, *Blacks and Whites* (1984), while the National Research Council publication *A Common Destiny: Blacks and Whites in American Society* (1989) is filled with information. Two newer accounts of the civil rights movement are Robert Weisbort, *Freedom Bound: A History of the Civil Rights Movement* (1989), and Taylor Branch, *Parting the Waters: America in the King Years, 1954–1963* (1988).

For American women in recent years, the best introduction is William Chafe, *The American Woman: Her Changing Social, Economic, and Political Role, 1920–1970* (1972). Jacqueline Jones, *Labor of Love, Labor of Sorrow* (1985), is also useful, as is Alice Kessler-Harris, *Out to Work* (1982). Also helpful are Sara Evans, *Personal Politics: The Roots of Women's Liberation in the Civil Right Movement and the New Left* (1979); Carol Stack, *All Our Kin: Strategies for Survival in a Black Community* (1974); and Susan Estabrook Kennedy, *If All We Did Was to Weep at Home: A History of White Working-Class Women in America* (1979). Jane Mansbridge, *Why We Lost the ERA* (1986), centers on the ERA; Susan Hartman, *From Margin to Mainstream: American Women in Politics Since 1960* (1989), discusses politics. A useful history of American women is Sara Evans, *Born for Liberty: A History of Women in America* (1989). Susan Faludi, *Backlash: The Undeclared War Against American Women* (1991), covers recent developments, especially in the media.

On recent immigration, Ronald Takaki, *Strangers from a Different Shore: A History of Asian Americans* (1989); Robert Daniels, *Asian America: Chinese and Japanese in the United States Since 1850* (1988); and Peter Kwong, *The New Chinatown* (1986) are useful regarding Asians. General information can be found in Alejandro Portes and Ruben G. Rumbaut, *Immigrant America: A Portrait* (1990), and David M. Reimers, *Still the Golden Door: The Third World Comes to America* (1985). On Miami, see Alejandro Portes and Alex Stepick, *City on the Edge* (1993).